Psychoanalytic Politics

T0270081

Psychoanalytic Politics

Jacques Lacan and Freud's French Revolution

second edition

with a new preface

Sherry Turkle

The MIT Press
Cambridge, Massachusetts
London, England

© 2024 Massachusetts Institute of Technology

"In Memory of Sigmund Freud" reprinted by permission from *Collected Poems*, by W. H. Auden, edited by Edward Mendelson (New York: Random House, 1976). Copyright © 1940, 1968 by W. H. Auden.

All rights reserved. No part of this book may be used to train artificial intelligence systems or reproduced in any form by any electronic or mechanical means (including photocopying, recording, or information storage and retrieval) without permission in writing from the publisher.

This book was set in ITC Stone Serif Std and ITC Stone Sans Std by New Best-set Typesetters Ltd. Printed and bound in the United States of America

Library of Congress Cataloging-in-Publication Data

Names: Turkle, Sherry, author.
Title: Psychoanalytic politics : Jacques Lacan and Freud's French revolution / Sherry Turkle.
Description: Second edition, with a new preface. | Cambridge, Massachusetts : The MIT Press, [2024] | Includes bibliographical references and index.
Identifiers: LCCN 2023035588 (print) | LCCN 2023035589 (ebook) | ISBN 9780262548175 (paperback) | ISBN 9780262378918 (epub) | ISBN 9780262378901 (pdf)
Subjects: LCSH: Psychoanalysis—France. | Psychoanalysis—Social aspects—France. | Psychoanalysis—Political aspects—France. | Lacan, Jacques, 1901-1981. | France—History—20th century.
Classification: LCC BF175 .T87 2024 (print) | LCC BF175 (ebook) | DDC 150.19/50944—dc23/eng/20231218
LC record available at https://lccn.loc.gov/2023035588
LC ebook record available at https://lccn.loc.gov/2023035589

10 9 8 7 6 5 4 3 2 1

To mothers and daughters who have sustained and delighted me:

Edith Bonowitz, mother of Harriet Turkle and Mildred Bonowitz

Rebecca Sherman, mother of Lily Harper Sherman

Contents

Preface to the New Edition

This book, written before personal computers, cell phones, or the idea of "online," nevertheless speaks to our most urgent conflicts about how to be human in a digital world.

My story's main character, the French psychoanalyst Jacques Lacan, continually asks: What is it to be a person? What is its essence? What do we give to each other as human beings that is specific to us—things not available to the world of machines?

Lacan's focus was on language, a system of symbols and meanings tied to the human body and its experiences. He was interested in formalizing psychoanalytic ideas (he had students searching for what he called *mathèmes* as analytic building blocks). Still, the fight that first made him famous was against theories that reduced the study of the human mind to biology or behaviorism. When I introduced Lacan to Noam Chomsky on a visit to America in 1976, Lacan tried to find common ground. He engaged Chomsky by telling him that they were both looking for formalisms, but Chomsky replied that he, Chomsky, was looking for a "language organ . . . something like the ear." Lacan's startled response: "Je suis poète—I'm a poet."

Today, Lacan's stand against reductionism inspires resistance to the idea that artificial intelligence could capture the essence of the human. Lacan would be fascinated by how digital technology might simulate human conversation so that people could not distinguish a machine from a person. But Lacan would insist, I think, that what came out of the device would be utterances in a different register from the erotically and relationally charged symbolic world of human language and meaning.

Lacan stresses how people can't escape specific shared experiences. They had once been small, and the world had seemed large and alien. They formed attachments and were often disappointed. They counted on touch, taste, and smell to make sense of things. They registered whether the body that first fed them had stiffened at their approach or bent toward them in delight. And most of all, they built a fragmented sense of self through the language spoken by people who loved or were indifferent to them. None of these things are true of machines. No matter how elegant the device, it cannot know the stakes of love given or withheld. For meaning to matter, you need a body. You need people who name and need or reject you.

So my story of the rise of a psychoanalytic culture in hyper-rational France reminds us of the specificity of the human when it comes to being a friend, a therapist, or a lover. And this is at a point of inflection in the development of generative artificial intelligence, a moment when there is so much talk of chatbots and robots stepping in to do these things.

The second flash point of current relevance concerns the politics of intellectual revolutions.

Lacan said he was leading a permanent revolution in psychoanalytic ideas, but he also was treated as a *Maître* (Master) by his students and colleagues. He behaved like an authoritarian leader while insisting that psychoanalysis is antithetical to any discourse of authority. The subversive psychoanalytic science Lacan proposed was at permanent war with its institutionalization. These days, radical intellectual movements ask where and how they can best thrive. Should they be in universities or try to grow outside of traditional institutions? Should they allow themselves to have leaders? Leaderless organizations are rarely effective, but the Lacanian narrative reminds us why it remains appealing.

Third, Lacan clarifies why sciences of mind, particularly psychoanalysis, needed to divorce themselves from a political reliance on medicine.

When I wrote this book, mainstream American psychoanalysis was a medical discipline. I wanted training as an analyst—but as a PhD psychologist, I would have to sign a waiver to use my analytic training only for research purposes. Lacan was a physician, but clear that psychoanalysis didn't need doctors as much as sociologists, linguists, and philosophers. Since the publication of this book, PhD psychologists have sued the American Psychoanalytic Association for the right to full training—and won. The odd promise of the "waiver" (that there could be an analysis that had nothing to do with "treatment")—those days are over. Lacan helped label them as hypocritical: Who would lie on a couch for four sessions a week if they didn't want help with some problem? What kind of analyst would see a "client" in pain but think only of research? If these analyses were done as described, they would be toxic. But of course, they were not done as described. When I asked about them, I was told, sotto voce, that, of course, the waiver was just for show. The actual instructions were to "just ignore the whole thing . . . it's just something you have to sign."

Lacan was allergic to that kind of talk among analysts, and for him, it meant they could not be analysts. And with this kind of thing going on, his excommunication from the International Psychoanalytical Association for unorthodox practice seemed all the more unfair. Early on, American psychoanalysts had made a political calculation that Americans were more likely to accept psychoanalysis if it were a medical specialty. Lacan helps us understand why the American solution was destined to fall apart.

These days, psychoanalysis and the talk therapies it inspired are no longer most people's treatment of choice. People like cognitive therapies or psychopharmacology because it makes you feel less vulnerable. But for Lacan, even reading a psychoanalytic text should put you in a position of vulnerability. When at one of our dinner meetings, I admitted that I was struggling with his theory of the mirror stage and how it leads to a permanent fragmentation of self, Lacan tried to help. He pointed to the smoky mirrors on either side of our banquette. In the mirror stage, Lacan explained, we see ourselves in one mirror, and it's as though we also see our smoky reflection in the other across from it, and on to infinity. There is no stable image. He wanted to help, but he added that he was not sorry that I was taking hours with my reading. He said that time spent with a psychoanalytic text is time for the text to work on you. It's self-reflective time.

Rereading *Psychoanalytic Politics* today, I am struck by what it took to create the world of Lacan readers who did indeed take that time. They had patience. They had a capacity for boredom. They were not afraid of the solitude of being alone with a difficult book. Today, these qualities are under assault. Our devices interrupt us up to twelve times an hour when we are at work. Because we have become used to multitasking, we are rarely immersed enough in reading for the idea of a text "doing its work" to make sense. But these are qualities worth reclaiming. It's in our ability to be alone with ourselves and recognize our limitations that we become capable of offering ourselves in relationships. The capacity for solitude is where empathy begins.

A final note on what brought me to this book: politics. When I wrote it in the late 1970s, I was concerned that the political energy of my 1960s' generation had dissipated. Many of my politically engaged friends declared victory when the Vietnam War ended. I thought that as a generation, we had turned our attention away from the inequalities of race and class, and toward the kinds of solutions that technology said it could offer. *And it was a time when people saw working on politics and "working on yourself" as two completely different realms.* I had been to France during my junior year of college, 1968–1969. By the early 1970s, I realized that French theorists and patients were not splitting off politics and therapy but tying them together through their interest in the psychoanalytic work of Lacan. It's what led me to this book. I wanted to study the integration of thought and feeling, politics and self-examination.

The French saw Lacan as integrating the world of psychology and politics because, for him, the self is formed through language. And language lives in the realm of symbols and society. As for the Marxist theorists of the Frankfurt School, society doesn't "influence" people; it comes to dwell within them. People become social with the appropriation of language, and it is language that constitutes them as subjects. In this way of thinking, self-knowledge doesn't take you away from political action but brings you toward it. Indeed, it should free you up to do it more effectively. In our current moment of political upheaval, I can't think of a timelier message.

January 2024

Acknowledgments

This book is about the emergence of a psychoanalytic culture. The themes raised by this sociology of a science of mind are not unique to any one place or time, but this book deals with a specific case: that of France in recent years. It grew out of a field experience in that country, and my greatest debt is, of course, to all my French informants who shared their experiences and opinions with me as well as their kindness, hospitality, and humor. In the world of French psychoanalytic culture, psychoanalyst Jacques Lacan had so special and central a role that his willingness to participate in my research, to discuss contemporary psychoanalytic history with me, was of crucial importance to my work. I am deeply grateful for his cooperation.

Of course, I owe a similar debt to my many other informants, who included nearly 150 practicing French psychoanalysts, each of whom added a new dimension to the story. But a rather special problem makes it difficult for me to thank them in the usual manner. Psychoanalytic history has been explosive, schismatic, deeply personal. Its controversies have often been played out in personal denunciations and more "political" sanctions, excommunications, and schisms within the framework of psychoanalytic institutions. In recent years, there has been a growing commitment within the psycho-analytic community to the open discussion of this history. However, when I did my fieldwork in the mid-1970s, the atmosphere was rather more conservative. At that time, many of my informants requested that their names not be mentioned in any reporting of my work. Since the absence of a name can convey as much information as its presence, a traditional list of acknowledgments seemed disrespectful of the privacy of those who had helped me. So, with the exception of Lacan whose special role demanded that his cooperation be acknowledged, I shall not thank my informants individually for their help, but I hope that each appreciates the depth of my gratitude. I have also followed the consistent policy in the text of not attributing quotations that come from my interview work, although, of course, I always cite an author when I draw from the public record.

I also owe thanks to my teachers and colleagues in the United States. George Goethals, George Homans, Stanley Hoffmann, Stanley King, and Laurence Wylie of Harvard University encouraged me to pursue my doctoral studies of the French Freud along a fieldwork model and gave me excellent advice and criticism as my work progressed. David and Evey Riesman offered thoughtful criticism as well as confidence and consideration through the years of researching and writing this book. Seymour Papert's extraordinary generosity as a reader and dialogue partner broadened the scope and greatly increased the quality of this work. My ideas about the sociology of sciences of mind, and in particular about what makes them "appropriable," owes much to our long conversations. He read many drafts of both the original book and the recent additions; he always provided encouragement and challenging advice. John Berlow read several drafts of the original manuscript. His literary taste and demands for clarity were particularly helpful in writing the sections of the book on Lacanian theory.

I also profited from comments on drafts and sections of this book by Daniel Bell, Saul Friedlander, Nathan Hale, Carl Kaysen, Kenneth Keniston, Martin Kessler, Leo Marx, David Misunas, Farrell Phillips, Robert Pindyck, Martin Roberts, Nancy Rosenblum, Stuart Schneiderman, Ralph Willard, Mary Kay Wilmers, and Robert Young.

Lola Kotsopoulos was of immeasurable assistance in the preparation of the index and notes for the new material in this revised edition. Her systematicity and dedication contributed moral as well as technical support.

I was fortunate during my time in France to have had the friendship of Anne Fresco, Janine Maucorps, and Patrick Miller, who made *depaysement* less painful. On my return to the United States, the frustrations of writing were made considerably easier by Mildred Bonowitz, Robert Bonowitz, and Susan Marsten.

As I was working on the final revisions of the new material for the second edition, my daughter Rebecca was born, on May 5, 1991. Her arrival slowed down my writing but increased my joy in life; I thank her for bringing to this book a new set of wonderful associations.

Boston, Massachusetts
August 1991

Preface: Psychoanalytic Politics in the 1990s

A rapid acceptance and even infatuation with psychoanalysis swept France in the late 1960s and 1970s after a long period of resistance to Freudian ideas. Until the late 1960s there had been a small but isolated psychoanalytic movement; then there was a rapid reversal of fortunes. French society developed a strong psychoanalytic thirst.

Ready to satisfy this thirst was a peculiarly French brand of psychoanalytic thinking embodied in the work of Jacques Lacan. *Psychoanalytic Politics* describes how his Cartesian, poeticized, linguistic, and politicized psychoanalysis constituted a French "reinvention" of Freud, congruent with the style of the French structuralist intelligentsia of the 1960s. I went to France in the early 1970s to study this indigenous psychoanalytic movement and its relationship to the surrounding intellectual milieu. But this framing of the problem proved insufficiently ambitious in relation to the situation I found on arrival. Beyond the development of a distinctly French psychoanalytic theory and practice, a larger social process was taking place: the widespread appropriation of psychoanalytic ideas about mind, the creation of a psychoanalytic culture.

Thus my interest turned from the history of a psychoanalytic movement to the study of a psychoanalytic culture. A psychoanalytic movement consists of analysts, their theories, their patients, their professional associations, and may include an intellectual community that analysts directly interact with and write for. In contrast, while a psychoanalytic culture includes the intelligentsia, it always goes beyond it to involve far less exalted folk. Psychoanalytic culture refers to the way psychoanalytic metaphors and ways of thinking enter everyday life. In the French case this means the kindergarten teacher who takes a training course that includes a watered-down Lacanianism, the lycéen who learns about Lacan when she prepares the new "Freud question" for the baccalaureate, the reader of the newly psychologized advice columns. From the point of view of the high-minded history of the psychoanalytic movement, the rapprochement of the Lacanian take-off and the flowering of psychologically minded advice to the lovelorn might seem an ignorant or vulgar juxtaposition. But a psychoanalytic culture is made up precisely of such little vulgarities, little pieces of this and that, taken up and woven into larger wholes.

My primary focus is on the sociology of the psychoanalytic culture, not on the history of the psychoanalytic movement. But, of course, the story of the movement has an important place in my narrative, and this for three reasons. First, the movement provides the seeds for the development of the culture; one cannot make sense of the culture without some knowledge of the movement. Second, the culture influences the movement as well as reflects it in a powerful "effet de retour," and I focus on those facets of the movement that illustrate how this works. Third, the study of the psychoanalytic movement raises issues that are relevant to understanding the social dynamics of other intellectual movements, for example the complex role of a *Maître* in the transmission of a body of ideas across generations and the resonance of ideas about mind with larger social and political forces. In *Psychoanalytic Politics*, I use sociological criteria in my choice of narrative focus when I discuss events and theoretical debates internal to the movement.[1] So, although I touch on the development of the French psychoanalytic movement as a whole, I stress the role played by Lacan and his followers not only because of their importance to the history of French psychoanalytic ideas, but because their work and lives most dramatically illustrate the sociological themes central to my story: the interactions between psychoanalytic theory and the politics of psychoanalytic movements and between a psychoanalytic movement and a surrounding psychoanalytic culture.

The fact that the French movement developed such powerful cultural projections depended in part on the fit between Lacan and the French intellectual milieu in the 1960s, particularly its preoccupation with the "decentered" subject. But the theoretical fit between Lacan and the intellectuals was not enough to explain the widespread popular diffusion of his ideas. Crucial to that diffusion was the relationship between psychoanalysis and a social demand at the time of the "May events" of 1968 and in the years that followed. During the events, there was a call for a psychologized politics and analysts were seen as its legitimate theorists; after the events, an aborted political movement played out its themes in a highly politicized psychoanalytic language. Lacan's work was central to the creation of this culturally and historically specific bridge between the psychoanalytic and political cultures.

Within the psychoanalytic movement itself, Lacan was a controversial figure. Disagreement over Lacan's unorthodox practices (in particular, his short sessions, sometimes of five minutes' duration) and his equally unorthodox ideas about psychoanalytic training precipitated three postwar schisms in the French psychoanalytic movement. And in the heat of yet another controversy, Lacan dissolved his Freudian School shortly before his death in 1981, an act that in turn produced a chain reaction of schisms so that at one point there were over thirty identifiable psychoanalytic groups in Paris.

In this second edition of *Psychoanalytic Politics*, the main body of the text stands (with some stylistic revisions)* as it was published in 1978, three years before Lacan's death and one year before the final crisis at the Freudian School, which in retrospect marked the beginning of the post-Lacan era. There are, however, two additions to the original book: a new chapter on the politics of the Lacanian movement during the last years of Lacan's life and since his death and this preface, a reflection on how and under what conditions a psychoanalytic movement gives rise to a psychoanalytic culture.

In the first edition of *Psychoanalytic Politics*, I used a comparison between France and the United States to explore the social factors that help explain the readiness of cultures to welcome psychoanalytic ideas. Here I enlarge on this comparative approach in two ways. One is to refer to the experiences of other national cultures, specifically Great Britain and the Soviet Union. The other is to look at a non-psychoanalytic example of how intellectual "movements" give rise to "cultures" in the understanding of mind. Since the late 1970s my interest in the cultural aspects of psychoanalysis has grown into a larger inquiry into the general sociology of sciences of mind. The quality of a theory that facilitates the generation of

---

*My revisions include removing sexist language; however, the masculine pronoun and the term "man" remain where I closely paraphrase authors who use them.

a culture from a movement needs a name: refer to it as that theory's "appropriability." Using the name focuses a general question: What makes some theories of mind more appropriable than others?

To answer this question I have found it particularly illuminating to juxtapose psychoanalytic models with another and currently fashionable approach to the representation of mind—the one that derives from computational thinking. Psychoanalytic and computational theories of mind could not be further apart in terms of their content. But in their form, these theories share something very important: both incite people to play with them in an active way.

In the case of psychoanalysis, what we play with are Freudian "things" such as dreams, slips, and jokes. Freudian ideas about slips became well known and gained wide acceptance for reasons that had little to do with positive assessments of their scientific validity and a great deal to do with the fact that they are almost-tangible ideas. They are ideas that function as "things" or objects. You can analyze your slips and those of your friends. They are manipulable and thus appealing. As we look for slips and play with them, both seriously and not so seriously, psychoanalytic ideas—at the very least, the idea that there is an unconscious—begin to seem more natural.

The Freudian slip as an "object to think with" provided one important way for psychoanalytic ideas to weave themselves into the fabric everyday life. Similarly, the play of manipulable and almost-tangible concepts stands behind the appropriability of computational theories of mind. To illustrate this point, consider a "slip" culled from Freud's own collection from both a psychoanalytic and a computational point of view.

At the beginning of a meeting, recounts Freud, its chairman rises to greet its participants and says, "I now declare this meeting closed." For Freud it is obvious that the slip is a source of information about the real wishes of the chairman: "The President secretly *wished* he was already in a position to close the sitting, from which little good was to be expected."[2] From a computational perspective, however, things need not be so emotionally complex. According to this way of looking at the world, people, like computer programs, can become momentarily derailed. When this happens and a slip occurs, it does not reflect secret wishes or hidden ambivalence. It may simply reveal the mechanisms of computation. The computational perspective on the chairman's slip begins with a view of the brain as a computer that contains information in something like a dictionary.[3] In an ordinary dictionary, the words *closed* and *open* are far apart. But when information is stored in a computer, it is common to represent opposites by the same symbol, with another symbol used to represent negation. In other words, *hot* = (–) *cold*: *dry* = (–) *wet*; and, of course, *open* = (–) *closed*. In the computer's storage medium, *open* and *closed* would be right next to each other, precisely because they are so far apart in meaning. Thus, in the case of a computationally modeled slip, all that has happened when *closed* is substituted for *open* is that a minus sign, a bit of information, has been dropped. As one of my students at MIT once put it, reflecting on Freud's example of the unhappy chairman: "All that has happened is that a bit has been dropped. There has been a power surge. No problem."

When what was once seen as a Freudian slip comes to be theorized as an information-processing error, there has been a shift in focus from meaning to mechanism. From the point of view of content, the two models, psychoanalytic and computational, are dramatically different. However, from the perspective of our inquiry into what makes theories of mind appropriable, what is most striking is not their differences but their similarities. Each offers accessible and manipulable "objects to think with." Each allows its objects to be easily anthropomorphized. To take the simplest case (which is the only case that matters when one looks for the reasons for a theory's appropriability), when one thinks about psychoanalysis, one can imagine the rational ego, the dirty id, and the censoring superego as inner personae. The theory offers a compelling cast of inner agents and games to play with them. Computational theory does so as well; one may be asked to imagine programs and subroutines as inner agents in a computer's "society of mind."[4] In the case of both theories, people imagine themselves in the roles of the psychic entities and acting out these roles feels enough like an acting out of the theories to give the sense of understanding them. Whether or not one really understands computational and psychoanalytic theories in their technical detail, each offers active experiences that break down resistance to seeing mind in its terms. So one way to describe the appropriability of specific theories of mind is to talk about the possibilities they offer for concrete manipulation.

From this point of view, Lacan's genius was that although he was an extremely abstract theorist, he also gave psychoanalysis a new set of concrete "objects to think with." His integration of linguistics and its notation into psychoanalytic discourse provided a highly manipulable object language. The play of equations, of little letters and big letters, of bars and ratios, of signifiers to signified, was easy to pick up and experiment with. Whether or not one thinks that this new language moved psychoanalytic thinking in a desirable direction, its cultural power was undeniable. It gave psychoanalysis new relevance to those who took text as their object; it opened up what Lacan termed the "Freudian field" to the larger study of discourse.

Toward the end of his life, Lacan worked extensively with images of complex knots whose configurations symbolized the structure of the mind as he understood it. He believed that the knots were more than a theoretical metaphor; they offered a theory in practice. As we shall see, for Lacan, the physical *manipulation* of the knots was both an aid to theorizing and an embodiment of the process of theorizing. Thus in this case, Lacan believed that the objects themselves carried the theory. They were quite explicitly his "objects to think with." Claude Lévi-Strauss wrote of the power of *bricolage*, a theoretical tinkering at the heart of a science of the concrete.[5] Lacan himself was a *bricoleur*; beyond this, he facilitated the work of *bricolage* on a cultural level.

Freud's theory of slips is a theory of why people make them: we try to repress unacceptable wishes but they break through all the same. It is also a theory of why people like to think about slips: they offer a way to get closer to these taboo wishes. And most central to my subject here, it is a theory of why people are attracted to Freudian ideas in general: they offer us a way to come close to aspects of ourselves, such as sexuality and aggression, which we censor but at the same time want to be in contact with, the uncivilized that makes us human. A similar dynamic stands behind the appropriability of computational ideas. If behind popular acceptance of Freudian theory was a nervous, often guilty preoccupation with the self as sexual, behind the widespread interest in computational interpretations of the self is an equally nervous preoccupation with the self as machine. Playing with psychoanalytic and computational theories allows us to play with aspects of our nature that we experience as taboo.

Discussing the appropriability of a psychological theory in terms of its ability to offer concrete "objects to think with" puts the emphasis on formal qualities intrinsic to the theory. But raising the question of what is taboo at a given moment in the life of a society points to the necessity of a different kind of analysis. We need to look at a science of mind in the context of the culture into which it is deployed. In other words, what stands behind the development of a psychoanalytic thirst? If we take the formal properties of psychoanalytic "objects to think with" as intrinsically appropriable, what social conditions encourage a psychoanalytic movement to grow into a psychoanalytic culture? What has to happen for psychoanalytic ideas to influence the way that not only professional psychologists, but the amateur psychologists that we all are, think about thinking?

A first set of conditions relate to an underlying sociology. A psychoanalytic culture is not something that a psychoanalytic movement can create in the outside world; the outside world has to be ready. In chapter 1, I describe how psychoanalysis flourishes during what Philip Rieff has called a moment of deconversion, that is, a time of rapid mobility and social dislocation, a time when the old rules and traditional, collective ways of interpreting experience no longer seem to apply. In a traditional society, it is the community and its values that cure; when tradition breaks down, they no longer can serve this function, and the individual must create a personal world of symbols and meaning. Reflecting on the social dislocation of American society, Peter Berger remarked that in twentieth-century America, "if Freud hadn't existed, he would have had to be invented."[6] From this point of view, it is not surprising that psychoanalysis was welcomed in an urban America that had to come to terms with geographic and spiritual rootlessness, with social mobility from within and immigration from without. In the United States, a psychoanalytic culture began to grow in the 1920s and took off in the years after World War II. In more traditional French society, a widespread psychoanalytic culture was a much later phenomenon.

Following this model, one can speculate about the causes of the continuing cultural reticence toward psychoanalysis in Great Britain. There, unlike in France and the United States, a strong psychoanalytic movement exists in relative cultural isolation. It barely penetrates British academic life, and for the most part, cultural criticism, political discussion, and social analysis proceed without psychoanalytic referent. British psychoanalytic theory of the object relations school increasingly dominates American clinical discussion, but this international success is nonetheless coupled with isolation at home.

To put it too simply, the British psychoanalytic movement is not situated in a British psychoanalytic culture. Perhaps British society has retained certain traditional values that have shielded it from the full implications of the process that Rieff called deconversion. This may be seen in the community of British intellectuals, few of whom have turned toward psychoanalysis as have their French and American counterparts. In the early history of British psychoanalysis, the Freudian movement was taken up by a certain literary culture through Bloomsbury, but things did not go much further than that. For some British intellectuals, the traditional virtues of rationality and logic, an intact sense of caste privilege, and the intellectual aesthetic of analytic philosophy have served as a shield against what they perceived as an unseemly Freudian onslaught. For others, the role of traditional intellectual values has been played by a style of Marxism hostile to psychoanalysis, which it condemns as reductionist and bourgeois.

The recent experience of the Soviet Union[†] gives a new opportunity to reflect on the experience of psychoanalytic thirst. There, since the late 1980s I have studied a situation in which psychoanalysis is in great demand despite the virtual absence of cultural supply. Freud had been unofficially banned since the 1930s, but with glasnost and the relaxation of censorship, there has been a race to republish his texts. In 1989–1990, over a million copies of the first official publication of Freud's essays were printed; they were sold before they made their way into bookstores.

In the Soviet Union today, people are visibly eager to understand their experience in psychoanalytic terms. Freud is one symbol among many others of democratization, free expression, and the growth of a new individualism in personal and economic life. The Soviet situation is intriguing because it is the mirror image of that in Britain. Again, to put it too simply, in Britain there is a psychoanalytic movement and no psychoanalytic culture whereas in the Soviet Union there is no psychoanalytic movement but there are the preconditions for a psychoanalytic culture. There is a widespread psychoanalytic thirst.

Of course, life in Moscow today is characterized precisely by a crisis of community and traditional values characteristic of a period of deconversion. With the Communist Party and its view of history delegitimated, the Soviet individual is thrown into the uncharted waters of having to define individual purpose. As Berger would say, something has to be invented or reinvented. On the side of reinvention, Eastern Orthodox religion is the main contender. But its appeal is conservative: the prospect of reintegrating the individual into a

---

[†]Note that this preface was written in 1991.

collectivity—and a collectivity that looks to the past. On the side of invention, there are classical models of free enterprise, social Darwinism, and a range of psychologies of the individual, among them psychoanalysis. In the Soviet Union today, psychoanalysis is perceived as an ideology for the invention of a new kind of person who can make it alone and who has meaning alone, without Party or state.

On my first visit to the Soviet Union in 1987, I met Soviets who held tattered Freudian texts, translated and printed in the 1920s and banned in the 1930s, as though they were precious religious icons. The analogy to icons is more than metaphoric. For the most part, Freud's works were kept in locked rooms in libraries. And when there was private possession, their reverent study needed to be kept a guarded secret. In 1988, I met philosophy students who had been analyzed by their elders, and their elders by their elders, a small and somewhat clandestine community that took its direction from Freud's earlier writings (largely because these were most readily available). By 1989, the situation was far more open. Among students, intellectuals, teachers, and therapists of all varieties, there was interest in and demands for analysis; indeed, there were repeated demands that I undertake training analyses during a three-week visit to Moscow. (My objections to this procedure were repeatedly challenged with the comment "Isn't that how Freud analyzed his first students on their visits to Vienna?")

By spring 1989, the question of publishing Freud was part of stronger demands in general for freedom of speech and press. The first publication of Freud in the Soviet Union since Stalin's ban was not by the state publishing office but by a member of the new class of free enterprise entrepreneurs—Marat Akchuran. Akchuran headed a small private business that, in the somewhat confusing lexicon of Soviet free enterprise, is called a "cooperative." In May 1989, he printed 100,000 copies of "Three Essays on Sexuality," using a text obtained from a small provincial library. But the law that established cooperatives did not permit these private organizations to publish books, a right reserved for state publishing houses. Freud's "Three Essays" became a test case to challenge that law.

The state bureaucracy seized all printed copies of the "Three Essays," claiming that Freud was still banned, these ideas were bad for youth, and the texts were pornographic. Finally, it claimed that only the state could publish books. In the Moscow of summer 1989, publishing Freud became a symbol not only of the right to repressed knowledge, but of individual economic rights in the marketplace of ideas. Only a few months later, in September, a state publishing house, "Prosvichenia," released a collection of Freud's essays that ran through two editions and sold 1,250,000 copies within six months.

Looking at different national case studies suggests that while one way of thinking about the sociology of psychoanalysis stresses the large social processes of deconversion, a second needs to be on the level of a more intimate sociology, namely in terms of the way that ideas come to connect with individuals, the "inner history" of sciences of mind. Deconversion creates the context for individualistic ideologies to flourish. But which ones will flourish? Which ones will be able to make a connection?

For one of these theories to be psychoanalysis, it must be able to present a formulation that helps people think through a historically specific problem. The process is dialectical because societies can also shape psychoanalytic theory into forms that are suited to their specific needs. In her study of comparative psychoanalysis, Edith Kurzweil noted, "Every country creates the psychoanalysis it needs, although it does

so unconsciously."[7] Appropriable theories must be available
for sculpting by the culture into which they are deployed
and psychoanalysis is no exception. In *Psychoanalytic Politics*
I explore the cultural plasticity of psychoanalytic ideas when
I discuss the many ways in which the "French Freud," whose
idiom invaded French life and language in the 1960s, was a
very different animal from the "American Freud" of the past
or of today. American psychoanalytic ego psychology, directed
toward an active adaptation of the patient to reality, toward
what came to be called "coping," brought Freudianism in line
with American beliefs about the virtue and necessity of an
optimistic approach. Aspects of the theory that could not be
brought into line were rejected or reshaped.

For example, American optimism would naturally rebel
against that part of the Freudian message that suggested an
early and irrevocable determination of character. Erik Erikson's work is a good example of how psychoanalytic theory
was able to take on a more acceptable American form. Erikson's emphasis on adolescent and adult development and on
a life cycle where early themes get to be replayed at later stages
suggests that we all get second chances, as do Heinz Kohut's
ideas about reparenting, another image that aptly fits American dreams. In America, where there is no strong intellectual
tradition on the Left, optimistic revisions of Freud focused on
an adaptation to a reality whose justice was rarely challenged.
In France, on the other hand, where there is a strong political
and intellectual Left, psychoanalysts became deeply involved
in radical social criticism, and French social criticism became
deeply involved with psychoanalytic thinking. In France,
Lacanian psychoanalytic premises became the common reference shared by Communist Party and non-Party Marxism,
utopian and anarchistic *gauchisme*, and feminism.

Thus the possibility for the growth of psychoanalytic cultures depends on the dual nature of psychoanalytic theory as both concrete and culturally malleable, on the presence of a moment of social deconversion, and on a crucial third condition I have already noted. Theories most easily pass into popular culture when they offer a way for people to "think through" a collective issue of political and social identity. In chapter 1, I introduce the notion of using a theory to "think through" a historical event by beginning with a non-psychoanalytic example. French existentialist writers began writing before the war, but it was only in the postwar years that history, in a sense, caught up with them. Their philosophy of extreme situations and actions for extraordinary individuals was resonant with the French experience of the Occupation and Resistance. Part of existentialism's popular appeal was that it provided a way to think through the issues of choice and individual responsibility that had been raised by the war years: to collaborate or not to collaborate, to betray or not to betray those who did.

The heart of my argument on the infatuation with Freud that followed the May events of 1968 in France is to propose a relationship between psychoanalysis and the May events that was in many ways similar to the one between existentialism and the Occupation and Resistance. Both theories offered historically appropriate "objects to think with," theoretical materials for a cultural process analogous to the concrete manipulations of Lévi-Strauss's *bricolage*.

In France, the events of May–June 1968 were an explosion of speech and desire. They called for the invention of new political forms that looked not to the politics of traditional political parties but to a politics of the person. For a short while the May events looked like a revolution in the making, but then suddenly they were over. After the events, people were left hungry for a way to continue to think about sexuality and self-expression as part of a revolutionary movement, for a way to think about the personal as the political and social. "Thinking through the events" required a theory that integrated society and the individual. Lacan provided that theory in his ideas about the transition from imaginary to symbolic realm, the transition from presocial to social with the acquisition of language.

Lacan's theory of the construction of the symbolic order allows for no real boundary between self and society: human beings become social with the appropriation of language and it is language that constitutes human beings as subjects. In this way of looking at things, society does not simply "influence" autonomous individuals but actually comes to dwell within them at the moment of the appropriation of language. In chapter 3 I note that Lacan, like Jean-Jacques Rousseau, described a powerful myth of passage that was able to serve as a framework for thinking about the individual and society in a very different way from Wilhelm Reich's discussion of a "natural man" deformed by crass society. In Lacan's version of the banishment from Eden, *there is no natural man* and therefore no way of thinking about society as coming afterward to thwart his nature. The infant is alienated in a first imaginary realm of mirrors and misidentifications and the imaginary always remains within us just as does the structure of the social order when we pass into the symbolic realm.

People who thought of themselves as being on the Left were able to read Lacan's theory of the social and linguistic construction of the self as supporting the notion that the "private self" is a construct of capitalism and that the distinction between private and public, the very touchstone of bourgeois thought, exists only as an invention of bourgeois ideology. This interpretation was surely far from Lacan's original intention—and such appropriations might well have seemed off the point both to him and to dedicated members of his psychoanalytic movement. But such appropriations are the stuff of psychoanalytic culture. The psychoanalytic ideas that are appropriated into that culture are not the ideas as written but the ideas as "read," the ideas as reconstructed by what, in the context of literary criticism, has been called an "interpretive community."[8] In the case of psychoanalysis as in the case of literature, displacing political and social effects from the text to its reading has the effect of moving the debate from the question of what a theory is to "what the theory does—in a particular place, for a particular public, . . . at a particular time."[9]

Lacanianism offered images that were good to think with for addressing the issues that surrounded the May events. The Lacanian mythology, the vivid and richly imaged portrait of the social and linguistic construction of the subject in the symbolic dimension, became a common idiom in French discourse in the years that followed 1968. Indeed, for several years, much of social thought situated itself in what one could term "Lacanian space." That is to say, French social and political theory tended to accept the fundamentals of Lacan's theoretical scaffolding, in particular, the notions that people are constituted by language, that our discourse embodies the society beyond, and that there is no autonomous ego. People who disagreed profoundly with each other and, indeed, who disagreed profoundly with Lacan nevertheless situated themselves in this space.

In sum, thinking through the May events required a theory that could integrate politics and the person. In the *après-mai*, this theory was psychoanalysis. When I speak of "thinking through the Resistance" by "thinking existentialism" or "thinking through the May events" by "thinking psychoanalysis," I am not describing a use of theory to *explain* social events but, rather, a way of using theory to "work through" powerful cultural images, to help to arrange these images into new and clearer patterns. In the case of the May events and psychoanalysis, people used contact with the theory to keep in touch with the stuff of which the events were made. For a person to use theory in this way does not require a full understanding of its subtleties. Understanding the power of theory in such cases constitutes a "sociology of superficial knowledge" that does not trivialize the meanings of that theory in the life of an individual or culture. In this spirit, the widespread phenomenon of "coffee table Lacan" is a serious object of study for social epistemology.

In the Soviet Union today, the people who talk so much about psychoanalysis often don't even *have* a psychoanalytic book to put on their coffee table, if indeed they have a coffee table at all. The psychoanalytic discourse there is impressionistic and fragmented, based largely on images of psychoanalysis frozen in the 1930s. And yet the images drawn from this "time-capsule Freud" serve urgent current purposes. Soviets *want* to talk about repression, the unconscious, the things they feel but were not allowed to say, the things that they have trained themselves not even to feel. In this context, psychoanalysis carries a heavy symbolic burden. Traditional Soviet psychiatric doctrine argued that all mental distress was born in the material illness of the body or in the individual's failure to integrate into the socialist collectivity. In a striking analogy with the meanings it carried in France in the years after May 1968, psychoanalysis became symbolic of the individual,

the idiosyncratic, the power of new and previously unliber-
ated forces for change. Psychoanalysis became symbolic of the
symbolic itself.

France offers a dramatic case to study the tension between
this "subversive" side of psychoanalysis and its widespread
social diffusion. If psychoanalysis is a subversive science,
undermining all accepted truths, what does it mean when it
becomes acceptable, "the thing to do?" Freud thought he was
bringing America a subversive doctrine, indeed he has been
widely quoted as referring to it as "the plague." Instead, cultural diffusion occurred at the price of normalization through
medical and social acceptability. In America today, Freudian
thought sometimes seems lost in a morass of self-help slogans
and therapeutic homilies. Popularization carries the risk that
the specificity of the psychoanalytic movement will be lost in
the psychoanalytic culture.

That risk is strikingly present in France today. At the end
of the 1950s, there were only about 150 psychoanalysts in
France; today analyst Gérard Mendel estimates that there are
15,000.[10] Unlike in America, where the number of patients
in classical analysis has decreased and analysts usually fill
their practices with patients in analytically inspired psychotherapy, most reports have it that French analysts are able
to find analytic patients. In a 1986 survey, 18 percent of all
French adults knew someone in psychoanalysis.[11] The figure
was highest for the middle classes (at 30 percent), but there is
widespread testimony about the general democratization of
the analytic cure, even from the provinces. Dr. Paul Mathis,
an analyst from Toulon, describes his full-time analytic practice within a community of analysts that has grown from two
members in 1960 to over a hundred today. He claims that his
clientele includes "doctors, lawyers, judges, high school and

grade school teachers, naval officers, and a few workers from the naval shipyards. The only people I have never seen in my office are policemen."[12]

This democratization of clientele goes hand in hand with a staggering level of coverage of psychoanalysis in the French popular media: in addition to literary publications, articles on psychoanalysis appear in newspapers, weekly magazines, women's magazines, and in the Sunday supplements. Along with democratization and popularization has come public discussion of the analytic cure by its patients. Eric Cantona, a young French soccer star, describes in *L' Express* how he had to cut his analysis short to make a career move from Auxerre to Marseilles:

> When I stopped, we had barely begun to explore the real questions, emotional problems, sexual problems, problems with my family. So I had to begin again—once again I felt a lack, no one to speak to, to really speak to. . . . When I am in analysis, it is like an oil change, I am in my best form, I play my best. Yes, I must start again. It's no longer a curiosity but a necessity. As a matter of fact everyone should have the courage to have done one. Everyone should at the very least read Freud and Groddeck.[13]

It is a public testimonial that is hard to imagine from an American baseball or British cricket star.

Beginning with Marie Cardinale's *The Words to Say It* in 1975, the French psychoanalytic novel or "report from the couch" became a new literary genre. Two of its most recent manifestations, *Seduction on the Couch* and *My Analyst and Me*, portray patients who have been sexually exploited by their analysts but then find salvation *through a second psychoanalysis*, this time with a more serious practitioner.[14] The popularization of psychoanalysis reflects its social normalization (it is perceived as helping with anxiety, loneliness, sports) as well as a fierce loyalty to the psychoanalytic method (a bad treatment can only be salvaged by a good and more rigorous treatment).

Is there a price for popularization? Lacan held a position that suggested that psychoanalysis, like anarchism, is a system committed to breaking down systems. The increasing integration of psychoanalysis into the everyday raises ever more sharply a question that weaves through this book. Does the continuing power of the psychoanalytic movement, like that of anarchism, depend on permanent revolution rather than social acceptability?

Today's French psychoanalytic culture stands in a complex relationship to this issue. In the years since Lacan's death in 1981, psychoanalysis has become increasingly accepted as a therapy and even as a privileged path toward personal salvation. In France, patients are able to find psychoanalysts through the yellow pages of the phone directory, through computerized information systems available on home networks, and through personal advertisements that sometimes include the analyst's photograph. The most well-known French analysts, including Serge Leclaire, Françoise Dolto, and Gérard Miller, turned (as did Lacan) to radio and television to bring their messages to the public. In all of this, however, French analysts struggle to find a way to maintain the radical specificity of their theory and practice. Perhaps paradoxically, it is the Lacanian analyst Serge Leclaire who has taken the most public position in favor of "specifying" the domain of psychoanalysis. His proposal is for analysts to regulate their own profession. His December 1989 call for an "Order of Psychoanalysts" was designed to ward off state certification. Some analysts favored the idea of an exclusionary professional association as a way to protect analysis from the perceived excesses of certain Lacanians—in particular, those affiliated with the psychoanalytic society headed by Lacan's son-in-law, Jacques-Alain Miller. Ever since it was founded in the year of Lacan's death, Miller's School of the Freudian Cause has been surrounded by controversy, most recently a lawsuit against Miller by one of the school's members, Gérard Pommier. Pommier accused Miller of taking information gleaned from patients in treatment and using it against him. Ironically, it was Miller who could have been the one suing for breach of confidentiality ten years earlier, when Miller's own analyst, Charles Melman, denounced him, setting off the chain reaction that led to a mass desertion of analysts from the School of the Freudian Cause.

In France, such continuing and it would seem endemic institutional crises within the psychoanalytic movement have been played out on the public stage, indeed, reported as front-page news. So at the same time that psychoanalysis has been normalized as a therapy in the public mind, it has continued to present itself to outsiders as a movement whose politics may put it in perpetual self-contradiction. For example, the passage of time has made it clear that the politics of self-authorization in the Lacanian movement (Lacan took a stand against institutional certification and insisted that only an individual analyst in training is in a position to declare himself ready for practice) was in conflict with the presence of a *Maître* whose authority authorized the self-authorization. Lacan, dead or alive, has remained the living legitimating presence.

The last years of Lacan's life, years in which he put his son-in-law Jacques-Alain Miller in the place of dauphin—much as Freud made his daughter Anna his Antigone—dramatized the tortured and self-contradictory nature of psychoanalysis as a family affair, whether by blood, by marriage, or by transferential bond. These underlying structural problems that plague the Paris circle, much as they plagued the Vienna circle of half a century before, show psychoanalysis struggling not only with the paradoxes of popularization but against itself.

The republication of this book raises the question of the current relevance of one of its major themes: specifically Lacan's critique of the ego. In his very first seminar in 1953, Lacan complained that the ego psychologists say "over and over again, 'We speak only to the ego, we are in communication with the ego alone, everything is challenged via the ego.'"[15] Lacan argued that the ego cannot provide any solutions for analyst or patient because it is the problem: "The ego is structured exactly like a symptom. At the heart of the subject, it is only a privileged symptom, the human symptom *par excellence*, the mental illness of man."[16] For Lacan, the ego never exists as a coherent entity. From the beginning, it is a composite of false and distorted introjections so that I and Other are inextricably confused in the language of the self. When you look inside there are mirrors and snapshots and patched-on labels. But there is no I.

In this book I place special emphasis on Lacan's critique of the ego, in part because it highlights the differences between the French and American psychoanalytic traditions. Some readers may feel that Lacan's critique is no longer relevant, believing that what Lacan had to say was once very useful but that denunciations of the "first wave" ego psychologists are no longer needed. I do not share that belief; Lacan's message about the decentered self seems more relevant than ever. First, even if psychoanalytic ego psychology has become far more philosophically sophisticated, there is the continued growth and popular presence of all of its noisy relations: the plethora of theories and therapies that assume the presence of an active, autonomous self. These run the gamut from what has come to be called American "humanistic" psychology to the flowering of such opportunistic offshoots as bioenergetics, biorhythms, and "being your own best friend." They each talk a somewhat different language, but their messages have something fundamental in common. They each promise self-improvement, without calling society into question, by stressing the reassuring and the individualistic. In the world of analytic theory, Heinz Hartmann may no longer be a major point of reference, but (to take only one example) Kohutian theory presents a self whose optimism, realism, and ability to stand aside from conflict makes it not dissimilar to the autonomous ego that Lacan took to task over a quarter of a century ago.

In addition, to come full circle and return to the cultural impact of computational models of mind, the growing presence of increasingly "intelligent" computers in everyday life has given new salience to questions about the centered ego and its autonomy. People now meet ideas about intelligent computers outside the realm of science fiction, in the plans and the products of industrialists, educators, and toy makers. In my research on the impact of these ideas on how people think about the human self, I have found a paradoxical, even a romantic reaction.[17] Many people react to intelligent machines and to computational images used for thinking about people by asserting the opposite, that is, that people can never be captured in a software program. Faced with the prospect of intelligent machines, they insist that people, unlike the machines, are not deterministic systems; they insist that free will exists, that there is an acting ego that slips through the net of science.

Thus it would be far too simple to explain away ego psychology as the "Americanization of psychoanalysis" or as though it were a historical accident beyond which we could easily move. Lacan noted that analysts themselves periodically greet the return of the ego with relief: "Ah! Our nice little ego is back again! It all makes sense now!"[18] What is true in the analytic world is true for the popular culture as well. Ego psychology is the psychological model that is closest to common sense. It is the psychological model that is closest to the way most people *like* to think about themselves. It is the version of the unconscious most acceptable to the conscious.

Lacan's critique of ego psychology relates directly to a struggle that touches each individual. To what extent is each of us willing to accept the presence within ourselves of an other, an alien, whether that other be linguistic, social, historical, or computational? To what extent are we willing to accept a subversion of our everyday sense of ourselves as autonomous actors, the makers of our own lives? Doing so takes extraordinary discipline because everything pushes in the other direction, including and perhaps especially, language. As soon as we use pronouns with verbs—"*I* do, *she* wants, *he* desires"—we speak the language of the *cogito*, without (if Lacan is right) being one.

For generations, people have argued about what was revolutionary in Freud's theory and the debate has usually centered on Freud's ideas about sexuality. These days, the idea that our sexual selves are present in everything we say, do, and think has passed into the world of things that most people take for granted. But Lacan's work underscores that part of Freud's message that is revolutionary for our time. The individual is "decentered." There is no autonomous self. What sex was to the Victorians, the question of free will is to our new fin de siècle.

Introduction: Freud's French Revolution

During May and June 1968, French society experienced a social explosion of near revolutionary proportions. A student protest in the Department of Sociology at the University of Paris at Nanterre escalated into a social movement that struck at every level of French society. In the space of weeks, not only the universities, but the factories, the theaters, the high schools, and the hospitals, too, were on strike. People rejected the authority not only of the government and the employer, but of the traditional opposition—the Left political parties and trade unions as well. The turbulent May days created the impression of a vacuum of power which made it look—if only for a short time—as if control of the French state could be taken by any group with sufficient organization and will. France was gripped by a paroxysm of the spoken word. There were confrontations and attempts at communication across generational and class lines that were unparalleled in her recent national life. The spirit of the May days was utopian, expressive, and festive. The ideology of the celebrants was to avoid traditional ideology. The fresh outlook of May downplayed traditional forms of structured political action and stressed an existential revolution of the person.

For most participants, May–June 1968 was a deeply moving personal experience, yet the May events, judged by standard revolutionary political criteria, were a failure. Power was not seized; within a few weeks, life in France returned to normal. The public buildings that had been occupied were washed and put back into order, the ubiquitous posters were stripped away, and the graffiti was sandblasted from the walls. By mid-June, Paris was cleaned up and returned to the tourists, its cobble-stones paved over—building blocks of the barricades frozen in cement.

At the time, observers of the French scene searched in vain for traces of the May events on French life. This book describes ways in which May 1968 marked and gave momentum to a profound though not immediately visible kind of change: the dramatic reversal of the relationship between psychoanalysis and French society and culture. In the course of the 1960s, the French attitude toward psychoanalysis swung from denigra-tion and resistance to infatuation in one of the most dramatic social reversals of an intellectual position in modern history. Until recently, it had been commonplace in twentieth-century intellectual history to contrast the American "overacceptance of psychoanalysis" with France's violent and sustained rejec-tion of it. In fact, the first to comment on the differences in the fate of psychoanalysis in France and America was Freud himself.

When Freud came to America in 1909, he was amazed. After confronting the skepticism of the medical and scien-tific communities in Europe, Freud found the America of 1909 a welcome terrain. Professors at Clark University seemed astoundingly unprejudiced and open, even to the point of giv-ing psychoanalysis a place in their lectures at a time when their European counterparts were ignorant or scornful of the new doctrine. "In prudish America," remarked Freud, "it was possible, at least in academic circles, to discuss freely and scientifically everything that in ordinary life is regarded as objectionable."[1] In the capitals of Europe, the situation was reversed: life was "sophisticated" and the universities puritanical. Freud could only wonder at the attitude of the Americans: "They don't understand that I am bringing them the plague."

Only five years after his American visit, Freud noted that something was going wrong in America. Americans were accepting psychoanalysis too *easily*, and Freud took this as a sure sign that they were misunderstanding it, watering it down, and sweetening it to their taste. To his mind, if the Americans really had been accepting the theory of infantile sexuality, for example, things would not have been going so smoothly. Freud believed that too easy an acceptance meant that psychoanalysis was being denatured, and he also believed the converse: resistance to psychoanalysis suggested that it was being taken seriously. For Freud, psychoanalysis was so deeply subversive of commonsense ways of thinking about the world that to understand it was to resist it. It was for this reason that Freud wrote that "the final decisive battle" for psychoanalysis would be played out "where the greatest resistance has been displayed."[2]

By 1914, it was already clear that it was in France, country of Mesmer, Bernheim, Charcot, Bergson, and Janet, with its long literary tradition of exquisite sensitivity to the psychological, that resistance to psychoanalysis was the greatest. French philosophers preferred Henri Bergson, the French church found it morally unacceptable, and French scientists found it shabby. Only the surrealists, who distorted and poeticized the theory to their taste and almost beyond Freud's recognition, had anything good to say about psychoanalysis.

"In Paris itself," reflected Freud, "the conviction still seems to reign . . . that everything good in psychoanalysis is a repetition of Janet's views with insignificant modifications, and that everything else in it is bad."[3]

Freud's juxtaposition of France and America seems to have been prophetic, as have his fears that in America the pressures of pragmatism might turn psychoanalysis into a watered-down eclecticism. In America, a too easy acceptance of an "acceptable," "medicalized" psychoanalysis went along with a downplaying of elements that Freud considered essential to his theory. For example, Freud's ideas about the unconscious and about infantile sexuality were diluted in the service of making them more palatable to American tastes. Psychoanalysis was torn from its base in cultural studies by the American Psychoanalytic Association's 1927 decision to limit its practice to medical doctors. The path was clear for its socialization, perhaps even its domestication, by American psychiatry. Few American psychoanalysts were interested in psychoanalysis as a subject for basic research. Most saw themselves as medical practitioners and tended to codify the rules of practice as they would codify the rules for any medical specialty. Today, American psychoanalysis may be paying a price for its early loss of independence from medicine. There is a lack of intellectual dynamism, a marked decline in the volume of analytic practice. In competition with the plethora of other therapies, few analysts can fill their practices with analytic patients.

In France, on the other hand, psychoanalysis had become the fiefdom of poets, novelists, and painters before the physicians had even expressed their interest. There was no French psychoanalytic society until 1926, and for nearly a quarter of a century it remained small, its members badly stigmatized by medical peers. Before World War II, the French had rejected psychoanalysis as a German inspiration, an object of distrust; after the war, it fared only a little better with a new image as an American import.

In the years since 1968, all of this has changed. Freudian thinking became a central theme in French intellectual life in fields as diverse as literary criticism, mathematics, economics, and philosophy. And the change has gone far beyond the intelligentsia: psychoanalysis has emerged as a social phenomenon. A small and insignificant French psychoanalytic movement has become a French psychoanalytic culture, deeply and broadly involved in politics and society. The number of French analysts has shot up dramatically, and public interest in psychoanalysis has climbed to new heights. Child-raising manuals, vocational counseling, education, and social work have all "gone psychoanalytic." Psychoanalysis became big news in French medicine, psychiatry, and publishing. One of France's most popular radio personalities even claimed to be doing mini-psychoanalyses over the airwaves.

Despite superficial similarities with the situation in the United States during the 1940s and early 1950s, when psychoanalysis enjoyed a certain hegemony in American cultural life, the contemporary French psychoanalytic movement is a new breed, more intensely engaged in questions about the nature of psychoanalysis, its status as a science, its relationship to linguistics, mathematics, poetry, and politics. The French psychoanalytic movement may have been a "slow starter," but its maturation has been explosive and dramatic. The psychoanalytic idiom has invaded French life and language, changing the ways people think about politics, discuss literature, and address their children. The degree of social infiltration of the psychoanalytic metaphor in France may be unique in the history of the psychoanalytic movement. Even in the United

States, things did not go so far. The extent of its colonization of intellectual and popular culture and its strong political flavor are only two of the many ways in which the new "French Freud" is a very different animal than "American Freud" ever was or is today.

In America, a special mix of optimism, individualism, and voluntarism contributed to the acceptance of a psychoanalytic *therapy* founded on the belief that people can change themselves by their own efforts if they want to. American individualism tends to represent the individual as a virtuoso or entrepreneur of his or her own self. Although it underscores autonomy, it does not assume that we each possess an inviolable inner core that constitutes our "human nature." Thus it is very different from traditional French ideas about individualism that focus on the individual's boundaries and isolation from others. French notions about the immutable self were hard to reconcile with an active notion of psychoanalytic interventionism. This is reflected in the contemporary French style of psychoanalytic theorizing, which emphasizes that psychoanalysis is an interpretive science in which images of analytic "listening" (*l'écoute*) and analytic understanding are more salient than promises of analytic "cure."

In America, on the other hand, individuals are taught that to achieve success, they must be willing to change. Unlike the French, Americans believe in the plasticity of the individual who could learn to conform; that which is not malleable, or suitable for reshaping, is often dismissed. Americans accepted psychoanalysis, but they shaped it to their image of what would be "helpful."[4] American psychoanalytic ego psychology, directed toward an active adaptation of the patient to reality, toward what came to be called "coping," brought Freudianism in line with American beliefs about the virtue and necessity of an optimistic approach.[5] This version of psychoanalysis, considerably more optimistic and conformist than Freud's own, could then be presented as a recipe for individual change and was particularly attractive to the nation of the "other directed."[6] It was able to assuage fears of being different or of being unsusceptible to "reform," and it promised that self-improvement was possible without calling society into question.

In America, where there is no strong intellectual tradition on the Left, the optimistic revisions of Freud focused on adaptation to a reality whose justice was rarely challenged. Those analysts who did try to use psychoanalytic insights as part of a critique of American life were exceptions to the general trend. But in France, where there is a strong political and intellectual Left, psychoanalysts became deeply involved in radical social criticism, and French social criticism became deeply involved with psychoanalytic thinking. In fact, psychoanalytic premises became the common reference shared by Communist Party and non-Party Marxism, utopian and anarchistic *gauchisme*, and by the radical anti-Marxism which burst forth in France in 1977 under the name of "The New Philosophy."

In America, where interpretations of psychoanalysis that stressed biological models gained a wide audience, the women's movement has seen Freud as one of history's great misogynists. Freud is read as claiming that passive and subordinate femininity is a consequence of the anatomical differences between the sexes. Anatomy is destiny, and there is little hope for women. In France, where Freud is read differently, the Marxist branch of the women's liberation movement actually called itself "Psychoanalysis and Politics."

In America, where individualist and conformist ideology was attracted only to that brand of psychoanalytic thinking that was supportive rather than subversive of existing institutions, psychoanalysis became a medical, psychiatric, and even corporate "insider." Thus, antipsychiatric stances that challenged the status quo of institutional psychology have tended to imply antipsychoanalytic ones. In France, the antipsychiatric movement has taken psychoanalysis as its ally, not its enemy.

Since 1968, French Marxism, French feminism, French antipsychiatry, and French psychoanalysis have become so tied up with one another that they resemble a complex knot—it is sometimes hard to tell where one strand leaves off and the other begins. But this has not always been the case. Through the 1960s, the French Left generally scorned psychoanalytic treatment as bourgeois self-indulgence and saw psychoanalytic ideas as reactionary instruments for psychologizing away social problems. But in the dismal aftermath of the May–June 1968 events, the French Left was in a shambles. During May, students took over their universities and workers their factories and tried to make them work by egalitarian models that placed the highest value on free and full expression of emotion and imagination. This experiment in a politics of speech and self-management may have been a powerful social expression of existential Marxist ideas, but its failure as a political action seemed to betray the weakness of its social base. Leftists who, in 1968, had confidently talked about new revolutionary classes and new forms of social action began to lose confidence in their analyses as 1968 turned into 1969 and then into 1970, and everyone realized how very little things had really changed.

When French sociologist Raymond Aron used the metaphor of psychodrama to explain what was happening in 1968, he was roundly criticized by the Left for "psychologizing away" the political importance of what was taking place. But after the events, the metaphor of psychodrama became common coin, not only among critics of the protest movement, but also among those who had participated most actively in it. People who had criticized Aron for psychological reductionism now turned to psychoanalytic ideas to explain what had happened and sometimes even began personal psychoanalyses to understand what it had all meant to them.

Indeed, my own involvement with French psychoanalysis began with a brush with the fallout from May–June 1968. I had spent 1968–69 in Paris as a student, and in the years that followed the 1968 events, I kept in touch with French students I knew had been active at the time. When I had first met them in the late 1960s, their hostility toward psychoanalysis had been obvious. But in the early 1970s, several of them began talking more and more about psychoanalysis, decided to go into analysis, and told me of others in their former political circle who were making the same decision.

To the American reader, something about this story may sound familiar. The fact that a group of French activist students of the troubled late 1960s searched for personal solutions when a political solution seemed to have failed might not seem surprising. After all, a similar phenomenon swept American campuses in the early 1970s as energies once spent on radical politics were redirected into encounter groups, religious cults, and the human potential movement. Of course, the situations in France and America have much in common. In both countries, political disillusionment was followed by an outburst of interest in a transformation of the spirit and the psyche. But there were also important differences.

In France the turn from political demonstrations to interest in things psychological was directed toward a highly theoretical psychoanalysis rather than to the medley of more mystical and occasionally visceral therapies popular in America. Even when the French students invoked the *spontanéiste* spirit of the May days, they maintained an intellectual rather than anti-intellectual or mystical idiom.

A second difference is that for the French student radicals of 1968, the turn to psychoanalysis had to be a gesture of considerable force because they, unlike their American counterparts, had grown up in a general intellectual culture that was markedly hostile to psychoanalytic ideas. And their political socialization on the Left *accentuated* this hostility. Although the new interest in psychology was a more dramatic about-face for the French, it was the Americans who tended to experience a sense of discontinuity between their political activism and a new turn to private, "psychological" solutions. In America, the turn toward psychology and the self was often accompanied by a disillusionment with and an abandonment of politics. In France, this was not the case. Somehow, French students and intellectuals maintained a sense of continuity as their activities and their language took on a new psychoanalytic tone. Given the almost total disjuncture between a psychoanalytic and a radical political discourse before 1968, it seemed clear that something new was going on.

This book tells the story of something that was new in France after 1968. It is the story of the emergence of a distinctly French reading of Freud, a new version of psychoanalysis that has served as a bridge between a politics of social activism and a politics of the person. In the aftermath of the May–June 1968 events, French psychoanalysis became more permeable to politics, and politics more permeable to it. A failure of radical politics led to the radical politicization, at least in its rhetoric, of a significant segment of French psychoanalytic thought, a politicization that accompanied its massive infiltration into French culture as a whole. The phenomenon was on a scale so large that it makes sense to speak of "Freud's French Revolution."

It would be a mistake, of course, to think of this revolution as a simple "result" of the 1968 events. Both the 1968 explosion and the more sustained psychoanalytic presence that followed reflect deeper social changes that had long been in process. At the same time, however, the form taken by the post-1968 psychoanalytic culture was powerfully influenced by the 1968 events.

One might expect the story of a psychoanalysis that has become an ally of the Left and an inspiration to radical feminists and antipsychiatrists to be stormy, ideological, filled with conflict. It is. The story of French psychoanalysis is punctuated by schisms and with the excommunications of dissidents within psychoanalytic and political parties. It is deeply involved with convulsive changes in the French asylum system, in the ideological line of the French Communist Party, and in the structure of the French university. The events themselves are exciting and the question of what that excitement is all about leads us to important issues about the nature of the psychoanalytic enterprise. The new French psychoanalytic culture was shaped by a social revolt whose trademark was the radical challenge to boundaries of all kinds, among them the line between psychology and politics. In 1968, students insisted that creating the context for a new authenticity in personal relationships was part of what a political revolution had to be about. Now, in the name of a "return to Freud," the challenge to traditional ways of dividing up experience continues. A significant current in French psychoanalysis has taken a "subversive" position in relation to its environment, calling into question the "taken for granted" ways of looking at the family, the child, what is private and what is public, and how people communicate with each other. The recent history of French psychoanalysis shows how this kind of radical movement comes under powerful social cross fire. The pressures on it all point in the direction of its social adaptation, of fitting into rather than challenging what is around it. In this sense, the French psychoanalytic movement is playing out, in a highly condensed and particularly clear form, the cultural experience of those intellectual movements, among them Marxism and Darwinism, which suggested ways of perceiving reality that profoundly challenge the status quo, what we may call "subversive sciences."

In the case of psychoanalysis, the pressures for normalization are not simply those imposed from the "outside" by society. They also come from the inside, from within psychoanalysis itself. Indeed, this book directly raises the question of whether or not psychoanalysis may carry within itself the seeds of its own neutralization as a radical, critical theory.

The psychoanalytic enterprise has lived with this powerful paradox from the very beginning. Freud was concerned both with his science and with the politics of its expansion, concerned both with the structure of the mind and with the social acceptance of his new therapeutic methods. But can a discipline that attacks the acceptable be socially accepted? In America, this contradiction has tended to be smoothed over: much of what was socially unacceptable in psychoanalytic theory was watered down as psychoanalysis moved toward a medical model that locates problems and the place for their solution within the individual. The impact of the medical legitimation of psychoanalysis has been so great that most Americans have stopped thinking about the existence of contradictions at all.

In France, the opposite has happened. The events of the late 1960s forced problems to the surface. Nowhere has the question of whether the vitality of psychoanalysis depends on its scientific research or on its therapeutic successes been posed more sharply. Nowhere has the question of whether "subversive psychoanalysis" can survive its social acceptance been so widely debated. And nowhere has the question of whether psychoanalysis suffers from a profound internal contradiction been raised so clearly.

Freud seems to have had considerable prophetic acumen. A decisive struggle about the future of psychoanalysis is being played out in France where the issues go beyond anything local to the French scene and often go beyond psychoanalysis itself. In this book, I look at the struggle from four different points of view which correspond to four distinct sections of the book, each of which has a somewhat different balance between theoretical discussion and anthropological description.

Part I treats the gap in the timing of this psychoanalytic "take off" in France and America as a puzzle to which there are no simple solutions. The nation which had produced Stendahl, Proust, Balzac, and Flaubert might well have been expected to embrace rather than reject Freud's insights when psychoanalysis was introduced in France at the turn of the century. Because one knows that the facts are otherwise, there is a tendency to accept the French resistance to Freud as obvious and to argue, for example, that French values emphasized the rational to a degree that made psychoanalysis unacceptable. But if things had gone the other way, that is, if there had been little or no resistance to psychoanalytic ideas and practice in France, one might well have been able to argue with equal persuasiveness that Freud's rational approach to the irrational made psychoanalysis a "natural" for the French. Here, the discussion of this problem of interpretation begins in part I with an examination of those French values and cultural traditions which have usually been blamed for the French hostility to Freud. They are of course a part of the story, but they are only one piece of the puzzle. The effort to understand the French resistance to Freud and the more recent French swing toward an "infatuation with Freudianism" demands a consideration of the social roots of a psychoanalytic culture and the specific ways that psychoanalysis has adapted to the French environment. Specifically, the work of French psychoanalyst Jacques Lacan represents a "reinvention" of Freud that is particularly French. With this introduction to Lacan as a base, the discussion opens out to how his psychoanalytic ideas allowed for new theorizations of the individual and society and to new forms of social criticism that captured the imagination of the French Left in the post-1968 years.

Part II treats the history and internal politics of the French psychoanalytic movement. The history of French psychoanalysis, like the history of Freud's circle, can be read as the emotionally charged story of individual personalities. Here the focus is on underlying structural problems that plagued the Vienna circle of the turn of the century as well as the Paris circle of fifty years later. This perspective leads to the question of whether the story of psychoanalytic politics is the story of psychoanalysis struggling against itself. Does the master-disciple relationship that is built into psychoanalysis subvert what is most subversive about it? Does the psychoanalytic society systematically destroy the theory that it believes itself to be protecting?

In part III, the perspective shifts from the politics in the world of psychoanalytic societies to psychoanalysis in the world of politics. In France, psychoanalysis has moved out of narrow professional circles and onto the larger social stage. For example, in the development of the French antipsychiatric movement and in the workings of the French university, conflicts within the psychoanalytic world, "psychoanalytic politics," have been projected as a "politics of psychoanalysis" whose results seem to be the erosion of traditional dichotomies between psychology and politics, madness and normality, a university-styled mathematical discourse and a poetry of the person.

Part IV turns directly to the issue of the popularization and normalization of psychoanalysis in the world of popular culture by looking at psychoanalysis and its popularity from both sides of the analytic couch. Since 1968, French people often find a psychoanalyst in places where they might once have expected to find a priest, a teacher, or a physician. Analysts lived through the May–June events to find that by the time the dust had settled, they were no longer marginal men and women but were very much at the center of things. For many people, psychoanalysis, which was once seen as subversive and alien, was now a welcome source of expertise for solving the problems of everyday life.

For some French psychoanalysts, recognition was a welcome change. For others, social acceptance brought new doubts. Some had long felt that psychoanalysis declined in the United States as a result of having been popularized and accepted without being understood. French psychoanalysts used to reflect on the situation in the United States with a mixture of scorn, pity, and disdain. Now they too face the problem of acceptance and acceptability. Some discuss popularity in apocalyptic terms. They fear that when psychoanalysis becomes the "thing to do" it means the end of psychoanalysis, that psychoanalytic subversiveness depends on psychoanalytic marginality. If psychoanalysis, like anarchism, is a system designed to break down systems, does the continuing power of the psychoanalytic movement thus depend on permanent revolution?

Such questions weave through our story, often expressed in controversies around the work of Jacques Lacan. Although the "French Freud" is not a person but a complex social and cultural phenomenon, its story does have Lacan as a central actor. In France, Lacan came to personify a conception of psychoanalysis not as a quasi-medical technique focused on "cure" but as a scientific discipline and a process of individual research and self-discovery that needs no further "therapeutic" justification. According to Lacan's way of looking at things, if anything that a medically oriented person would call a cure comes at all in psychoanalysis, it comes *par surcroît*, as a kind of bonus or secondary gain. This therapeutically indifferent perspective on the psychoanalytic enterprise goes hand in hand with a radical critique of the psychoanalytic institution. For Lacan, becoming and being a psychoanalyst involve processes of scientific discovery and personal development that have nothing to do with having a particular academic degree, with belonging to the bureaucracy of a psychoanalytic institute, or with following a set of rules on how to conduct psychoanalytic sessions. Lacan himself refused to follow the rules of accepted psychoanalytic technique. For example, the orthodox length of the analytic session has long been set at around fifty minutes. Lacan shortened or lengthened it according to what was happening with a particular patient on a particular day, thus using time as well as speech to punctuate the analytic discourse. By 1978, controversy over Lacan's unorthodox practice and his equally unorthodox ideas about psychoanalytic training had precipitated three schisms in the French psychoanalytic movement.

In the psychoanalytic school that Lacan himself founded in 1964, the Freudian School of Paris, there were no requirements for admission to candidacy (such as an MD or a PhD), there was no standard curriculum for becoming an analyst, and there were no prescriptions about the conduct of an analysis. Lacan insists that there be no distinction between a didactic or training analysis and any other: for a future analyst, as for any analysand, standards of discipline or routine imposed from outside the relationship between analyst and analysand can only distort and distract. The underlying belief is that, if psychoanalysis is to survive and grow as a living science, the only rule must be that there be no set rules. When Lacan's belief that "Only the analyst can authorize himself as an analyst" is put into practice, this means that the psychoanalytic society or training institute does not intervene in an analysand's decision to see patients as an analyst. The decision is intensely personal; its privacy is protected. In Lacan's conception, psychoanalysis is seen more as a calling than as a career, and no institution can certify the fact that an individual feels a powerful sense of vocation that comes from within.

Lacan's emphasis on psychoanalysis as a calling and his insistence that psychoanalysts must turn away from their preoccupations with institutional forms toward an intense and personal re-examination of Freud's original texts all suggest the metaphor of psychoanalytic Protestantism. For Lacanians, Freud's work is the psychoanalytic Bible and derivative commentaries must be cast aside. Also to be abandoned are institutional forms that support the psychoanalytic church rather than psychoanalytic theory. Lacan's sessions of variable length and his belief that only an analyst can authorize his or her practice exemplify his iconoclasm in relation to the doctrine and bureaucracy of the psychoanalytic establishment.

Although Lacan himself has gotten caught up and tangled in the contradictions of psychoanalytic politics, much of "Freud's French Revolution" has been triggered by the Lacanian psychoanalytic "Protestant Reformation."

The fact that Lacan's perspective on psychoanalysis has, at least in theory, been resolutely anti-institutional has made it easier for Lacan's ideas to filter through the world of French radical politics. And it was largely through Lacan that psychoanalysis was rehabilitated for radicals after 1968. But the reconciliation was due to more than Lacan's well-known stands against bureaucracy. Lacan's psychoanalytic theory effectively neutralizes some of the complaints that Marxists have traditionally lodged against psychoanalysis. For example, the Marxist complaint that psychoanalysis "adapts" people to bourgeois society seems to have been disarmed by Lacan's insistence that only a perversion of psychoanalysis conceives of itself in terms of adapting people to the social status quo. He sees psychoanalysis as a form of truth seeking, and from his vision the Left has been able to extract a notion of psychoanalysis as a facilitator of political consciousness-raising. A second Marxist reproach has been that in the face of human misery psychoanalysis focuses on the individual ego, not the society. For Lacan, the coherent, autonomous ego is an illusion, and one of the goals of psychoanalysis as a science is to explain its psychological and social construction. This view of psychoanalysis clearly places Freud's contribution, like that of Marx, at the center of interest for those who want to understand the individual in society. A third objection has been the alleged biological determinism of psychoanalysis. Does anatomy or the individual's place in the system of production make destiny? Lacan's reading of Freud is militantly antibiological, shifting all descriptions from a biological-anatomical level to a symbolic one. According to Lacan, Freud never meant to say anything about anatomy, and where he seems to be talking about anatomy, he is really talking about how culture imposes meaning on anatomical parts. For Lacan, when Freud seems to be talking about organs, he is really talking about information. In short, the French connection between Marxism, feminism, antipsychiatry, and psychoanalysis has been mediated by Lacan.

My belief in Lacan's centrality to my story became much deeper in the course of my field experiences in France. My research strategy was to talk to as many people as possible who lived in and around the new French psychoanalytic culture. Some of these conversations were informal, for example, with students in the cafés outside of university lecture halls, with activists after political meetings, and with patients in the waiting rooms of psychiatric clinics. Other conversations, with French psychoanalysts and physicians, usually in their offices and scheduled between patient hours, tended to be more formal and structured. Typically, the interviews with psychoanalysts were conducted in two or three one-hour sessions. Some went on much longer than that. In the cases of about a dozen analysts who were deeply involved in psychoanalytic politics—on the Left, in the antipsychiatric movement, or in the university—our conversations extended over many months. I also interviewed journalists and media professionals who had made careers out of "selling psychoanalysis" and a broad sample of people living in Paris (from high school students to housewives) to whom it was being sold. These interviews, together with personal observations of the worlds of education, medicine, and psychiatry and the analysis of written materials, constitute an ethnographic investigation of French psychoanalytic culture in the 1970s, that is, at the height of Lacan's cultural influence.*

The use of the term "ethnographic" emphasizes the similarity of this project, which looks at French psychoanalysis as a complex cultural phenomenon, to investigations by anthropologists in "traditional" societies. Although the subjects are quite different, the intent is similar: to take an intensive fieldwork experience and distill from it those elements that make the life of a society (or of a subculture in that society) intelligible and meaningful to someone outside of it. No ethnography can be a complete mapping of a society's spirit and structure; no one account, no one perspective can tell the whole story. Here the focus is on several related issues that raise questions for the sociology of science and the sociology of knowledge. Part I asks: Why now? And why Lacan? Why has psychoanalysis come into such prominence in France today? And why is the French Freud so different from the American Freud? Part II looks at the French experience to explore the possibility of a contradiction between what is radical in psychoanalytic theory and its institutionalization in psychoanalytic societies. Part III shows how Lacan has helped to forge a new relationship between psychoanalysis and antipsychiatry,

---

*Of course, doing an ethnography of a psychoanalytic culture meant studying organizations and situations where people are in relationships of unusual intimacy and intensity. Many of the people I interviewed did not feel free to have conversations which touched on such emotionally charged relationships without the promise that their names would not be used in the reporting of the material. In the pages that follow I have adopted the policy of not attributing any quotations that come from my interview work, although, of course, I always cite an author when I draw from the public record.

and psychoanalysis and the university. Part IV looks at the diffusion of the theory into popular culture, stressing how the social image of psychoanalysis can come into conflict with the theory itself. Understanding Lacan's impact on "The French Freud" is important to exploring each of these themes.

Indeed, for many French people Lacan's name is synonymous with psychoanalysis. At certain moments in the life of a society, there is a fit of spirit and situation that makes a certain thinker (or rather, the way in which others perceive the main issues raised by what they understand to be their thought) particularly relevant. Their thought furnishes categories that people use to think about their own social experience. In other words, their catchwords act as a kind of cultural mnemonic. Lacan is such a thinker, and thus, much of his influence, particularly in the public at large, is not due to his ideas being read and fully understood.

In fact, Lacan is an extraordinarily difficult thinker. The chances of understanding his writing in all its complexity depend not only on a deep acquaintance with the work of Freud but also on a familiarity with existential philosophy, French literature, structural linguistics, and anthropology. Also required is an ability to pick up fine distinctions between French and German renderings of psychoanalytic concepts and an acquaintance with Hegel and his French commentators.

Some of Lacan's followers came to his work with the dedication and intellectual culture that permit them full access to it, but such scholars do not account for his enormous influence. A much larger group finds itself deeply engrossed in Lacan's writing, although it cannot understand the fine points of the theory. They find Lacan "good to think with," experiencing the texts as evocative of important things about themselves.

This is an example of Lacan's psychoanalytic Protestantism at work outside the confines of the psychoanalytic institution. These readers make Lacan "their own."

A third group approaches Lacan by assimilating a prepackaged set of Lacanian slogans. Their understanding is on the level of anecdote, recipe, and cliché. For many people I interviewed, particularly among the students, Lacan is a reference point for thinking about psychoanalysis, literature, and politics, even though they would have been at great pains to give a vaguely coherent description of the basic elements of his theory. Although they thought of themselves as *lacaniens*, they sometimes could do no more than parrot the famous Lacanian "formulas" (such as "The Unconscious is structured like a language" or "The Unconscious is the discourse of the Other"). It is tempting to dismiss these people as mere charlatans, but taking them seriously illuminates the "sociology of superficial knowledge" and helps to decipher some elements of an emergent modern mythology.

Lacan's centrality to the French psychoanalytic culture is nowhere as apparent as within the psychoanalytic community itself. In the course of my year and a half of fieldwork in France in the mid-1970s, I interviewed over one hundred French psychoanalysts, and Jacques Lacan was a powerful presence in conversations with most of them. Often it seemed that they fantasized Lacan as the ultimate destination for their communications to me. This was as true for the many analysts who have broken away from Lacan as it was for analysts in his school. Communication with Lacan is a problem for both groups. For members of Lacan's school, communication with Lacan could be difficult: dialogue with a living *Maître* posed tremendous problems. For analysts outside of the Freudian School, communication with Lacan could be almost impossible. Lacan considered himself abandoned by three successive generations of students and colleagues, often by the very people with whom he had worked most closely, that is to say, his own analysands. The possibilities for dialogue were shut down, the feelings ran too high, the history was too charged.

The French psychoanalytic movement is caught up in the myths and images of its history, which is dominated by relationships with Lacan. The successive schisms in the French psychoanalytic movement, each based explicitly or implicitly on a judgment about Lacan, have left a bitter legacy. Lacan dominated the French psychoanalytic scene, either by his presence or absence from any group of analysts. He was cherished, feared, hated. Few analysts were neutral about him. Desire for some audience with Lacan seemed implied when French psychoanalysts would ask me: "Avez-vous déjà vu Lacan?" ("Have you already seen Lacan?"). In this almost inevitable question, the *déjà*, the time marker, was always present. The question was, after all, "Have you *already* seen Lacan, or are you going to be seeing him; are you or are you not in a position to carry my message of apology, or love, or recrimination, or self-justification, back to him?"

In this book, an overview of Lacan's ideas is presented in part I, which discusses the "reinvention" of Freud in France and its relationship to radical ideologies. Additional elements of Lacanian theory are presented within the discussions of the social worlds in which they are influential. These are the worlds that make up the French psychoanalytic culture. Part II looks at the world of analysts and their psychoanalytic societies; part III examines the worlds of antipsychiatry and the university; part IV scans the world of popular culture. In each of these different contexts, different aspects of Lacan's thought are more salient than others. For example, in the history of the schisms in the French psychoanalytic movement, Lacan's ideas about psychoanalytic training and the rules of psychoanalytic technique dominate the controversy, while other ideas, his linguistic theory for example, are present only as shadows. The story of psychoanalysis in the French university, on the other hand, makes no sense without some appreciation of how Lacan roots psychoanalytic theory in mathematics and linguistics. Thus, from chapter to chapter, Lacan's ideas emerge in shifting patterns of foreground and background. The reader comes to know different sides of Lacan in different settings, just as someone living in France and touched by the social worlds around psychoanalysis would come to know him.

Students of French society, indeed the French themselves, have gotten used to a cycle of intellectual fads that quickly come and go on the Paris scene. On a superficial level, the Lacanian "terrorism" in contemporary French intellectual life does not seem far removed from this French-styled dilettantism and thirst for the new. After its 1963 move from the Saint Anne Hospital to the Ecole Normale Supérieure, Lacan's seminar became a meeting place for the most prominent figures in Parisian intellectual circles, among them Marxist philosopher Louis Althusser, literary critics Roland Barthes, Julia Kristeva, and Philippe Sollers, philosophers Michel Foucault and Jacques Derrida, and anthropologist Claude Lévi-Strauss. Since the 1966 publication of Lacan's *Ecrits*, the number of people attending the seminar has multiplied at an extraordinary rate; by 1978, up to a thousand people tried to get into the law school auditorium where it was held. It became the meeting place for *le tout Paris*. Is the Freud-Lacan enthusiasm just a fad? Is it different from previous, evanescent intellectual flirtations that have swept Paris before it? I believe that it *is* different.

To begin with, psychoanalytic thought is socially embedded in both therapeutic practice and in its own psychoanalytic societies, thus generating a group of practitioners and institutions with large stakes in the perpetuation of the doctrine. In addition, recent French social changes have created a new environment in which psychoanalytic ideas about the individual are welcome because people seem to find them relevant to their experience. Such changes include those in the role of religion, in people's sense of privacy, in education and child raising, and in the life of the French family. They are not easily reversible. The extent to which the enthusiasm for psychoanalysis will continue to center on Lacanian thought is a more complicated question. Lacan's ideas are powerful, but some of their appeal is certainly due to his own personal charisma. Now that he is gone, his ideas may become less seductive. On the other hand, Lacan's ideas are resonant with important traditions in French intellectual life, and as this ethnography of the contemporary French psychoanalytic culture unfolds, it will become apparent that they are also peculiarly adapted to complex interactions with ideas and events on the French political and social scenes.

Although on the surface the popularization of psychoanalysis in France has many similarities with how Freud was marketed to Americans, the French response to the mass diffusion of psychoanalytic ideas, which only a few years ago were considered occult and esoteric, is taking place in a very different context. The most important differences seem to be the high level of politicization and the influence of Jacques Lacan. Having to deal with Lacan has sharpened theoretical debate in French psychoanalytic writing and has opened it to a broad world of scientific, philosophical, and social concerns. Although many French psychoanalysts are violently opposed to how Lacan did his clinical work, they can still view his experiments as a positive response to the threat that psychoanalytic work will run itself down into "routine analytic practice" that is no longer fresh and alive. In 1974, one analyst, whose attitude toward Lacan was generally very critical, made his last point by saying: "Lacan invents and invents, but his patients are in *analysis*." And even analysts who had bitter ten-year feuds with Lacan expressed a desire to attend his seminar again, as if to recapture closeness with some kind of touchstone. Many felt that by continually reminding them of what was most subversive in Freud's vision, Lacan offered them some respite, if not final relief, from the "American dilemma" of psychoanalysis becoming "the thing to do."

Thus Lacan expressed a challenge to the psychoanalytic "routine" on a theoretical and institutional level and often served as a bridge between psychoanalytic and political radicalism. His radical critiques of theories of the ego and of traditional psychoanalytic societies have inspired others to go even further in challenging political institutions as well as psychoanalytic, psychiatric, and educational ones. But Lacan's impact has certainly not been all in the direction of keeping psychoanalysis "subversive." For many people, the fascination with Lacan is a fascination with the writing, the style, the public display, the politics, the sense of being *au courant*. In debates about psychoanalysis, structuralism, and politics, the Lacanian discourse often helps to keep things on a highly abstract level. Ironically, a theory that aspired to bring people back to what is most subversive in the Freudian notion of the unconscious often ends up by enlivening cocktail party talk.

In France, a controversial person, a revolution in psychoanalytic theory, and some highly politicized social involvements— all dedicated to keeping psychoanalysis subversive—are in tension with psychoanalytic popularity and popularization, which tend to normalize the doctrine. This tension defines what is most unique on the French psychoanalytic scene. This work begins with an attempt to understand the social world within which the French psychoanalytic movement was able to grow into a new, rich, and complex psychoanalytic culture.

I The French Freud

1 The Social Roots of Psychoanalytic Culture

This book treats the new French psychoanalytic culture as "Freud's French Revolution." It is revolutionary in many ways: in its dramatic difference from what came before, the turmoil of its coming into place, in the scope of its penetration into French life. One cannot take the full measure of its influence by a simple count of analysts and their patients. It is necessary to look at how a psychoanalytic language, even a popularized one, has affected how people think about themselves, about philosophy, about politics, about the future of universities, about literature, about madness and despair, and, of course, about families and children. It is because believing in psychoanalysis touches on so many aspects of life, and calls so many assumptions into question, that psychoanalysis has some claim to being a subversive doctrine. Because it is subversive in this sense, resistance to it can come from many quarters. It is present, for example, in France's early response to Freud. From the beginning, the French opposed psychoanalysis from so many directions that it is appropriate to speak of an "anti-psychoanalytic culture."

This chapter puts the contemporary French psychoanalytic culture into perspective by looking at the inhibiting antipsy-choanalytic culture that preceded it, the elements of which were equally complex and interdependent. The expression "antipsychoanalytic culture" does not imply that it came into being in *response* to the introduction of psychoanalysis. Quite the contrary. The opposition was already in place at the time of the introduction of psychoanalysis at the beginning of the twentieth century.[1] In domains where psychoanalytic ideas might have found a clientele, there were secure establishments that saw little need for anything new. And apart from being new, psychoanalysis was particularly threatening.

French psychiatrists tended to look at the sufferings of their patients as the result of either organic lesions or moral degeneration. In either case, the boundary between the "healthy" doctor and the "sick" patient was clear. Freud's theory makes it hard to draw such lines by insisting that if psychiatrists knew themselves better, they would find more points in common with their patients than they might have thought. In Henri Bergson and Pierre Janet, French philosophy and psychology each had a national hero with strong claims to have already treated the themes that Freud was raising. They also claimed to have treated them in better taste (e.g., without Freud's "excessive" reference to sex) and to have treated them without having to call in a foreign theorist. Moreover, French philosophy and psychology were involved in drawing and consolidating the line between them, and in deciding which aspects of the mind each would take as its province. Psychoanalysis did not respect such lines. It went beyond traditional psychology and claimed the right to intrude into problems that philosophers considered their professional preserve: the reality of free will, the reliability of intuition, and the autonomy of consciousness.

Thus the hostility of professional establishments in medicine, psychology, and philosophy and the offended sensibilities of chauvinists and moralists helped to build a French antipsychoanalytic culture. But the culture also gained its strength from a quieter yet more pervasive kind of opposition. Psychoanalysis was profoundly discordant with a firmly in place system of social relations and values which, by giving people confidence that meaning and support could be found in the social order, encouraged ways of thinking about the individual that referred to outer rather than inner realities. This chapter examines how this social system worked, how it found expression in the pervasive cultural hostility toward psychoanalysis, and finally how it broke down, setting the social groundwork for the development of a psychoanalytic culture. This effort requires an overview of nearly a century of cultural, social, and psychiatric history. Of necessity, its presentation will be schematic and general. But its purpose is modest: to provide a few reference points for thinking about what kinds of social conditions facilitate or militate against the development of a widespread interest in psychoanalysis as a theory and as a therapy.

A first reference point is the radically different initial response to psychoanalysis in France and America: psychoanalysis captured the American imagination a full fifty years before it stirred up a comparable level of interest in France. Comparing what was happening in these two societies at the time of the introduction of psychoanalysis at the turn of the century teaches a great deal about the social roots of psychoanalytic culture. Psychoanalysis was welcomed in America, particularly in urban America, which had to come to terms with rootlessness, with geographic and social mobility from within, and with immigration from without. In the American nation of immigrants, psychoanalytic absorption in the history of the individual helped to compensate for the absence of a collective past. Many Americans shared an insecurity about their *parvenu* status that encouraged continual self-examination and the strong desire for self-improvement.[2] In addition, America's lack of a coherent national culture helped psycho-analysis achieve a greater social role. The Americans had no strong national psychiatric tradition and no national univer-sity structure that could institutionalize a single accepted way of thinking about philosophy and psychology. And American middle-class affluence could support a relatively expensive self-improvement industry.

Historian Nathan Hale has presented the thesis that psy-choanalysis became important in America during the crystal-lizations of two crises: there was a crisis of "civilized" morality in social life and a crisis of the "somatic style" in the treatment of nervous and mental disorders.[3]

"Civilized" morality, with its insistence that progress depended on the control of sexuality and that "mind" should govern sensual nature, operated as a coherent system of related economic, social, and religious norms. It defined correct behav-ior and correct models of the "manly man and the womanly woman" and served as a powerful ideal of conduct. But, accord-ing to Hale, by the time that Freud visited America in 1909,

> religious and cultural conservatives complained of a crumbling of moral codes, a new mass society bent on business and pleasure. Subjects that respectable families would never have mentioned a decade before now were being publicly talked about. Some were shocked at the academic nudes displayed in fashionable maga-zines. Darwinism, relativism and pragmatism were "blasting the Rock of Ages' and destroying a reverence for moral truths once believed to be eternal. A few Americans asked whether their coun-try was progressing or degenerating.[4]

By the early twentieth century, models of the human mind which had provided the psychological underpinnings for "civ-ilized" morality had been challenged. "The faculties of Will,

Conscience, and the concept of the unified and responsible Self were no longer adequate descriptions of what was known about human personality."[5] And the economic and cultural factors that had fostered late nineteenth-century "civilized" morality were also changing.

New attitudes toward sexuality and religion developed simultaneously with urbanization and increased affluence. America was moving from an economy of deficit and saving to one of surplus and abundance. Particularly in the rapidly growing cities, which presented the immigrant from Europe or the American countryside with widely varied patterns of behavior,

> a new kind of character had to emerge, no longer dedicated to austerity and sacrifice but to leisure and rational enjoyment. . . . The sharp moral codes of the small town—close-knit neighbors, churches, "society"—were replaced by relative anonymity and isolation.[6]

G. Stanley Hall, Freud's host for his 1909 visit to America, informed Freud that he had come at a good "psychological moment."[7] In the present context, it is more to the point that Freud came to America at a good "sociological moment" as well.

When individuals feel enmeshed in a network of stable social relationships with family, ancestry, and religion, they can use these relationships to make sense of experience, and when they are in pain or distress, these relationships become natural reference points for trying to understand what is happening and sources of support for finding a way out of trouble. But with mobility of place, profession, and status, and a new instability of values, old ways of looking at the world no longer apply. Individuals are thrown back on themselves and may be more receptive to theories such as psychoanalysis which search for meaning in dreams, wishes, fears, and confusions. In a stable society, people feel that they understand how things work. The rational and conscious are deemed trustworthy. When life is in greater flux, daily experience continually suggests the presence of processes hidden from awareness. Society appears more opaque, and the idea of an unconscious acquires greater reality. In this situation, psychoanalytic theory and therapy become more "culturally appropriate."[8] Sociologist Philip Rieff has called this change in the character of the community "deconversion" and has described how the shift to a social environment where each individual must create his own meaning creates the possibility for the "psychoanalytic moment."[9] In Rieff's terms, Freud had come to America during a period of deconversion—that is, a time when "civilized" morality and the traditional forces of community and cohesion which had kept it in place were all in jeopardy.

From this point of view we can appreciate why, at the turn of the century, some aspects of the new psychoanalytic theory made sense to Americans. The violent and sexually charged unconscious which it was discovering "bore an uncanny resemblance to the precise opposite of the values of 'civilized morality'" just at the time when they were coming under social attack.[10] But what makes sense in one society might make nonsense in another. And in France, the psychoanalytic perspective on the world seemed profoundly out of step with social realities. At about the same time that the American middle class was trying to make its peace with new self-doubts and insecurities, French bourgeois society was more secure than ever about its sense of itself as the model and matrix for French society as a whole. The French bourgeoisie had triumphed over the workers in the insurrection of the Paris commune in 1871 and had set up the Third French Republic, a sturdy political creature whose seventy-year tenure has been referred to as "the Republican synthesis" because of the close fit of the

political system with social norms and values and with a well-
articulated vision of the world.[11] Ancestors were known by
their names and by their habits, the past was secure, and the
future was rooted in it.[12] This, at least, for the bourgeoisie. So,
at a time when American society was increasingly receptive to
new ways of looking at the world that focused on the *self*, the
French bourgeoisie was concerned with reinforcing its own
experience of France as a self-contained, organic, interdependent, well-cemented *society*. The bourgeois school and family
instilled "character": a sense of privacy, morality, civic duty,
and historical continuity. French schools taught children to
feel a sense of solidarity with the French community, civilization, and race. Many French primary school texts carried a
frontispiece in which the Gauls, Charlemagne, the medieval
and modern kings, the Napoléons, and the great leaders of
the Republican governments were pictured holding hands in
a great chain whose final link was the student to whom the
book presumably belonged. A favorite image of France was as a
beehive where each individual family was a cell, each helping
to construct a whole that was greater than the sum of its parts.
The individual was encouraged to feel roots in social space and
time. Psychoanalysis threatened this reassuring sense of continuity by insisting that civilization (even French civilization) is
the origin of our discontents and that the past can live within
us as an insidious rather than benign presence.

In traditional French bourgeois society, the call to values
of collectivity coexisted with a sense of privacy that was built
around maintaining rigid boundaries between self and others. French sociologist Michel Crozier has gone so far as to
characterize all of French social life, from the corporation to
the family, as "bureaucratic." And he sees this bureaucratic
style as the expression of a shared "horror of face-to-face

confrontations."[13] People seemed willing to live with cumbersome bureaucratic mechanisms for getting even the smallest things done in order to protect their privacy. Even within the family, there was much formality and distance; in many French bourgeois homes, it was not uncommon for children to address their parents in the formal *vous* form.

By the time of the introduction of psychoanalysis around the turn of the century, bourgeois-dominated French society presented itself as in a state of equilibrium so well balanced that it often seemed more like a stalemate. Indeed, the French bourgeoisie liked to think of itself as *le juste milieu*, the balanced middle-of-the-road in political, personal, cultural, and economic matters. Although France had industrialized, the bourgeois social hierarchy was still based on traditional patterns of status, deference, and family ties. Although the state was secular, for many people the Catholic Church was a national presence that served to cement political and spiritual life. And although the French bourgeoisie ran corporations as well as the more traditional small businesses, they adopted many of the characteristics of the old aristocracy, in particular, a disdain for the aggressive "entrepreneuring" associated with modern capitalism. They called it *grimpage*, "climbing," and thought it in extremely poor taste. Indeed, in the French bourgeois society being described here, what was and what was not "in good taste" was extremely clear; people did not have to struggle with an ambiguous sense of the rules of the game as was beginning to happen in America.

It is not surprising that people with a clear sense of what was right and wrong, of what was appropriate and what was inappropriate, were not interested in theories that suggested the relativity of all values. The French were offended by Freud's psychoanalytic "moral neutrality" just as they were by Max Weber's sociological "value neutrality." Both theorists saw the world with a relativism that went against the French cultural grain. In its stability and security in what it stood for, French bourgeois society was not ready for psychoanalysis. But Freud challenged more than "civilized" morality. He also challenged the "somatic style" in neurology and psychiatry, a style that was particularly well rooted in French medicine. The somatic style attributed breakdowns in mental functioning to physical causes, most specifically to brain lesions. Neurologists hoped to relate the symptoms of patients to specified pathological conditions. This mechanistic view of mental disorder had been encouraged by the discoveries of German and British investigators in the 1870s in the localization of brain functions. The cerebral cortex seemed a mosaic of overlapping areas, each defining a specific function. In the later nineteenth century, in France and America, the norms of the "civilized" moral order such as judgment, reason, and control were each associated with psychological categories such as Will and Conscience and given a somatic base. They were believed to be located in the frontal lobes of the cortex along with the other "superior" functions and to inhibit the action of the "lower" centers where the primitive drives and instincts, including the sexual passions, were located. But by the time of Freud's visit in 1909, this coherent social psychological-physiological system was in crisis in America. The problems of classifying mental disease on physiological grounds had become increasingly apparent, as had the fact that neither gross lesions nor metabolic dysfunctions seemed to be present in the most important varieties of insanity.

Nathan Hale recounts that in America "the somatic style and 'civilized' morality exhibited roughly the same historical pattern. They became dominant in the 1870s, rigid in the

1880s, and were in a period of crisis by 1909."[14] In France, however, the Gallic version of "civilized" morality was not in crisis at the turn of the century and neither was the traditional style of French psychiatric theory and practice that was moral and rational as well as somatic. The terrain that psychoanalysis might have occupied as a theory of irrational processes was already taken by Bergsonianism and the terrain that it might have occupied as a therapeutic model was dominated by a psychiatry that seemed more consonant with French social life and social values.

Psychiatry, like literature, is a medium onto which social values can be projected as themes and preoccupations.[15] In its moral, rational, and even chauvinistic view of the world, the French psychiatry in place at the time of the introduction of psychoanalysis expressed the social values of the Third Republic. French writers in the nineteenth and early twentieth centuries took family, nation, religion, community, and regionality as major touchstones for their work. So did French psychiatrists. Like French social theorists and novelists, French psychiatrists presented being "rooted" in the harmony and security of life in the rural provinces as a near prerequisite for mental health.[16] Even as France was industrializing, her psychiatrists insisted on an irreconcilable conflict between modern industrial society and the nature of the human spirit. And although Descartes's neurophysiology of emotional states had long been discredited, nineteenth- and twentieth-century French psychiatrists seemed to agree with him that an innate intellectual core was the basis for a shared human nature. Cure was often represented as the triumph of intellect through "reasoning" a patient back to his senses.[17]

This major, "rational-intellectual" tradition in French psychiatry had always coexisted with a minor tradition which focused on cure by passage through an altered state of consciousness, such as a hypnotic trance, and through the manipulation of a powerful relationship to a healer. This minor tradition existed as an underground current that would surface from time to time to trouble the habitually calmer waters of traditional French psychiatry. In the mid-eighteenth century, there had been such an eruption in Mesmerism. In the late nineteenth century, there was another. French psychiatrists became interested in hysteria and hypnosis, and Jean Martin Charcot turned the Paris hospital of the Salpêtrière into an international center for their study. However, it emerged that Charcot had induced by suggestion much of the hysteria that he then claimed to cure by hypnosis, and by the time of his death in 1893, his work had been discredited. French psychiatry turned its back on the study of hysteria and hypnosis as it had done after the heyday of Mesmerism. It was the chilliest possible atmosphere for the introduction of psychoanalysis.

And indeed, when Freud's work was introduced, French psychiatrists saw it as dogmatic, arbitrary, barbaric, immoral, exaggerated, and speculative. They also dismissed its radically "psychological" explanations for the etiology of illness. Although the French had access to and had even produced some of the studies that had led to disillusionment with the somatic style in America, French neurology remained stony and confident, firmly rooted in the national university and hospital system. Neurologists dominated psychiatry; until 1968, psychiatry was not even a separate discipline in France.

In making their criticism of the "unscientific" Freud, French psychiatrists tended to compare him to Pierre Janet. Janet was the "complete" French psychological theorist, concerned with the rational, the moral, and the organically real. His theory of the origin of neurosis was rational (he believed that neurotic symptoms could be explained by their inability to deal with complex realities) and moral (strength is equated with successful control over impulses, a failure of this is moral weakness). He divided psychic life into ranked classes with "rational" acts on top and "socio-personal" acts at the bottom of the hierarchy. Even his therapeutic strategies confirmed the biases of the French psychiatric community. He combined moral treatment with "Cartesian" intervention: isolation from family to calm patients, rest to restore the powers of their will, work to strengthen the lower levels of their psychic organization, firm persuasion to convince them of their errors in judgment, and education to develop their rational potential to the fullest."[18] Janet presided over the Fourteenth International Congress of Psychology in Paris in 1900, the year that Freud published *The Interpretation of Dreams*. The International Congress reflected Janet's distaste for the issues that Freud was raising: it concerned itself entirely with the psychology of consciousness, perception, and sensation.

Janet believed Freud's radical psychological theory for the origin of hysteria to be unfounded and unscientific. Although Janet possessed great psychological insight, he, like Charcot, was unable to rid himself of the belief that hysteria was a manifestation of heredity, organically based. In addition to his scientific objections to Freud, Janet questioned the morality of psychoanalysis. In Janet's eyes, Freud was a pansexualist who equated man with beast when he spoke of man's uncontrollable passions. Janet was not alone in such moral objections. In a study of the introduction of psychoanalysis in France, Anne Parsons concluded that French psychiatrists at the turn of the century, like most other French intellectuals, deemed Freud's theory unacceptable on value grounds rather than on scientific ones. The rejection of Freud was a "moral act."[19] Psychoanalysis, like the tango, another foreigner that had invaded at about the same time, was morally shocking and very un-French, and even those physicians who served as its early champions found it somewhat offensive. In 1923, Professor Henri Claude opened his psychiatric service at the Saint Anne Hospital to a psychoanalytic consultation by Dr. René Laforgue, but by 1924 Claude was describing psychoanalysis as "shocking to the delicacy of intimate feelings" and "unadapted to the French mentality."[20] Claude was tormented by the opinions of the analysts whom he "harbored" in his service. When, during a conference on a patient, Marie Bonaparte, herself trained by Freud, argued that the young girl's phobia for slippery bars of soap was related to fantasies of playing with her father's testicles, Claude, enraged, roared out that *his* daughters would never think of such a thing.[21]

The catalog of French moral objections to Freud was extensive. Psychoanalysis was on a bad footing with Catholic doctrine. It allowed the individual to blame others for his failings and abdicate responsibility for individual action. Suggesting that sexual forces lurked as motivations in family relationships threatened the strong loyalty to the French bourgeois family and its complicated system of interfamilial alliances. Freud's notion of the unconscious conflicted with the importance that the French put on the possibility of the rational control of one's life and on the conscious manipulation of one's own talents.

The French objections to Freud did not fade away in the decades that followed the introduction of psychoanalysis. Even by the 1950s and 1960s French psychiatry was decidedly antipsychoanalytic in its reliance on moral authority, rational argumentation, and the invocation of shared social principles as well as its reliance on tranquilizers, sleep cures,

antidepressants, and electroshock.[22] Even as the stability of
French rural society was in the process of crumbling, French
psychiatry continued to express its nostalgia for a simpler,
more rooted life in the provinces. French psychiatric studies
spoke of the pathology inherent in urban life and warned that
leaving "organic and alive" rural settings for "artificial" urban
ones would have only the most deleterious effects on mental
health.[23] Given the problems of French urban life, there is no
reason to dismiss this position. But by taking it and expressing
it in what was often a passionate rhetoric, French psychiatry
served to bolster a social ideology that glorified rural life and
traditional values. Psychiatric writing described the geographi-
cally mobile as carriers of psychopathology, and the psychiatric studies on *les transplantés*, "the transplanted," made them
sound like a rare and somewhat dangerous species of plant
rather than the pioneers of a new industrial society. Psychoanalytic models that spoke of the self rather than of support from
community, nation, church, or etiquette were of little interest.
Later chapters make it clear that in the years after World War
II, a small, highly committed group of young psychiatrists,
psychologists, and literary scholars were deeply involved in
reworking psychoanalytic theory, but the climate was such
that neither the general public nor the psychiatric mainstream
was highly enthusiastic.[24] "Scientific" critics objected to psychoanalysis for its lack of an organic model of mental functioning; "moral" critics objected to the analyst's neutrality
that denied his patients warmth, encouragement, and a model
of good moral and social values. And while one group of moral
critics objected to Freud's "coldness," another group found
him too "warm," and criticized Freud for coddling people who
were not really sick and for encouraging hedonism.[25] To scientific and moral criticisms were added political and religious

ones. The Communist Party and Catholic Church took firm stands against psychoanalysis, which greatly influenced Communist and Catholic psychiatrists, as well as a large constituency of potential patients.

A content analysis of the French psychiatric literature from 1954 to 1966 by sociologist Carol Ryser documented this French psychiatric reticence toward psychoanalysis.[26] The values which Ryser found to be dominant in both French general culture and in the writings of French psychiatrists were hostile to any psychological (and by extension, psychoanalytic) focus in treatment. The dominant values stressed rational control, realism, and an individualism that insists that other people stay out of one's private business. In a spirit remarkably similar to Descartes's and to that of the nineteenth-century French psychiatrist Jean-Etienne Esquirol, who spoke of madness as a "false idea," French psychiatrists through the mid-1960s described emotional disturbances as disturbances of the intellect and encouraged their rational control in terms that suggested a moral imperative. Ryser found that the psychiatric literature associated psychoanalysis with values that were relatively unimportant or negatively valued in French psychiatry and in French general culture. For example, psychoanalytic treatment was frequently portrayed as a violation of individual privacy.

In 1967, Ryser predicted a gloomy future for psychoanalysis in France based on her analysis of the antipsychoanalytic values which dominated French society and psychiatry. She predicted the continued unpopularity of psychoanalysis in France because it was profoundly out of synchrony with deep and pervasive French values. In fact, things went in just the opposite direction. In the years immediately following her research, psychoanalysis "took off" in its popularity in France.

And this "take off" was not limited to intellectual and professional circles. Looking at psychiatric and cultural values in the
mid-1960s gave little hint of the explosion that was to come.
For although it is true that a therapeutic model has to fit in
with dominant social values, these values are not static entities. They themselves must remain relevant to social experience. And in France, that experience was changing and had
been changing for a long time.

The notion of deconversion suggests that psychoanalysis has special relevance for a community in the process of
rapid social change. One way of looking at the "time lag" in
the French and American enthusiasm for Freud is to suggest
that this kind of process was well underway at the time when
psychoanalysis took root in America over half a century ago,
but that in France the extraordinary synthesis of state, society, and individual that marked France's Republican period
successfully warded off most attacks to the status quo. That
stability was attacked in the years before the Second World
War, but the serious damage began with the war itself. The
fact of French collaboration with the Nazis left little room
for images of French society as an organic whole: the bourgeois politics of *le juste milieu* was attacked by the Right and
the Left. France's "aristocratic" values in business crumbled,
and the fragmentation and mobility of industrialization and
urbanization forced themselves on her. The new sweep of economic rationalism, beginning with the First Plan at the end
of World War II but only fully implemented with the coming
of Charles de Gaulle and the end of the Algerian War, shook
what equilibrium was left in "the stalemate society." The traditional French family business gave way to new industries
based on the American corporate model, and the percentage
of the population working in agriculture and living in rural

villages fell from 50 percent before the war to less than 15 percent in the mid-1970s.

The accelerated urbanization of France brought drastic changes in the ecology of French villages and cities. The nostalgic weekend return to roots in the provinces grew at a cadence equaled only by the general flight from them. In cities, traditional, longstanding neighborhoods were undermined by the mass influx of rural migrants and foreign workers, and in the country, social life was disrupted by the exodus of young people and by the influx of city people who used country property for weekend homes. There was marked erosion of the "village" quality of French urban and rural life. There was crisis in organized religion, in public education, and in the traditional ways of doing business. A managerial revolution led to the emergence of a new class of technocrats whose status was based on skills, performance, and profit rather than cultivated manner and family name.

The prewar response to the strains and crises of the Republican synthesis had been in terms of traditional political ideologies. The postwar response was less traditional. The existentialists wrote about the loneliness and confusion of the new, more fragmented social experience. Their response to social disintegration shifted the emphasis from the society to individual personal responsibility. They attacked the bourgeois order for denying what they felt history had made obvious: that each person must define his or her own values. The existentialists began writing before the war, but it was only in the postwar years that, in a sense, history caught up with them. Their philosophy of extreme situations and of extreme action for extraordinary individuals was resonant with the French experience of the Occupation and the Resistance. Part of existentialism's popular appeal may have been that it provided a way to think through the issues of choice and individual responsibility that had been raised by the war years. These were, most dramatically, to resist or not to resist the Germans, to betray or not to betray those who did. But as a theory of the self, existentialism did not go very far toward breaking away from the Cartesian heritage. Its psychology tended to portray individuals as rational, conscious actors who could understand the basis for their actions. It remained firmly rooted in a philosophy of individual autonomy and rational choice.[27]

Existentialism offered a vision of the individual which stood between the Cartesian culture which had been and the psychoanalytic culture which was to come. But as time went on, and the war years became more distant, a rationalist philosophy of the extreme situation no longer responded sufficiently to the times. Psychoanalysis goes beyond the study of the individual in extreme situations to focus on individuals as they face the banality and the pain of the everyday. And in the more fragmented, less emotionally secure life of the postwar years, many found the everyday increasingly hard to face. New overcrowded urban complexes cut people off not only from family ties but also from the lives of neighbors. The attendant social disorganization in old and new French urban centers were reflected in increases in violent crime, suicide, alcoholism, and drug addiction. Gradually, in the course of years, the French public began to hear about these and other problems in terms of a new "psychological" vocabulary. The difficulties of everyday life, of family life, of urban life, were discussed as problems of *le psy*, the shorthand expression used in French to refer to all things psychological. This psychologization of the problems of daily life was a giant step beyond existentialism toward setting the stage for a full-blown psychoanalytic culture.

People experienced shifts from rural/traditional to urban/industrial patterns in the life of the French economy, of work, and of the family in changed notions of individual privacy and in new insecurities about education, child raising, religion, and sexual behavior. When individuals lose confidence in their ability to understand the world around them, when they feel split between private and public identities, and when social "recipes" no longer offer a sense of meaning, they are apt to become anxious consumers of reassurances about their "authentic" subjectivity, their hidden "inner life," and their deepest interpersonal experiences. People seem to respond to what Max Weber described as the "world's disenchantment" by becoming fascinated with the mysteries of their interior alchemy. In France, this turning inward had a dramatic impact on traditional notions of the family.

With the breakdown of other communities and the dissolution of intermediate social circles, such as clubs, church groups, and local cafés, the French family is suffering under the strain of becoming too important. In villages, where male society used to center around cafés and clubs, social life has drifted from these male refuges to the family. In cities, inhabitants of the new high-rise housing projects complain of the isolation and loneliness of life within them, and have little choice but to turn toward the family as a source of psychological support. But particularly in the cities, the French family means the French nuclear family, and its resources are limited. Now, under pressure, it is searching for a new definition of itself in terms of a psychological function.

Family historian John Demos has argued that the emergence of a self-contained "hothouse family" in late nineteenth-century America set the stage for the American acceptance of Freud.[28] Now the French too are developing a "hothouse family," turned in toward itself. In France people used to talk about *la famille souche*, the economic unit of the family as the basis of national strength; now one hears about the family as the *lieu privilégié d'épanouissement*, a privileged setting for personal growth and self-actualization. French parents are concerned that they don't know how to make the switch, and their disorientation is reflected in a new interest in child psychology. When society is accepted and understood, parents' function is to *civilize* the child. When society is in disarray, romantic notions of *l'enfant sauvage* emerge. The youth revolt of 1968 brought to the surface profound parental uncertainties about the rational and authoritarian child-rearing codes which had gone unquestioned for generations. Parents no longer felt secure, as had their parents before them, that they understood the world for which they were raising their children.

These anxieties about child-rearing were similar to those expressed by Americans who, in the years after World War II, began living in a culture which was more "child oriented" than anything the French had ever been able to understand. In France, these anxieties did not really surface until the 1960s, but when they did, uncertainty led French parents to search for new experts just as American parents had done several decades before. And as in America, they turned to psychoanalysts, psychiatrists, and psychologists. In the late 1960s and early 1970s in France, there was a proliferation of psychoanalytically inspired articles, advice columns, and radio and television programs on how to raise children. The demand for the *experts du psy* has led to a new economic climate in which the number of psychoanalysts being trained could proliferate and in which the number of psychologists, group leaders, and psychological counselors of all sorts could similarly explode. Private institutions that could respond to the demand for expertise have blossomed as part of a new and profitable industry, heavily psychoanalytic in tone, that has sprung up around the troubled relationships between parents and their children. In the public sector, child-treatment centers that had been primarily pedagogical in focus (e.g., offering speech therapy and remedial reading classes) were transformed into centers of psychoanalytically inspired psychotherapy. Teachers began to refer students to them whom, a few years earlier, they might simply have disciplined.

In the course of the 1960s, psychological and psychoanalytic experts became more involved in education, and as they helped the family adapt to new pressures, they tried to do the same thing for the schools. The French educational system has to deal with the effects of the society's serious racial problems and class inequalities; the schools stagger under an overload of students they do not have the resources to teach. Psychological expertise is sometimes used to legitimate a process of "tracking" students which weeds out enough of them to make the situation tolerable for the system.[29] As time went on, the analytically trained professionals in the schools began to be seen as role models for educators. And when, in the late 1960s, the traditional French model of education, like the traditional French model of child raising, was attacked for being too abstract, rigid, and impersonal, many teachers began to identify with "psychoanalytic knowledge," more relative and relational than the "right or wrong" knowledge of academe.[30] Some tried to recycle professionally as psychoanalysts, but this was beyond the means and desires of most who simply tried to redefine teaching as a *profession du psy*.

Like the educational establishment and the family, the church is another social institution in trouble which is trying to use psychologization as a strategy to achieve flexibility. By the mid-1960s in France, the church was in crisis, its influence undermined by its continued opposition to abortion and contraception in the face of their popular acceptance.[31] For over a decade, the church had sought sources of renewal outside of itself. It had looked to ecumenical movements and social action. By the late 1960s, it began to look to a "psychological" perspective on religious work. Very quickly, the psychological perspective became a frankly psychoanalytic one. A growing body of Catholic thought stresses that, despite the fact the church had condemned psychoanalysis for half a century, psychoanalysis is compatible with Catholicism. Whereas in the early 1960s the priesthood tended to represent psychoanalysis as a sure precipitant of divorce, by the 1970s the clergy were as likely to describe psychoanalytically inspired counseling as a possible solution for a marriage in trouble. Even more important, they were doing some of that counseling themselves. Psychoanalysts became role models for clergymen as well as for teachers and parents. Increasing numbers of clergy began psychoanalytic training, and even more became convinced that the only possible future for the priesthood was to turn it too into a *profession du psy*.[32]

There is a French cliché: "The more things change, the more they stay the same." And there is a tradition of writing about French society that has elevated this cliché into something of a paradigm, working out the "real" continuities through apparent changes and focusing attention on the persistence of tradition in what only "seem" to be new and less traditional settings. But in the postwar years, students of French society have been obliged to note that much that had been considered "immutable" in French life has been highly subject to change when barriers to change were lifted. For example, the political instability of the Third and Fourth Republics was often attributed to the French "character." However, from the perspective of the more stable Fifth Republic, it seems that constitutions

which encouraged government by crisis rather than by compromise may have served as barriers to stability. Similarly, the
"characteristic" French ambivalence toward industrialization
(the maintenance of a strong rural tradition and a reservoir
of aristocratic traditions in industry) faded markedly when
the state no longer took artificial measures to keep families
on the farms and foreign labor outside of French borders. The
new enthusiasm of the church toward psychoanalysis suggests
that the end of the French resistance to Freud can be at least
partially explained by the removal of barriers which had previously blocked the acceptance of psychoanalysis. In the case of
psychoanalysis, the forces in the opposition were formidable,
including not only the Catholic Church but such powerful,
assertive institutions as the highly centralized French educational system, which kept Freud out of the curriculum, and
the French Communist Party, which virtually blacklisted it for
Marxists. Today, high school students study Freud as part of
their standard curriculum and are asked to write about him
to pass their baccalaureate examinations. And later chapters
describe in greater detail how psychoanalysis was given a new
seal of approval by a "culturally liberal" French Communist
Party. It is not surprising that there should have been a great
breakthrough of interest in psychoanalysis when such road-
blocks were removed. The social groundwork had been laid
for some time and had been reflected in other intellectual
movements.

In the 1940s and 1950s, existentialism had clearly expressed
the idea that society could no longer be counted on for a sense
of values and individual purpose. In the early 1960s in France,
the art of the new novel and new cinema went even further.
Their emphasis on radically individual languages and formal
description often seemed intent on rejecting the existence of a

society or even a shared reality that would be able to mediate our perceptions. The social changes reflected in the work of existentialists, new novelists, and new filmmakers are those that, by isolating and psychologizing the experience of the individual, pave the way for the emergence of a psychoanalytic culture. Clearly, these changes were all well underway before the 1968 turning point in the emergence of Freud as a significant social presence in France. The events of 1968, with their insistence on the continuity of politics with the world of everyday personal relationships, did not themselves forge the social basis of the psychoanalytic culture, but they did serve as a watershed. They marked and demarcated the importance of changes that had already occurred. In this sense, the events had a Januslike quality: they were analogous to attempts to re-create the illusion of community where it has disappeared, but in their form of expression that denied traditional boundaries between people, between the private and the public, and between the taboo and the permissible, they looked ahead to something new.

In the post-1968 years in France, a psychoanalytic language that refers the visible back to the invisible, the manifest back to the latent, the public back to the private, has become part of the standard discourse on the family, the school, and the church. Previously "private" concerns such as abortion, contraception, and sex education became the focus of public debate. Their consideration brought the psychoanalysts, perceived as the experts of the private, onto the public stage, where they offered people a language for thinking and talking more openly about such issues. The language that we use to talk about a problem is inseparable from the way in which we think about it. Many French people seem to feel that traditional moral, political, and religious philosophies no longer offer sufficient guidance, and the use of a psychoanalytic framework for thinking about public and personal problems has contributed to a new sense of privacy in which rigid boundaries between public and private have been softened.

In the midst of all this change, the French, who have always been used to a highly structured sense of the "rules of the game," were left with few social prescriptions. Family traditions and rituals were no longer secure, once coveted diplomas and titles no longer fulfilled their promise of prestige or even employment, religious faith and institutions were in crisis. When individuals sought anchoring points for their lives or help in dealing with distress, it was hard to find them in the experience of a community, in a set of established institutions, or in a faith. They had to look within and to personal relationships. In this personal sphere, psychoanalysis in both France and America offered itself as a way of addressing new insecurities. It also responded to the lack of norms by offering new experts for social problems that traditional formulas (religious ones, for example) no longer seem able to handle. In sum, psychoanalysis emerged in France as it did in America as the "therapy of deconversion."

Sociologist Peter Berger, who has sketched the outline of the correspondences between psychoanalysis and the social opacity and loss of community that characterize twentieth-century America, has reflected that, in America, "if Freud had not existed, he would have had to be invented."[33] One might say that in recent years the French *have* invented their own Freud. The next chapter, however, makes it clear that although France and America both developed a psychoanalytic culture, each "invented" a different Freud, one who matched the national texture of its social, intellectual, and political life.

2 "Reinventing" Freud in France

Understanding the emergence of the French psychoanalytic culture must recognize three kinds of developments. First, there were the social changes which seriously challenged a long-standing French belief that people could look to the collectivity and its traditions for some sense of who they were and where they were going. Second, there was the development of a psychoanalytic theory with the right cultural credentials. And finally, there was a breakthrough into a more popular psychoanalytic culture. Chapter 1 looked at the breakdown in traditional functioning at the social base which allowed psychoanalysis to take root. This chapter looks at the second and third of these strands of development, at the Lacanian "French indigenous" psychoanalytic paradigm that came to dominate the French scene and at the catalytic role of the May–June 1968 events.[1] The 1968 events translated existential Marxist ideas into a kind of social action which raised questions about the world to which psychoanalysis seemed to offer some answers.[2] The May events themselves were explosive and ephemeral, but among other effects they may have had, they were midwife to something more long lasting: they facilitated the breakthrough of the French psychoanalytic *movement* into a new, widespread psychoanalytic *culture*, and helped to shape it in the process.

The discussion of the American appreciation of Freud introduced the idea that a developing psychoanalytic culture can be shaped by its surroundings. In fact, when Freud expressed his first surprise that the Americans were enthusiastically accepting the psychoanalytic "plague," he was underestimating the degree to which psychoanalysis can adapt to its environment. Psychoanalysis has become culturally specific in several ways. First, cultures can "pick and choose" among its elements, bracketing those that seem most threatening or least useful. For example, the Americans might have been ready to accept a kind of therapy that focused heavily on early childhood memories, but not ready to accept fully the idea of infantile sexuality; they might have been ready to accept the existence of an unconscious, but unready to accept the power that Freud attributed to it.

Second, psychoanalysis can be a screen onto which a culture projects its preoccupations and values. Early twentieth-century American social theorists, such as Dewey, Mead, Peirce, and James, shared an optimistic and therapeutic outlook on the world. These thinkers of the "American Enlightenment" set the stage for the Americanization of psychoanalysis, which was dominated by a celebration of an autonomous ego that could change if it tried. Freud believed that since neurosis was the result of deep-seated psychological and social determinants, cures could only be protracted and partial. Freud's pessimistic tone suggested that psychoanalysis could help people to endure the paradox and tragedy of human life, but "endurance" was no substitute for the sense of wholeness that Americans felt they had lost with urbanization and the end of the frontier and that they hoped to recapture through a therapeutic culture. Freud's American interpreters shifted the emphasis to a new therapeutic optimism. Their response to Freudian pessimism was to shrug off the suggestion that the individual is not master of his or her own house, free to act and choose no matter what the problems or environment. Although the Americans welcomed Freud to their shores, Freud's theory could not stretch far enough to meet American demands for therapeutic optimism and voluntarism. In the end, he was "not enough," and Americans strained to produce more optimistic, instrumental, and voluntaristic revisions of his work.

Third, psychoanalysis is shaped by social institutions. In the story of what happened to psychoanalysis in the United States, the fact that the "American Freud" was nearly monopolized by physicians, a social group under the greatest possible pressure to emphasize the useful, took the general American preference for the pragmatic and raised it to a higher power. In France, the psychiatric resistance to psychoanalysis allowed it a long period of incubation in the world of artists and writers before a significant breakthrough into medicine, a pattern which reinforced the French tendency to take ideas and invest them with philosophical and ideological significance instead of turning them outward toward problem-solving.

In its susceptibility to cultural influence, psychoanalysis is not unique. Most intellectual movements undergo some form of cultural adaptation to different national settings. But psychoanalysis is not just an intellectual position: its extension as a therapeutic strategy makes it especially sensitive to its environment. In order to be effective, therapies must be relevant to a culture's prevailing modes of making sense of experience.[3] In this, therapeutic strategies are similar to religious beliefs. One would not expect the national versions of psychoanalysis to be any less varied than the national versions of Calvinism. An American patient, nursed on the Horatio Alger story and on dramatic tales of biological or spiritual ancestors battling it out at the frontier, can respond to a picture of the psyche which emphasizes the struggles of the ego with the demands of a difficult reality. A French patient who has been doing *explication du texte* and memorizing literary aphorisms since grade school might be more receptive to a psychoanalysis which presents itself as a form of textual analysis on the unconscious. This chapter keeps the cultural specificity of psychoanalytic cultures in the foreground as it looks at how Freud was "reinvented" for the French.

Historian H. Stuart Hughes has remarked that the French resisted psychoanalysis until they had produced Jacques Lacan, an "indigenous heretic" whose structuralism and linguistic emphasis were resonant with the French Cartesian tradition.[4] Lacan's structuralist theories emphasize the possibility of discovering universal laws about individuals and society through our experience of ourselves. Lacan denigrates "humanistic" philosophy and psychology that treat people as actors who will their actions and instead sees them as submitting objects of processes that transcend them. Lacan's affirmation of the centrality of language to thought and his emphasis on logical and mathematical formalization is meant to lay the groundwork for a unification of knowledge. Lacan has underscored these Cartesian qualities in Freud where they were apparent and has read others back into Freud where they were at best implicit. The French tradition in psychology has always been poetic, and there had been much objection to Freud's didactic style, which the French felt did great injustice to the protean symbols with which he dealt. The French preferred authors like the philosopher Gaston Bachelard who treated such symbols more "aesthetically." Lacan's style, which is closer to Mallarmé's than to Freud's, satisfies the French taste for a poetic psychology. And his work is so elusive, so intentionally hard to pin down, that no one could accuse him of not letting protean symbols emerge in all their richness and ambiguity.

The Lacanian paradigm is structuralist, emphasizing individuals' constraints rather than their freedoms; it is poetic, linguistic, and theoretical rather than pragmatic and tends to open out to a political discourse which raises questions beyond the psychoanalytic. French intellectual life is among the most ideological and politicized in the world, and Lacanism's strong political valence helps to mark it as "French indigenous." Lacan's anti-institutional biases, his critique of "adaptationist" ego psychology, and his emphasis on the way in which society enters the individual as the individual enters the world of symbolic speech have facilitated a new dialogue between Marxism and psychoanalysis in France. In its structuralist, linguistic, poetic, and political emphases, Lacan's is truly a "French Freud."

I begin a discussion of Lacan, the theorist, with a distinction between two styles of theorizing, both of which can be found in Freud's work. The distinction is between a search for meaning and a search for mechanism. In Freud's early work much of the discussion is about how to find a new level of meaning in what people do, say, and dream by a method not unlike textual analysis. Psychic phenomena are discussed in terms of processes that constantly remind the reader that the phenomena themselves are linguistic: for example, one analyzes the dream as a rebus. In Freud's later work, different concerns are dominant. He focuses on the mechanisms of negotiation between internal entities—id, ego, and superego—which now join censors, instincts, and drives to act in hidden but highly structured processes which are presumed to underlie behavior.

To many, this later, "psychological" theory seemed more concrete, more scientific, more attractive. To Jacques Lacan, it opened the door to compromising the Freudian pursuit of meaning with an unfortunate preoccupation with mechanism. To his mind it represented a dilution of psychoanalytic thought, and he has devoted much of his career to the relentless criticism of such tendencies.

For example, in the 1950s Lacan turned sharp critical fire on the fashion of that time to look for bridges from psychoanalysis to behaviorist psychology. When the *International Journal of Psychoanalysis* published an article by the American psychoanalyst Jules Masserman, who argued that experiments which conditioned autonomic responses to word commands (and imagined word commands) were important to psychoanalysis, Lacan was outraged. He accused the editors of the journal of "following a tradition borrowed from employment agencies; they never neglect anything that might provide our discipline with 'good references.'"[5] Lacan himself was clearly not impressed with behaviorism's credentials for the job:

> Think of it, here we have a man who has reproduced neurosis expe-ri-mental-ly in a dog tied down to a table and by what ingenious methods: a bell, the plate of meat it announces, and the plate of potatoes that arrives instead; you can imagine the rest. He will certainly not be one, at least so he assures us, to let himself be taken in by the "ample ruminations" as he puts it, that philosophers have devoted to the problem of language. Not him, he's going to grab it from your throat.[6]

For Lacan, what is essential in psychoanalysis is the relation of the unconscious to language and symbolic behavior: in these areas, models of stimulus and response have nothing to contribute. Lacan's hyphenation of "experimentally" leaves little doubt that he intended such reverberations as the suggestion that experimental methods in psychoanalytic domains leave the essential behind (ex-mental) or go around it (perimental). Lacan insists that Masserman was mistaken in his claim that when the thought of a word is used as a stimulus in a conditioning experiment, the word is serving as an "idea-symbol." Lacan describes this mistake as a failure to distinguish between using a word as a mere sign and using it as a symbol. A sign conveys a simple message complete in itself. A symbol evokes an open-ended system of meaning. For Lacan, the confusion of sign and symbol by a psychoanalyst is deeply troubling because it compromises Freud's "Promethean discovery" of the unconscious, its laws and the effects of symbols. "To ignore this symbolic order is to condemn the discovery to oblivion and the experience to ruin."[7]

Lacan does not limit his critique of what he saw as mechanistic interpretations of psychoanalysis to behaviorism. For Lacan, explicit ex-pe-ri-mental-ism is only an extreme case of a way of thinking which includes psychoanalytic ego psychology as well. Indeed, Lacan found the Masserman case worthy of attention precisely because he felt it represented

> everything produced by a certain tendency in psychoanalysis—in the name of a theory of the *ego* or of the technique of the analysis of defense—everything, that is, most contradictory to the Freudian experience.[8]

As far as Lacan was concerned, the same shift of concern from meaning to mechanism which had led analysts to the search for Pavlovian or Skinnerian principles had also led them to an exaggerated concern for the whereabouts and activities of a set of psychic structures whose existence was at best problematic. Of course, of all such structures it is the ego that has occasioned the greatest interest from psychoanalysts. In Freud's later writings, the ego emerged as that agency which is turned out toward reality, and theorists who followed him, among them and perhaps most importantly his daughter, began to focus their attention on its vicissitudes. To them, the ego seemed almost a psychic hero as it battled off id and superego at the same time that it tried to cope with the world of the everyday. Anna Freud wrote of its powerful artillery, the mechanisms of defense, which helped the ego in its struggles but whose overly rigid use caused it new problems. And Heinz Hartmann gave the ego a property that was to prove decisive for psychoanalytic technique when he asserted that the ego had an aspect that was not tied up with the individual's neurotic conflicts. As perceived by the French, the concept implied a voluntarism that seemed anti-Freudian. This "unhampered" aspect of the ego seemed free to act and choose, independent of constraints, including social constraints. It almost seemed the psychic locus for a notion of the "Will" or for the seat of moral responsibility. And they felt that it was from the germ of this idea of a "conflict-free zone" that a new way of talking about psychoanalysis gradually emerged and became most powerfully rooted in the United States. This was to talk about a therapeutic alliance: the analyst's role was to become the ally of the "healthy" ego forces in their struggle to dominate instincts and drives.

Lacan's many-sided attack on this position provides an excellent introduction to the foundations of his thought. First, he attacks the ego psychologists' concept of a "healthy part" of the ego. How, asks Lacan, can they know which "part" is "healthy"? Is this not tantamount to assuming that the goal of psychoanalysis is to bring the patient to see the world as the analyst sees it? Lacan rejects this as a goal of psychoanalysis along with the associated formulation that "the purpose of analysis is achieved by an identification with the analyst's ego."[9] To Lacan's way of thinking, the analyst must engage in a continual process of putting himself into question and must never let his or her sense of reality become the measure of all things for the patient. Going even further, Lacan attacks the very idea that the health of the ego can be defined *objectively* in terms of an adaptation to *reality*. In one essay, Lacan asks us to imagine that his desk were capable of speech. The desk explains how well adapted it is to reality in the shape of Lacan's papers and person. The desk sees its reality as all reality and cannot know whether it is adapted to reality or reality to it. Why should things be easier for an ego? Lacan acknowledges that the ego and not the desk is the "seat of perceptions," but this does not give it an "objective" platform from which to view the world.[10]

Lacan traces most of ego psychology's problems and contradictions to this idea that there is an "objective," "knowable" reality:

> One understands that to prop up so obviously precarious a conception certain individuals on the other side of the Atlantic should have felt the need to introduce into it some stable value, some standard of the measure of the real: this turns out to be the autonomous ego. This is the supposedly organized ensemble of the most disparate functions that lend their support to the subject's feeling of innateness. It is regarded as autonomous because it appears to be sheltered from the conflicts of the person (*non-conflictual-sphere*).
>
> One recognizes there a down-at-heel mirage that had already been rejected as untenable by most academic psychology of introspection. Yet this regression is celebrated as a return to the fold of "general psychology."[11]

Lacan's own conception of the ego suggests that far from deserving a role as a trustworthy ally, it must be profoundly mistrusted because it is unable to discriminate the subject's own desires from the desires of others. According to Lacan, the ego is not autonomous, but subordinated and alienated to the objects (people and images) with which it has identified during its development. Lacan places the genesis of the ego's confusions at its time of origin in what he calls the "mirror phase" of human development; while other analysts were talking about setting up alliances with the ego, Lacan was insisting that the ego is the carrier of the neurosis and that allying with the ego is like consorting with the enemy.

For Lacan, the psychoanalytic approach to the ego must be "with daggers drawn"; the analyst must relate directly to the unconscious. When Lacan speaks of the psychoanalyst as the "practitioner of the symbolic function" he means that the analyst must be the practitioner of the language of the unconscious, a language of poetry and puns, wordplays, and internal rhymes.[12] In this language, there is no line between what is said and how it is said: style is indissociable from substance.

Lacan himself was at his most stylized and substantive at his seminar, a Paris ritual that lasted a quarter of a century. Once every two weeks many hundreds of people came to listen to a performance that defied categorization. Lacan described his seminar as a place where *ça parle* (the id speaks) and in many ways his discourse is like the flow of language of a person in analysis, dense with associations and unexpected transitions. But Lacan's seminars were much more than free associations. In these meticulously prepared presentations, we also hear Lacan speak with the voice of the analyst, interpreting his own discourse as did the early Freud of *The Interpretation of Dreams*. Unlike the early Freud, though, the line between the interpretation and the material is not always drawn. Interpretation is embedded in the discourse itself, often couched in wordplay and literary device. For example, Lacan speaks of people as *par-lêtres*. The term means "talking beings," but can also be heard as meaning "by the letter," playing on the structuralist notion of people as constituted by language. Lacan coins the phrase *père-version*, "father-aversion," and plays on the idea that it is also perverse. One of Lacan's most important theoretical tenets is that in a single act the child accepts both the name of the father (in French, *le nom*) and the father's saying "no" to the child's sexual attachment to the mother (in French, *le non*). So, when Lacan called his 1973–74 seminar "Les Non-Dupes Errent" (Those who are not duped are in error), he was playing on the other two ways of hearing these sounds, as "the father's *name*" and as "the father's *no*."

For Lacan, this wordplay is not a frill, but is at the heart of what he considers the psychoanalytic enterprise. He wants his communications to speak directly to the unconscious and believes that wordplay, where causal links dissolve and associations abound, is the language which it understands. All psychoanalysts use language as the medium of the analytic cure and are interested in its study. But Lacan's interest in language expresses something much more specific: Lacan believes that the study of the laws of language and the laws of the unconscious are one and the same, that *the unconscious is structured as a language*. And of course this means that linguistics is the cornerstone for all psychoanalytic science.

Thus Lacan is led to couch his fundamental theoretical ideas in terms of how different kinds of relationships of signification are built up. For Lacan, even the infant's first desire for the mother signifies something beyond itself: it signifies the wish to be what the mother most desires. In French, the ambiguity between desiring someone and the desire to be the object of that person's desire is beautifully expressed in the possessive form "de" ("of"). *Désir de la mère* means "desire for the mother" as well as "the mother's desire." (In English, we must constantly remind ourselves that desire for a person and the desire to be the object *of* desire are both always present, each implied in the other.)

The infant does not just want to be cared for, touched and fed, but wants to actually *complete* the mother, to be what she lacks and can be presumed to want above all else: the phallus. In Lacan's work, the phallus does not stand for the penis itself. It stands for the infant's absolute and irreducible desire to be a part of the mother, to be what she most desires. We shall see that for Lacan it comes to stand, even more generally, for the kind of desire that can never be satisfied.

The child's relationship with the mother is fusional, dual and immediate, dominated by the desire to lose self in other. The presence of the father (as presented by the mother to the child) excludes the possibility for fusion. The child's desire to be its mother's desire gives way to an identification with the father. Lacan tells us that this identification takes place through an assimilation of the father's name, which as we have already pointed out, is a homonym in French with the father's "no."

In "classical" Freudian terms we have just described the *repression* of desire for the mother. Freud's models of how this process takes place were sometimes psychological, sometimes hydraulic, sometimes energetic. What Lacan has done is to translate repression into linguistic terms as a process of metaphor formation. One signifier (father's name) comes to substitute for another (desire for the mother and desire to be the object of her desire).[13] Of course, what is being signified, the phallus, remains the same. But two important things have happened. The relationship between signifier and signified has been mediated: they are now more distanced from each other. And the old signifier (desire for the mother) and what it signifies are "pushed down" to a deeper level: they are now unconscious. The father's name now only signifies the phallus through a chain of signification that has an invisible link, the desire for the mother. In the course of a lifetime, the individual builds up many chains of signification, always substituting new terms for old and always increasing the distance between the signifier that is most accessible and visible, and all those that are invisible and unconscious, including of course the original signifier.

This model of repression as metaphor formation illuminates Lacan's way of talking about the psychoanalytic process as a science of interpretation. Its goal is not stated in terms of "adaptation to reality," but as the restitution of the associative chains of signification. Since these chains have been built up by complex wordplays, breaking the code requires skill with words. Lacan was being quite genuine when he summed up his advice to a young psychoanalyst as "Do crossword puzzles."[14]

But the formation of the parental metaphor, or, more classically, the repression of the desire for the mother through the "mechanism" of castration anxiety, is not a random link in the associative chain of signification. It is Lacan's version of what is taking place in the resolution of the Oedipus complex. And at the heart of what is going on is the development of the child's capacity for a new way of using signification. The child is learning how to use symbols. Lacan marks the enormous difference between the pre-Oedipal and post-Oedipal ways of signifying by naming two different orders of signification. The first order, associated with the immediate, dual relationship of child and mother, is called the "imaginary" (*imaginaire*) order. As when Narcissus bent over his reflection, self yearns to fuse with what is perceived as other. The second order, in which signification is mediated by a third term, the father, is called the "symbolic" (*symbolique*) order. Like the world after the Tower of Babel, there is no longer a one-to-one correspondence between things and how they are called. The symbol has intervened. The word is no longer the thing.

The imaginary order takes its name from Lacan's description of a "mirror phase" of development which extends from when the child is about six months old to when it is about eighteen months old. During this time, the child comes to see its body, which is still uncoordinated and not fully under its control, as whole rather than fragmented by identifying with its mirror *image* in much the same way that it identifies with its mother's body and with the bodies of other children. Lacan believes that all of these unmediated one-to-one identifications are *alienating*. The child is actually subordinated to its image, to its mother, to others. Lacan associates imaginary significations with dual, fusional, and alienating relationships and contrasts them with very different significations which can take place in the symbolic order. Symbolic signification, of which the "father's name" metaphor is an example, is mediated rather than fusional. It is social, not narcissistic. According to Lacan's way of looking at things, the Oedipal crisis is a crisis of imaginary signification. It marks the child's entrance into the world of the symbolic through the formation of the parental metaphor. The laws of language and society come to dwell within the child as it accepts the father's name and the father's "no."

This discussion has presented the transition from imaginary to symbolic as though an imaginary "stage" gives way to a symbolic one. But this is not the case. The entrance into the symbolic opens the way for symbolic significations, but the imaginary identifications which began during the mirror phase have become paradigmatic for processes of identification. The subject continues to identify itself with people and images in a direct, fusional mode in which self is lost in other. And it is through these identifications that the subject constructs the alienated self which Lacan calls the *ego* or *moi*. Of course this *ego*, built out of alienating identifications, has nothing in common with the sturdy, helpful being described by the ego psychologists. Quite to the contrary, for Lacan the *ego* is the bearer of neurosis and the center of all resistance to the cure of symptoms. The symbolic order always partakes of the imaginary because the primary identification of the self as a misrecognition constrains all further constructions of the self. The self is always like another. So the imaginary construction of the ego "situates the agency of the ego, before its social determination, in a fictional direction, which will always remain irreducible for the individual alone. . . ."[15]

All of the objects of imaginary identification function as substitutes for the absolute object of desire, long repressed, long forgotten, what Lacan calls "the absolute desire for the Other."[16] This desire can never be satisfied. Even at the end of a successful analysis the subject is faced with the impossibility of completing the chain of signification back to an accessible and irreducible reality. Knowledge and the absolute, final truth are irrevocably cut off from each other. "The symptom, ever more loaded with its content of knowledge, is cut off from its truth. And that which severs them from one another is precisely what constitutes the subject."[17] Psychoanalysis cannot undo this inevitable frustration. It can only bring the individual to an understanding of how the experience of "something missing" is at the very core of being. And indeed, Lacan acknowledges this final, frustrating state of affairs when he defines a third order which is beyond the symbolic realm of language and beyond imaginary construction. This reality which we can never know is what he calls the "real" (*réel*). Trying to describe the real in words is itself a paradox because definitionally the real lies beyond language. It is defined within the linguistic system as something beyond and outside of it. It is the precategorical and prescientific, the reality that we must assume although we can never know it.[18]

Even this very brief look at Lacan's ideas should leave little doubt that they would provoke strong feelings. Later chapters discuss both his excommunication from the International Psychoanalytic Association and the devotion of his followers. It is not uncommon for a French psychoanalyst to have made loyalty to Lacan the theorist a matter of personal principle despite his or her most profound reservations about Lacan the clinician or even about Lacan the man. In my own interviews with French psychoanalysts, many who neither approved of Lacan's short sessions nor of his ideas about self-authorization in psychoanalytic training felt that his theoretical perspective had brought them back to fundamental truths which served as sources of renewal in their lives as analysts.

Lacan's turn to linguistic referents for psychoanalysis and his interest in psychoanalysis as a science of interpretation gives him an appeal far beyond the psychoanalytic community itself. It is particularly strong in the world of literary criticism where "traditional" psychoanalytic approaches have all too often degenerated into unrigorous and reductionist speculations about an author's "Oedipal" preoccupations or use of sexual symbolism. Lacan offers literary critics the possibility of something new. In his seminar on Edgar Allan Poe's "The Purloined Letter," Lacan does not use analytic categories to solve textual problems. Instead, he takes the Poe story as a pretext for using analytic questions to open up altogether new kinds of literary and psychoanalytic issues.[19] The story has intrinsic appeal for Lacan: it offers "the letter" as an image of the power of the signifier. All of the actions of all of the characters in the story are determined by the presence of a letter, a signifier whose contents are unknown. Thus, like a typographic "letter," and like Freud's description of a "memory trace," the purloined letter is a unit of signification which takes on meaning by its differential opposition to other units. Lacan's seminar on Poe focuses on the generation of meaning from such oppositions and on the ability of pre-existing symbols to structure human action. Implicitly, it also raises the problem of the real. Even the "letter," the unit of signification, is not irreducible; it can bear meaning through associations and history that go beyond its differential oppositions with other (like) units. In other essays in the *Ecrits*, Lacan treats the work of Marguerite Duras, the Marquis de Sade, Jorge Luis Borges, and Molière, among scores of other authors, and explores many relations between psychoanalysis and literature. Lacanian perspectives on the problems of signification, on the structuring properties of desire, on the power of symbols in forging human action, and on the homologies between unconscious laws and linguistic laws, have deeply influenced the generation of French literary critics which included Roland Barthes, Julia Kristeva, and Philippe Sollers, and have swept Continental literary circles. Indeed, the first interest in Lacan in the United States came not from the psychoanalytic community, but from students of literature.

In this book, the focus is not on Lacan and the French literati, but on his relevance to another group. This is his appeal to people who consider themselves to be on the Left. Using the expression "people on the Left" calls for some disclaimers.

Although the discussion here will include some special reference to Communist Party intellectuals, the term "the Left" is
not only meant to designate the Left of official political parties. Rather, it is used to refer to a group of mostly middle-class
people, somewhat intellectual in their interests and preten-
sions, who do not necessarily hold much in common beyond
the fact that they would identify themselves as "people on the
Left." Some belong to the Communist Party, although others
who consider themselves "on the Left" feel that Party members
are definitionally excluded from the Left. Some identify with
the small, Marxist and anarchist student groups which sparked
the May days. Some identify with the existential Marxism of
groups like Socialisme ou Barbarie. Some are more influenced
by the opinions of the trendsetting *Le Nouvel Observateur* than
by the ideas of Marx, Trotsky, or Mao. For most French people
who consider themselves "on the Left," the cultivation of anti-
Americanism is a habit of long standing, and another common
element is a strong antibureaucratic and anti-establishment
bias. Lacan has appeal on all of these counts. For over a quarter of a century he remained relentlessly critical of American
psychoanalysis, politics, and culture and of all psychoanalytic
establishments. His attacks have frequently had a tone closer
to that of a political campaigner than to what we usually associate with psychoanalytic scholarship.

Freud began a tradition of psychoanalyst as cultural critic,
and Lacan often crossed the line between scientific criticism
of American ego psychology and more politically charged
attacks on the American values which helped to ensure its
acceptance. For example, he described the American psychoanalytic community as "a team of *egos*, no doubt less
equal than autonomous" which are "offered to the Americans to guide them towards happiness, without upsetting

the autonomies, egotistical or otherwise, that pave with their non-conflictual spheres, the *American Way* of getting there."[20] In his 1953 essay "The Function and Field of Speech and Language in Psychoanalysis," Lacan combined his attack on the United States as a nation where individuals were subjected to "human engineering" in the service of social control with an attack on the bureaucratization of the psychoanalytic establishment. He described the psychoanalytic establishment as "terrified" and defensively walled off from "the fresh air of criticism" by

> a formalism pushed to such ceremonial lengths that one might well wonder whether it does not bear the same similarity to obsessional neurosis that Freud so convincingly defined in the observance, if not in the genesis, of religious rites.[21]

And in the 1970s, things were not much different: Lacan was still using "American Psychoanalysis" as a shorthand for any mechanistic approach to psychoanalysis and was referring to the International Psychoanalytic Association as the SAMCDA, his acronym for "The Society of Mutual Aid to Combat the Psychoanalytic Discourse."[22]

Lacan's anti-American and antibureaucratic positions were not irrelevant to the social breakthrough of the French psychoanalytic culture in the late 1960s. At the height of the Vietnam War, anti-Americanism and the denigration of all establishments were rallying cries for the French student movement. Lacan's connections to these issues made it easier for the psychoanalytic culture to take some of the momentum from energies generated and then frustrated by the May days and their aftermath. But the vigor and political valence of the French psychoanalytic culture which emerged after 1968 was not a simple function of its ability to pick up on Lacan's iconoclasm and the student movement's anti-American and anti-institutional themes. In the years following the May–June 1968 events, French psychoanalysis came to be reconciled with two ideological currents, existentialism and Marxism, with which it had formerly had hostile relations. Jean-Paul Sartre had denounced Freud's notion of the unconscious as an insult to human freedom; generations of Marxists had denounced psychoanalysis as a weapon of the bourgeoisie. But by the 1970s French Communists were reading favorable commentaries about psychoanalysis in Party organs, and Sartre had written a biography of Flaubert of Freudian inspiration. To understand the role of the events of 1968 in mediating these changes, it is important to understand how in the twenty years between the end of World War II and the 1968 social revolt, existentialism and Marxism forged their own marriage in a way which prepared the ground for both of them to approach psychoanalytic thought with fresh interest.

For the "classical" Marxist, individual psychological processes are epiphenomenal because events are determined by a society's class structure and means of production. However, after World War II, the classical "economist" reading of Marx began to appear insufficient for understanding what had happened to Communism in the Soviet Union. If capital was defined only in terms of the private ownership of the means of production, the Russian system, which appeared to be a form of state capitalism, seemed a contradiction in terms. As it became increasingly apparent that the critique of capitalism had to be based on more than legal or purely economic ideas about ownership, more Marxists turned to Marx's early writings in which the emphasis was on the concept of *alienation* rather than ownership. The alienation of the early Marx is a psychological state which could be present whether or not one was in the presence of a stock exchange or working in a factory. One could be alienated in Moscow as well as in Detroit, in a university as well as on an assembly line. This notion of alienation was very appealing to intellectuals because, if a revolutionary class was defined in terms of its alienation, alliances between workers, students, and intellectuals could make real political sense. It was embraced by postwar French Marxists caught up in the burgeoning existentialist movement. Under the influence of existential philosophy, Marx's *1844 Manuscripts*, Gramsci's writings, and Georg Lukacs's humanistic Marxism, a native species of French existential Marxism was born. This marriage of political and philosophical currents was to be extremely relevant to the events of May 1968, which played out many existential Marxist ideas in political practice.

French existential Marxists were committed to the ideas that the essence of revolutionary action was self-management and local control of political power and that the socialist revolution would lead to a blossoming of the individual personality. Following Marx's vision of a world where the barrier between mental and manual labor would break down, they believed that socialism should mean the end to alienation. These beliefs in self-management and the end of alienation became focal points of the May–June 1968 actions when students seized control of their high schools and universities, and workers took over their factories. They wanted to run all institutions as participatory democracies where self-expression would be given free rein. In their writings, the existential Marxists tried to work out the theoretical connections between self-management and the problem of alienation, but the actual experience of May gave new life to the issues. Existential Marxists had long speculated about how a revolution of self-management might unfold, but it was *doing* it in

1968 that brought the centrality of individual psychology into relief. Attempts at self-expression in structures of democratic self-management led to preoccupations with the self. Existential Marxism when played out in social practice seemed to pave the way for the psychoanalytic culture.

The May actions stressed that a liberated politics could only emerge from liberated interpersonal relationships and that structured, impersonal political organizations could not respond to the problems of alienation in an over-structured society. The May 1968 alternative to traditional political organization was the *comité d'action*. "Action committees" sprang up everywhere: in universities, factories, theater groups, high schools, hospitals. They were not intended to develop a coherent program for a new society; they were to *be* that new society in embryo. They presented an image of the future socialist society as a society of continual, free, spontaneous creation. In such a society, action would not emerge from planning, but from people relating fully to each other as complete human beings rather than as fragmented social actors. One of the dominant ideas put forth during May was that the form and the relational context of politics was politics itself. Like Lacan, the May celebrants saw style and content as indissociable. People tried to act on a belief that unalienated thought and action required political structures that were designed to destroy structures. They participated in the action committees as "antistructures" and focused their attention on expected changes in their psychological states. The result was a new concern with the self and with personal relationships.

During May–June 1968, the streets of France were flooded with people talking to each other as they claimed they had never talked with each other before. They spoke of their sexuality, of their dissatisfactions with family life and formalities, of their desire for more open communication. The hierarchies and bureaucratic structures which are so much a part of French life were, for a moment, forgotten. Questions about authenticity and alienation were experienced as real, immediate, almost tangible. Even a brief experience of doing without the typical social roles gave special meaning to trying to understand how these roles stand in the way of intimacy.

In the years before 1968 in France, there had already grown up a small psychoanalytic movement animated by lively theoretical controversies, an intellectual community increasingly receptive to Freud's ideas, and a psychiatric establishment that was less hostile to them. The pieces were in place for a new relationship to psychoanalytic ideas. But while psychoanalysts and intellectuals alone can make a psychoanalytic movement, they cannot themselves make a psychoanalytic culture. The popularity of existentialism during the 1940s and 1950s had been fanned by its resonance with the decisions people had to make during the war. The issue of individual commitment took on a quality of concreteness and personal urgency. Now, the widely shared experience of May called long-established patterns of life into question and prepared the ground for a new cultural interest in individual psychology. In the years after May, there was great popular demand for psychoanalytic ideas, for psychoanalytically inspired advice, and even for psychoanalytic therapy.

The explosion of interest in psychoanalysis after 1968 was foreshadowed by many of the May slogans and graffiti, which expressed the desire to get close to immediate experience and emotion and to break down the boundaries between reality and fantasy, the rational and irrational. To many observers, May seemed to be a kind of surrealism-in-political-action. Freud's first French admirers had been the surrealists, and during May, as in surrealist writings, psychoanalytic slogans were put to use as utopian rallying cries: "Take your desires for reality. . . . A policeman dwells in each of our heads, he must be killed. Liberate psychoanalysis." In the course of the 1968 events, many radical students moved from indifference or hostility toward psychoanalysis to a new, more ambivalent relationship. Long-standing Leftist criticism of psychoanalysis as bourgeois ideology and upper-class luxury paled before popular demands for contact with psychoanalysis. Wilheim Reich became a *Maître à penser*; long nights of political debate were held in a Sorbonne lecture hall, newly rechristened *L'Amphithéâtre Che-Guevara-Freud*.

To many, May 1968 was experienced as a festival of speech and liberated desire and it seemed only natural to turn to psychoanalysts, whom they perceived as the professionals of both. Students asked analysts to join them in their struggles. Medical students wanted help in creating a new "human relations curriculum" for medical schools, psychiatry students wanted support in their revolt against their almost entirely neurological university training, and politicized students in the social sciences and humanities were in search of new critical vantage points. Psychoanalysts were asked to leave the consulting room and to join in what was happening on the streets. These developments will be examined in greater detail in chapter 7 on psychoanalysis in the university.

Political participation has always raised special problems for psychoanalysts: the orthodox have gravely emphasized psychoanalytic neutrality, but for many analysts, there was a real tension between the therapeutic imperative of presenting a neutral screen and their own sense of themselves as citizens. Psychoanalysts had debated the pros and cons of different

kinds of political visibility in seminar rooms, salons, and journal articles for many generations. In 1968, there was pressure
to act. Some analysts closed their offices, put up signs: "PSY-
CHOANALYST AT DEMONSTRATION." Some were hostile
to the events and charged patients for analytic sessions that
they missed. Others simply did nothing, watched, and waited
it out.

On May 23, 1968, Paris's *Le Monde* published a manifesto
in support of the students signed by seventy psychoanalysts.
The manifesto emphasized that the May actions were politically motivated. The analysts who signed the manifesto were
particularly interested in making this point because they knew
only too well that many of their colleagues were already using
analogies with the Oedipal drama to explain the events in
terms of collective psychopathology.

There was strong reaction to the manifesto within the psychoanalytic world. The French psychoanalytic societies were
torn by conflict over what the events were about and how
analysts should participate in them. Analysts challenged the
hierarchies of the psychoanalytic societies at the same time
that they struggled with their positions in the social movement as a whole. French analysts of all persuasions were
confronted with questions about psychoanalysis and politics
and about the role of the analyst as social critic and revolutionary activist. Finding a role was no simple matter. There
was first of all the traditional problem of "neutrality." Would
political participation compromise the analytic position? Second, even those analysts who wanted to participate found
themselves faced with a student movement that was highly
ambivalent about a psychoanalytic presence. Attitudes toward
psychoanalysis were in transition; the situation looked totally

confusing. Analysts were alternatively denounced as legitima-
tors of the status quo, cited in revolutionary slogans, criticized
as "superpsychiatric policemen," and asked to speak on sexual
and political liberation.

Lacanian analysts played a large role in the May movement:
they identified with the students, and the students identified
with them. In 1968, bridges between Lacan and the Left were
strengthened by Lacanian connections with Marxist circles at
the Ecole Normale Supérieure. This association dated back to
the early days of Lacan's seminar and had become closer and
more visible in 1963 when Marxist philosopher Louis Althusser
invited Lacan to bring his seminar to the Ecole Normale. The
link to Althusser's circle had greatly increased the recruitment
of politically involved people to Lacan's Freudian School and
began to break down the long resistance of French Marxists
toward psychoanalysis via a detour through Lacan's *Ecrits*.
Lacan had certainly not been giving garden-variety political
speeches in his seminars at the Ecole Normale, but by June
1968, his thought was sufficiently associated with radical student groups that the dean of the Ecole asked him to leave on
the grounds that his seminar was "politically disruptive." University administrators saw Lacan as a political threat and university students saw his anti-American and anti-institutional
theoretical positions as an inspiration.

To a student movement in the throes of challenging the
hierarchy of the French university system, the Lacanians—
who had attacked the Americans, broken rules, and attacked
hierarchy in the psychoanalytic world—seemed the natural
allies of such struggles. Lacanian experiments in antipsychiatry
seemed to anticipate the spirit of May, and students turned to
Lacanian analyses of group and institutional process for ideas
on how to run action committees.[23] A political form inspired

by the voluntarist tradition of worker self-management put itself at the tutelage of a structuralist psychoanalytic science. The action committees became a place for "bridge building" between existential Marxism and psychoanalysis, but there were many others, both during May and after.

Many people who had been caught up in the May actions turned to Lacan in the years after the events for help in theorizing many aspects of their aspiration to have made a revolution of speech and desire. They were able to turn to Lacan for help in thinking through the relationship of individual and society. This chapter has characterized Lacan's French "reinvention" of Freud by situating it in relation to some important currents in French social and political life. The next chapter shows how Lacan's theory (and in particular his theorization of the transaction between imaginary and symbolic, the transaction that marks man's entrance into society and that marks society's entrance into man) opened out to new connections between psychoanalysis and political ideas.

The surrealists had hoped to use psychoanalysis as a form of utopian thought. They tried to plumb psychoanalysis for images of a future that could draw on a world of dreams and desire. Much to Freud's dismay, they took the existence of a powerful, primitive unconscious as an aesthetic measure of contemporary society. The flattened experience that characterizes modern life stood accused by the images of freedom that the surrealists read into Freud's thought. In May 1968, and in its aftermath, utopian political currents reenacted this scenario, this time with the ideas of Lacan, Reich, and Marcuse as well as Freud. In Lacan's own biography, things had come full circle. In the mid-1930s, at about the same time that Lacan was beginning his study of the problem of paranoia, Salvador Dalí was deep in research on a similar theme. From

Dalí's work came a characterization of the paranoid style as the appropriate stance for people in modern society. Lacan and Dalí each claimed to have been greatly influenced by the other; Lacan joined the prewar circle of surrealist writers and artists in Paris. And so, if now in 1968 psychoanalysis was to be turned into a form of social criticism and in this sense to be returned to the surrealists, who but Lacan could accept the gift?

3 May 1968 and Psychoanalytic Ideology

In the May–June 1968 events, the struggle and the search was less for new governmental forms than for oneself. French bureaucratic society had called forth its antithesis: an anti-structural movement which created the context for a radical exploration of the self and a new, more encompassing mode of human relations. May seemed like a time out of time, a mythic moment which could be related directly to other such moments in French political history. Just as the Paris Commune had identified itself with the revolutionaries of 1789, even to the point of adapting the revolutionary calendar as its own, so the 1968 events looked to the Commune, another spontaneous uprising which aimed for the reconquest of urban centers, the dismantling of hierarchy, and the transformation of people into the "masters of their lives and of history, not only in political decisions, but in daily life."[1] If the May movement was romantic in its use of the symbols of the Commune—the barricades, the red and black flags, the general strike—its new mythology was even more romantic: that of a return to Eden.

From the perspective of May 1968, life in Paris did seem a return to a simpler, less differentiated society. One participant put it this way:

The festival finally gave true vacations to those who had never known anything but work days and days off from work. The hierarchical pyramid melted like a sugar cake in the May sun. People spoke to each other, understood each other "*à demi-mot.*" There was no longer a division between intellectuals and workers, but rather there were only revolutionaries in dialogue all over. . . . In this context the word "comrade" took its authentic meaning, truly marking the end of status separations. . . . The streets belonged to those who unpaved them. The suddenly rediscovered daily life became the center of all possible conquests. The people who worked in the now-occupied offices declared that they could no longer live as before, not even a little better than before. . . . The measured time of capitalism stopped. Without the train, without the metro, without the car, without work, the strikers were able to regain the time that they had so sadly lost in factories, on the highway, in front of TV. You strolled, talked, learned to live.[2]

The experience of May contrasted an unstructured model of society with the differentiated, structured system of everyday social life with its "masks" identifying status and role in the social and political hierarchy. During May, the movement drew strength from its Rousseauian metaphor: Paris became as a giant canvas and graffiti was its political language. The politics that it described was inseparable from a rediscovery of the capacity for love, imagination, and relationship that "normal" society with its rules and roles seemed to have eroded. The walls cried out that politics had to be made by "reinventing language" and that it had to be made in every person: "Revolution must be made in men before it can be realized in things."

In May, the mythology of a return to Eden with its (anti) rules, (anti)structure, and (anti)law was expressed in a hostility toward the dominant, structuralist intellectual methodology. In the course of the 1960s, a structuralist orientation had been incorporated into the work of thinkers in highly diverse fields:

anthropology, psychology, literature, history, and political theory, creating a constellation of famous names in French intellectual life (Lévi-Strauss, Althusser, Foucault, Barthes, and, of course, Lacan) whose prestige and army of students created an atmosphere of a structuralist takeover and sometimes, in their domination of intellectual debate, of structuralist terrorism.

Common to all these thinkers was a vision of people that stressed the determination of their action by forces that went beyond their conscious control. This vision was diametrically opposed to the voluntaristic, humanistic spirit of May. But the very sharpness of this polarization during May gave rise to a more complex relationship between radical political thought and structuralist ideas in the years that followed. There was a new entente and this chapter examines how psychoanalytic thought contributed to it, often by the misuse as well as the use of Lacanian ideas. Then the discussion turns to a larger phenomenon of which the new relationship between radicalism and structuralism is only one case: the general use of Lacanian metaphors to build bridges between psychoanalysis and politics. There have been numerous appropriations of a Lacanian discourse on the French radical Left, some by Maoists who focus on superstructure and the workings of the symbolic order, some by naturalists who look to the power and primitivism of the imaginary. Beyond this, there was the French Communist Party's long-awaited reconciliation with psychoanalysis, made through a Lacanian-inspired interpretation of Freud which stresses his kinship to Marx as an epistemologist and scientific pioneer.

Structuralists usually trace the origins of their movement back to the linguist Ferdinand de Saussure, who insisted that the meaning of language was to be found not in the thoughts of a speaker nor in the words that he used, but rather in their relations with one another and to the system of signs itself. The speaking subject was not the individualistic, autonomous Cartesian "I" because every "I" invoked the whole system of language, starting with the implied, reciprocal "you." Man's "commonsense" understanding of his "I" as an intentional actor had little to do with what was really going on. The Saussurian tradition saw people as the object of rules and laws that are built into everything in and around themselves, most notably into the microstructure of their language. Its most powerful message was that people are not their own center.

This notion of each person's determination by structures that transcend the individual altogether was antithetical in spirit to the voluntarist flavor of the May uprising, which asserted the primacy of desires and ideas. Indeed, the students were trying to create a revolutionary moment at a time when any classical Marxist-structuralist analysis of the economic and political conjuncture would have insisted that the time was not ripe. The students inclined toward a voluntarist notion of people making their own history: structuralism was associated with mechanistic determinism, and both were unfavorably counterposed to humanism. "Down with structuralism" became a student slogan. Structuralist theory was analogized to the modes of repression of contemporary institutions. In structuralist linguistics, for example, the speaker seems to disappear, the focus is on the relations of syntactical elements, on language "talking to itself." And thus, critics claimed, functioned the French university, which went on according to its own laws, its own code, without attention to or consideration of its human subjects, the students.[3]

During May, the students refused the knowledge of the university, and they struggled for access to a kind of knowledge more profoundly in touch with central human conflicts, feelings, and pain. Here, touching on these concerns, was a thinker who, while a "structuralist," seemed to have a theory that could help. The students' call was for a road back to Eden where word and thing were one. Lacan had, it seemed to some, theorized the road out of Eden by showing how the knowledge of the university, of society, of the symbolic order is "what comes instead of truth after the object has been lost."[4] Lacan's notion of psychoanalysis as a reconstitution of an associative chain of signification offered a model of a road back to earlier, more primitive signification. Where Lacan wanted to reconstitute links, there were some who saw in the dual, fusional, sexually charged imaginary order those things that bourgeois society denied but that they felt were essential to being human; and they wanted a way back. During May, social challenge came to be viewed as analogous to the analytic experience: as a liberating ritual whose goal is to trace a way back to a truthful idiom. And this would require the liberation of language. People spoke of May as *la prise de la parole*, "the seizing of speech," and of *l'imagination au pouvoir*, "power to imagination."

Of course, Lacan was not the only psychoanalytic theorist seen as relevant to the "new" social desire for a return to primitive, sexual sources of energy and for a new relation to language. Reich's theories about how society warps man's natural sexual energies and Marcuse's analysis of how modern life flattens man's experience of himself and his language were, at least during the events, even more central than Lacan's ideas. The concerns of the French students echoed the themes of the American cultural and sexual revolution of the 1960s. Indeed, to American observers of the French scene in 1968, the emphasis on spontaneity and the liberation of action, speech, and sexuality during the events did not seem very far away from "doing it" in America.

More significant differences emerged after the events themselves. In America, many veterans of the 1960s—left without a movement or a strong radical intellectual tradition—turned to the politics of self-absorption. Their turn from politics to the self carried with it the clear implication that it was possible to take care of the inner world without paying much attention to the outer. Encounter therapies, bioenergetics, and Hindu-styled mysticism were very much the order of the day. With no appreciation of social constraints, pessimism dissolves; openness and honesty alone are expected to breed contentment across the land. And with the flowering of a new crop of self-help therapies, Americans were told that they could be as self-reliant in their search for heightened consciousness as in their search for business success. The self-help movement seemed peculiarly "American" both in its lack of political perspective and in its anti-intellectualism. It insists that language (which it tends to refer to rather flatly as "verbalization") keeps us away from our "true selves" and all that matters is our feelings.[5]

In France, the experience of May had quite a different effect. A social movement which had denigrated structuralism as "deterministic," and therefore reactionary, became increasingly interested in the problem of how society enters the individual, in how the boundary between society and individual is broken down. The question was not new. At the end of the First World War, a group of Marxist social theorists in Germany, who called themselves the Frankfurt School, tried to understand how bourgeois Europe had survived the revolutionary crisis of 1914–19.[6] According to materialist Marxist theoreticians, the "objective conditions" had been "ripe" for revolution, but no revolution had occurred. Traditional Marxism did not seem to be enough. The Frankfurt School set a new agenda for Marxists: to study the question of subjectivity in revolution. This meant moving away from ego psychology models which looked at how the social order "influenced" the individual to a deeper and more dialectical analysis. Theodor Adorno stated the project as follows:

> While they [the revisionists] unceasingly talk of the influence of society on the individual, they forget that not only the individual, but the category of individuality is a product of society. Instead of first extracting the individual from the social process so as to then describe the influence which forms it, *an analytic social psychology is to reveal in the innermost mechanisms of the individual the decisive social forces.*[7]

Lacan is a practicing psychoanalyst, not a social theorist, but in a very important sense his work responded to the proposed agenda set by the Frankfurt School. He insists, as did Frankfurt's critical theorists, that to talk of "social influences" on the individual neutralizes one of Freud's most central contributions: the recognition that society doesn't "influence" autonomous individuals, but that society comes to dwell within them. Lacan's theory of the construction of the symbolic order, when language and law enter man, allows for no real boundary between self and society: people become social with the appropriation of language, and it is language that constitutes people as subjects. Leftist intellectuals have read this to suggest that the notion of a private self is itself a construct of capitalism. The distinction between private and public, the very touchstone of bourgeois thought, exists only as bourgeois ideology. Alienation is not psychological or social; it is both, and at the same time: society is discovered within the individual. The prevailing form of subjectivity, then, has an objective base. In the symbolic order the individual is determined by the social relations in which he or she is enmeshed, but the symbolic order is itself the history of man, which has hardened into what we accept as nature.[8] In this way, Lacan's theory offered a structure for thinking through the problem of the individual and society by theorizing the moment of transition from presocial to social man, the moment of "Oedipization," the passage from the imaginary to the symbolic.

Other structuralist writers, among them Claude Lévi-Strauss and Jacques Derrida, had reflected on this Rousseauian theme of the fall from a state of nature to a state of society where language was no longer direct, immediate, and transparent to its object. But Lacan's work on this theme was particularly subtle, provocative, and vivid. Like Rousseau, he had described a myth of passage that was able to serve as a framework for thinking about the relationship between the individual and society in a way that Reich's discussion of "a natural man" deformed by a crass society could not. What is perhaps most striking in Lacan's version of the banishment from Eden is that *there is no natural man* and therefore no way of thinking about society as coming *after* to thwart his nature. The infant is alienated in the imaginary realm and the imaginary remains with us.

In Lacan's treatment of the Oedipus myth, fears and desires that others have interpreted as relating directly to real parts of the body (castration anxiety, penis envy) and real or mythic family events (the primal scene) are understood in terms of language. For Lacan, the Oedipal crisis begins with the child's growing comprehension of the sexual rules that are embedded in its culture's linguistic terms for family and relatives. It is the kin terms (e.g., the way in which a father passes down his name to daughter and son), not body parts or any one event, that determine what is to follow. As elsewhere, Lacan is careful to distinguish between symbolic agents (such as kin terms), which can serve as structural markers, and body organs and real people, which cannot. So, for example, the penis can take its role in psychic development only when it is transformed into a symbol, the phallus, which is a signifier, a carrier of information about the set of meanings *socially* conferred on the penis. In the linguistic sense, the phallus serves as a distinctive feature that separates two classes of objects, men and women. In our society, these classes are not equal, and the phallus, as signifier, is the carrier of this information about social inequality. According to this way of looking at things, penis envy is not a biological imperative, but is a socially specific jealousy. Lacan's reading of Freud has paved the way for a reconciliation of the French women's movement with psychoanalysis. For Lacan, anatomy is not equivalent to destiny: it is associated with it through a series of linguistic transformations, themselves rooted in social structure. That social structure is patriarchal, typified in the "Daddy-Mommy-Me" Oedipal unit.[9]

If Lacan's Oedipus myth begins when the child first understands kinship terms, it ends when the child accepts a prescribed place, not just in the kinship system, but in the shared discourse of language and society. The child's "asocial," dual, and fusional relationship with its mother is foresworn for the world of symbolic discourse, where a third term is interposed between signifier and signified. The father becomes this third term and we enter the symbolic dimension by accepting his name and interdictions. Through him, we accept social law and language that now live within us as presences: "Man speaks then, but it is because the symbol has made him man."[10]

Lacanian psychoanalysis established a context for people struggling toward a reconsideration of self, society, and politics to think through their concerns. May proved their number was legion. After May, the call for a "Return to Nature" swelled the ranks of French movements, which opened out to a variety of political actions. Some romanticized Lacan's imaginary realm and looked to the mad as those closest to nature and freest from social constraints. They laid the foundation for a highly politicized French antipsychiatric movement. Some moved into the French ecology movement, whose strong politicization contrasts markedly with its American counterpart, which until the antinuclear issue, tended to be more Thoreauian. Some thinkers took Lacan's symbolic order—the "dictatorship of the signifier"—as paradigmatic of all social repression and conceived "back to nature" as a return to the imaginary. For others, the analytic process was a means, not of returning to the imaginary, but of establishing a new relationship to it, a relationship which could itself be revolutionary. Lacan's theory does not allow for a simple choice between different realms of experience. It dynamically situates what is most human about people at the point of tension between imaginary and symbolic. The individual and the social order are inextricably bound.

In the post-1968 years, Lacanian themes were all the more salient to the Left because of its newly found interest in structuralism. Sartre had criticized structuralism in the name of the Left for its ahistoricity and consequent inability to explain change, particularly revolutionary change. But the May 1968 experience left many bitterly skeptical about existential assertions of man's freedom to create his history and ready to accept the structuralist emphasis on large areas of man's life that lay outside of his conscious control. What had seemed reactionary in structuralism now seemed merely realistic. Leftists reconsidered structuralist methods. And since the letdown after May left many with a desire for self-examination, the structuralism they turned toward was psychoanalytic. Of course, this meant Lacan. According to Lacan, it has been clear since Freud's *Interpretation of Dreams* that people are inhabited by a law that they do not constitute but that constitutes them. They are inhabited by the signifier; they didn't create it:

> Symbols in fact envelop the life of man in a network so total that they join together, before he comes into the world, those who are going to engender him "by flesh and blood"; so total that they bring to his birth, along with the gifts of the stars, if not with the gifts of the fairies, the shape of his destiny; so total that they give the words that will make him faithful or renegade, the law of the acts that will follow him right to the very place where he *is* not yet and even beyond his death. . . .[11]

This powerful image of a subject "decentered" by its relation to the symbolic opposes both the view of people held by the existentialists, who focus on the "cogito" and on individual freedom, and that of the ego psychologists, who treat the ego as an active autonomous unit.

In the post-1968 years there was a clear intent on the part of those who had been inspired by existential Marxism to try to build bridges to structuralism. The intent was clear, but the task was not easy. Existential Marxism had always stressed the intentionality of the individual actor while structuralism looked at the individual as the bearer of timeless structures that undermine his autonomy. But the desire for a rapprochement was great on both sides. While the students were busy berating themselves for their naiveté and lack of a more rigorous understanding of social forces, the structuralists were looking for a reconciliation with radicals. In France, intellectuals almost definitionally consider themselves to be "on the Left," and in France in 1968 it was almost unthinkable, except for loyal members of the Communist Party, to be "on the Left" and against the events which had swept the entire country. The events had made a passionate, humanistic statement and structuralist thinkers wanted to be part of it. Intellectual historian Mark Poster, writing of the more conciliatory position that structuralists took toward humanism after 1968, remarks that it is not clear if the structuralists had always believed that their work had radical implications or if the events of May had forced them to invent some.[12]

Michel Foucault, for example, had used a structuralist methodology to write about the cultural history and philosophy of medicine and psychiatry. He had long been considered the most antihumanist of all the structuralists. In Foucault's view, even philosophy is determined outside of man's conscious ability to will it. This position, which puts even those human productions people consider most within their control outside of it, made Foucault the special object of attack by humanists, who went so far as to characterize his antihumanism as the stance of a "prophet of the end of man." But in the years after May, Foucault became something of a hero to May veterans. His work on the asylum, on psychiatry, on prisons, on medical repression, became central to their newly developing interests in the politics of medicine and madness.[13] And Foucault did far more than meet existential humanism halfway by making a very substantial concession to voluntarism. Two years after the 1968 events, he suggested that in his work the whole point of finding structures (which he had always presented as immutable) was to be better able to be rid of them:

> What the students are trying to do . . . and what I myself am trying to accomplish . . . is basically the same thing. . . . What I am

trying to do is grasp the implicit systems which determine our most familiar behavior without our knowing it. I am trying to find their origin, to show their formation, the constraint they impose upon us; I am therefore trying to place myself at a distance from them and *to show how one could escape*.[14]

Thus the structuralists eased their integration into the good graces of the Left by suggesting that structures they had once discussed as immutable might be evaded by those armed with the right kind of knowledge.

Lacanian theory took a central role in building many bridges between the intellectual traditions of structuralism and existential Marxism and in making new connections between them and a long tradition of French romantic thought. Looking at these connections, one is struck by the diversity of interpretations and even some apparent misinterpretations of Lacan that were used. For some, psychoanalysis, no longer conceived of as a therapeutic enterprise, could expose the implicit social constraints embedded in metaphoric and metonymic chains and thus, to borrow from radical political terminology, provoke change by sharpening contradictions. For other, more utopian thinkers, the psychoanalytic enterprise was interpreted as a possible way back to the imaginary.

As already noted, some thinkers on the Left "appropriated" Lacanian metaphors by reading Lacan's description of the constitution of the subject on the basis of a lack (*manque-à-être*) as referring to the sad fate of the subject in capitalist society. Lacan himself makes no clear statement that would support a view that the subject in a socialist society would not be equally entrapped by the impossibility of reaching the object of its desire; nevertheless, Lacan's picture of the crisis of the subject was taken as an image of the fate of the individual in capitalism. By the early 1970s, this idea had become a commonplace in radical pamphlets and political meetings: "The Being of the humanist-subject was solid, self-evident, the Being of the Lacanian subject vacillates and is in crisis."[15]

For the authors of this statement, a radical political group called Scription Rouge, Lacan's theory of the divided, decentered ego does not describe something inherent in the human condition, but simply an artifact of capitalism. In any case, Lacan never pretends that psychoanalysis can "repair" the break that constitutes the subject. It can only bring the subject to an understanding of its inner discontinuities and ruptures. For those who link these discontinuities to the plight of the subject under capitalism, Lacanian psychoanalysis is a form of political consciousness-raising. Through analysis, the capitalist subject can learn that its crisis extends to the very deepest levels, and in so doing achieve a higher level of personal and political consciousness.

The "crisis of the subject" is seen as representative of significant political vulnerability in the capitalist system. In France there is a tendency to see most psychotherapy and non-Lacanian branches of psychoanalysis as working to limit this crisis. Lacanian psychoanalysis, on the other hand, is seen as its perpetual reflection, and thus as socially revolutionary.

This embracing of psychoanalysis as political consciousness-raising is a far cry from the traditional leftist attack on psychoanalysis for "adapting" the subject to social oppression. Lacan, radically indifferent to the notion of "cure," opposes the goal of the analysand's adaptation and stresses personal discovery instead. This discovery may include the realization that he is exploited and the realization that, in his lack of a coherent "self," he is not very different from people whom he has been classifying as "crazy."

During May, the "power of the word" had meant the power of the word to change things, the belief that self-expression (in the schools, in factories, and in the streets) could lead the way to social change. This concern with the efficacy of symbolic behavior contrasts with traditional "economist" Marxist assumptions about the material conditions for revolution. In the late 1960s and after, belief in the power of the word became a major theme for theoretical reflection. This reflection took many forms: there was a widespread interest in everything linguistic, there was a fascination with Maoism and the Chinese Cultural Revolution, which stressed the importance of ideological superstructure in the revolutionary movement, and, of course, there was Lacan. The *Dazibao* of the Cultural Revolution and the *affiche* of the May revolt could be synthesized and understood through the Lacanian prism which made the point that "it is the world of words that creates the world of things."[16]

The idea of using the symbolic order as a stage for political action was taken up by Philippe Sollers and Julia Kristeva, both highly influential French literary critics and political writers. In the early 1970s, Sollers situated the political problem for the French Left as the integration of psychoanalysis and Marxism. Sollers admitted that the task of constructing a Marxist psychoanalysis was painfully difficult because "psychoanalysis caught the plague in the USA and Marxism came down with cholera in the USSR."[17] The Left was caught between the plague and cholera, but it had no choice but to work on the problem. Fascism, claimed Sollers, has been conquered only superficially; it lives on and can be extirpated by its ideological roots only if it is understood more profoundly. This understanding demands a political psychoanalysis: "A politics without psychoanalysis or a psychoanalysis without politics in modern industrial capitalism runs the very risk of fascism." For Sollers, the "existence of fascism is the material proof that Marxism cannot do without psychoanalysis."[18]

But a mechanistic psychoanalysis or a mechanistic Marxism will not be able to address the problem. For Sollers, a solution lies in looking to the new psychoanalysis of Lacan and the new Marxism of Mao. In a talk that he gave in December 1973, Sollers emphasized how Lacan and Mao had broken with what had come before. Although other psychoanalysts like Reich had grappled with the problem of fascism, they lacked methodological and political rigor. In Reich's case, speculation had ended in "metaphysical substantialism." But Lacan was different. He had rejected mechanistic interpretations and had put the accent on language, from which point "could begin a true pursuit of Freud's discovery."[19] Mao, too, had rejected mechanistic models of Marxism through his emphasis on ideology and Cultural Revolution. And of course, Mao's concerns about propaganda and the class nature of literature all reflected his interest in language.

Sollers's call is for a psychoanalytic politics and a politicized psychoanalysis. The task of the analyst is not to turn political militant, but, following Lacan's lead, to move from an empirical and antitheoretical philosophy to a new commitment to language and dialectics. The analyst pursues a "truth operation" by becoming a dialectician in the analytic act.[20] The political militant, on the other side, must participate in a regeneration of dialectical studies that are open and sensitive to the impact of psychoanalysis and its study of the symbolic. This assimilation of psychoanalytic understanding into political work leads to his "truth operation": ideological struggle. And finally, for those who work, as Sollers does, on the level of language, there is another "truth operation." Their task is the transformation of language. Language, the realm of the symbolic, is the intersection of the historical, social, and subjective fields, the place where the dialectic process between ideology and language is played out. The practice of a writer, too, can produce "truth effects."[21]

Sollers puts the accent on Lacan's concept of the symbolic as it theorizes the transformation of language in literary acts. Julia Kristeva, too, hopes for this transformation, a new politics of language. She believes it can come through confronting the symbolic order with what she calls "the semiotic," which is "chronologically anterior and synchronically transversal to sign, syntax, denotation, and signification . . . we can imagine it in the cry, the sounds, the gestures of the baby. In the adult discourse, the semiotic functions as rhythm, prosody, word game, the no-sense of sense, laughter."[22]

The world of the semiotic is close to the world of the Freudian unconscious. Kristeva envisages it drawing revolutionary potential from a praxis analogous to Lacan's notion of psychoanalysis as the transaction between symbolic and imaginary. Kristeva believes that the semiotic is revolutionary if it confronts the symbolic thesis of meaning and structure, thereby serving as antithesis to the symbolic.[23] Politically revolutionary acts must open up politics to the presymbolic, to what came before structure and socialization. To do this, revolutionaries need psychoanalysis, for "the subject of a new political practice must be the subject of a new discursive practice," in which language may dissolve, structures may disappear, language may approach "the limit of language."[24]

In all of this one sees how different people on the Left, and for very different reasons, found a way to situate themselves in what might be called "Lacanian space." That is, they found in his ideas, particularly in his formulations of the symbolic and the imaginary realms, a way to get a *prise*, a grasp of what they considered to be the most significant political problems. But when one speaks of the French "Left," or of *gauchistes* (the term usually used to stand for non–Communist Party left-ists), the reference is to a large and diverse group. In 1968 it included people who considered themselves Maoists, Trotsky-ists, existentialists, anarchists of all varieties, and situation-ists, a new school of "action-theorists of daily life." This cast of characters is as contentious as it is large; during the May days, they were united mainly in their opposition to the Com-munist Party, which was seen as the greatest impediment to action. So it is not surprising that at the same time that some of them, like Sollers and Kristeva, were able to take their *prise politique* by focusing on Lacan's conception of the symbolic, others situated themselves differently in Lacanian space. Some, for example, theorized the refusal of the symbolic alto-gether and looked toward what might be construed as a return to the imaginary. For the structuralist thinkers, people begin to be truly human with their entrance into the symbolic order (a position most sharply expressed by Communist Party phi-losopher Louis Althusser, who wrote of the transition into the symbolic as "the extraordinary adventure . . . transforming an animal born of man and woman into a human child").[25] For others, it is just the contrary. Leaving the order of flux and fusion is seen as a loss. Entrance into society and structure is seen as a tragedy. Only a return to the imaginary, to a "pre-Oedipal" state, could spell the end of sociopolitical repres-sion, of the "Dictatorship of the Symbolic." Out of the May days grew a current of political naturalism which hurled itself against Althusserian structuralism.

The naturalists saw the goal of politics to be the return to man's freedom, to his sense of being a passionate animal.

They glorified a model of a presymbolic age of direct, fusional relationships, of spontaneity, of primitive, unmediated desire. They decried "phallocentrism" and denounced the family as the bearer of hierarchy and taboo. They looked to children, primitive peoples, and most of all to the mad, as examples of people in touch with the power of the presymbolic. What these marginal groups were assumed to have in common was that they had not yet been fully "Oedipized," that is, that the symbolic—language, structure, and society—had not yet entered them. They were still in Eden.

One of the most powerful and one of the most popular expressions of post-1968 naturalism was in *Anti-Oedipus: Capitalism and Schizophrenia* by Gilles Deleuze and Félix Guattari. The book, as its title indicates, is a diatribe against Oedipization, a refusal of the moment when society enters man. Deleuze, a philosopher, and Guattari, a Lacanian psychoanalyst and antipsychiatric activist, were often referred to as the R. D. Laing and David Cooper of French antipsychiatry. They began their collaboration after the events of May–June 1968. Their concern with how the May revolution of speech and desire had played itself out led them to an inquiry into the role of speech and desire in revolution. Although their attack on Oedipization is also an attack on psychoanalysis whose theory is built around the Oedipus complex, it relies on Lacan's particular way of theorizing Oedipization as the process by which society enters the individual. Chapter 6 examines their politics of schizophrenia in some detail. Here, it is important to note it as part of a naturalistic current that exalted the schizophrenic's proximity to the imaginary, to fusional relationships, and to flux as a *privileged political position*. In Deleuze and Guattari's characterization, the schizophrenic makes no separation between personal and social experience: his personal expressions are themselves political expressions. For the schizophrenic, word and thing are one, saying is doing. The relationship between word and action, wish and action, is direct and immediate.

Deleuze and Guattari see these qualities as virtues shared by the political style developed during May 1968, when roles, specialized functions, and the boundaries between political, emotional, intellectual, and artistic expression were dissolved. Indeed, Guattari described the groups whose spontaneous fusion precipitated the May events as harbingers of a new schizo-culture where there will be no barriers between politics and the individual and where the division of labor between the specialists of saying and specialists of doing is blurred.[26]

The naturalistic current of political thought expressed in *Anti-Oedipus* takes off from what was a powerful theme during May, a theme best expressed in the wall slogan: *Sous les pavés la plage*, "under the cobblestones, the beach." There was a call for a return to a more direct, simpler experience, the return to Eden. This naturalism stressed that if allowed free expression, man's natural desires, energies, and creative imagination would be a revolutionary force. Kristeva spoke about this force as the semiotic and said that it had to confront the symbolic in order to serve the revolution. Naturalism insists that desire alone will be enough. The naturalist current, too, was able to draw on Lacan, this time through a very partial reading, which focused on and idealized his concept of the imaginary and chose to see him as the theorist of a revolution of the primacy of desire.

Breton's *Surrealist Manifesto* had drawn on Freud to postulate a future "sur-reality" emerging from the resolution of dream and reality. Now Lacan, a follower of Freud and companion of the surrealists, was being subjected to a similar interpretation.

While Breton believed that reality could be transcended, the new naturalists—sur-symbolists, as it were—thought there was a way to go beyond Lacan's order of law and society. They envisaged a politics of the Lacanian imaginary.

The imaginary was not the only evocative metaphor Lacan gave to the rather inchoate politics of May. In particular, activists from May 1968 identified with his concept of the "intransitive demand." Lacan emphasized that for him a subversive aspect of psychoanalysis is its "short-circuiting" of the usual cycles of supply and demand. The analyst makes the first move: he offers the possibility for analysis. The offer permits the analysand to make the next move: the formulation of a demand, a desire for analysis. Lacan made an ironic résumé of this process when he said: "In short, I have succeeded in doing what in the field of ordinary commerce people would dearly like to be able to do with such ease: with supply, I have created demand."[27] Lacan believes that this demand, the desire for analysis, has a radical quality: "his [the analysand's] demand is intransitive, it carries no object with it."[28] When one demands nothing in particular, one expresses "pure desire"; this global desire allows the analysis to work. Only when desire is so pure, so intransitive, so without prior object can it release the powerful forces of past demands that have never been met. The parallels between this formulation and the language and politics of May were not lost on its partisans, who used the concept of the "intransitive demand" to justify actions in political and social life that were, in their way, without concrete object. They believed that the offer of action can create a demand for radical change no matter what the economic and social conjuncture. The sentiment is well expressed in the May slogan: "I take my desires for realities, because I believe in the reality of my desires."

This projection of Lacanian theory onto the social field demands consent to the proposition that what is meaningful practice in the clinical situation is meaningful practice in politics as well. The connection is not obvious. Frequently in the post-1968 years when the connections between political analysis and Lacan's psychoanalysis seemed strained, one sensed that they were invented. Using Lacanian psychoanalytic discourse as a referent served to legitimate political discourse. And sometimes, when even invention failed, people on the Left relied on metaphor, myths, and images of Lacanian radicalism. Although Lacan's personal political views were not notably to the Left, he acquired, and perhaps actively cultivated, an image as a "cultural radical," a man sympathetic to unpopular causes. There is, for example, Lacan's reputation as an iconoclast in psychoanalytic politics, his short sessions, his attack on the psychoanalytic establishment, his consistent attacks on the Americans. There is Lacan's association with the surrealists, which meant a lot to people who had just experienced a political event that many saw as a kind of surrealism-in-action. There is the Lacan who criticized the "discourse of the university" before such talk had become popular. There is the Lacan who signed manifestos in support of the striking students in May 1968, and the Lacan who sided with jailed student leaders. There is the Lacan who warned the students not to be seduced by the government's attempts to cool them out with promises of dialogue and participation: "There is no such thing as dialogue, it is a swindle."[29] And of course, there is the story, so much a part of the folklore that it even made its way across the Atlantic to be reported in *The New Yorker* magazine, of Lacan putting student leader Daniel Cohn-Bendit in the back of his own Jaguar and successfully smuggling him across the border into Germany.[30]

Thus far the discussion here has been in terms of ideas, of people looking to psychoanalysis after political disillusionment in a search for philosophical and ideological continuities. In conversations with people who moved into the Lacanian orbit after a heavy concentration on politics, other more personal concerns came to the surface as well. But whatever the individual's primary motivation, new interest in psychoanalysis after 1968 was legitimated by the quickly assimilated social image of Lacan as a *gauchiste* and of psychoanalysis as a "radical thing to do." For many, the turn to psychoanalysis by people whose political aspirations had been dashed was reminiscent of "conversions" from politics to psychoanalysis after the Soviet Union's invasion of Hungary in 1956. In both 1956 and 1968, political disillusionment led to a new focus on the self. The parallel is striking, but the differences are even more so. When the generation of 1956 made psychoanalysis a part of its lives, the break with politics was absolute: many left or were expelled from a highly structured party. But for the generation of post-1968 converts, there was an easy slide between political and psychoanalytic worlds. Not only did many former May activists go into analysis, but many became analysts themselves. Most did not seem to feel that they had made an exclusive choice, and there was a filtering back of psychoanalytic language to wider political circles on the Left and a filtering into psychoanalysis of radical political concerns.

Some people concerned about the future of radical politics in France feared that the slide between politics and psychoanalysis had been too easy and that "Freudo-Marxist" or, more commonly, "Freudo-Lacanian" jargon was simply covering over the fact that people once involved in working in factories and organizing workers were no longer doing so and that a "real" political language was being smothered under the weight of psychoanalytic jargon and Lacanian mythology. This point was made by a satirical pamphlet, written in comic book style, which appeared shortly after the events.[31] The story is simple: a student revolution explodes, and the government decides that police repression might encourage it, so more subtle tactics are used. The government turns to its "Laboratory of Psychoanalytic Toxicology" and makes it clear that the main advantage of using psychoanalytic weaponry to distract the radicals is that they do not even know that they are being distracted. As the students theorize about the politics of desire, they continue to think that they are involved in political action. The social movement winds down as energies are refocused onto the production of psychoanalytically inspired radical ideology. The story ends with order restored and revolution displaced onto intellectual fads. The radicals have been reduced to consumers of "their" Godard, "their" Lacan, "their" Foucault. Psychoanalysis has helped turn politics into radical chic, and the pamphlet concludes that "a radical critique dissolves in its own delirium."

Not everyone "on the Left" accepted that the politics of the future cannot be the structured politics of political parties and government ministers and economic crises. In particular, the Communist Party, certainly the single most powerful group in French oppositional politics, most assuredly did not agree. We should remember that in May 1968, the Party denigrated the students' concerns as petit bourgeois, advanced nothing but standard economic demands from their position in the trade unions, and did everything they could to support a return to order. Not seeing the situation as "revolutionary," they were the closest allies of the Gaullist forces within the movement and gambled that playing a "legitimate" game during the events would enhance their post-crisis position. That gamble paid off handsomely. And so, coming out of the May–June experience, partisans of May saw the Communist Party as a saboteur that had been willing to sacrifice a social revolution to assure its integration into the normal game of French politics. The Communists, in turn, continued to see the *gauchistes* as petit bourgeois romantics who relied on spontaneity and poetic ideology as a substitute for the hard and necessary work of building a working-class basis for political action.

Given their very different political philosophies and sense of what is appropriate for concrete political action, it is not surprising that the Communist Party members and non-Party leftists tended to read Freud and Marx quite differently. What is interesting is that, after passing through very different Marxes and very different Freuds and very different political expressions, many Communists, as well as many *gauchistes*, ended up in the orbit of Jacques Lacan. By 1968, the French Communist Party that had denigrated psychoanalysis for nearly half a century was itself engaged in a process of rapprochement. While the non-Party Left was using Lacan's theory of the symbolic and his notion of the decentered subject to build its bridge to psychoanalysis, the Communist Party had been using Lacanian structuralism to build some new bridges of its own.

Marxists have traditionally reproached psychoanalysis for building up an anthropology in terms of the individual instead of in terms of the political, economic, and historical situation. In France, this classical critical position was first exemplified in the work of Georges Politzer, who, in 1924, defended Freud's scientific ambitions while criticizing his lack of interest in history and economics.[32] Politzer maintained this position throughout his life. In 1939, only a few years before his death at the hands of the Nazis, Politzer reaffirmed his belief that psychoanalysis had been a fiasco, that although Freud had touched on a critical field for scientific study, he had never grasped the true relation between the laws of individual psychology and the laws of historical development.[33]

Politzer's charge that psychoanalysis was fundamentally in error because it tried to explain history by psychology, rather than psychology by history and economics, was taken up by eight Communist Party psychiatrists in 1949 in a collective statement of self-criticism: "Psychoanalysis, a Reactionary Ideology."[34] They insisted that in the postwar era Politzer's critique was more timely than ever. Psychoanalysis was being used as an arm of reaction: American psychoanalysts were "managing" peaceful relationships between workers and employers, and the international psychoanalytic movement was representing struggles for national liberation as expressions of pathological "aggressive drives."

The French Communist Party hardened its position on psychoanalysis during the Cold War 1950s when the Soviet Union intensified criticism of psychoanalysis as an American product and emphasized its own brand of behaviorist psychology. But with the 1960s came de-Stalinization and a new ideology of peaceful coexistence. It was no longer obligatory for Party members to criticize everything Western. The French Communist Party began to integrate itself into the political game of the Gaullist regime and tried to make this transition smoother by taking less rigid positions on intellectual matters. Party intellectual Roger Garaudy was allowed to lead an effort for dialogue and reconciliation with existentialists, socialists, and Christians. But interestingly enough, the new, vigorous Communist dialogue with psychoanalysis did not emerge from Garaudy's eclectic and humanistic perspective, but from

a movement that grew up in direct opposition to it: the "theoretical antihumanism" of Louis Althusser. Althusser, a party
member and professor of philosophy at the Ecole Normale
Supérieure, advanced a structuralist reading of Marx that dismissed the early Marx and his philosophical, humanistic concern with alienation. Althusser was not interested in Marx's
youthful speculative anthropology; he was interested in Marxism's structure as a science.

When one considers how the classical Politzerian line criticized psychoanalysis for psychologizing social conflict, it is
not surprising that the Communist entente with psychoanalysis came through Althusser, who counterposes psychoanalysis
to psychology. This position often seems strange to Americans,
who are used to thinking about psychoanalysis as a contribution to psychology. For Althusser, however, the future of psychoanalysis as a scientific discipline, and its good relationship
with Marxism, depends on purging it of psychology. Althusser
argues that as a psychologist, Freud was interested in how an
individual's problems begin in his family relationships, a point
of view which is incompatible with a Marxism which locates
the origins of conflicts in the economic and social order. The
Althusserian reconciliation is made by interpreting Freud on
a level of abstraction at which the psychological detail of his
theory is seen as a secondary and dispensable carrier of his primary discovery as a philosopher: the discovery of a totally new
kind of knowledge. When Freud recognized the unconscious
as an object of study he defined a new science, a new way of
knowing about people and society. From this epistemological
perspective, Freud and Marx have a lot in common because
Althusser also sees Marx's primary contribution as the discovery of a new object of knowledge and a new way of knowing.
Althusser's interpretation of Freud and Marx as scientifically

homologous theorists whose contributions are compatible and mutually supportive relies heavily on Lacan's reading of Freud.

Althusser articulated this "epistemological" point of contact between scientific socialism and scientific psychoanalysis in his 1965 article "Freud and Lacan" which appeared in the official Party magazine, *La Nouvelle Critique*. Althusser begins his article by admitting that for a Communist to write an article about the long maligned Freud must mean that something new has come up. That something is Jacques Lacan. Among psychoanalysts, says Althusser, only Lacan in his theory of the decentered self saw, understood, and put forth the theoretical consequences of Freud's radical break with psychology. Marxists had spent two decades criticizing a humanistic, psychologizing, biologizing Freud, but finally Lacan made it clear that this was not the true Freud at all.

Of course, Althusser admits that Freud himself was partly to blame for all of those generations of confusion. In Freud's writing, there are serious lapses into psychologism, but Althusser urges sympathy for Freud's equivocations. He sees them as analogous to Marx's equivocation between humanism and the new structuralist science of history. Althusser explains that Marx and Freud each invented a new science; each discovered a new object of knowledge, the mode of production and the unconscious. Inventing a new science obligates the inventor to construct a new theoretical space within which to situate it.[35] But when the inventor creates that space, he must fashion it out of the materials of the past, that is, from scientific concepts that were constituted to serve entirely different ends than his own. Thus Freud and Marx both were weighted down by the cultural baggage of their time. Freud "thought" his discovery in concepts borrowed from the biology, mechanics, and psychology of his day; Marx "thought" his discovery using Hegelian notions of the subject.[36] In "Freud and Lacan" Althusser is trying to rethink Marxism without any reference to Hegel's absolute subject, and he sees a kindred spirit in Lacan, trying to rethink psychoanalysis without reference to a unified conception of self or ego.

> Since Marx we know that the human subject, the political, economic or philosophical ego is not the center of history—we even know, against the Enlightenment philosophies and against Hegel, that history doesn't have a necessary "center" in our ideological misrecognitions of it. In his turn, Freud showed us that the real subject, the singular essence of the individual is not made of an ego centered on the "me" (le moi), on consciousness or on existence . . . that the human subject is decentered, constituted by a structure which also has no "center" except in the imaginary misrecognition of the "me" (moi), that is to say in the ideological formations where it finds recognition.[37]

According to Althusser, both he and Lacan are trying to save fundamentally subversive structuralist sciences from their neutralization in an eclectic humanism.

Althusser wants Marxists to follow him in a return to Marx and to follow Lacan in a return to Freud, but urges clarity about which Marx and which Freud they are returning to. Althusser rejects the early Marx of the *1844 Manuscripts* who had not yet broken free of a humanistic Hegelian influence; of course, Lacan's reading of Freud is equally selective. Althusser agrees with Lacan that the metapsychology of the later Freud opened the way for the unfortunate assimilation of psychoanalysis by sociology, anthropology, and biology as a fellow "discipline" that they misunderstood and neutralized.

Althusser's 1965 article extended the Communist interest in Lacan beyond the small circle of his own students. Although in the mid-1960s, the Party had sided with Garaudy's humanist positions, it also basked in the sunshine of Althusser's intellectual renown. After 1968, Althusser became far more prominent in the Party, and it was through him that Lacanianism became important to the Party's post-1968 intellectual.

By 1974, the Communist press had published its first book which officially condoned psychoanalysis: *Pour une critique marxiste de la théorie psychanalytique*.[38] Despite its title, the book is an appreciation rather than a criticism of psychoanalytic theory, which is not surprising since two of its authors are members of the Freudian School. The authors do not repudiate Politzer's criticism but simply link it to one form of psychoanalysis that they variously classify as "psychological," "American," and "reactionary." The authors make it clear that in their view, Althusser is right: Politzerian criticisms do not apply to Freud as read by Jacques Lacan.

Party intellectuals have given Lacan's antihumanism their theoretical seal of approval, but other, more stylistic considerations have powerfully contributed to his success among Communists.[39] Lacan's popularity was certainly enhanced by his tendency to dismiss American psychoanalysis as "highbrow astrology," "psychological confusionism," and "bastardization."[40] In 1964, Lacan went so far as to blame the Soviet Union's rejection of psychoanalysis on the fact that the Americans had distorted it, a position which made it easier for the Communist Party's rapprochement with psychoanalysis to be via Lacan and his school.[41] The Party was able to sidestep the issue of Soviet intransigence to psychoanalysis during the 1950s and 1960s because France's most renowned psychoanalyst was willing to see it as an understandable response to the denaturing of psychoanalysis by the Americans. By focusing on Lacan, the French Communist Party was able to emphasize that its approval was for an indigenous psychoanalytic movement, altogether different from that of the Americans.

Thus, in the years after 1968, a range of people on the French Left became interested in psychoanalysis as ideology, and there is no doubt that a freer circulation between political and psychoanalytic worlds was facilitated by having Lacan in common. This new "circulation" meant that people did not feel constrained to make choices between leftist politics and psychoanalysis. The result has been some breakdown in long-standing barriers between Marx and Freud, between structuralist and voluntarist readings of these thinkers, and between those who believe that history is determined by the material conditions of existence and those who tend to think in terms of how words change things.

This investigation of French psychoanalysis has until now been exploring the lay of the land: identifying those aspects of French society, politics, and intellectual culture with which it has had to contend and through which it has developed its distinctively "French" form. This has placed the focus on psychoanalysis as it operates *outside* of its own professional world, as a social theory, a theory of politics and culture. But Freud had many agendas for psychoanalysis: it was to be a social theory, a scientific discourse, but it was also to be organized as a worldwide therapeutic movement. The internal structure of its earliest organization was itself highly political. It was directed by a secret committee, with purges of deviant members, with local and international organizations in a tight, well-defined hierarchy. When a theory becomes concerned with conquest and with control over who can be its "certified" proponents and practitioners, it becomes caught up in political dynamics that have little to do with its subversive ideas and which in fact may tend to erode them. The following chapters turn to the history of the French psychoanalytic movement and tell a story of internal contradiction that seems more poignant than any tale of co-optation from the outside could ever be. The French psychoanalytic movement is a laboratory for studying how internal contradictions in the psychoanalytic movement, and especially in the psychoanalytic institution itself, can undermine psychoanalytic science.

II Politics in Psychoanalysis

4   For or Against Lacan

Psychoanalysts have been organized into psychoanalytic societies ever since Freud created the Wednesday Psychological Society and gave it its mandate: "to teach, practice and spread psychoanalysis." Indeed, much of the character of psychoanalysis as a movement is shaped by the fact that it is housed in local institutions and overseen by an international association, all of which have the job of preserving and protecting it. In the United States, the psychoanalytic society—a curious amalgam of university, masonic lodge, literary school, professional association, political party, and church—has not been seriously challenged. But by 1978 in France, three schisms in the psychoanalytic movement, each precipitated by Jacques Lacan, challenged the traditions of psychoanalytic societies and psychoanalytic training.[1] The stories of these schisms raise fundamental questions about the tension between scientific activity and its institutionalization: Does the essentially political nature of the psychoanalytic institution subvert the development of psychoanalysis as a science? Is the psychoanalytic society a contradiction in terms?

The two previous chapters told the story of how Lacan's "return to Freud" became central to French psychoanalysis and opened out toward utopian thought and social criticism.

This chapter and the one that follows look at the history of the French psychoanalytic movement where Lacan's ideas have been equally central to challenging the psychoanalytic institution itself. The focus of these chapters on the politics within psychoanalysis is not on personalities, nor indeed on psychoanalytic theory, but on how the history of psychoanalysis in France has been paradigmatic of enduring paradoxes in the psychoanalytic movement since Freud.

Because of Freud's fears for the young and the threatened psychoanalytic movement, he set up the International Psychoanalytic Association in 1910 as a hierarchical structure designed to protect his orthodoxy. No wonder, then, that it ran headlong into conflict with Lacan, who sees the essence of psychoanalysis as the refusal of any established truths. Indeed, as we describe the history of French psychoanalytic politics, it will become apparent that Jacques Lacan was always riding a collision course with the internationally organized psychoanalytic movement. For example, to the psychoanalytic establishment, it became dogma that the perpetuation of Freud's contribution depended on the "orthodox" conduct of the training analysis. Tampering with it was anathema. And yet, beginning in the 1950s, this is exactly what Lacan was doing in his experiments with short analytic sessions. Lacan saw patients for varying amounts of time and sometimes for as little as five minutes. His belief is strong that in analysis, nothing should be routine or predictable, and this includes the duration of a session. His experiments were not wanton provocation of the establishment on a particularly sensitive point. Lacan believes that experimental technique is part of the open attitude that is necessary to psychoanalysis as a scientific enterprise: "One remains loyal to tradition because one has nothing to say about the doctrine itself."[2] Under no conditions, insists Lacan,

can psychoanalysis identify itself with a "tried" technique or a set of "true" principles. The touchstone for a true return to Freud is the rejection of all certitudes.

The Freud to whom Lacan is returning is the early Freud of *The Interpretation of Dreams*, *The Psychopathology of Everyday Life*, and *Jokes and the Unconscious*. Lacan sees this early Freud as a thinker of radical doubt and discovery, one who was deeply involved in his self analysis and in a continually renewed process of questioning his own language, knowledge, and presumed basis for knowing. As already noted in chapter 2, Lacan is more critical of the later Freud whose metapsychology shifts the focus from meaning to mechanism. This Freud continued to work, to create, even to change his mind; but at the same time, he embarked on an enterprise of codification of theory, protection of orthodoxy, and lobbying for expansion of his movement. But is such codification, orthodoxy, and lobbying compatible with the growth of a scientific activity?[3]

Lacan has argued that they are not and puts forth images of a psychoanalytic science unfettered by orthodoxy and of a psychoanalytic training unfettered by institutions. No institution, says Lacan, but only the analyst can authorize him or herself in the analytic vocation. He asserts that the analytic discourse has been deteriorating because of an emphasis on technique rather than on theory and understanding: "Meticulousness of detail is passed off as rigour, and rule confused with certainty."[4] But he insists that no amount of allegiance to technique or doctrinal orthodoxy, which is relabeled as "classicism," can save psychoanalysis,

> if the concepts on which it is based are ignored. It is our task to demonstrate that these concepts take on their full meaning only when oriented in a field of language, only when ordered in relation to the function of speech.

> At this point I must note that in order to handle any Freudian concept, reading Freud cannot be considered superfluous. . . .[5]

In Lacan's writing we see the insistence that psychoanalytic knowledge, like personal religious knowledge, cannot be reduced to the transmission of certifiable, outward "signs"; there is also the call for a personal relationship to an inspirational text. The conflict between this psychoanalytic Protestantism and the established church was inevitable, although the exact form of the confrontation was shaped by personalities and historical accident. Indeed, by 1963, Lacan and his followers had been definitively excommunicated from the International Psychoanalytic Association. The roots of that excommunication go back further than Lacan's first experiments with unorthodox practice. They go back to the very introduction of psychoanalysis in France and its marriage at that time, not with medicine but with poetry.

In France, psychoanalysis was first championed by the literati. And although they may have misunderstood psychoanalysis in their eagerness to use it for their own artistic purposes, they wanted its support and claimed it as their own. André Gide even insisted that he had been practicing Freudianism for twenty years without knowing it. Although Freud was appalled by Gide's claim, its impact could not be undone by counterclaims. For good reasons or bad, in France psychoanalysis was identified with literature and especially surrealism.[6]

By 1921, psychoanalytic societies already existed in Vienna, Zurich, Budapest, Berlin, London, and America, but there was nothing in France. Freud sent an emissary to Paris, hoping to remedy the situation. His emissary was Madame Sokolnika, a Polish analyst who had studied with him, Ferenczi, and Jung. Madame Sokolnika's arrival in Paris evoked little interest from physicians, but she became the pet of the literati, particularly of the surrealists. In fact, it was Paul Bourget, a member of the surrealist circle, who introduced Madame Sokolnika to her first contacts in the medical world.

In the early twentieth century, French physicians were as reticent toward psychoanalysis as French poets had been enthusiastic. Even the handful of physicians who saw themselves as the champions of psychoanalysis were ambivalent. When eleven analysts founded the first French psycho-analytic society in 1926, the Paris Psychoanalytic Society (Société Psychanalytique de Paris), most of them started a new psychiatric society at the same time: Psychiatric Evolution (L'Evolution Psychiatrique).[7] This second association was supposed to introduce psychoanalysis to French medicine in a more "acceptable" form. Instead, Psychiatric Evolution became a center of resistance to psychoanalytic study, and it drained off a great deal of energy from the young psycho-analytic society. With the exception of Madame Sokolnika and Princess Marie Bonaparte of Greece, whom Laforgue had encouraged to study with Freud in Vienna, the Paris Society was made up exclusively of physicians with limited psycho-analytic practices who associated psychoanalysis more with surrealism than with science. Their training had been some-what haphazard even by the standards of early psychoanaly-sis. Some of the founders of the Paris Society had been trained by Madame Sokolnika, others had made quick pilgrimages to Vienna, others had remained in France, where they worked for brief periods with visiting Freudians such as Otto Rank and Max Eitingon. Tradition has it that some of them were not analyzed at all.[8]

René Laforgue's ambivalence was typical of the group. He seems to have felt that psychoanalysis was interesting but a bit shady. As editor of *La Revue Française de Psychanalyse*, Laforgue did not want to put Freud's name on the cover of the journal for fear of "loss of respectability." It took the personal intervention of Freud to "persuade" Laforgue that a psychoanalytic journal had to admit its adherence to *le freudianisme* whether or not that would be looked on with favor in polite society. Laforgue's insistence that the Psychiatric Evolution medical society would help reduce resistance to psychoanalysis seems to have been a rationalization for other motives. Laforgue also hoped that Psychiatric Evolution would help French psychoanalysis to retain a certain independence in relation to the authoritarianism of the young and growing psychoanalytic movement. Years later, he wrote: "From the very start I felt that something didn't seem right in the group around Freud. Psychiatric Evolution permitted us to avoid some of the psychoanalytic dogmatism whose roots I didn't understand."[9] Laforgue had reason to feel that he and his colleagues would do well to shy away from the scrutiny of the Vienna circle because the Paris Psychoanalytic Society was a breeding ground for psychoanalytic unorthodoxy as well as ambivalence. The isolation of the Parisian psychoanalysts and their skepticism about psychoanalysis itself made deviation their rule. Perhaps most significantly for the future, French psychoanalysis was torn between its identification with poetry and with medical professionalism.

The seeds of a conflict between this early Freudian tradition in France, distrustful of "Germanic" dogma and authoritarian organization, and the larger psychoanalytic world had been planted during the prewar period. But the conflict did not occur. As we have seen, most of the enthusiasm for psychoanalysis was outside of the professional psychoanalytic world. The "official" French analysts were few in number (on the eve of World War II, there were only twenty-four). Their marginality to the French psychiatric establishment and to Freud's psychoanalytic establishment protected them from a confrontation with outside orthodoxies. Their ambivalence about psychoanalysis and their lack of interest in monitoring one another's work protected them from conflict within.[10] For example, it was well known that Laforgue's practice was highly idiosyncratic, but nobody minded very much.[11] After the war the mood of amused toleration for deviancy would end. The group would be larger, its members would develop a greater stake in psychoanalysis as a professional identity, and there would be more contact with the medical community within France and the international psychoanalytic community beyond. Informality among a handful of colleagues who could see each other as artistic or scientific pioneers would turn into demands for discipline among a larger group that felt a need to train and certify medical practitioners. The ways in which psychoanalytic methodology and knowledge should be transmitted would become a lively arena of conflict, which is still central. For example, should it be transmitted by the means appropriate to poetry, pragmatic medical technique, or formal science?

If psychoanalysis is seen as a kind of "action-surrealism," worrying about how an analyst might be certified seems absurd. The poet has powerful means at his disposal to change how we think, how we look at ourselves, and how we live, yet we do not think about "certifying" a poet. But if we look at psychoanalysis as a medically associated therapeutic discipline, the problem of certification becomes crucial. We think of a "patient" in a different way than a "poetry reader." Patients are defined as vulnerable, and we put a premium on their protection by controlling who is allowed to practice on them. In the history of the French psychoanalytic movement

Lacan was central to how French psychoanalysis confronted the tension between psychoanalysis as a hierarchical church and psychoanalysis as a personal vocation. He was equally central to the working through of a second tension between psychoanalysis in the service of medicine and psychoanalysis as a form of interpretation and art. For he, more than any other analyst, lived fully in both worlds.

Lacan was born on April 13, 1901, to a family belonging to the Parisian *haute bourgeoisie*. He studied medicine and then psychiatry as a devoted student of Clerambault.[12] In 1932, Lacan received his Doctorat d'Etat in psychiatry with a thesis on the relationship of paranoia to personality structure.[13] All through the 1930s, Lacan's literary productions oscillated between studies in classical psychiatric journals and essays and poems in surrealist publications.[14] He was interested in paranoia, in language, fantasy, and the formal character of symptoms, and all of these concerns were deeply in harmony with the concerns of the surrealists. Lacan frequented the prewar Paris circle of artists and writers, among them Georges Bataille, André Malraux, and Jean-Louis Barrault.

In 1934, after an analysis with Rudolf Loewenstein, Lacan joined the Paris Psychoanalytic Society, and in 1936 he presented his theory of the "mirror stage" to the Fourteenth Congress of the International Psychoanalytic Association at Marienbad.[15] With this, his first communication to an international audience, Lacan established himself as an important, original thinker who subscribed to no orthodoxy. While the rest of the psychoanalytic movement was starting to follow Anna Freud in her emphasis on the ego and its power to marshal mechanisms of adaptation and defense, Lacan was saying that the ego really did not exist as a coherent entity at all. Lacan stresses that the ego is formed by a composite of false and distorted introjections so that "I" and "Other" are inextricably confused in the unconscious language of the self. Picked up by the Paris Psychoanalytic Society, Lacan's ideas gave French analysts a very different way of talking about the ego than was becoming common coin in the rest of the world. Lacan taught the French analysts to see the ego as the distorted reflection of mirrors within mirrors. The ego psychologists were in error: the "reality principle" was "the expression of a scientific prejudice most hostile to knowledge."[16] And the psychoanalysts who tried to borrow from existential philosophy were equally in error with their belief in "a self-sufficient consciousness" and the "illusion of autonomy."[17]

The Vichy years and the Nazi occupation decimated the Paris Psychoanalytic Society: there were deaths, a resignation, the Swiss analysts who had been working in Paris left for Geneva, and Loewenstein moved permanently to New York. In 1945 the Paris Psychoanalytic Society had eleven full members in Paris, its original size when Madame Sokolnika had presided over its foundation nineteen years before.[18] Only four of the original founders remained: René Laforgue, Marie Bonaparte, and Georges Parcheminey in Paris and Angelo Hesnard at Toulon.

The Paris Society responded to its depopulation by aggressively recruiting candidates and by committing itself to expansion. By 1951–52, it had seventy new analysts in training, and these candidates were analyzing another hundred patients in supervised "control cases." Training at the Paris Society had always been fairly informal, but now size started to strain the system of tutorials and individual arrangements for supervision. A training institute had to be created, and in planning for it a long implicit tension in the Paris Society between different models of a psychoanalytic society became explicit. The first model was of an organization for training and certifying medical practitioners who were all committed to the same technique. The other model called for a looser structure which would facilitate training, not in a medical specialty, but in a way of listening that demanded creativity and commitment rather than certification in an acquired skill.

On June 17, 1952, the Paris Society moved ahead on its plan to start a separate training institute. Sacha Nacht, whose mandate as president of the Paris Society was about to end, was made the first director of the new Psychoanalytic Institute. He chose three of his students as its scientific and administrative secretaries and, together with his inner circle, prepared the Institute's curriculum and administrative statutes. Both were violently contested, the curriculum for its rigidity and the statutes because they would assure the Nacht group of an automatic majority in all administrative and educational decisions. The ambition of the Nacht group was to obtain official state recognition for the Institute's psychoanalytic diploma, which would be reserved to physicians. This ambition contradicted long-standing practice at the Paris Society as well as its 1949 training statutes, written by Lacan, which specified that nonmedical candidates could receive full psychoanalytic training and full rights to practice.[19] The idea of an exclusively medical diploma enraged Marie Bonaparte, who herself was not a physician and who was a passionate advocate of lay analysis. Princess Bonaparte's rage was a significant political factor, particularly since it was she who was providing most of the funds for the new training Institute.

The Nacht proposals precipitated a period of discord among the senior analysts of the Paris Society. Jacques Lacan, Daniel Lagache, and Marie Bonaparte joined together in opposition to the Nacht group. Nacht resigned from the directorship, and

Lacan was given the job of temporarily heading the Institute in order to mediate a compromise between the factions. By the end of 1952, while the Nacht group was in the minority and was talking of schism, Marie Bonaparte suddenly threw her weight behind Nacht, and the balance of power in the Paris Society again tipped dramatically. It seems that Bonaparte had been slighted because Lacan did not plan to give her any special role in the Institute. Nacht was more diplomatic, and Bonaparte's support made the difference. On January 20, 1953, even as Lacan was elected president of the Paris Society as a whole, Nacht and his partisans were reinstated as the officers of the new Psychoanalytic Institute, which they proceeded to set up according to their rules.

During his brief tenure as interim director of the Psychoanalytic Institute, Lacan took strong exception to Nacht's conception of psychoanalysis as a discipline within neurobiology. Lacan argued that the elucidation of the rules of human exchange which were latent in speech situated psychoanalysis at the very center of the human sciences, irreducible to neurobiology or to anything else. Students of psychoanalysis should be judged not only in terms of their therapeutic efforts but also for their part in artistic, philosophical, and basic scientific endeavors.[20] Lacan warned his colleagues that the kind of psychoanalytic society that Nacht was trying to create would stunt the growth of psychoanalytic science by its defense of orthodoxy.

The Paris Society was divided into two opposing camps, and many analysts found themselves on the same side for different reasons. Some sided with Lacan, although they despised his clinical practice, usually because they found Nacht's authoritarianism and medical ideology intolerable.[21] Some sided with Nacht, although they found him reprehensible, because they found Lacan even more threatening. There were objections to Lacan's practice: "How can he possibly analyze the transference in five-, ten-, or twelve-minute slices?" There were other objections that Lacan was less interested in psychoanalysis than in taking over the French psychoanalytic movement by "the speedy manufacture of little carbon copies of himself." After all, deviant psychoanalytic schools grow by a process not unlike cell division. Each training analysis leaves two analysts where before there had been one, and the analysands of a heretic are presumed to be heretics as well. There was certainly a widespread feeling that a Lacan-dominated psychoanalytic society meant giving psychoanalysis back to surrealism and losing the bit of medical respectability it had so painfully gained.

There were serious attempts to monitor Lacan's practice, to force him to lengthen his sessions, and to keep the number of his analysands down. At the beginning of 1953, the Paris Society had put forth a set of rules for acceptable practice in the training analysis. Candidates would not be allowed to begin supervised analyses until they had been through at least twelve months of a training analysis with at least three three-quarter-hour sessions a week. Needless to say, by these criteria Lacan's students, often seen for much briefer intervals, would never become analysts. So Lacan promised to follow the new rules—not because he agreed with them, but because he didn't want to sacrifice the careers of his own students.

In March 1953, the new Institute finally opened, announced its rules, and distributed its catalog. The conflict in the ranks of the senior analysts was sharpened when the students joined in the controversy. According to the plans of the new Institute, a candidate for membership in the Paris Society would not only have to complete a personal analysis and two supervised control cases as before, but would also have to go through a three-year program of study with many required courses which would have to be paid for session by session. There was an uproar and much resistance to requirements, to a standard curriculum, and to the idea that psychoanalytic education could be reduced to a "lowest common denominator." Some of the candidates were already professors of philosophy and resented having to share schoolroom benches with physicians taking their first course on elementary Freudian theory.

Most Americans are so used to the idea that psychoanalytic training, like medical training, takes place in a structured setting that the controversy about the rules for the Paris Psychoanalytic Institute may be hard to understand. But the fact that Americans are used to seeing psychoanalysis in the same light as other professions may simply indicate a clouded vision, although widely shared. In their dismay over the new classroom exercises, the Paris students were perhaps seeing some things more clearly. The new Institute (like any bureaucracy trying to make rational plans for its future) made statements about the "average length of a training analysis," and students objected that "average" had nothing to do with the exploration of the unconscious.[22] The new Institute asked candidates to sign pledges not to practice psychoanalysis until officially authorized, and students pointed out that the call for a "legal" signature in a context where people were trying to break down internalized "legalities" by the strength of the spoken word was deeply disruptive. In any case, several of the students who were practicing psychiatrists had been using psychoanalytic techniques in their work with patients for many years. Was the new legal agreement not to practice asking them to lie, or was it asking them to stop their work? The students complained that infantilizing psychoanalysts-in-training could not produce good psychoanalysts. In a successful psychoanalysis, the analysand must work toward breaking free from relationships of infantile dependence and come to recognize the integrity of his or her own viewpoint. How could this process happen in an institution which asked students to behave "like minors and grade schoolers"?[23] When the students spoke of these problems, they faced the worst contradiction of all. The psychoanalytic institution made circular use of its own theory and responded to students' complaints by claiming that the students were poorly analyzed.

The student revolt in the Paris Society grew in strength and things came to a head when the students learned that the senior analysts were also quarreling. The situation was volatile, and all of the complicated issues began to crystallize around one thing: Lacan's short sessions. The Paris Society's Education Committee first raised Lacan's short sessions as a problem in 1951, and the short sessions probably kept him from the presidency of the Society in 1952, but did not lead to open conflict. But now, in the context of a heated discussion of orthodoxy, standardized training, and organizational discipline, the short sessions became the focus of controversy. In January 1953, Lacan had promised to obey the rules for "standard sessions." A quarter of a century later, the question of whether or not Lacan really kept his promise in 1953 could still lead to a heated discussion. In either case, the rumors that he did not were widespread enough to detonate the explosive situation in the Paris Society.

On June 2, 1953, at a scientific meeting of the Paris Society, a Nacht partisan attacked Lacan for inciting the student revolt. Others retorted that the student movement was in opposition to the authoritarianism of the new Institute and had nothing to do with the quarrels of the senior analysts. Another Nacht supporter responded that "even if Lacan didn't instigate the conflict, he was still responsible for its existence."[24] The discussion that followed this heated interchange was embarrassing to all sides. It came out that the Nacht group had misreported the results of elections and had used its administrative role to steer students away from analysts in the Society whom it considered undesirable. And Lacan came close to admitting that he was not keeping his pledge to renounce short sessions.

The Paris Society was split between Lacan's accusers and those who felt that the issue was really not Lacan at all, that the controversial short sessions were being used to mobilize support for an otherwise unpopular authoritarian faction and mask a deep malaise in the Society. On June 16, 1953, an administrative session of the Paris Society gave Lacan a vote of no confidence. Lacan resigned from the presidency, and the Society's vice president, Daniel Lagache, refused to take over. Lagache, Juliette Favez-Boutonier, and Françoise Dolto resigned from the Society and announced the creation of a new psychoanalytic group, the French Psychoanalytic Society (Société Française de Psychanalyse, Groupe d'Etudes et de Recherches Freudiennes). Lacan and Blanche Reverchon-Jouve also resigned from the Paris society and joined the new group.[25]

With the dissidents gone, along with approximately forty analytic candidates who left with them, the Paris Society was free to run its Institute according to the original Nacht plans. While Nacht was trying to gain for psychoanalysis an official status as a medical subspecialty, the new French Psychoanalytic Society planned to keep itself and the field open to audiences beyond medicine, and to strengthen psychoanalysis as an area of humanistic and scientific research. Indeed, in their founding statement its members say their purpose is to "fight for scientific liberty and humanism." But this same document, which proclaimed that "humanism has no strength without militancy," went on to say that "there seemed to be no reason for the new Society not to be recognized by the International Psychoanalytic Association at its next congress in London."[26] Things were not to be so simple, however. Humanistic militancy would not necessarily satisfy the International Association's demands for psychoanalytic discipline.

None of the analysts who left the Paris Society thought that doing so would jeopardize their affiliation with the International Psychoanalytic Association. When Nacht's group was in the minority, the story had gone around that Anna Freud had felt that in the event of a schism recognition would be no problem. The Lacan-Lagache faction did not think that their case would be different. But by July 6, 1953, Lacan had already received a letter from the general secretary of the International Psychoanalytic Association informing him that he could not attend the business meeting of the Eighteenth International Psychoanalytic Congress in London, where his case would be discussed: "the meeting is only open to members . . ." and "we are sure you are aware that this step [of resigning from the Paris Society] also means loss of membership in the I.P.A."[27]

Lacan and Lagache tried to marshal support in the international psychoanalytic community. They emphasized that they had left the Paris Society in order to protest authoritarianism in the psychoanalytic institution, which they felt was getting in the way of psychoanalysis itself.[28] But the central executive of the International Association seemed uninterested in anything except the one point that the dissidents claimed was not at issue, that is, Lacan's unorthodox practice in the conduct of training analyses. At the administrative session of the London Congress, at which the case of the

French analysts was discussed (the Nacht group was present; the Lacan-Lagache group was not), Heinz Hartmann and Anna Freud held fast to the decision already made: the dissidents were to be excluded and a special committee would look into the whole matter.[29]

The tone of the administrative session at London was curt.[30] Discussion centered around psychoanalytic discipline and on the necessity for psychoanalysts to keep their differences to themselves. When Gregory Zilboorg, an American analyst, pointed out that there had been a schism in the New York Psychoanalytic Society without anyone's being excluded from the International Association, the reply was legalistic: unlike the American case, France had no national Psychoanalytic Association to "cover" the dissidents. When several analysts, among them Michael Balint, suggested that the dissidents should at least be given provisional membership pending the investigative committee's final report, the suggestion was brushed aside with an implied reference to Lacan's unorthodoxy. When Rudolf Loewenstein reported that he had firsthand reason to believe that the Paris Society had acted in an authoritarian manner (even now, he reported, they were not living up to their responsibilities to the students of the dissenting analysts), there was no particular concern. And Anna Freud said that efforts on behalf of the dissenters' students would probably be wasted energy because it "is a well known fact" that someone who has had irregular training is usually impossible to supervise later.[31]

Anna Freud's remark made it clear that as far as she was concerned, losing these colleagues and their students meant no great loss to psychoanalysis. In any case, she claimed that the dissidents had closed down the possibility for compromise by letting "the outside world" know that there had been a conflict. The implication here is that the psychoanalytic movement, like an authoritarian political regime, has to present itself as sure, certain, undivided. If controversy cannot be hidden, it has to be eliminated by the decisive exclusion of the dissenters. This position is certainly incompatible with a view of psychoanalysis that sees it as an enterprise requiring continual self-criticism and challenge.

During the very first few months of the French Society's existence, in September 1953, Lacan presented a paper, "The Function and Field of Speech and Language in Psychoanalysis," to a group of French-speaking psychoanalysts in Rome. The paper, usually referred to as "The Discourse of Rome," opened up psychoanalysis to a new realm of linguistic research, which would become central to Lacan's later work. The Discourse of Rome was also an occasion for Lacan to reflect on his recent experience with the psychoanalytic establishment:

> The mere fact that one could claim to regulate the training of psychoanalysts in so authoritarian a manner posed the question as to whether the established modes of this training did not produce the paradoxical result of maintaining them perpetually as minors.
>
> Certainly the highly organized initiatory forms which, for Freud, were a guarantee that his doctrine would be transmitted are justified in the situation of a discipline that can survive only by maintaining itself at the level of an integral experience.
>
> But have these forms not led to a dispiriting formalism that discourages initiative by penalizing risk and turns the reign of the opinion of the learned into a docile prudence in which the authenticity of research is blunted before it finally dries up?[32]

Lacan insisted that the transmission of psychoanalysis must be involved with perpetual challenge to anything that might be deadening to its vitality. This vision of psychoanalytic teaching is not compatible with the view of the psychoanalytic institution that he attributed to Nacht and his supporters, that is, "rather like that of a driving school, which not content with claiming the unique privilege of issuing the driving license, also imagines that it is in a position to supervise the making of the car."[33]

Thus, in the course of the 1953 schism, Lacan had raised the serious issue of whether or not a rigid professional society could supervise a psychoanalytic science, but such issues were not to be taken up by the International. Two years later, at the Nineteenth Congress of the International, President Heinz Hartmann simply announced that the committee that had studied the dissident group had recommended that it be excluded from membership in the International because of its "insufficient training facilities." This initial decision had been handed down, and the issue of recognition was to haunt the ten-year history of the new French Psychoanalytic Society.

Many analysts who participated in the early years of the new Society as members or as candidates still refer to them warmly as a golden age. Theoretical research flourished, links to other disciplines were established. But the shadow of the International hung over the group. The French analysts wanted recognition. One might ask why. French analysts, whether or not they belonged to the International, had no official status, so recognition was largely symbolic. But to French analysts, who knew that medical colleagues and much of the public considered them charlatans and quacks, any symbol of legitimacy was precious.[34] There were also more practical concerns: some members of the French Psychoanalytic Society were concerned that it could not compete with the Paris Society for analytic candidates if it could not promise them international standing as analysts. Some feared that the Cold War or Algerian War might create an intolerable political situation; they wanted international credentials that would make it easier for them to leave France if necessary. And finally, Lacan and his students wanted to bring their brand of psychoanalytic theory and research to an audience outside of France.

The new terrain of psychoanalysis as a linguistic science in close touch with structural anthropology and mathematics, was important, uncharted, and exciting, but Lacanians feared isolation from the mainstream of the psychoanalytic movement. They knew that when other new currents in psychoanalysis had not maintained a dialogue with the establishment, the new researches often were perceived by the majority of psychoanalysts as "non-Freudian." Many Lacanians felt that it would be better to work on the International "from the inside."

So in 1959, the French Psychoanalytic Society decided to try again and thus began a courtship of the International Psychoanalytic Association that many of the members of the Society saw as a psychoanalytic "pilgrimage to Canossa." The analysts were not asking for forgiveness from a pope, but from a psychoanalytic church. The French Society requested affiliation and sent a report of their research and training activities over the past six years. The central executive of the International claimed that the report was insufficient and formed an ad hoc committee, under the chairmanship of Pierre Turquet, to investigate further.[35]

After two years of interviewing French psychoanalysts and their candidates, the Turquet committee submitted its report. The French Psychoanalytic Society rushed its negotiators to Edinburgh, where the International was holding its Twenty-Second Congress. They were told in language, which they saw as betraying the regression of the International toward traditional medical psychiatry, that the International intended to ferret out "unhealthy" forces in their group and that their "healthy" forces were not yet strong enough even to justify an *application* to the International Association as a regular psychoanalytic society. All they could do was become a "study group" under the close supervision of the International.[36] And the supervision would begin with a set of nineteen rules that the study group would have to follow if it ever wanted to become a regular member society in the International. These rules became known as the Edinburgh demands.

In the Edinburgh demands the psychoanalytic establishment forgot its own history as it responded to what it found threatening about the Lacanians. Many members of the French Society considered Lacan's seminar in psychoanalytic theory as a complement to personal analysis. What would have happened to psychoanalysis if Freud's analysands had not also been his students? Yet the seventh demand forbade students from attending any course given by their analyst without special permission. By the early 1960s, young physicians from around the world, particularly from the Mediterranean countries, South America, and French Canada, were coming to France to study with Lacan. What would have happened to psychoanalysis if the physicians who had come to Vienna to study with Freud had needed letters of permission from their local medical societies? Yet demand nineteen treated foreigners who came to France as if they were children who had no right to make this decision alone. The French group was not allowed to train foreign students without authorization from the psychoanalytic institute in their home countries.

It seems obvious that the Edinburgh demands, like the study committees, secret reports, special cases, and discreet legalisms that had come before, were motivated by a desire to exclude Lacan from the International. But during these eight years, this had not been allowed to surface clearly. It was only after the last round of discussions at Edinburgh when the members of the French delegation were already at the London airport that the latent was made manifest. They discovered that a twentieth demand had been inserted in the Edinburgh document as article thirteen. Article thirteen demanded that Jacques Lacan and Françoise Dolto be phased out as training analysts.

The French Psychoanalytic Society was not able to deal with the Lacan issue with greater forthrightness than had the International. Indeed, for a while, all effort seemed directed toward trying to deny that it would have to deal with it at all.[37] The Society tried to protect Lacan with special statutes at the same time that it reassured the International that it was following all the Edinburgh rules. Wladimir Granoff, Serge Leclaire, and François Perrier made up a negotiating "troika" that tried to work out compromises between the International's article thirteen and the French Society's loyalty to Lacan. It was an impossible job. Lacan was not following the "rules," and there was a growing faction within their own group that was looking forward to a showdown in order to rid themselves of him.

In January 1963, the Turquet committee made yet another visit to Paris (more interviews with analysts and candidates, more warnings) and wrote yet another report for the central executive of the International. These visiting analysts were deeply disturbed by the world around Lacan. They found his theory "overly scholastic" and too centered on the early Freud. They found his conduct of the training analysis unorthodox as to time and non-analytic in its reliance on "intellectualization." They found that Lacan manipulated rather than analyzed the transference.[38]

Despite the diplomatic efforts of Granoff, Leclaire, and Perrier, a showdown over Lacan could not be avoided. The

International was willing to trade official recognition for a price, and that price was Lacan. As a therapist, Lacan was considered irresponsible; as a training analyst, he was considered a menace to the future of French psychoanalysis because his large numbers of students threatened to take it over. The Edinburgh demands had been a warning; they had spoken of "phasing out." Now there was an ultimatum. Lacan had to be forever excluded from training.[39] And if it did not happen by October 31, 1963, the French Psychoanalytic Society would lose all rights to the International's recognition. Lacan was cornered, and again French analysts had to take sides.

Some analysts with whom I spoke about the split said they had been grateful for the clear choice. They had had enough of Lacan.

> If sessions of variable length only mean shorter and shorter sessions—and this was the case for Lacan—three minutes, four minutes, five minutes, then the whole idea of punctuating analyses by time as well as speech is really just letting an analyst be as sadistic as he wants.

> If Lacan heard about a talented student or philosopher, or if he saw a new interesting face at his seminar, there would ensue a courtship to seduce the person into beginning an analysis with him. How could he talk about psychoanalysis as "refusing the patient's first demand"? It was *Lacan* who made the first demand.

> You were either totally loyal or you were out of favor. One false move and you were out of the charmed circle. When people were fragile, no wonder there were so many suicides.

Others felt that it was out of the question to abandon Lacan. As in 1953, his supporters were behind him for very different reasons. Some defended Lacan's practice:

> The laws of the unconscious don't reveal themselves in forty-five minute intervals, and so neither do Lacan's sessions.

Some stressed that the fight over Lacan was no longer the point because the fight was about an approach that he had already passed on:

> If Dolto and Lacan were to die, right here and now, what could we do with the heritage they have left us. . . . And would this heritage be as irritating to the psychoanalytic establishment as their persons?[40]

And yet another group insisted that the struggle was about the legitimacy of the International Association as a psychoanalytic body:

> Being recognized was just a way of being told that you were obedient enough to be trusted with maintaining the status quo.

By October 13, 1963, well within the time limit set by the International, the Education Committee of the French Psychoanalytic Society removed Lacan's name from its list of training analysts.[41] A month later, on November 19, 1963, the decision was ratified by the majority of the Society, on which Leclaire and Perrier, its president and vice president, announced their intention to resign their posts. The following day Lacan walked into his regular seminar at Saint Anne Hospital and began by announcing that it would be his last. He claimed to have been misunderstood and misrepresented. He had tried to present psychoanalysis as a science which must reject simple models of "truth and falsity," and where, as in all sciences, "each chapter follows on to a next chapter." But now, hurt and disappointed, he doubted that this kind of truth, "shifting, deceptive, slippery," had been transmitted to those whom he had believed were listening to him and studying with him. He claimed that he had stayed out of the machinations of the psychoanalytic politics that had been going on around him for the two previous years in order to allow his truth its "needed space and purity." But now the shock and the pain of the news that Lacan had just received was visible and audible: "I have never, at any moment, given you reason to think that for me there was no difference between a yes and a no."[42]

With the "no" vote, the French Psychoanalytic Society split in two, and the president of the International made their schism official by naming the majority faction of the Society as members of a "new" French Study Group that had the right to train candidates. Within a year, this anti-Lacan group became a new psychoanalytic society, the French Psychoanalytic Association (Association Psychanalytique de France), which was officially welcomed back into the fold of the International at its Congress at Amsterdam in July 1965.[43] It had taken twelve years, but the International had finally found a formula for the definitive exclusion of Lacan and his followers.

Lacan's critics accused him of attempting a cheap *coup de théâtre* at Saint Anne, for in fact the seminar *did* go on. Symbolically though, it left its hospital setting and moved to the Ecole Normale Supérieure, where the balance of Lacan's audience began to shift away from psychiatrists and toward philosophers, anthropologists, linguists, mathematicians, and literary critics. Increasingly, Lacan seemed to feel that Freud's truth could be better understood by people whose first concern was not medicine and therapy but philosophy, poetry, and science, and could be better presented outside of an analytic society than within one. Lacan did found another psychoanalytic society, his own, but he tried to make it a psychoanalytic society "with a difference." In June 1964, Lacan founded the Freudian School of Paris (Ecole Freudienne de Paris). The Freudian School would have no analytic hierarchy, and indeed, it would not be a closed circle of analysts at all, but a meeting place for the freest possible contact between psychoanalysts and members of other disciplines.

The International had rewarded French analysts for their anti-Lacan politics, but in doing so, had acted as a political body and had placed itself in a contradiction from a psycho-analytic point of view. Its list of recognized training analysts for the new French Psychoanalytic Association included many analysts trained by Lacan. No psychoanalytic logic could justify this position. The International had made it clear that, as far as it was concerned, Lacan was not fit to train analysts. By what right were candidates who had been trained by him, and him alone, now fit to be analysts and to *train* analysts? The International seemed to be saying that if you had been analyzed by Lacan, but had renounced him, then you were fit to be a training analyst. If, on the other hand, you had been analyzed by Lacan and chose to stay with him, you, like he, were unfit and were to be excluded. The illogic of the position was not lost on the French analysts. Lacanian François Perrier reflected on the problem as follows:

> The fact that the French Study Group [the group formed preliminary to the constitution of the new, recognized French Psychoanalytic Association] includes a certain number of people who owe the substance of their training to the very person who was excluded in October, clearly shows that the only criteria for being selected by London and Chicago [London is the headquarters of the International; Chicago was to be the site of its next Congress] as a "good French analyst" is how one is presumed to have marked a ballot cast last December. If this were not the case, the application of analytic principle alone would require that all of the poorly analyzed [that is, the Lacan analysands] would have to regress down the hierarchy to the level of candidates smitten-with-nonliquidated-transference-loves, that is, until they did another analysis with a true training analyst. . . . Unless, of course, the only proof of a liquidated transference is when an ex-student shows the capacity to take an active role in the condemnation of his *"Maître."*[44]

The imperative behind the International's position clearly seemed more political than psychoanalytic. And the form it had taken seemed theological; it was on this point that Lacan insisted when he reconvened his seminar in January 1964.

> They [the Executive Committee of the International] specified that there would never be affiliation without the guarantee that my teaching would never, ever again, be a part of analytic training.
>
> So we have here something comparable to what in other contexts is called major excommunication. But even in that case, it is not made irrevocable.
>
> It only exists as irrevocable in a religious community . . . the synagogue. . . . Spinoza was the object of its *kherem*, an excommunication similar to a major excommunication; then, a while later, he was the object of a *chammata*, which consists of adding the condition of irrevocability. . . .
>
> I am not saying—but it is not out of the question—that the psychoanalytic community is a Church. But without doubt, the question arises if we are dealing with the echo of a religious practice.[45]

The story of Lacan's exclusion from the International brings unresolved tensions in the psychoanalytic movement into sharp relief. One is a tension between scientific inquiry and client-centered professionalism. All scientific societies inevitably combine two functions between which tension easily arises. These are the pursuit of truth and the protection of the profession. While belonging to an authoritarian medical association might not necessarily interfere with a surgeon's technical skill, there are good reasons to think that belonging to an authoritarian psychoanalytic organization can undermine the work of the analyst. Where an accommodation to authoritarianism often means learning to tune out the contradictory and the complex, the analyst's task is to listen without censor. While in most organizations it is commonplace to smooth over painful confrontations, in the particular case of psycho-analytic organizations, attempts at polite obfuscation, such as the legalisms, secret negotiations, and hidden agendas that had marked the Lacan excommunication, are in deep con-flict with psychoanalysis itself. In dealing with the individual, the analytic process continually fights to make even painful things clear, but when psychoanalytic societies do not live up to this standard, the question is raised whether their behavior is compatible with the doctrine they claim to be protecting.

By 1964, the Lacanians were on their own, and their strug-gles were no longer with Freudian orthodoxy and the Inter-national. Later, however, Lacan became ensnared in many of the same contradictions of psychoanalytic politics that he had criticized in others. There was soon to be a third schism that pitted Lacanian against Lacanian. Its story suggests that the problems of psychoanalytic politics are not simply the incom-patibility of psychoanalytic science with authoritarianism and with demands for blind allegiance to Freudian technique. The problems may be more fundamental. Psychoanalytic science may be incompatible with allegiances to any *Maître* and with loyalties to any institution.

5 Psychoanalytic Societies and Psychoanalytic Science

After Lacan's excommunication his followers set about trying to create a nonauthoritarian, nonhierarchical psychoanalytic society. The story of their difficulties points to a contradiction more fundamental than that between psychoanalysis and an authoritarian psychoanalytic institution. Lacan himself pointed to this contradiction, one that is inherent in the very existence of a psychoanalytic society. For Lacan, the analyst can never make his sense of reality the measure of all things for the patient. For an analysis to work, the analyst must refuse all certainties and refuse to be the "subject who is presumed to know" the truth about another. But Lacan asks: "What does it mean to have an organization of psychoanalysts and the certificate it confers—if not to indicate to whom one can go to find someone who will play the role of this subject who is presumed to know?"[1]

The contradiction between the way psychoanalysis tries to subvert all "truths" and the need for organizational discipline goes back to the time of Freud. During the period of debate over the work of Sandor Ferenczi and Otto Rank, Karl Abraham, Freud's "model" disciple, promised his teacher that he would act objectively. "I promise you, dear Professor, in advance, that it will be done on my part in a nonpolemic and purely factual manner and only with the wish to serve you and our work, which is identical with your person."[2] Thus, when psychoanalysis established itself as a psychoanalytic "movement," it tended to identify not just with a field of research but with Freud himself, and for Abraham, the disciple, behaving in "a purely factual manner" had become identified with serving the interests of the teacher. And the promise of loyalty could be given *in advance*. This of course is the point of contradiction: a successful psychoanalysis might be expected to break down that kind of loyalty to a *Maître*, particularly when he is one's own analyst.

In "Group Psychology and the Analysis of the Ego," Freud described the libidinal mechanisms that provide the cement for such organizations as the church and army, but he might as well have been describing the International Psychoanalytic Association or any psychoanalytic society.[3] Freud pointed out that organizations are held together by the ego's alienation in transference loves. Since a successful analysis dissolves such investments and liquidates the transference to the analyst in the analysis itself, psychoanalysis may face an internal contradiction similar to that faced by anarchism. It may subvert all structures, including its own: its therapeutic goal is to analyze the irrational bonds which tie us to our past and to those around us. Nevertheless, Freud saw fit to distribute ceremonial membership rings to the secret committee which was to serve as the nucleus of his new psychoanalytic movement.

If psychoanalysis identifies itself with an individual or a "cause" rather than with a field of research, the presence of the *Maître* may overwhelm the science; yet, the psychoanalytic movement was first constituted on the basis of a transference relationship to Freud, and loyalty to him continued as the touchstone of psychoanalytic discipline in the International Psychoanalytic Association. The Lacanian dissidents work as a school constituted around another theorist. Indeed they have often been reproached for an allegiance to Lacan that compromises their allegiance to Freud. It is not surprising that over the years, they have become preoccupied with the role of the *Maître* in the psychoanalytic institution.[4]

Critics of psychoanalytic dissidents are fond of explaining the latter's "heresies" by saying that the dissidents are poorly analyzed and proving that by pointing to their dissidence. The perspective on psychoanalytic politics presented here suggests that the opposite is true. Schism is not a sign of an unsuccessful analysis. It can be a positive sign because the successfully analyzed patient would resist the role of an unquestioning disciple, even of Freud himself. By the very effect of psychoanalysis on its members, any organization of psychoanalysts may carry within itself the seeds of its own destruction. It is in this sense that "to speak of psychoanalytic societies is a contradiction in terms."[5]

After two schisms and twelve years of fighting with psychoanalytic institutions, the Lacanians were well aware of their problems and were weary of psychoanalytic politics on the international or on any other level. Once they were on their own in early 1964, they tried to form a psychoanalytic institution that was as little like a traditional psychoanalytic society as possible. The mission of the Freudian School as Lacan first founded it was to "reconquer" psychoanalysis from both the psychoanalytic institution and from bad theoreticians.[6] It would be the first psychoanalytic society to leave the responsibility of whether or not someone was "ready" to be an analyst to the individual: "Only the analyst can authorize himself as an analyst."[7] Yet within a very few years the Freudian School itself was deeply entangled in the contradictions of its need for and its need to reject a *Maître*. It split, like the Paris Psychoanalytic Society and the French Psychoanalytic Society before it. As before, the particular way in which this happened had much to do with personalities and circumstances, while at the same time the schism reflected more fundamental tensions in the psychoanalytic institution.

From the very start, membership in the Freudian School was open, informal, and without prerequisite. Anyone could join, whether or not one was an analyst, wanted to become an analyst, or had any intention of being psychoanalyzed. There were no required courses for analysts in training. People simply participated in those study groups that interested them. In the traditional psychoanalytic society, there is a complex hierarchy of analysts but the major distinction, so important to the story of the Lacan controversy, is between those analysts who are certified to train other analysts (by analyzing them in a "training analysis") and those who are not.

At the Freudian School there was no special group of analysts who were authorized to train other analysts: there was no distinction between a training analysis and a personal analysis. The Freudian School's sharpest break with the traditions of the psychoanalytic institution was that the decision to use an analysis as a step toward becoming an analyst was considered to be a completely personal decision.

This, of course, is the policy of "self-authorization." When an analysand at the Freudian School felt ready to see patients as an analyst, he or she simply notified the School's secretary and was then listed as a "practicing analyst" in the School's membership roster. This implied no "guarantee" of the analyst by the School since the decision to begin practice and to arrange for supervision belonged to the analysand alone. Most

Lacanians insist that this policy was a direct expression not only of the essential privacy of the decision to become an analyst, but also of the current state of law in France:

> In France analysts have no legal status. Anyone can legally call himself an analyst, and if he finds a patient, he is *de facto* an *analyste praticien* (a practicing analyst). We list on our roster people who have made a certain kind of decision. We are not judging them, we are simply stating a fact.

The idea of self-authorization directly challenges what is for most the reassuring notion that psychoanalysis, like other professions, and particularly like other medical specialties, works with a clear standard of quality control. What seemed obvious to Lacanians about self-authorization was bitterly opposed by almost everyone else. Outside of the Freudian School the policy of self-authorization was generally seen as irresponsible to the public at large for refusing to maintain a standard of quality and for refusing to recognize that analysts who are "listed" at the Freudian School are implicitly legitimated:

> It is impossibly naive, and among all his faults Lacan is not naive, to think that someone who appears in an official publication as "X, practicing analyst and member of the Freudian School of Paris" is not seen as someone legitimated as a clinician by the weight of Lacan's prestige.

Many saw the problem of self-authorization as a case where the translation of Lacanian analytic theory into actual practice gave rise to unintended consequences. Other analysts refused the idea that Lacan was doing anything "unintended" and saw his intent as directly political. For one, Lacan's policy "has always been political: to seduce the intellectuals, the newspapers, the magazines, so that the only psychoanalysis you can read in France is Lacanian." In our interviews many spoke of Lacanian self-authorization as a policy designed for the quick manufacture of disciples. Over and over I heard the phrase "to turn out little Lacanians by assembly line."

The tension between theory and its practical implementation was pervasive at the Freudian School. Perhaps the best example of the gap between theoretical intent and institutional reality at the School is the story of "the pass" (*la passe*).[8]

For Lacan, a better understanding of how an individual in analysis comes to know that he or she is ready to assume the role of analyst is central to the development of psychoanalytic theory. Lacan sees the decision to become an analyst as analogous to the act of becoming a poet. It is the assumption by the individual of a new, particularly intimate relationship to language. From a traditional point of view, the question of the "readiness" of an analysand to be an analyst has been posed in terms of progressing toward a healthy resolution of neurotic conflict and in terms of the acquisition of skills and technical knowledge. From a Lacanian perspective, psychoanalytic readiness is a relation to "the word."

Lacan wanted to find a way of bringing information about the development of this new relation to language out of the personal experience of the psychoanalyst and into the collective experience of psychoanalysis. What complicates the picture is that this should take place in the setting of a psychoanalytic society dominated by a *Maître*. In this situation, the individual cannot help but strive for the approval and appreciation of the *Maître*, and the process of research, of "information gathering," becomes highly charged. This much, at least, seems intrinsic to the situation.

In the "pass" procedure itself an analyst gives an account of his training analysis to three other members of the School, his "passers," all of whom are themselves currently in analysis. These passers then "pass" what they have heard to a committee of senior analysts, a committee that always includes Lacan. This committee would review the information gathered, not in a spirit of judging their fellow analyst's capacity to practice or train but in order to decide whether the analyst had reached the maturity needed to use his or her own analytic experience as research.

When Lacan presented the idea of the pass to the Freudian School, the reaction was violent and almost uniformly negative. Some analysts felt that the pass would compromise the confidentiality of the analytic relationship and would undermine the analytic transference. Others objected that, since Lacan would be a permanent member of the passing committee, there was no doubt that "he is the one who will decide." Others feared that the pass was a way for Lacan to monitor the analytic practice of school members. ("He can check up on whether you are following his line by being right there next to you, as though he were on the couch next to your patients.")

Although some Lacanians felt that the experience of the pass would not disrupt analysis since it would simply become grist for the analytic mill, others objected that the pass might injure relationships with patients. The passers are chosen by analysts at the Freudian School from among their analysands. Are patients to feel successful when they are chosen as passers by their analysts? Successful at what, for whom, and why? Some Freudian School analysts warned that being chosen as a passer might well become a hidden agenda for analytic patients.

> The task of the passer is really to listen with an analytic sensitivity, so it is natural for me to choose someone whom I believe has that sensitivity. But this communication to my analysand has an effect on his analysis; it is like a wild, out-of-control interpretation. And perhaps worse, it can have an uncontrolled effect on other

analysands who were not chosen, and who may feel that they were
not chosen because they are not "good" enough.

With or without the pass, belonging to an analytic society would be expected to create tensions about position in
the group among its members. The pass as it was put forth
by Lacan complicates matters by making the implicit explicit.
Lacan established the pass as a process which can lead to collective recognition within the Freudian School. This can be
seen as recognition for having given a personal testimony that
might ultimately contribute to the theoretical understanding
of the experience of becoming an analyst. This needs courage,
particularly because the testimony itself—a recounting of the
individual's analysis—will have to be examined and may perhaps be found wanting. The individual's presentation will be
considered on the basis of its theoretical sophistication; good-
will and the success of the analysis are not enough. This judg-
mental component considerably aggravates the problems with
the pass. Lacan has made no attempt to avoid these tensions;
he deals with them by accepting and even symbolizing them.

After the presentation, the passing committee votes on
what they have heard; a pass can be "successful" or "unsuccessful." The recipient of a successful pass is recognized as
having important theoretical abilities and is given the title of
"School Analyst," the same title as the analysts who judged
him. It should be underscored that the title of School Analyst
recognizes an analyst's abilities as a theoretician and has nothing to do with his qualifications to train other analysts. At the
Freudian School all analysts can train other analysts.

When Lacan first proposed the pass, there were objections
not only to how it might affect relationships with patients
but also to how it might impact on the life of a psychoanalytic society committed to an open, egalitarian structure and

to the idea that everything important about psychoanalysis is embedded, not in institutions or their hierarchies, but in personal desire and commitment. Lacan had recoiled from any notion of hierarchy for clinicians (where others felt certification procedures to be justified on the basis of public responsibility): here though, he was instituting a hierarchy on the basis of theoretical sophistication.

Lacan's "Proposal of October 9, 1967," in which he put forth his argument in favor of the pass, makes it quite clear that if an analyst were not a theoretician or did not even want to try to become one he was resigning himself to a rather mediocre fate:

> Because if one has the courage, why should one aspire to less? Let us not forget that the School Analysts are those who contribute to the advancement of psychoanalysis. Why not begin as soon as one is ready? On the other hand, some people will more modestly be content to work as simple analysts. The School will involve itself with them in a positive way and will give them the title of Member Analyst of the School without the necessity for the member to make any formal request.[9]

The same psychoanalytic society that had hoped to reconquer psychoanalysis from the organizational imperatives of the psychoanalytic establishment was now setting up a hierarchy of its own, which distinguished between the School Analysts who courageously contribute to the advancement of psychoanalysis and those who are more "modestly" content to "simply stand and wait." They also serve, but it was hard not to infer that they serve a rather inferior function. Despite official Freudian School ideology to the contrary, Freudian School analysts with whom I spoke did tend to speak of "School Analysts" as a higher grade of analyst, if only because they were more valued by Lacan and were presumed to be close to the *Maître*.

Lacan had violently denounced psychoanalytic "religion" after his own excommunication, but now that he had his own school, his colleagues bitterly complained that it too seemed to be developing characteristics of a church, complete with dogma, "mysteries," and a pope. The School had started out with an organizational structure which gave Lacan a five-year term as president and set up a five-member "directory," charged with making important policy decisions for the School. But under Lacan's presidency, the directory was never consulted and there has never been talk of electing a new president. One by one, the directory resigned, either in protest or in simple adjustment to the fact that things were not to be as they had once seemed. One analyst described the situation as it had developed in the mid-1960s in the following way:

> Debate was stifled just when it might have been most productive. Lacan sent out every kind of signal that disagreement was not welcome on the things that he considered really important. And a paradox was created. Lacan was constantly exhorting a return to Freud, but most people found it more comfortable to accept his interpretation once and for all, and the book that became dog-eared was not Freud's *The Interpretation of Dreams*, but Lacan's *Ecrits*.

The Freudian School seemed well on its way to becoming the Lacanian School. By giving up the personal re-examination of Freud's texts and by putting Lacan in the position of "the subject presumed to know," it seemed that many of Lacan's followers were compromising Lacan's own psychoanalytic "Protestant Reformation." Freud's acceptance of the position of *Maître* with his disciples had led to contradiction between the development of the science and loyalty to the founder. Some of Lacan's colleagues felt that now Lacan too was falling into the same trap. By allowing his students to regard him as a *Maître*, he was helping them to subvert what his own theory stood for: "As for the *Maître*, he was caught in the trap of what he had offered. He gave no resistance to the temptation to create his line and to have the School's psychoanalytic heritage stamped with his seal alone."[10]

By 1968, and the publication of the first issue of the official journal of the Freudian School, *Scilicet: Tu peux savior ce qu'en pense l'Ecole Freudienne de Paris*, the policy of a united front behind Lacan's ideas was confirmed by an editorial policy unique in psychoanalytic literature. All of the articles in *Scilicet* are published anonymously except for those written by Lacan. The members of the Freudian School publish as a "school," but the words of the *Maître* are set aside, for as one cynical Lacanian put it: "How else are the rest of us supposed to know what to think?"

What we know of Freud's relationships with his disciples suggests that the way in which psychoanalysis is transmitted can menace psychoanalysis itself if an identification with the "cause" and with the *Maître* is not questioned. Although Lacan was able to point this out theoretically, it now seemed that the worst sins of Freud, the father, were being visited on Lacan, the son.

By the late 1960s, a significant group of analysts at the Freudian School was finding its atmosphere barely tolerable. They tried to make Lacan reconsider his stand on the pass. He was intransigent. The voting of Lacan's "Proposal of October 9, 1967" on the pass became a focal point for conflict. But as had been the case in 1953, when the issue was the creation of an Institute of Psychoanalysis, and as had been the case in 1963, when the issue was removing Lacan from the list of training analysts, the specific discussion of the pass only served to detonate an already explosive situation. And in 1969, as in 1953 and 1963, the underlying issues were brought to the surface through a controversy about what goes on during psychoanalytic training.

Lacan believes that the critical element (the "knot") in the training analysis and the one most difficult to analyze is the analysand's desire to be an analyst. This *désir de l'analyse* touches on the many sides of the analysand's desire for his or her analyst, a desire to be the analyst, to be loved by the analyst, and to be an analyst oneself. It is also tied up with the analyst's own desire to be an analyst, which is in turn related to a love for his or her own analyst. The "knot's" difficulty carries its own reward. If analysts commit themselves to grappling with its tangles, it can be a source of renewal in their analytic vocation, because each time it arises analysts must call into question how they were "parented" as analysts and their desire to parent other analysts. For Lacan, this continuing investigation into psychoanalytic filiation constitutes a permanent criticism of the psychoanalytic movement, the kind of criticism necessary to deal with the problems of the *Maître*. But at the very same time that Lacan was saying that the mark of true analysts is their continual challenge of their training and desire to train, he was also insisting that *the training analysis is the only pure analysis.*[11]

But there seemed to be a contradiction: how could analysts continually call their desire to train into question if the official line of the psychoanalytic school flatly asserted that a training analysis was the only "pure psychoanalysis"?

One analyst who was at the Freudian School during the debate on the pass and on "pure psychoanalysis" put his feelings this way: "I abhor a situation where someone who goes into analysis has reason to feel that he is not getting 'the real thing' (and indeed, his analyst has reason to feel that he is not giving 'the real thing') if he doesn't end up an analyst." On the other side, those more sympathetic to Lacan felt that "pure psychoanalysis" was only meant to emphasize that it was in the training analysis that one could best examine the crucial analytic "knot" which tangled the transference to the analyst with the desire to be the analyst and to be an analyst.

In January 1969, in a crisis atmosphere, the text on the pass came to a vote. The two sides were at loggerheads. Lacan would not budge an inch on what he felt to be an issue of theoretical principle, a "truth" for which he must do battle. Lacan seemed to be making the kinds of unconditional demands for fidelity that characterized Freud's relationship to his circle. These demands contradicted Lacan's own teaching about the need for each analyst to maintain his own sense of discovery, doubt, and judgment and never, under any circumstances, to abandon them for an institution or a *Maître*.

The text on the pass was voted on by a badly divided Freudian School, and ten of Lacan's closest followers and friends left to form a new group, known as the Fourth Group (*Le Quatrième Groupe*). These "Lacanians without Lacan" hoped to preserve what they felt was most important in Lacan's teachings about psychoanalysis as a science and a calling without having to suffer, as one of them put it, "the agony of watching Lacan himself undermine his own teaching."[12]

Lacan's unwillingness to compromise did not end with the 1969 split and the formation of the Fourth Group. Indeed, in the 1970s, Lacan's positions, particularly on the importance of mathematical formalizations of psychoanalytic theory, became increasingly intransigent even as they left more and more of his disciples behind. When members of his school objected that some of his actions seemed to be contradicting his long-held beliefs, Lacan insisted that he had "no need to explain himself on the matter."

Of course, there is great irony here because Lacan, more than any other theorist, has pointed out the incompatibility between that kind of statement and psychoanalysis itself. We have seen that Lacan has gone so far as to say that the tension between the individual's truth-seeking and a transferential allegiance to psychoanalysis as a "cause" must be worked out in every analysis. This is the analysis of "desire for analysis," the fundamental "knot." Lacan points out that, to the extent that Freud demanded unconditional loyalty, discipline, and obedience from his followers, he was subverting an important aspect of psychoanalysis even as he was trying to establish it. But when Lacan demands loyalty without "having to explain himself," he is doing the same thing. By 1978, almost fifteen years after the foundation of the Freudian School as an attempt to create an anti-institutional psychoanalytic institution, there was widespread talk about the "return of the repressed."

In this case, what was returning is a very deep paradox in the psychoanalytic enterprise. Though psychoanalysis tends to destroy the transferential cement that holds together an organization, it also needs the psychoanalytic institution. The institution protects the individual analyst from what might be intolerable personal pressures if all there was in psychoanalysis was relationships between individuals, and it ensures the perpetuation of the movement. So the psychoanalytic institution, for the "good of psychoanalysis," strikes back at dissenters. In doing so, it maintains transferential bonds that successful psychoanalysis aims to dissolve and retards the development of psychoanalytic science which requires individual independence. Lacan, arguing a position in terms of personal allegiance to his school, is to a certain extent replaying the struggle in Freud's circle between allegiance to psychoanalysis, which would entail a commitment to independence, and allegiance to Freud as the father of the movement. Psychoanalysis lives and relives this paradox.[13]

The presence of a living *Maître* dominated the history of the Freudian School. But a *Maître* can play a dominant role as much by his absence as by his presence. It has often been said that Freud's domination "stopped" the development of new psychoanalytic ideas by his disciples and by those who broke away. In France, the presence of Lacan as a *Maître* allows the parallels with Freud's circle to emerge and makes it easier to discern patterns in psychoanalytic history.[14] For example, in the story of those who stayed with Lacan at the Freudian School, it became clear that getting away from psychoanalytic authoritarianism was not as simple as breaking away from the International. Now, turning to the story of those who left Lacan, it will become equally clear that getting away from the domination of a *Maître* is not so simple as renouncing him. This last point is made dramatically by looking at the French Psychoanalytic Association, formed in 1963 in what was perhaps the most bitter of all the schisms.

The Association has remained small, beset with conflicts about its identity and with little renewal of its leadership. Part of the difficulty is that the Association shares its "establishment" image with the Paris Psychoanalytic Society and its "academic" image with the Freudian School, and each of these competing groups overshadows it, one on its medical "Right," the other on its university "Left." But although looking at the Association as a group without an exclusive clientele is one way to explain its troubles, there seems to be more going on. Members of the Association speak of having made the "moral" choice in 1963, but some of them feel trapped in the role of children on good behavior. One Association member wondered, "If the desire to please the International didn't lead us to a certain simplicity. . . . We were so afraid of wild analysis [*analyse sauvage*] that we have ended up with safe and wise analysis [*analyse sage*]."

In addition, when they cut themselves off from Lacan, the brilliant young Lacanians who formed the Association left themselves indelibly marked by Lacan's ideas but almost unable to have any contact with him. Many of them had been among Lacan's most cherished disciples. The break was angry and embittered. During the debate over whether Lacan should be barred from training, it was his student Jean Laplanche, later of the Association, who argued that Lacan's presence was incompatible with the functioning of an analytic society.[15] The bitterness has continued. In a 1967 article, "Against Lacan," another former student, Didier Anzieu, condemned Lacan as a danger because he kept his students tied to an "unending dependence on an idol, a logic, or a language," by holding out the promise of "fundamental truths to be revealed . . . but always at some further point . . . and only to those who continued to travel with him."[16] These attitudes are representative of how most members of the Association talk about Lacan.

Even more than a decade after the split, an inquiry about Lacan at the Association still brings forth a barrage of invective ("Lacan lied to us." . . . "Lacan discouraged students from working together for fear they would disagree with him." . . . "Lacan wanted his students to be children.") In his "absence," Lacan remains a powerful presence, a reference point, a preoccupation. This kind of situation does not facilitate the development of theory or even of self-expression.

Wladimir Granoff is an analyst at the Association who feels that the study of psychoanalytic schisms raises questions of a psychoanalytic order. The *Maître* is a father and thus he is also the law, the doctrine. Granoff tells the following story:

> I will never forget an evening at Françoise Dolto's home shortly after the schism of 1953, the year of the explosion at the Paris Psychoanalytic Society. Françoise Dolto, Blanche Reverchon-Jouve, who has since died, Lagache, Lacan, Perrier, and myself had gotten together. And Lacan, while chewing on a slice of ham said to us: "It seems that I was their [the Paris Psychoanalytic Society's] doctrine. And that when I left them really I dealt them a low blow. Now, you all better watch me carefully so that I don't do the same thing to you."[17]

Indeed, Granoff believes that psychoanalytic history does repeat itself and has been repeating itself since Freud. Dependence on the *Maître*, conflict with the *Maître*, followed by a preoccupation with the *Maître*, are the themes that organize that history. In his own case, Granoff, who admits being a principal instrument for Lacan's excommunication, did not speak about the 1963 schism and his role in it for ten years, a silence which meant that he was unable to express himself about the theoretical issues with which he was most deeply concerned.[18] Finally, when Granoff did present his own seminar, it focused on the politics of the psychoanalytic family. The accent was on the relationship to psychoanalytic parents, what it meant to leave or stay with Lacan, to leave or stay with Freud, to follow a master or abandon him.

What can be said about this preoccupation with the excluded father when it operates in the analytic institution?

In June 1973, *Le Coq Héron*, a small, independent journal of psychoanalytic reflection, held a meeting on "the schisms." The participants ranged from young analysts who did not even have a clear idea about why the Fourth Group had been formed, to men and women who might have been their analysts'

analysts and who had done battle in over two generations of psychoanalytic politics: Dolto, Clavreul, Granoff. In the midst of a heated discussion of whether each of the schisms was over-determined by analytic issues or whether the actions of individuals were decisive in determining the outcomes, someone remarked that "the schisms have always been good for those who stayed with Lacan and have always been bad for those who left him." Even with an audience that included members of three analytic groups that were placed in the "losing" camp by this comment, there was not one objection.

It is not only the French Psychoanalytic Association, but other products of anti-Lacan splits which have had difficulty finding an identity that is more than an assertion of what they are not, a problem that certainly plagued the dissidents who broke off from Freud. For example, the Fourth Group spends much of its theoretical energies arguing against Lacanian positions, and for ten years after its break with Lacan, the Paris Society handled its hostility by pretending that Lacan did not exist. Certain analysts at the Paris Society even went so far as to forbid their candidates from attending Lacan's seminar. After the second schism, though, things loosened up; the Paris Society seemed to be freed from its role as "official" center of resistance to Lacanianism. Further away than all the rest from its break with Lacan, it is more open to constructive dialogue with his ideas, and it was able to pass its former role on to the Association and the Fourth Group, where the wounds are fresher.

What seems to weaken the vitality of those who leave Lacan is not that he is gone but that he continues to be present in a way that is preoccupying but not easy to talk about. Indeed, the anti-Lacanian groups almost seem to be constituted by the taboo on Lacan's presence, or as one analyst put it, "Almost by the requirement that his name not be spoken." Lacan might say that in such groups he is "foreclosed," his term for a brutal and total repression.[19] If the schisms seem to be bad for those who have left Lacan perhaps this is because they have given themselves a larger problem than Lacan's presence could ever have imposed. They come together by an agreement *not* to discuss something, and as one Association member put it, "This unsymbolized residue can poison the group."

The unsymbolized is at the root of neurosis. In the case of an hysteric, it can paralyze, but psychoanalysis can cure by bringing it to awareness and symbolization. There is an effort today among French psychoanalysts to confront publicly what has in the past been considered unspeakable. After ten years of silence, Wladimir Granoff gives a seminar in which he recounts his part in political machinations when Lacan was excluded in 1963 and what that has meant to him as an analyst. A veteran of three schisms, François Perrier gives a talk on the "Didacticized Psychoanalyst" and speaks of the personal costs of psychoanalytic politics. For over a half a century, psychoanalysts have spoken about the need for political neutrality, but perhaps they have defended themselves against facing the damage done by their own internal politics by externalizing the problem. Psychoanalytic politics seems to be more capable of compromising analysis than participation in a political party ever could be.

So far, the focus has been on the story of tensions between psychoanalytic institutions and psychoanalytic theory; there is however, another story to be told. This is the story of psychoanalytic politics and personal pain. French analysts are fascinated by the story of Victor Tausk and his relationship with Freud. Freud seems to have found contact with Tausk's brilliance painful. He refused to see him as a patient and referred him to Helene Deutsch, whom he had in analysis at that time.

However, Deutsch became so involved with Tausk that she began to speak more and more of him in her own analysis. Freud was hearing more about Tausk than he could stand and told Deutsch that she had to choose between continuing her analysis with him and continuing to see Tausk as a patient. Deutsch chose to continue her analysis with Freud and dismissed Tausk. Tausk committed suicide shortly thereafter. The translation of Paul Roazen's 1969 book on Tausk's suicide was devoured in Parisian analytic circles, as was Kurt Eissler's rebuttal to Roazen, commissioned by the American psychoanalytic establishment.[20] In interview after interview, I heard echoes of the Tausk story. ("Was Freud so taken up with psychoanalysis that he couldn't see that in giving Deutsch an either/or choice he was himself not acting as a psychoanalyst?" "Were the analysts around Tausk so involved with the cause and with Freud that they did not see that Tausk was being driven to suicide?") Sometimes the Tausk story seemed to be used as a reproach to Lacan, who, like Freud, was suspected of not being able to tolerate students of independence and spirit. More often it introduced a statement about the human cost of psychoanalytic politics:

> It was horrible to be in the middle of an analysis with Lacan . . . loving him and hoping he loved me . . . and hear all around me how Lacan loves that one as a son. . . . I wonder if he loves me as much . . . how he drove that one to suicide. . . . I wonder if I am capable of killing myself . . . how he invited that one to work on his texts with him. . . . Perhaps I am not intelligent enough . . . how he turns on people if they express their anger. . . . My God, is it possible that he will abandon me in the middle of all this. . . . And then, there was the split.

The pain of psychoanalytic schism was not all on the side of the patients. Lifelong friendships between analysts were destroyed, and many suffered great personal loss as students with whom they had worked for over a decade vowed never to speak to them again.

French analysts often find it painful to talk about their pasts, and it has been hard for them to talk to each other across it. But a new generation of French psychoanalysts has come of age in the years since the last schism, and it has little tolerance for life in the shadows of psychoanalytic history. Still, the protagonists of that history—its heroes and its villains—are their analytic fathers, mothers, grandparents. Although the events seem far away and motivated by unfamiliar passions and people, French analysts cannot make them foreign to themselves because no matter who they are, where they come from, and to which group they belong, they are born of these events. Myths of origin are not easily erased in any society, and in the case of psychoanalysis, where each analyst relates back through his or her analyst to a chain of analysts before, metaphors of birth, ancestry, and filiation are particularly powerful. The new analytic generation in France is not denying its past, but it is not letting the past poison the present by leaving it unspoken: there is a growing spirit of communication across schools and generations. Since 1974, a new context for such dialogue has been created. It is called "Confrontations." Each month, one analyst speaks to the group, usually on themes raised by a book that he or she has written. Discussion ensues. The formula seems simple enough, but on the French analytic scene, where encounters between analysts can carry a high ideological and emotional charge, the apparent simplicity is deceptive. Confrontations was organized by several analysts at the Paris Institute, but it has no affiliation with any psychoanalytic society. Indeed, Confrontations presents itself as being in the position of a "third party" to the tensions between analyst and psychoanalytic institution, a *"rendez-vous en un lieu*

hors-lieu," a meeting place that is outside of the space that analytic societies have traditionally occupied.

Participants in Confrontations have included Jean Laplanche
and Wladimir Granoff of the Association, Christian David and
René Major of the Institute, Michèle Montrelay, Serge Leclaire
and Moustapha Safouan of the Freudian School, and François
Perrier and Nathalie Zaltzman of the Fourth Group. Membership in Confrontations has mushroomed. Many hundreds
of analysts attend each meeting, and some claim that there,
for the first time, they are speaking to other analysts in their
"own" voice rather than through a position they feel constrained to take because it is the trademark of "their society."

Confrontations undoubtedly gets much of its élan from
energies frustrated and unspent at the Freudian School. The
story of the pass revealed the beginnings of a serious sense of
frustration at the School because Lacan seemed more interested in psychoanalytic theory than in clinical practice. A
substantial group of analysts at the School began to think of
themselves as "mere practitioners" who were of little concern
to the *Maître.* In the same spirit, Lacan's growing involvement
with developing mathematical formalizations ("mathemes")
of psychoanalytic theory, has increased the frustration of the
practitioners. Lacan has also moved toward more intensive
collaboration with non-analysts, particularly with a circle
of philosophers and mathematicians around his son-in-law,
Jacques-Alain Miller. As we shall see in chapter 7, Lacan has
become increasingly interested in the transmission of psychoanalytic knowledge in the university. In reaction, many
Lacanians gravitate toward Confrontations, which seems to be
filling needs that the Freudian School is not attending to. One
young analyst, who considers himself Lacanian but who has
made his intellectual home in the Fourth Group and Confrontations, made it clear that in Lacan's *Ecrits,* he continues to

find sources of personal renewal and greater clarity about his direction as an analyst, but that the newer, and more mathematical theory, "does not relate to what Lacan has taught me are my concerns as an analyst: death, sex, desire, the way I feel language in my body. . . ."

Confrontations is trying to do what the Freudian School once tried to do, that is, to circumvent what seems to be an inevitable contradiction between psychoanalysis and the psychoanalytic institution. Like the Freudian School, Confrontations is trying to create an institution that is not an institution; unlike the Freudian School, it is doing so by refusing any responsibility for training analysts. So, Confrontations refuses to be a psychoanalytic society as Freud defined it. If the French have ended up at this extreme in order to maintain a sufficient number of degrees of freedom in the psychoanalytic institution, it may be because the Lacanian presence has redramatized the problem of master and disciple that tore apart Freud's circle and that reflects fundamental contradiction in the psychoanalytic institution.

Beginning with Freud, the unique father, psychoanalysis has been passed down directly from analyst to analysand. Every analyst alive today is Freud's descendant. The transmission of psychoanalysis poses great threats to psychoanalysis if the means of transmission lead to the reinforcement rather than the dissolution of the transference. Yet this is just what Freud's role as *Maître* may encourage. Each analyst's debt to Freud would be great if all that was owed was a method of professional practice. But there is much more at stake. The training of an analyst is also the personal analysis of his or her neurotic conflicts, a way out of suffering and pain. Thus, the method of the transmission of the professional technique is both the method of the "cure" and the method of theory building in the science.

The Lacanian presence underscores the tension that exists between Freud and every major psychoanalytic theorist who has come after him. The transference to Freud as a father is overdetermined. Psychoanalysis is so deeply steeped in the mythology of paternity that a requirement for the development of psychoanalytic science carries the echo of ritual murder. Disputes among psychoanalysts challenging Freud's ideas are far more highly charged than disputes within other scientific disciplines. Loyalty to a father is always at stake. The progress of the field is confused by these complex Oedipal issues. Even Lacan, who certainly disagrees with Freud on many points, claims legitimacy comes only from his "return to Freud." Trapped between the problem of the *Maître* and the problem of going beyond the *Maître*, psychoanalysis faces enduring paradoxes.

French psychoanalysis is in the process of breaking down the barriers that have separated psychoanalysis from its own history and from the fact that much of that history is political. This process has not occurred in a vacuum. The French Freud is also struggling to break boundaries between psychoanalysis and politics and between psychoanalysis and science. Two major sites of these struggles are the antipsychiatric movement (based in clinics throughout France) and the universities. In both the world of mental health politics and in the world of the university, the positions of the different French psychoanalytic societies on psychoanalytic theory, technique, and transmissibility have been played out on a larger social stage. The conflicts over psychoanalytic ideology turn out to have larger political implications, as psychoanalytic politics is played out as a politics of psychoanalysis.

III Psychoanalysis in Politics

6 Psychoanalysis as Schizoanalysis:
Antipsychiatry

The actual translation of psychoanalytic ideas into social actions other than the psychoanalytic act itself has taken place in many arenas, but perhaps nowhere as directly as in the area of mental health.[1] It is here that many people have found it possible to pursue both their interest in social action and their new, growing concern with language and psychoanalysis, a legacy of 1968 and its "cult of speech." Some of the political struggles of May, in particular the opposition between the Communist Party and the non-Party Left, continue to be expressed in the politics of mental health, even a decade after the events themselves. Thus mental health is a field where conflicts already discussed in the realm of ideas are played out on everyday ground. Conflicts between Communists and *gauchistes*, between traditional "medical" psychiatry and Lacanian psychoanalysis, between Lacanian "utopians" who seek a return to the imaginary and other Lacanians for whom this is an irresponsible and psychotic politics, are all a part of this chapter's story.

In the context of the politics of mental health, a contradiction that has plagued psychoanalysis since its beginnings—the contradiction between psychoanalytic theory and therapeutic

practice—becomes a central concern. Freud himself recognized
this tension and insisted that only psychoanalytic theory could
go beyond the tendency of all therapy to respond to the social
pressure to make people's lives "a little bit better," or as Freud
put it, to transform "misery into common unhappiness."[2] In
Freud's view, "the recognition of our therapeutic limitations
reinforces our determination to change other social factors so
that men and women shall no longer be forced into hopeless
situations."[3]

The tension between revolutionary theory and reformist
politics is not unique to psychoanalysis. It has been faced by
other movements as well. Among Marxists, for example, the
epithets of "opportunist" and "sectarian" have been used to
refer to "errors" in the degree of compromise with the establishment, the first term referring to too much compromise,
the second, to not enough. In fact, the term *gauchiste*, which
in common French parlance has come to mean people on
the non-Communist Left, was originally a Communist Party
term of opprobrium for too little compromise with the realities of governing. It derives from Lenin's attack on German
revolutionaries for their failure to involve themselves in parliamentary and trade union struggles for fear of loss of revolutionary purity. Lenin entitled his polemic against their
policy, *Left-Wing Communism: An Infantile Disorder*, which is
translated into French as "Le Gauchisme: Maladie Infantile du
Communisme."

We recall that during May, it was the non-Party, *gauchiste*
political style that dominated events. This political style, much
to the disapproval of the conservative, establishment Communist Party, fought hierarchy and put forth self-expression
as a significant political statement. This approach, buttressed
by Lacanian ideas about the destructive impact of hierarchy

on truth-seeking processes and existential Marxist ideas about local control and self-management, was easily exportable into the area of mental health. There have been efforts to organize former mental patients into action committees to fight against psychiatric repression, and efforts to organize patients, mental health workers, and community members to gain control of mental health facilities under slogans of self-management.

The challenge to the medical hierarchy within health facilities is seen as a stepping stone to a global challenge to therapeutic institutions which locate social problems in the individual. In particular, critics of the medical hierarchy object to the notion that a mental health service has "knowledge" to dispense to the individual in order to effect a "cure." Since the individual's suffering is largely a reflection of social injustice, "cures" call for social action. It is on this issue that radical political actions begin to pick up the themes of radical psychoanalytic ideology. Lacan's criticism of the medical model in psychoanalysis gets played out as a challenge to therapeutic *replatrâge*, "plastering over" social problems as psychiatric ones.

In France, there is a tradition of harsh criticism of the asylum system by liberals and the Left, and in the aftermath of the 1968 events, an alternative model of community mental health (previously developed by a group of medically oriented psychoanalysts in Paris's thirteenth *arrondissement* and characterized as "psychoanalysis minus the couch") became national health policy.[4] The asylums were being emptied and psychiatry moved out into the community. Through the community programs, psychoanalysts could now be central to the psychiatric establishment, but some analysts tried to use this new arena as a stage from which to intensify their critique of its repression. The community mental health model had long been supported by the Left, but by the mid-1960s many felt that the new model could be as dangerous as the traditional asylum: it gave psychiatry its biggest chance ever to invade the school, the workplace, and the private life of the individual. School psychologists can legitimate the tracking of working-class children out of the academic system, and psychiatrists in the factory can label political activists as "maladjusted" and help to get them fired. Since the victims of institutional psychiatry are often poor and ill-equipped to protect themselves, it is they who may be in danger from the society rather than the other way around: when a community mental health center turns people into patients, the transformation can mean a net loss of rights. When patients, often frightened and unsure, make an effort to fight back, their efforts can be classified by the medical profession as "resistance to treatment." Political militants who work in the politics of health point out that this endless, circular return to "illness" as explanation for dissatisfactions increases the powerlessness of the working-class patient-subject in capitalist society; "neutral" medical ideology turns out not to be politically neutral after all.

The problems raised by the community centers gave radicals strong issues around which to organize. And since the Communist Party supported the centers and their medical orientation, it was also a new focus for conflict between the Communist and non-Communist Left. But theirs are not the only old quarrels to find their way into the new arena. Internal divisions among psychoanalysts also have been projected onto antipsychiatric politics. For example, while some community treatment centers had come under traditional psychoanalytic tutelage and had a medical orientation, others had come under the control of Lacanians, who used them as bases for a distinctly nonmedical and antihierarchical psychoanalytic practice. Thus the state health system was divided into psychoanalytic units with radically different kinds of functioning and radically different "schools" of analysts. The Lacanians were obviously in a good position to make political alliances on the non-Party Left. And if much of the conflict between *gauchistes* and Communists in the politics of mental health seems like old wine in new bottles, this is partly because Lacanian psychoanalysis was in such an excellent position to carry old political quarrels onto the new psychiatric stage. Lacanians were also well placed to make psychiatry's political struggles more salient to the French Left as a whole. And indeed, the radicals against psychiatry who work in the context of community mental health are only a small part of a large, highly ideological movement in France which can properly be called "antipsychiatric" and which makes up a whole world of its own. The world of French antipsychiatry ranges from working-class nurses organizing in provincial psychiatric hospitals to Parisian intellectuals primarily interested in Lacanian theory. It is radical—often Marxist—in its orientation. And chiefly because of Lacan's centrality, it sees itself as psychoanalytic. In all these regards, it is very different from its Anglo-Saxon counterpart.

While some French antipsychiatric activity is theorized in fairly straightforward notions about psychiatry interfering with civil liberties or about medical "neutrality" being used to mask political repression, other activity is cast in terms of more complex and often extravagant theorizations that use the schizophrenic's situation as a take off point for more global social criticism. These theorizations develop the structure for a politics of schizophrenia whose implications reach far beyond the psychiatric institution. Since 1968, Lacan's discourse on the constitution of the subject, the antipsychiatric discourse on the politics of madness, and the Marxist discourse on the crisis of the subject in contemporary capitalism have become interwoven. What follows is an effort to pull apart these separate strands—the dominant themes—of the new French antipsychiatric movement.

A first theme, one already touched on, centers around Jacques Lacan's impact on antipsychiatry. Lacan has expressed views that go far toward supporting antipsychiatric positions, for example, his oft-cited statement in the *Ecrits* that "man's being cannot be understood without reference to madness, nor would he be man without carrying madness within as the limit of his freedom."[5] Psychiatric theory is traditionally based on a pejorative concept of madness in which madness is perceived as a deficit, a *lack* of rationality, a state of being *less* than what one could be. In Lacan's work, we find the echo and indeed the amplification of those elements in Freud which were most subversive of such traditional psychiatric notions. Lacan's maxim of a "return to Freud" tries to purge all normative, psychiatric values out of psychoanalysis. For Lacan, the goal of psychoanalysis is the bringing to awareness of underlying contradictions (what Lacan calls "the truth of the subject"), which can never be confused with the acceptance of social norms.

A second theme is the rejection of the intellectual and social status quo through use of a "subversive discourse," which echoes the Rousseauian characterization of language as anti-Edenic, and the struggle in May 1968 to "reinvent language." The antipsychiatrists place themselves in a relationship of potential identification with the mad insofar as they claim to have a message that cannot be communicated in ordinary ways. Like the schizophrenic, they have to destroy ordinary language in order to communicate. Some, like Lacan himself, work in a highly controlled intellectual structure and express this identification with the psychotic in a highly theoretical way; others, more involved in political situations where they are treated as deviant and dangerous, have developed a theory of their own situations that likens them to the situation of the schizophrenic.

A third theme is the emergence of theories, many inspired by Lacan, that are explicitly antipsychiatric and political. Here, we shall look at "schizoanalysis," a theory elaborated by Gilles Deleuze and Félix Guattari in their book, *Anti-Oedipus: Capitalism and Schizophrenia*, which was discussed briefly in chapter 3.[6] Their book, like most current French antipsychiatric thinking, builds on the base of Jacques Lacan's contribution, in particular his radical critique of theories of the ego. In the case of antipsychiatry, Lacan's support comes most directly from the way in which he demolishes the notion that there is a "normal" self that is autonomous, coherent, its own "center."

We have seen that for Lacan the origins of the self are imaginary in a quite literal sense. The baby confuses others with its own mirror reflections, and since the self is formed from a composite of introjections based on such misrecognitions, it can hardly constitute a unified personality, even for "normal" people. According to Lacan, we all experience a profoundly "divided self." In questioning the integrity of the "I," Lacan challenges assumptions that are solidly built into "ordinary" thought and "ordinary" language. In fact, it almost is impossible to express such a radically "anti-ego" theory in ordinary language: the language's pronoun structure reflects our culturally embedded notions about subjectivity. From the moment that we begin to write or speak, we are trapped in formulations such as "I want," "I do," "I desire." Lacan's reading of psychoanalysis is subversive in the way it undermines the formulations of the self that are implicit in our language, and it puts each speaking subject in an intimate relationship with the fragmented self experienced by the schizophrenic. Thus the notion of the decentered subject is a crucial link between Lacan and the antipsychiatric movement, which refuses to view madness as something completely alien to "normals."

Lacan's support for antipsychiatry comes from the *form* of his writing as well as from its content. His associative, poetic style is intended not only to shock or to force a closer reading by slowing his reader down (although he does intend these) but also, more important, to challenge commonsense notions of the "self."

Our everyday language reinforces our "commonsense" understanding of our experiences as subjects, so theories of the mind which are directed toward subverting our usual way of thinking about ourselves have adopted strategies to fight the normalization that everyday language imposes. A first possible strategy has been to make mathematical models that are acceptable ways of "setting up one's own language." Any reader who has even glanced through the *Ecrits* will surely know that Lacan's work is studded with such "formalization." He uses symbols, signs, charts, and diagrams to express himself without referring to ordinary language. And by the 1970s, Lacan tended toward a greater emphasis on mathematical models of psychoanalytic theory and new topological symbolizations such as knots.

A second strategy has been to use ordinary language in a highly unconventional way. Lacan relies heavily on punning and word games. He also coins words that have no definitions other than his own and then tends to define them only contextually. Even when Lacan borrows what might superficially seem to be standard technical terms from other disciplines, he often uses them in ways in which their normal definitions are not applicable.[7]

A third strategy involves the invention of a new level of discourse. Using a new kind of discourse to break the reader's usual "set" is not an uncommon strategy for subversive intellectual movements of the twentieth century. It characterizes the work of Wittgenstein, Joyce, and the surrealists, as well as that of Lacan. In each of these cases, the text is not there simply to transmit content or to convince you of an argument, it is there *to do something* to the reader. The text serves to help the reader reject standard notions about the nature of knowing. Wittgenstein takes up this idea in *The Tractatus*, when he compares his work to a ladder that is to be discarded after the reader has used it to reach a new level of understanding.[8] Similarly, when Lacan gave his seminar in Paris, he claimed to be putting himself in the place of the analysand and his audience in the role of his analyst. His spoken "texts" and his written statements were designed to provoke the listener or the reader into a self-analytic experience. The *Ecrits* are not meant to be read; they are meant to be lived with. These three strategies—inventing a new language, unconventional usage, a therapeutic discourse—are all part of Lacan's psychoanalytic subversion and have powerfully influenced the new French school of antipsychiatric exposition.

When Gilles Deleuze and Félix Guattari wrote *Anti-Oedipus*, they, like Lacan, were trying to make their text a "therapeutic" instrument. We cannot know if the book's readers were changed by their experience, but there is good reason to think that they were provoked. The book became a *cause célèbre* in Paris in 1972–73.

Let us look at what confronts the reader when he opens to the first page of *Anti-Oedipus*:

CHAPTER 1. THE DESIRING-MACHINES

It is at work everywhere, functioning smoothly at times, at other times in fits and starts. It breathes, it heats, it eats. It shits and fucks. What a mistake to have ever said the *id*. Everywhere *it* is machines—real ones, not figurative ones: machines driving other machines, machines being driven by other machines, with all the necessary couplings and connections. An organ-machine is plugged into an energy-source machine: the one produces a flow that the other interrupts. The breast is a machine that produces milk, and the mouth a machine coupled to it. The mouth of the anorexic wavers between several functions: its possessor is uncertain as to whether it is an eating-machine, an anal machine, a talking machine, or a breathing-machine (asthma attacks). Hence we are all handymen: each with his little machines. For every organ-machine, an energy-machine: all the time, flows and interruptions.[9]

This discourse assaults, its language breaks language apart, fragments all person markers and tries to transform the reader's way of thinking about his or her personhood. Its power seems to depend more on involvement with its language than on agreement with its individual propositions. Deleuze and Guattari present us with an image of a world where complexity and fluidity seem to defy language and its structure.

Deleuze and Guattari take Lacan's ideas about the decentered subject and carry them several steps further than he does. Although Lacan believes that the self is constituted by imaginary misrecognitions and rupture, he still works to diagram and even mathematically express the relationship among its elements. But Deleuze and Guattari describe a self of such flux and fragmentation that a methodology of trying to grasp discrete relationships between determinate objects is clearly missing the point. For them, the self is a collection of machine-parts, what they refer to as "desiring-machines": "The desiring-machines pound away and throb in the depths of the unconscious: Irma's injection, the Wolf Man's tick-tock, Ann's coughing machine, and also all the explanatory apparatuses set into motion by Freud, all those neuro-biologico-desiring machines."[10] Each person's machine parts can plug and unplug with the machine parts of another: there is no self, only the cacophony of desiring-machines. In human relationships, one whole person never relates to another whole person because there is no such thing as the "whole person." There are only connections between the desiring machines. Fragmentation is a universal of the human condition, not something specific to the schizophrenic.

But psychoanalytic notions of the Oedipus complex seem to demand that one think in terms of one-to-one relationships. Indeed, Deleuze and Guattari think that it is with Oedipus that psychoanalysis went wrong:

> Psychoanalysis is like the Russian revolution; we don't know when it started going bad. We have to keep going back further. To the Americans? To the First International? To the secret Committee? To the first ruptures, which signify renunciations by Freud as much as betrayals by those who break with him. To Freud himself, from the moment of the "discovery" of Oedipus? *Oedipus is the idealist turning point.*[11]

Freud's position on who are the actors involved in the Oedipal drama seems fairly clear: it is played out in a triangle of child, mother, and father and results in the internalization of a parental superego. For Lacan, Oedipus is not about a moment in the family drama or about forming a new psychic entity. It is about the child's development of a new capacity for using symbols as signifiers; it is about entering the symbolic dimension, with its new relationships to language and the world. The dynamics of the Oedipal drama are not played out by people as such; the meaning and import of the drama are to be discovered in the linguistic functions for which the people stand as signifiers. For Lacan, passage into the symbolic dimension requires that certain structural conditions be met that are associated with the formal properties of the Oedipal drama. Most important, there is triangulation. But the Deleuze and Guattari model of the unconscious as infinitely open and infinitely fragmented rejects any notion of Oedipal triangulations, whether the elements being triangulated are literal, biological parents or Lacan's more abstract symbolic elements.

Deleuze and Guattari advance a "politics of schizophrenia." They regard schizophrenia as a privileged experience and believe that the schizophrenic, in the grip of this experience, is in touch with fundamental truths about society. The schizophrenic is in a position to teach us about our political reality. R. D. Laing has written of the mad as the sane in an insane world, but his work emphasizes the schizophrenic experience as spiritually privileged. Deleuze and Guattari focus on other aspects.

For them, the first way in which the schizophrenic is privileged is epistemologically. The schizophrenic has not entered the symbolic dimension: he has not accepted the epistemology of signifier to signified. In Lacan's terms, the schizophrenic has refused to Oedipize. Deleuze and Guattari point out that by virtue of this refusal he remains close to the primitive truth of the desiring-machines, not trapped within the Oedipal prison in which the complexity and fluidity of the unconscious are distorted, frozen, and flattened.[12]

Deleuze and Guattari also present the schizophrenic as privileged politically because, essentially, capitalism cannot tolerate the multitude of possible relationships that can exist among the desiring-machines. The schizophrenic is in touch with a level of desire whose nature is irreducibly subversive:

"Despite what some revolutionaries think about this, desire is revolutionary in its essence . . . and no society can tolerate a position of real desire without its structures of exploitation, servitude and hierarchy being compromised."[13]

Society cannot tolerate the free circulation of this revolutionary desire. It imposes clear limits on it, constraining the relationships among the desiring-machines, enforcing order where there is only flux. Society constructs the family as "the agent of this psychic repression."[14] The repression must be massive because the danger is absolute:

> If desire is repressed, it is because every position of desire, no matter how small, is capable of calling into question the established order of a society: not that desire is asocial, on the contrary. But it is explosive; there is no desiring-machine capable of being assembled without demolishing entire social sectors.[15]

The danger is absolute and it is also increasing. Deleuze and Guattari argue that the more complex a society becomes, the more disordered, "decoded" it becomes. Its structures of Oedipization are increasingly strained and threaten to crack. The absence of Oedipization is schizophrenia, the ultimate form of decoding. Thus they argue that capitalism is threatened by widespread social schizophrenia and must respond by repression. Capitalism tries to replicate within itself more ordered and coded forms of social organization.[16] It does this where it can, for example, in the family, where the father can take the role of a residual despot. It does this in its increasingly narrow notion of appropriate behavior. The family, the privatized individual, the psychoanalytic subject within the Oedipal unit, all of these are capitalism's constructs to constrain desire and mask social disorder. The schizophrenic is in a special political situation because he or she stands outside all of these.

It is clear that, according to this analysis, we must look beyond psychoanalysis to understand desire in the social field because psychoanalysis is tied to the notion of Oedipus, and Oedipus is tied to the capitalist family, to the powers which hide social disorder and the boundaryless nature of desire. You cannot understand something by using concepts that contribute to its camouflage. The essence of desire is that it refuses representation, and that is what Deleuze and Guattari believe the psychoanalytic process is all about:

> Free association, rather than opening onto polyvocal connections, confines itself to a univocal impasse. All the chains of the unconscious are biunivocalized, linearized, suspended from a despotic signifier. The whole of desiring-*production* is crushed, subjected to the requirements of *representation*, and to the dreary games of what is representative and represented in representation.[17]

Psychoanalysis can certainly show us a part of ourselves, but only the part that exists within the "Daddy-Mommy-Me" matrix. But there is much more. All desire is not produced in the closed family system. Desire also is produced in the social field, part of a historical-political situation. This is what psychoanalysis misses out on, and Deleuze and Guattari suggest something new: schizoanalysis.

Schizoanalysis is not accidentally so-called. "Schizo" means that it is a process of decoding and analysis rather than an attempt to create a new order or synthesis. "Schizo" means that it resembles the way in which a schizophrenic is able to experience. Its goal is to analyze how the social field is invested with unconscious desire, something that schizophrenics are presumably in touch with since their vision has not been narrowed by the demands of Oedipization. Deleuze and Guattari also liken schizoanalysis to curing rituals in primitive societies, where healing involves a political, social, and economic analysis of the community and its neighbors and does not impose Oedipal solutions by reducing every new situation to the framework of "Daddy-Mommy-Me." Indeed, they describe such cures as "schizoanalysis in action."[18] Schizoanalysis and primitive curing analyze desire in the social field, whereas psychoanalysis, by insisting that desire exists only in the person, reduces much social conflict to the level of the individual.

Schizoanalysis presents an aspect of schizophrenic functioning as a way to explore the true nature of our society's contradictions and at the same time it suggests that our society's contradictions are part of the genesis of schizophrenia. Deleuze and Guattari argue that schizoanalysis is in this sense unlike other antipsychiatric theories that have remained trapped in the notion of Oedipus and see the origin of schizophrenia as within the family. They charge Gregory Bateson with being "American familialist" because Bateson claimed to have found schizophrenia-producing *social* mechanisms at the same time that his social analysis never went beyond the family.[19] R. D. Laing comes under even sharper fire for similar reasons:

> This contradiction is perhaps especially perceptible in Laing, because he is the most revolutionary of the antipsychiatrists. At the very moment he breaks with psychiatric practice, undertakes assigning a veritable social genesis to psychosis, and calls for a continuation of the "voyage" as a process and for a dissolution of the "normal ego," he falls back into the worst familialist, personological, and egoic postulates, so that the remedies invoked are no more than a "sincere corroboration among parents," a "recognition of the real persons," a "discovery of the true ego or self" as in Martin Buber. Even more than the hostility of the traditional authorities, perhaps this is the source of the actual failures of the antipsychiatric undertakings, of their co-option for the benefit of adaptational forms of familial psychotherapy and of community psychiatry, and of Laing's own retreat to the Orient.[20]

So even the antipsychiatrists are bogged down in bring-ing everything back to the Oedipal Holy Family. Deleuze and Guattari see their job as getting antipsychiatry unstuck and politicized. They present the schizophrenic as someone whose language is particularly transparent to the real connections between the language of the unconscious and the language of race, class, police repression, student revolt, rape, and war, that is to say, the language of politics. Schizophrenics do not have successful Oedipization to wall them off from the con-nections between self and society. These same connections are present in each of us, but most people never see them. Oedip-ization builds a wall in front of them, which psychotherapies that remain in the Oedipal framework only serve to reinforce. Schizoanalysis is a way for each of us to uncover these connec-tions by rejecting the false coherency of the "whole self." The point of all this is not to go crazy, but to schizophrenize, that is, to become aware of fragmentation, disorder, and the fact that there is no boundary between the politics of desire being played out in the self and that which is continuously being played out in society.

Deleuze and Guattari describe schizophrenization as a voy-age, and of course, the metaphor suggests the language of Laing. But we have seen that this is where the resemblance ends. For Laing, the schizophrenic's voyage resembles a long acid trip. Laing's politics of schizophrenia is a politics of expe-rience. For Deleuze and Guattari, by contrast, schizophrenics' special position derives from their escape from the epistemic constraints of the symbolic and the structurally similar politi-cal constraints of capitalism. The schizophrenic voyage is political and epistemological rather than moral and aesthetic, as for Laing. Willingly or not, and whether or not it makes them "happy," schizophrenics have refused the usual manner in which capitalism stamps and controls our psyches.

Deleuze and Guattari say that they meant their book to finally close the old "Freud-Marx" debate by arguing that studying the psyche and studying the social field are not activities that can meaningfully be separated. In practice, however, *Anti-Oedipus* sparked new interest in the Freud-Marx question. Many saw schizoanalysis as a political complement to psychoanalysis. Others, like sociologist Robert Castel, saw it as a work that laid a theoretical basis for opposition to what he sees as a growing Left-Lacanian-antipsychiatric "establishment," despite its appreciation by that same "establishment."[21] In his book, *Le Psychanalysme*, Castel attacks the way in which psychoanalysis is now taken as "definitionally" subversive by the French Left. He complains that although psychiatry has become the focus of strenuous critical activity by the Left, psychoanalysis and particularly Lacanian psychoanalysis is usually deemed irreproachable. The role of psychiatry in repression and social control is taken as self-evident, but when psychoanalysis seems to be guilty of the same sins, the assumption is that it has been compromised by outside forces.

Castel argues that psychoanalysis is not so guiltless as all that: it is not simply co-opted (*récuperé*) by others; it itself does quite a bit of recuperating. Like historian Michel Foucault, Castel points out that psychoanalysis has inherited the asylum's role of social control and does the job well, more subtly than other, more obviously repressive psychiatric techniques.[22] For example, in challenging the standard medical division between normal and diseased states it establishes a continuum model for thinking about pathology: we all suffer from the same processes; some of us simply handle them better than

others. The continuum model makes it possible to describe
a whole spectrum of behaviors as prepathological, including
behaviors that a given society at a given time finds bizarre,
immoral, or politically inconvenient. Thus, Castel argues,
psychoanalysis carries within itself the germs of its use as an
agent of social control. So when we discover psychoanalysis
being used in this way, we should not be surprised. But what
is shocking from Castel's point of view is that the Left seems
too taken up by Lacanian mythologies even to look around.

Castel is particularly offended by the way in which the
uncritical infatuation with psychoanalysis extends to antipsychiatric circles. For example, Castel points out that in a special
1970 edition of *L'Idiot Internationale*, a radical "antipsychiatric" newspaper, "psychiatry is executed without concession
but the references to psychoanalysis are always reverential."[23]
And to add insult to injury, the closing pages of this same
edition place even the Chinese Cultural Revolution under
Freud's patronage: "The history of man is the history of his
repression."

As Castel rightly points out, in the Parisian intellectual context much of antipsychiatry is really intellectual and social play.
The sense of antipsychiatry as play is reinforced by the roman-
ticism of much of the French antipsychiatric movement. For
example, the group around the Clinique de la Borde at Cour-
Cheverny (which has included Guattari and the Lacanian-
influenced antipsychiatrists, Jean Oury and Jean-Claude Polack)
publishes a magazine, *Cahiers pour la folie*, that features literature and visual art by mental patients. Many people are critical
of the *Cahiers*, and describe it as "smug," "self-congratulatory,"
"dishonest," and an "adventure in surrealism."

Many psychiatrists, analysts, and mental health workers reproached the *Cahiers* for denying mental patients their

"rightful feelings of sadness" by portraying their experiences as consistently poetic. One nurse in a psychiatric hospital outside of Paris criticized the approach: "It is no help to patients to present them with images of themselves in which there can be no self-recognition." Others objected that the *Cahiers* presented a glamorized image of what life is like at an "antipsychiatric" hospital such as the Clinique de la Borde. Although the showpiece of French antipsychiatry in terms of its staff, ideology, spirit, and sense of experimentation, la Borde, like other mental hospitals, relies heavily on medication and electroshock treatments in its daily activities. Critics object not just to the use of electroshock, but to the way in which antipsychiatrists seem to have invented new theoretical justifications for old methods: "When you ask them about electroshock they talk about regression at the moment of coming to. . . . This is self-serving nonsense." Reflecting on the *Cahiers*, one psychiatrist said:

> I know that it passes for humanism, but I find it dehumanizing. I know how psychotics are, I worked, lived among them. They are sad, isolated, resigned, overwhelmed by boredom . . . for one Artaud, how many patients stay in the hospital for all of their lives and never get up out of a chair? For each Gramsci who writes letters from prison, how many prisoners are completely brutalized, crushed, who think of nothing but the rhythm of the day, the rhythm of meals—because that is what it means to be confined: breakfast is over at ten in the morning and the women stay behind, seated around a table, not talking to each other, waiting for lunch at noon.

The May days romanticized playfulness, spontaneity, and fantasy in politics. The spirit of play in the French antipsychiatric movement may be seen as a part of the May legacy. For example, in 1973 a meeting was held at Gourgas to facilitate an encounter between political and psychiatric "militants," but it had less the quality of a meeting than of an antipsychiatric "Woodstock," where the heroes were not rock stars but the stars of the antipsychiatric establishment: Lacan, Guattari, Oury, Polack, Gentis. Gourgas buzzed with rumors about who might or might not be showing up.

At Gourgas, the festival atmosphere seemed to inhibit rather than to facilitate discussion. Participants became bitter when they realized that organizing the sessions meant a lot of work, and there seemed to be an implicit contract not to challenge the people who serve as the "mythic" cement for the antipsychiatric movement. For example, the Villejuif affair, perhaps the most widely known antipsychiatric action of that year, did not come up for discussion.

In 1973, a group of student nurses at the Villejuif Hospital outside of Paris, one of the most backward mental hospitals in all of Europe, had started a newspaper for the hospital's patients and staff. The newspaper had carried articles that criticized conditions at the hospital and was banned by the hospital's administration. A scandal followed: the Parisian press published a series of exposés on Villejuif. Most notably, a special joint issue of *Cahiers pour la folie* and *Recherches* (a journal on which Guattari worked) was devoted to Villejuif and published the design of the keys to the hospital's infamous "closed" Henri Colin service. The gesture was dramatic: the hospital authorities had to change all the locks. They also fired the group of nurses who had started the newspaper and who were the chief suspects in the "keys" affair. Neither the *Cahiers* group at la Borde nor the *Recherches* collective organized a support movement for the nurses. Publishing the keys had been satisfying symbolically, but taking responsibility for the unemployed nurses required a more serious kind of political organization. Although these nurses were present at Gourgas, participants claimed that discussion of their problem seemed to be fastidiously avoided: "It was something people didn't want to talk about—you couldn't touch it."

The events at Gourgas serve to dramatize some of the contradictions in the French antipsychiatric movement. Although it attacks mythologies of "normality," it substitutes mythologies of deviancy of the excluded, of revolutionaries, gangsters, and psychotics. All are given a privileged status for being "outside the law" of capitalist society or "outside the law" of Lacan's symbolic dimension.

Not everyone in the antipsychiatric movement is carried away by these highly theorized ideas and by antipsychiatric "actions," such as the Gourgas meeting, which can easily slip into actings-out of nostalgia for the lost unity of the May days. A new movement has grown up that can be best described as a "grassroots" antipsychiatry. There is a well-published and publicized antipsychiatric elite around Lacan and around the Clinique de la Borde, but grassroots organizers assume that the real political struggle has been abandoned by the psychoanalytic-antipsychiatric-*gauchiste* "superstars." Indeed, the biggest complaint of the grassroots people is that the antipsychiatric theorists and their showplace institutions romanticize psychosis and show more of a penchant for prose than for the door-to-door organizing that could actually make a difference in the fight against repressive psychiatry.

The grassroots efforts center around local organizing of former patients in neighborhood groups, of workers and patients in mental hospitals, and around antipsychiatric publications.[24] These publications tend to be less glossy and more short-lived than those that appear in Lacan's *Le Champ freudien* series at Seuil or in the *Textes à l'appui* series at Maspero, where the big names of "official" antipsychiatry publish. One center of grassroots publication is the Solin publishing house, whose offices in Paris's Latin Quarter also serve as a bookstore and a meeting place for radical health organizations. The locale is a drop-in center for people who want information about such things as where to get sex counseling or a legal abortion, how to start a small newspaper for mental patients in a provincial hospital, and how to find a therapist whom they can afford. This enterprise is directed by Bernard de Frémenville, a young psychiatrist who has given up psychiatric practice to work full time as a journalist and as something of an impresario in the politics of madness.

Solin publishes an antipsychiatric magazine called *Gardes Fous*, the "guardians of the mad." Gardes Fous also is the name of a group that tries to join together political militants interested in the problems of madness with the new group of mental health workers who are starting to see the problems they face in the psychiatric system in terms of larger political conflicts. Gardes Fous is particularly interested in fighting against the romanticization of mental illness, which it feels has become endemic. For Gardes Fous, action against repressive psychiatry must be on the level not of poetry but of politics. The group points out that psychiatry uses a cover of medical expertise and the pretense of "neutrality" to legitimate its *technical* solutions to crises in the capitalist school, family, and prison. The army and judicial system use psychiatry to label troublemakers as "sick" in order to get them out of the way. Psychiatry's value to the ruling class as a subtle, "scientific" form of social control makes it a good terrain for political organizing.[25]

Gardes Fous is trying to support challenges to establishment psychiatry as they develop in hospital settings. Such challenges have become more frequent since 1968. Psychiatric hospitals have been torn apart by internal battles in which groups of personnel attack the institution. Nurses led the protests at psychiatric hospitals in Brie, Caen, and Villejuif, often using a rhetoric of protest heavily marked by psychoanalysis. Teachers, speech therapists, and physical therapists have led strikes in institutions for children with special needs. These protests have been met with the government's traditional weapons: isolating and firing of "troublemakers," calling police into the institution, and personal harassment. When they are unionized, mental health workers often belong to the country's largest union, the Confédération Général du Travail, which is controlled by the Communist Party. And as we shall see, although Communist Party intellectuals have latched onto the Lacanian bandwagon, the Party's practical labor union politics opposes disruptive movements in psychiatric institutions. So in the psychiatric setting, workers often have to organize without their traditional union support. That is where Gardes Fous comes in. The Gardes Fous strategy is to begin organizing at the lower level of salaried personnel in the psychiatric hospital, *les gardes fous*, whose role in the system is to maintain an order that exploits them as it maintains the submission of their patients.

Gardes Fous tries to organize patients in the same groups as the hospital workers because if just the latter are organized, things can rapidly turn against the interests of the patients. If the hospital is viewed as a factory, nurses and staff are the exploited workers and patients are the merchandise, the objects produced by exploitation. It is hard to avoid this industrial metaphor for the psychiatric hospital, because it corresponds to a certain reality, but this reality is central to a basic problem. The workers in psychiatric hospitals have low pay and terrible working conditions. When they organize, their immediate interests often contradict those of the patients. For example, from the point of view of an overworked psychiatric nurse, it makes a lot of sense to oppose liberalization of hospital policies. Reductions in patient medication and increases in patient privileges usually mean more work for the nurse. Thus it often seems that the only way to improve institutional psychiatry is to set its politics in the context of the larger social struggles of the peasants and workers who tend to be both the inmates of mental hospitals and their "guardians." In the years after 1968, French radicals frequently did present psychiatric concerns as the most appropriate vehicle for general political organizing. One of their arguments, and one which is shared by Gardes Fous, is that in advanced industrial capitalism, the community that was once represented by the state is in dissolution. Citizens are no longer in what used to be the "normal" relationship with a moral community. In the eyes of the state, the citizen, like the madman and like the political dissident, is in a perverse relationship to the normal order. The citizen has more reason than ever to identify with the political radical and with the psychotic because the state relates to them all in the same terms.

Psychiatric issues are therefore in no sense concerns that the citizen and the militant can be interested in but exterior to. The psychotic has gone further than some in his experience of the crisis of the capitalist subject, but the psychotic's fragmented experience corresponds to a mass phenomenon. The psychotic's symptom is seen as an expression of a socially shared malaise. Thus it is not a question of "curing" patients but of using their situation to sharpen a societal analysis. By reflecting on the psychotic's situation, political activists will better understand their own.[26]

In Gardes Fous, like other French antipsychiatric efforts, there is a tendency to view psychoanalysis—especially "non-adaptationist," Lacanian psychoanalysis—as relevant to such reflection on the crisis of the subject in capitalism. This, of course, is their point of tangency with radical political groups that have tried to use Lacan as a theorist for antipsychiatric actions within institutions.[27] In some settings, politicized Lacanian experimentation reached a point where the staffs of institutions for psychotic children refused to "Oedipize" their charges, allowing a fluidity of symbolic and sexual behavior for both patients and staff which certainly went beyond what most members of the society consider to be "normal" or even tolerable. Even where things did not go so far, many health facilities have developed an increasingly charged politics both within the institution and in relation to the outside—to the social security system, to parent groups, to labor unions, and to the Communist Party.

From even this brief description of the new politics of mental health, it should be clear that its actions would be viewed as noisome by an establishment party, playing the game of electoral politics and worried about alienating its not particularly radical constituency. Such has been the reaction of the Communist Party, which is as opposed to this kind of antipsychiatric politics as it was to the politics of spontaneity in May 1968.

In the politics of mental health, the Party has a cautious and conservative position. It supports what most of its constituency seems to find reassuring and helpful on a day-to-day basis. Working-class people do not want to throw physicians out of mental health centers. On the contrary, they see physicians as a reassuring sign of quality care. They do not want to discard the hope that they can go to a mental health center for treatment and symptom relief. They want and need to be free of symptoms so that they can hold their jobs. They resist the idea that their illness is a symptom of social injustice because to them the idea suggests that illness is not "real," that it is "in their heads." In many ways, the more medical the psychiatry, the more reassuring it is. And working-class people surely do not see how they can be helped by creating chaos in mental health institutions. The feelings of resistance to seeing health care as a sphere for political or psychoanalytic enlightenment were perhaps most adequately summed up for me not by a Communist Party position paper but by a woman I interviewed in the waiting room of a community mental health center outside of Paris. She was a ticket taker on the Paris subway. Her son was dyslexic. The mental health center where he was being seen was split between Communist and radical Lacanian factions. She said that she wanted "a real doctor on the job, not just one of those psychoanalyst troublemakers. They want to talk, talk, talk, but they can go to hell. I want my son to learn to read."

By supporting attitudes such as hers, the Communist Party is accumulating considerable political capital. Radical movements that envision a new order cannot be guided by the day-to-day practical problems that are the chief concerns of most people. Their theoretical guideposts often lead them to actions that might seem counterintuitive and even counterproductive if one were only calculating the greatest good for the greatest number in the shortest run. Party intellectuals are encouraged to explore Lacanianism in its theoretical structure as a science, but the practical politics of mental health is an entirely different matter. There, the Party supports a liberal psychiatric establishment, supports a "responsible" medical brand of psychoanalysis, and attacks the *gauchiste* mental health politics of the 1970s with essentially the same position they used to attack the *gauchiste* labor politics of the 1960s. This is to point out that it is easy for people who have nothing to lose to try to tear everything down. If striking factory workers lose their jobs, the student who instigated the strike does not suffer, and similarly, privileged bourgeois Leftists can be cavalier about subverting all possibility for treatment in a public mental health center, because if they were in trouble, they would never have to use it.

One young Communist who joined the Party after 1968 was not defensive about the Communist disinterest in a movement to "democratize" a hospital service in a Communist-controlled municipality in the Paris suburbs:

> I don't think that all of those Lacanian-trained philosophers know anything about mental illness or hospitals or how to run them, and I don't think they care. I think they are interested in theories and whether you are doing the young Freud or the old Freud, the young Marx or the old Marx. The Party is a serious operation, it needs to care about people's real problems. It has to protect itself from all of this theorizing when it comes to practical political action.

And of course, in their turn, the *gauchistes* accuse the Party of opportunism, of putting together a politics designed to "please," even though "pleasing" in the short run means acting against the real long-term interests of its constituency. Many are also very annoyed about the way in which the Communist Party is using its intellectuals' interest in psychoanalysis in order to appear to be what it is not. According to one activist I interviewed:

> It is Machiavellian. The Communists can have Althusser doing all of that fancy stuff, and then in practice, they support a conservative establishment that tries to convince people that their problems are in their head, not in the society. The Party made a great discovery. If you let your intellectuals use a psychoanalytic language, you can do anything you want. . . . It is a cheap way to look "Left" while your actions are to the Right.

During May–June 1968, the Communists thought they were siding with their constituency when they opposed May and its disorder, but things became confused when more people than they expected turned out to be angry enough (often at something they could not define) to support the May actions, at least for a time. In the sphere of mental health, the conflicts between traditional medical psychiatry and psychoanalytically inspired antipsychiatry are not yet played out. But the pressures at work to "normalize" the antipsychiatric initiatives do not just come from the outside—from traditional medical establishments and from the conservative Communist Party. They also come from within.

In the case of both the antipsychiatric and psychoanalytic "Left" there is a common problem: in France, it is hard to keep radical chic out of radical politics; in this psychiatric politics is no exception. Antipsychiatry, like psychoanalysis, has come into fashion among French bourgeois intellectuals. People who thought that they were joining an anti-establishment movement gradually find themselves lionized by the Left liberal press, solicited for articles, asked to write books about "antipsychiatry from the inside." After May 1968, student leaders told stories of publishing compacts signed on the barricades. In the 1970s it was antipsychiatry that became news.

The fact that antipsychiatric ideas have been picked up and popularized among the Parisian intelligentsia raises the question of what happens to serious and even potentially subversive ideas when they are integrated into café society. Support can mean trivialization. One young psychiatrist who was trying to raise money for liberalizing a psychiatric service that dealt with prisoners and delinquents put it this way:

> Refusing to play the game can mean the loss of vital support; playing the game can mean losing contact or real rapport with the

people you meant to be helping. They're not following your publicity or going to your cocktail parties. They are too busy suffering. They are in the situation full time, not part time like you.

The pressure on most people within the antipsychiatric movement is to capitalize on publicity and to get the support that comes from a sympathetic article in *Le Nouvel Observateur* or from having a Jacques Lacan or a Michel Foucault say something good about your cause to people who "matter." Such processes of normalization take place in all societies, but the Parisian concentration of students, intellectuals, and ideologists creates a particularly charged hothouse atmosphere where radical thought turns easily into radical chic.

Freud feared for the future of psychoanalysis because he was afraid that "the therapy might destroy the science." In the case of a psychoanalytically inspired antipsychiatry, the radical critique of a therapeutic approach may focus on polemic and can also leave the science behind. Antitherapy may turn out to "destroy the science" as surely as therapy ever did. The next chapter turns to the setting in France where the question of the health of psychoanalytic science has been posed most directly. The setting is the university.

7 Psychoanalysis as Science: The University

Freud gave his authority to the view that, while psychoanalysts had something to contribute to almost all academic disciplines and the universities had everything to gain from their collaboration, psychoanalysis itself could easily do without being taught in official places.[1] But the question of what psychoanalysis does need for its development is not so clear. The May–June 1968 events in France propelled analysts into the university and precipitated fundamental challenges to Freud's position.

During the events, students had torn traditional concepts of university education to shreds, and one student group after another came to look to psychoanalysts as those who were best qualified to help them pick up the pieces. Students attacked the traditional university discourse as cold, abstract, and politically insensitive. They wanted a more personally and politically relevant education, and in the post-1968 atmosphere, a radicalized psychoanalysis seemed like the very thing to fill the bill. Students objected to the French university's pretense to "absolute knowledge," and as we have seen, Lacan's presentation of psychoanalysis as a science that refuses all certainties seemed attractive. But the interest in having psychoanalysis taught in the university did not come only from students. It came from psychoanalysts as well.

The schisms in the French psychoanalytic world had raised again and again the question of psychoanalytic training, of how to transmit psychoanalytic knowledge. Thinking about this question demanded a serious look at the nature of psychoanalytic "knowledge." Is it artistic or scientific? Is it empirical or theoretical? For Louis Althusser and for Lacan, a science is not defined by its praxis or technique but by its theory. The praxis of psychoanalysis (the analytic cure) is simply that moment in the life of the theory when, having developed its technique (free association, analysis of the spoken text), it can enter into theoretical and practical contact with the unconscious, its specific object.[2] Lacan, of course, always stressed that the specifics of technique in psychoanalysis (how much time you spend with analysands, how many times a week they come to see you, whether you see them on the "outside") are not subject to immutable, "scientific" rules. Only the theory constitutes the science, and only the science is subversive as a new epistemology, a new way of knowing. In fact, by the mid-1960s, Lacan was saying that what was essential to psychoanalysis as a science could be separated from its clinical practice and formalized mathematically. Others violently disagreed, insisting that research in the science of the unconscious required a clinical contact.

Debate about the nature and transmission of psychoanalysis had long been taking place within the psychoanalytic societies, but when the university opened up to psychoanalysts after 1968, the questions were asked again, this time in a somewhat different form. Was university involvement a good or a bad thing for psychoanalysis? What kind of university involvement was appropriate? What should be taught, and who should teach? What of psychoanalysis is transmissible or should be transmissible outside the context of personal analysis? What have analysts become when they place themselves not behind a couch but behind a lectern? Can analysts "profess" psychoanalysis, or as one analyst asked, does this make them "monstrous hybrids," playing a charade which calls psychoanalysis itself into question?[3]

After 1968, the position of most non-Lacanian analysts seemed to be that it was all right for analysts to teach psychoanalytic theory in the university if they taught it in a highly abstract, scholarly way, much as another educator might teach literary theory. The Lacanians felt that this method of discourse was untrue to the essential nature of psychoanalysis, but the alternatives were not clear. They made some attempts to use their presence in the university to subvert what they saw as its rigid, absolute approach to knowledge; their university participation was often an ambivalent exercise in which they sometimes seemed to be working to make it not work. But beginning in 1973, Lacan took a new interest in teaching psychoanalysis in the university as his conviction grew that the future of psychoanalysis lay in its formalization into mathematical statements which he calls the psychoanalytic "mathemes" (les mathèmes). The development of the mathemes by mathematicians, philosophers, and linguists might— even if only for practical reasons—best take place in the university. As a consequence of Lacan's position, non-analysts, whose presence Lacan had already encouraged at the Freudian School, began to take a larger and larger part in a Lacanian program in psychoanalytic studies at the University of Paris at Vincennes. In 1976, in a major departure from his previous positions, Lacan participated in the expansion of that program to include a diploma in clinical psychoanalysis. Now the non-analysts were training clinicians as well as theorists, and the tension between psychoanalytic science and psychoanalytic clinical activity, long a major theme in the politics of the psychoanalytic societies, was being played out on a new stage.

The psychoanalysts came into the university in response to many different student clienteles with many different demands. There were, first of all, the medical students who wanted psychoanalysts to help them design a new curriculum, one that was more sensitive to the human dimension of medical practice. In 1968, the teaching of medicine in the French university was a caricature of all the worst features of the French educational system. Gifted medical students got clinical experience during an internship after medical school, but students who performed less brilliantly in the competitive examinations for the internships began their "internships" when they practiced on their first patients.[4] The closed, elite French system produced scandalously few physicians. In 1968, France had the fewest physicians per capita of any country in Europe.

Like most French students, French medical students were getting an irrational education, but unlike most, their irrational education led to secure jobs and social prestige. Lenin once said that you could tell that a situation was revolutionary when even waiters and hairdressers were willing to join a general strike. Medical students had little reason for taking risks and the student occupation of the Paris Medical School came almost a week after the first occupations of the Sorbonne. Even though they were latecomers, the medical students—the waiters and hairdressers of the French student movement— did ultimately join the May actions.

From the very first days of the student takeover at the medical school, a student-faculty study group on "human sciences" in medicine began to discuss the possibility that, in a revised medical curriculum, psychoanalysts might lead sensitivity training groups for medical students. Previously, psychoanalysts had been virtually excluded from the training of French physicians, and at first many medical students found the idea of analyst-professors shocking. Soon however, the analytic presence became one of the most taken for granted elements in student plans for medical school reform. Indeed, the medical students' discovery of psychoanalysis and their sensitization to politics seemed to develop together.[5] They looked to a psychoanalytic contact to help them understand the social suffering that might lie behind a symptom by making it easier for them to "relate to their patients as people." This interest in psychoanalysis, at first conceptually primitive and palliative in aim, soon led to a more fundamental criticism of the role of medicine and medical workers in society.

During the summer of 1968, the psychoanalyzed physician began to be discussed as a political ideal: he or she would not be threatened if unable to isolate a physical cause for a "medical" problem and would feel freer to consider possible social and psychological factors with the patient. He or she would be comfortable with the idea of denying immediate symptom relief if that meant losing the opportunity to get to the real root of the patient's problem. Ulcers, high blood pressure, insomnia, gynecological problems were all discussed as "signifiers" of social exploitation. The physician must learn, as the analyst had learned, to follow the chain back to its source: anger at society. The symptom was an alarm signal: "If the physician accepts the role of just cutting it off when it signaled an emergency, he would be accepting contemporary society and its constraints."[6] The analyst did not dismiss the symptom, but his or her first priority was helping the patient to understand its message. This must be true, argued the students, for the physician as well. A medical school action committee put forth the slogan: "Psychoanalysis must inform the behavior of each physician."[7]

One physician who had been a medical student during May 1968 spoke out for the "physician's right to carry political consciousness-raising as well as Band-Aids," but it was very clear that his model of consciousness-raising was psychoanalytic: "Can the physician serve, as an analyst might, to bring the patient progressively to the point where he can criticize his conditions of existence and recognize that his body symptom is a revolt against an insupportable social situation? . . . I believe he can."

The idea that medical treatment could be allied with social criticism became associated with Lacan. One student put it this way: "Without Lacan's critical approach a physician would simply use psychoanalytic techniques to get his patients to identify with him, and they would end up just as alienated from themselves." The Lacanians however, were not unchallenged in bidding for student sympathies. The "Human Sciences" committee at the medical school formed a psychoanalysis subcommittee and many reports about what went on indicated that analysts used it as a place to carry on their own quarrels and to compete for the attention of students. Students used images of street vendors and street walkers to describe these efforts to win their favor: "It was like watching the opening of a new sales campaign to market psychoanalytic societies. We were solicited, hustled by the members of both groups [the reference here is to Lacanians and non-Lacanians], each trying to convince us that the plague infested the other side."[8]

Although the psychoanalysis subcommittee was criticized at the medical school as "theater" and "psychodrama," it seemed to intrigue even some of its sharpest critics. For example, one medical student who wrote a thesis about psychoanalysis at the Paris medical school during the May days criticized the subcommittee for playing a game in which "the students furnished the analysts with disorder which the analysts then rearranged into psychoanalytic order," but he also described it as a place to "touch base" with "ultimate realities," as a "kind of amulet."[9] The tone of his remarks reflects the language that was circulating around the Paris medical school in 1968. There was little challenge to psychoanalysis by medical students during May; they were too busy "discovering" it.

In 1968, the situation in French medical education was bad, but the situation in psychiatric education was worse.[10] Since psychiatry was not yet considered an autonomous discipline in France, all psychiatrists were trained as neuropsychiatrists. This, of course, reflected the traditional somatic bias in French psychiatry. To become a neuropsychiatrist the medical student had to take one of three options, each highly unsatisfactory from the point of view of someone who wanted to practice psychiatry. One possibility was to compete for one of the few highly prestigious university internships in general medicine. These internships offered little opportunity to study psychiatry, but interns could arrange their schedules in such a way that by the end of their internship they would be qualified in neuropsychiatry. The internship had the further advantage of being the only path to a career in academic medicine. A second possibility was to compete for internships in a psychiatric hospital. Like the general medical internships in university hospitals, these positions carried a stipend, but there was a good chance that the new psychiatrist would spend the rest of his or her career in the asylum system as a Médecin des Hopitaux Psychiatriques, a physician in the French civil service.

Civil service psychiatrists were treated as pariahs by other physicians and by other psychiatrists. A third option was to take courses toward a certificate of advanced study in psychiatry. Many considered this the least desirable of all the options because here a student had no official hospital duties, no pay, and no clear route of access to patients.

Clearly, there was a crisis in psychiatric education. Out of the May days at the medical school came a proposed solution: a new Psychiatric College that would offer one course of training to a new *autonomous* psychiatric profession. In the college, psychiatry would be autonomous from neurology but in the closest possible relation to other behavioral sciences (psychology, sociology, anthropology, psychoanalysis), which would also be taught there. Coursework would be integrated with practical experience for *all* students, not for just the elite, and faculty positions would be open even to physicians who had not taken the standard track in academic medicine. Indeed, the college faculty itself would not be exclusively medical because it would be part of a larger entity: a new Critical University of Human Sciences. In this regard, the proposed reforms resonated with the spirit and concerns of May: integration of theory and practice, dissolution of hierarchical boundaries. The Critical University was to train psychiatrists and psychologists in the same institution according to a "common language and knowledge" and ultimately to merge the two professions.[11] Psychoanalysts dominated the Critical University's planning sessions, and there was no doubt that the "common language and knowledge" being discussed were largely psychoanalytic.

At first, discussions of the Psychiatric College had a strong political flavor, highly critical of status hierarchies among mental health professionals. By October 1968, though, most of the politics had fallen out of the project and the college had become a vehicle for negotiating liberal reforms for psychiatry.[12] Many reforms were achieved: psychiatry was made autonomous from neurology; the Médecins des Hopitaux Psychiatriques were integrated into the regular French hospital system and their salaries were tripled; psychoanalysts were given the possibility of teaching posts in the university; and a psychoanalytically inspired pilot program in community mental health was recognized as official government policy for all of France. These reforms were not negligible, but once they were won, the plans for a Psychiatric College fell apart. The psychiatry students did not see much change in their situation, and psychologists were left to carry on alone with the project of a Critical University.

By 1970, the Critical University had been more or less reduced to a Department of Clinical Human Sciences and to an Institute of Clinical Psychology at the Censier campus of the University of Paris.[13] The Institute of Clinical Psychology offers a two-year program after a master's degree that leads to a state diploma as a clinical psychologist.[14] But at graduation, students of psychology face a paradox. They are licensed psychologists, but have been trained by a faculty of which nine-tenths are psychoanalysts who have not necessarily had any formal training in psychology. Their professional careers depend on their contact with psychoanalysis since getting a job as a clinical psychologist in France usually requires that the applicant has had personal analytic training.[15]

In spite of (or perhaps because of) the domination of their profession by the psychoanalytic world, the number of psychology students has skyrocketed, tripling in the five years after 1968. The number of students seems to be limited only by the lack of space in psychology departments. Faculty members say that their students are drawn to study psychology because they dream of psychoanalytic careers. As one of them put it, "Since '68, psychoanalysis is like God (*le bon Dieu*)."

Each week, over two hundred analysts come to teach at Censier. Some of them seem troubled by their students' demands for an analytic presence.

> I agreed to come to Censier to teach one section of a course for first-year students on "The Interview." I thought I would spend the first part of the semester on how to take a thorough psychological history. But the students would have none of it. They said they wanted to learn about the evocative power of total silence in the interview. I refused and half the class left my section in search of a teacher who would let them play analyst.

The students are equally frustrated: they are surrounded by psychoanalysis but are told that they may not take courses that deal specifically with it until their fourth year of study in psychology. Psychoanalytic knowledge is represented as too explosive to teach to the "unprepared," yet when the courses come, they are abstract and didactic. Students call it "the psychoanalytic tease."

Jean Laplanche, a former student of Lacan's and one of the founders of the Department at Censier, feels that given the conditions of its birth, "out of the protean forms of the events," it was inevitable that the psychology students' desire for psychoanalysis would be "immoderate" and "excessive." But Laplanche feels that the Censier response to that desire has been exemplary, allowing a strong analytic presence without compromising analytic "extraterritoriality" since "the primary references for the analyst are not in the university but in the analytic society and the process of analysis itself."[16] Laplanche takes pride in maintaining a delicate balance which from the point of view of many students seems more like a clumsy balancing act.

Censier psychology students describe themselves as "second-class citizens in a psychoanalytic ghetto." Trapped between medical and psychoanalytic power, neither of which they possess, they have little room for expression except in the interstices of their own institution. This was illustrated by a self-analytic group at Censier which was constituted as a course. The members' only task was to develop an agenda and analyze how the group went about making and implementing decisions, but the group found it impossible to make any decisions at all. At one point, the group's anxiety over whether or not it would ever be able to decide on an agenda became so great that it made an extravagant gesture toward "potency": it officially constituted itself as a legal corporation and established a bank account in order to manage its small academic budget. After forming the corporation, all the group members seemed to feel better for a while, although nobody was sure why they needed to form one. The group denigrated psychoanalysis but was deferential to the analysts invited to speak. Group members felt trapped in the double bind that seems to plague the Censier psychologists in general: their only contact with power is through that held by analysts. They are frustrated but cannot express anger to the analysts on whom they depend and with whom they identify. They have to turn their anger against themselves.

Laplanche thinks that psychoanalysis needs to be in the university because pressure from academics will force psychoanalysts into greater rigor and precision.[17] But this reasoning, along with the Censier formula of maintaining a psychoanalytic "presence"' with no psychoanalytic training, sidesteps one of the important issues raised by teaching psychoanalysis in a university: Can there be psychoanalytic researchers who do not practice as analysts and who are not part of the professional organization of analysts? In medicine, fundamental theoretical contributions are most frequently made by university research scientists who are not engaged in the practice of medicine. Can psychoanalysis work along similar lines?

Traditionally, psychoanalysts have answered no—psychoanalytic theory is indissociable from psychoanalytic practice. For example, in the United States, psychologists, anthropologists, and sociologists have felt authorized to borrow some psychoanalytic concepts for their own purposes but as far as most analysts are concerned, the *real* psychoanalytic teaching and research is among them and in the psychoanalytic institution. This situation has remained fairly stable in the United States. In France, on the other hand, the lively ferment surrounding the May events and the emergent psychoanalytic culture opened the question. Some Lacanians came to see the university, and not the psychoanalytic society, as the most fertile ground for the further development of psychoanalytic research.

Laplanche hopes that the university will keep psychoanalysis intellectually honest, but there is no fundamental challenge to Freud's assumptions about what psychoanalysis can and cannot "do without." But when Lacan talks about the possibility of a psychoanalytic matheme, he is arguing that there is a psychoanalytic science that is deeply rooted in other scientific disciplines and that can be formalized and transmitted apart from going through the process of a personal analysis.

Lacan's particular explorations of psychoanalytic science (what he calls *Le Champ freudien*, "the Freudian field") are controversial, not to mention opaque. It is not my purpose here to pass judgment on them. Even if Lacan's particular theories turn out to be false, his general position that psychoanalytic research can be the province of the non-analyst may well be true. Looking to non-analysts to make fundamental discoveries about the science of the unconscious has far-reaching implications for psychoanalytic theory, for the politics of the psychoanalytic institution, and for the relationship between psychoanalysis and the university. What, for example, are the implications of the position that psychoanalytic theory can be expressed in theorems that are removed from the analytic experience, or that developing these theorems (or even understanding them) requires a deep understanding of mathematics and linguistics?

In this case, psychoanalysts would not be in the university to do it a *favor*. On the contrary, the new "psychoanalytic scientist" would probably need the resources of the university in order to do his or her work.

The existence of a fertile psychoanalytic science apart from the world of psychoanalytic societies and clinical practice clearly would mean drastic changes in the organization of psychoanalysis. The resistance of most analytic societies to the possibility of such a science—in France, this is expressed as resistance to even the *idea* of a psychoanalytic matheme—is motivated by more than the natural resistance of institutions to things that force them to change. There is first of all a moral question. Analytic societies see themselves as more than professional training centers or centers of intellectual activity; they see themselves as guardians of a set of ethical standards. Psychoanalytic societies, like medical schools, train practitioners, but whereas physicians need licenses to practice, psychoanalysts do not. Many psychoanalysts feel that the analytic society carries the moral burdens of a medical school with none of the legal protection; and they fear university programs in psychoanalytic "science" because their very existence may encourage students to think that theoretical knowledge is enough to practice psychoanalysis, that a personal analysis is not necessary.

In France, there is another kind of resistance to the idea of psychoanalytic science. This resistance is associated with a specific hostility toward Lacan's new preoccupation with mathematical formalization. The Freudian School itself became split between those who were intrigued by the possibility of a psychoanalytic matheme and those for whom the idea of the matheme contradicts a belief that psychoanalytic research can only take place during privileged moments of discovery in the analytic process.

Be that as it may, Lacan acted on his belief: after the May–June 1968 events, he agreed to bring the teaching of psychoanalysis to the experimental campus of the University of Paris at Vincennes and helped to staff a Department of Psychoanalysis with a substantial group of non-analyst faculty. The Department of Psychoanalysis was conceived of as an experiment within an experiment. Although the idea of an experimental campus for the University of Paris had been around for quite a while, the May events provided the impetus for one of the fastest pieces of university construction in the world. Vincennes was begun during the May events; by the following fall, it was open to students.

Edgar Faure, the Minister of Education who presided over the Vincennes project, seemed to have learned a lesson from the May days. The University of Paris at Nanterre had been the birthplace of the Leftist *groupuscles* whose actions precipitated the 1968 conflagration. Getting to the Nanterre campus meant crossing some of the most horrifying slums of Paris. It was not a place where sociologists could easily be lulled into recollecting Marxism in tranquility. Although it is hard to assess the exact degree of intentionality involved, it is certain that Faure was hoping to neutralize students politically by the unique open admissions policy of Vincennes (unlike other French universities, you could enroll at Vincennes without a baccalaureate) and eclectic subject offerings (film, psychoanalysis, semiotics, etc.). One Vincennes literature student put it this way: "The administration talks about an experimental university, but the only experiment going on here is to see whether the government can take a group of Leftist students and keep them out of trouble by giving them a playground to fight over."

The government's intentions may well have been to isolate radicals and to put them out to pasture, but its success seems more a result of student complicity than government cunning. During the first two years after Vincennes opened, its students literally tore it apart in a struggle over whether or not to participate in student-faculty administrative committees for university management. The Communist Party favored participation: the non-Communist Left saw the committees as a way of buying off the radical movement by throwing it a cheap "democratic" crumb.

Even as the battle over participation on the student-faculty administration committees was raging, many Vincennes students and faculty members started to feel that even by getting involved in this struggle they were playing into the government's hands.[18] They were being kept busy in campus politics, and this was keeping them "out of trouble." Students were enraged at the government's strategy, angry at themselves for being such "easy marks," and frustrated by the failure of the May events to "change anything." They also were bitter about their premature enthusiasm over Vincennes: they had a "liberal" university, but graduating from it did not confer the national French university diploma. In degree-conscious

France, that is a high price to pay for a playground. The students turned their anger against the very physical materials of which Vincennes was built. Many of the Paris universities are subjected to a permanent and very high level of vandalism, but at Vincennes, things went to the extreme. Library bookshelves were used for bonfires, doors ripped off classrooms and lavatories, closed-circuit televisions torn apart. Their hollow shells and the twisted forms of uprooted wrought iron desks stood like sad pieces of surreal sculpture.

This was the environment that hosted the Freudian School's first efforts to bring Lacanian psychoanalysis into the university. Lacan had long insisted on a radical disjuncture between university and psychoanalytic knowledge. Theoretically, at least, the Lacanians agreed that their presence in the university should constitute a permanent criticism of the traditional university and its form of knowledge. They saw themselves as involved in a long-term strategy of "subversion," but they disagreed about what to do in the present. For example, many Lacanians felt that it was wrong to give courses, exams, and credits because that might imply that psychoanalytic knowledge could be measured and tested by an absolute standard. In a first phase of the history of the Department of Psychoanalysis at Vincennes, the analysts became caught up in conflicts over what price they were willing to pay for a place in the university.

These conflicts at Vincennes resonated with long-standing disagreements among Lacanians about how "subversives" should conduct themselves in the everyday world of normalized institutions. Of course, the issues most resembled those that had surrounded the schism of 1963, when the question was whether Lacanians should remain outside of the establishment or should join the International and try to change it from within.

During this first phase of Freudian School activity at Vincennes, the department was led by Dr. Serge Leclaire, one of Lacan's closest disciples. As president of the French Psychoanalytic Society in the early 1960s, Leclaire had spearheaded Lacanian efforts to win recognition from the International Psychoanalytic Association. Thus Leclaire had long been a partisan of bringing Lacanian thought to a wider circle of people by participating to whatever degree possible in "established" institutions. The International Association had been one such place; in 1969–70, Leclaire believed Vincennes to be another.

Dr. Jean Clavreul, another member of Lacan's inner circle, also was at Vincennes. Clavreul had long been critical of Leclaire's efforts to win recognition from the International Association. From his point of view, Lacanism could gain nothing from compromising with the establishment. During the first phase of conflict at Vincennes over departmental status, exams, and course credits, Leclaire and Clavreul resumed their old roles and disagreed about playing by the rules of the university, just as they had disagreed about playing by the rules of the International. Once again Leclaire argued that what was most important was entering the institution and getting their message heard by large numbers of people. Since the message was subversive, it would carry its own consequences. To him, refusing to give course credits was an empty gesture. And once again Clavreul argued that analysts must remain marginal to institutions that were potentially "normalizing." Becoming part of the bureaucratic and conservative International would have distorted Lacan's message and playing the university game at Vincennes would cause the analysts to be swallowed up in the traditional university discourse. Analysts could not "certify" a psychoanalytic course credit.

When it came down to a vote, the faculty of the Department of Psychoanalysis was overwhelmingly against giving course credits, but the students were overwhelmingly in favor of getting course credits for their work. The department ended up giving course credits, but gave them to everyone who signed up for a course. This solution was no solution because it took all the value out of the "value units" (course credits) that everyone was fighting about. It pleased neither students, faculty, nor administration.

Leclaire stayed at Vincennes for only a year and left feeling that the Lacanians were playing the same cat and mouse game with the university that they had played with the International Psychoanalytic Association. Leclaire felt that in both situations the Lacanians were condemning themselves to isolation and impotence by insisting on marginality. In any case, it now seemed clear to him that the costs of university participation were higher than he had imagined.

Students at Vincennes (like students at Censier, except perhaps a little more so) tended to fantasize their studies as psychoanalytic experiences, and students spoke of their psychoanalytic "credits" as though they were canceled checks to an analyst. Jacques Hassoun, a Freudian School analyst at Vincennes, wrote about a string of classroom incidents that he found disturbing. Students told him they could not follow what was going on in class, but came because sitting there evoked childhood memories; other students, the most brilliant, would go through periods when they couldn't follow the simplest arguments; students who had never missed a single class decided to begin personal analyses and never returned to class. Hassoun worried that he had become that "monstrous hybrid," neither psychoanalyst nor teacher.[19] His concerns were widely shared. Another Vincennes analyst reflected an often expressed sentiment when he lamented the fact that he "was sick of seeing my classroom used as a couch."

Leclaire left Vincennes, but most of the others stayed on despite their reservations. They taught what was on the surface a diverse set of courses, but there really was only one subject: Lacan. There were courses on Lacanian texts, Lacanian concepts, even a full course on one Lacanian page. Jacques-Alain Miller, Lacan's son-in-law, taught a course on new books relevant to Lacanian thought. One student spoke of it enthusiastically: "Take this course with Miller, and you get as close as you can to Lacan's ideas about the latest bestsellers."

For many students, "getting close to Lacan's ideas" or "getting close to those who are close to Lacan" was what Vincennes was all about. One Vincennes student named Victor pushed his identification with the *Maître* to the point of giving his own Lacanian-style seminar. It was listed in the 1973–74 Department of Psychoanalysis catalog as "Dialogue with one's own madness—a pirated edition of the Seminar." On a hospital ward, there often is a patient whose symptoms are recognized as a particularly acute expression of the contradictions of the institution. He or she often receives special attention and tolerance from staff and other patients. Many Vincennes students and faculty seemed to regard Victor as a symptom student. His extravagant behavior seemed to express tensions at Vincennes from which they all suffered.

I first met Victor during a seminar at Vincennes whose members were discussing the relationships between psychoanalysis, science, and mathematics. The seminar met in a room that was virtually demolished. The lights had been torn from their fixtures and formed an array of unfixed swinging bulbs. Twisted chairs and tables were chained to one another and to the floor so that they too would not be uprooted. There was a "No Smoking" sign on the wall and no ashtrays in the room, yet almost everyone was smoking and grinding out cigarettes on the carpet. Vincennes students see Vincennes carpets as hypocrisy—"Who ever heard of a ghetto with carpets?"—and seem untroubled about destroying them. The walls of the classroom were covered with writing, some of it from a struggle between *gauchistes* and the Communist Party, most of it about psychoanalytic politics: "Miller: Despot's Buffoon," "Have pleasure here and now—liquidate psychoanalysis," "Lacan = Paranoia."

Toward the end of the seminar, Victor began a monologue on Lacan as the prophet of paranoia. He was not interrupted for fifteen minutes. The class heard him out and then disbanded. Class members reflected on what had happened:

> Victor is an exaggeration of everything we all feel. Psychoanalysis in a classroom is painful for me. Victor expresses his pain. I keep quiet, but I feel it too. Victor is a student, but he is in analysis with one of his teachers. Victor wants to be an analyst, probably will be, but uses his Vincennes experience to pretend that he already is one.

If Victor was a symptom student for the contradictions of the first phase of Vincennes history, then Lacan's visit to Vincennes in December 1969, may well have been its symptom class.

Lacan came to give a lecture, but he was interrupted by objections and catcalls from the floor. The objections focused on the question: Why can't Vincennes students be psychoanalysts after they graduate? Lacan tried to explain that psychoanalytic knowledge could not be transmitted like regular academic knowledge but the students were not interested in hearing that answer. Like the students at Censier they resented being close to "psychoanalytic power" without sharing it.

The group became increasingly agitated, and in a gesture of hostility and frustration one of the students began to strip. Lacan turned to the half-nude student and shook with rage. He accused the students of having become pawns in the government's game by becoming fools, impotent court jesters, the regime's harmless isolates. "The regime shows you off and says: 'Look at how they play!'"[20]

Lacan was not alone in feeling that student "play" was a sign that the government had successfully defused student politics. The idea that Vincennes was the government's garbage dump for radicals was widespread. In 1973–74, the Department of Psychoanalysis listed a course entitled "The Praxis of Garbage," which students and faculty members commonly referred to as "The Praxis of Vincennes" or "The Praxis of the Department of Psychoanalysis." And when the department was given a bit of extra money for the 1973–74 academic year, one of its faculty commented: "That's just the government paying us off for keeping Marxist troublemakers preoccupied with their unconscious."

If the first phase of the Vincennes story was dominated by what it means to put a radical psychoanalytic discourse in a normalizing university structure, the second phase was dominated by a question about the nature of the psychoanalytic discourse itself: What are the limits of our ability to formalize psychoanalytic theory meaningfully? Lacan had ended his personal participation in the Vincennes department after his very turbulent afternoon there in 1969. But in the summer and fall of 1974, he took a sudden new interest in the department. The psychoanalytic presence at Vincennes had been created in his image, and it could not have been pleasant for Lacan to hear it continually referred to as garbage. But the reasons behind Lacan's change of heart went beyond pride.

His new concern for psychoanalysis in the university came out of his desire for research on psychoanalytic mathemes by mathematicians, philosophers, logicians, and linguists. If the future of psychoanalytic theory lay in mathematical formalizations developed independent of psychoanalytic practice, no psychoanalytic society, no matter how eclectic, could hope to serve as its exclusive intellectual base. In July 1974, Lacan seemed to decide that the intellectual home for psychoanalysis had to be the university. Even though Vincennes was chaotic and marginal, it was at hand. Lacan announced that the Vincennes Department of Psychoanalysis had failed as a "pilot" project—he was going to take personal charge of its reorganization. He named himself the scientific director of the department and made Jacques-Alain Miller, a philosopher who was not then an analyst, its new chairman.

The Vincennes department was renamed *Le Champ freudien*, "the Freudian field" of research in structuralist psychoanalysis.[21] In order to carry such a heavy burden, the department was refounded on new principles that stressed the psychoanalytic matheme and the necessity of psychoanalytic research. From then on teaching in the new Department of Psychoanalysis would have to be justified on the basis of research in process. All scheduled courses were canceled and the Vincennes faculty or anyone else wishing to teach there would have to submit a research plan as a proposal for a course. Lacan named himself, Miller, Clavreul, and Charles Melman, a Freudian School analyst who until then had not been at Vincennes, as a Scientific Committee to judge the proposals. Beyond that, the Miller-Clavreul-Melman triumvirate would be in charge of implementing the new directives for *Le Champ freudien*.

The Vincennes faculty was outraged. The Lacan "takeover" seemed arbitrary and dictatorial. No one denied that some action was needed, but there was widespread objection to the way in which Lacan had stepped into the department, declared its activities null and void, named new directors for it, and set up a faculty review process. Apart from the question of Lacan's right to do this, there was anger and anxiety about the review process itself. To some, asking for a research project description of a few pages as a basis for judgment seemed a pretense; they suspected that the review would be based on personal associations and on how interested each faculty member was in the matheme. Most of the Vincennes faculty thought that the review would go far toward getting rid of the analysts who would not follow Lacan in his new mathematical orientation. Non-analysts seemed more and more to be on center stage.

In protest, some faculty members refused to submit projects and resigned. Others had their projects rejected by the triumvirate for reasons that did not address the real issues: "too succinct," "insufficiently elaborated," "come back with more details next year" was the language with which analysts who had been teaching in the department for years were told they could no longer remain. For example, Luce Irigaray, a Freudian School analyst and Vincennes faculty member, had just published a book on psychoanalysis and feminine sexuality when the Vincennes crisis broke and proposed to give a course on its themes.[22] Her project was rejected. Many felt that Irigaray's book had displeased Lacan and that he was using Vincennes to settle personal scores. The Irigaray incident sparked some of the most violent discussion of the Lacan coup. Many found Lacan's peremptoriness to be intolerable, and once again, analysts had to take sides for or against Lacan.

As had happened with the pass, Lacan insisted on the validity of his position in a way that seemed to contradict his lifelong belief that there could be no certitudes in psychoanalytic matters. Lacan was more adamant than ever about not having to offer any explanations for his actions. All explanations were to be found in the urgency of elaborating the mathemes.

In October 1976, the Freudian School held a three-day meeting on the mathemes. For three days, the mathemes were brought to bear on every conceivable problem: Freud's case of Dora, Borromean knots, Hilbert's operator, James Joyce, and traditional psychiatric nosology. There was a matheme of perversion, a matheme of phobia, a matheme of the mytheme. Equations, ratios, arrows, diagrams of knots, and Venn diagrams covered the blackboards. The audience reaction ranged from enthusiasm to indignation. "An insult to the intelligence. This is a case of the emperor's new clothes. Why doesn't anyone say that the emperor is naked?" Some felt guilty at understanding nothing or very little of something that "everyone important seems to feel is so crucial."

The skeptics did more than grumble: the celebration of the mathemes was punctuated by strong dissenting statements. In his talk, Serge Leclaire reminded the group that the psychoanalytic act is an "affair of speech" (*parole*), and in relation to this speech, the mathemes, important though they might be, are best seen as "graffiti." They are traces, testimonies, but still *written* expressions of an essentially *verbal* act of rage or passion or pain or pleasure.

Despite colleagues' fears that the mathemes might stifle psychoanalysis before they got a chance to be the key to its transmissibility, Lacan was committed to them as fundamental to the scientific expression of psychoanalysis. He described them as the expression of the knowledge within psychoanalysis that can be expressed "without equivocation" and said that in order for psychoanalysis to define itself in relation to science it must develop such statements at its base.[23]

The problem is whether Lacan's idea of the matheme is to be interpreted literally or metaphorically. Jacques-Alain Miller takes the literal point of view, and has made it a trademark of the Department of Psychoanalysis at Vincennes. He sees the mathemes as equational and describes them by analogy to a book on symbolic logic. If you take such a book and decide that you want to translate it from one language to another, there are some things in it that you have to translate and other things that do not need translation because they stay constant in all languages: these latter, claims Miller, are analogous to the mathemes.[24] They are formulas made up of "little letters" because only such symbols lack all signification of their own. Miller quotes Hegel's phrase that "the Mysteries of the Egyptians are mysteries to the Egyptians themselves." For Miller, without the mathemes, psychoanalysis would only be able to form a society of initiates guarding a secret and "the Mysteries of the psychoanalysts would be mysteries to the psychoanalysts themselves."[25] If there are no mathemes, the fundamentals of psychoanalysis will remain ineffable. No mathemes means no real scientific community for psychoanalysis.

Some of the analysts who were skeptical about "a psychoanalysis of little letters" were nonetheless sympathetic to the mathemes taken as a metaphor for new and higher aspirations for their discipline. They felt that the mathemes, like Lacan's interest in topology (particularly in the structure of complex knots), were attempts to use concrete materials to add precision as well as texture to overly ambiguous psychoanalytic theory. Lacanian François Roustang reads Lacan in this way, and according to him, a huge gulf separates what Lacan means by the mathemes from what his disciples have understood him to mean. Miller and his circle see the mathemes as formulas that need to be discovered. When and if they are discovered, psychoanalysis will become scientific; if they are not, the analytic world will live in a growing cacophony that will destroy it. Lacan, on the other hand, first posed the problem of the matheme as a question: "Is a psychoanalytic matheme possible?" Roustang argues that all such interrogatives are necessary in order to situate, define, and elaborate psychoanalysis in relation to science: "In other words, it is the questioning about the possibility of the matheme which is envisaged as the necessary condition for theory, that is to say for theorization and transmissibility."[26]

Roustang's position is attractive because it allows one to separate the intention of creating a formalized, scientific core for psychoanalytic theory from a particular, highly committed concept of what it might be. But Roustang's effort to read Lacan's "real intentions" as an aspiration to a scientific spirit may be missing the point. Lacan may be very precisely rejecting the value of discussing science in a generalized sense and telling us that the only way to approach the problem is to set about making a particular theory, however hard that might be. Even if in the end we find that the theory was prematurely formulated it may be better to be precisely wrong than vaguely right.

Even if Lacan is correct in his belief that psychoanalytic theory suffers from too much ambiguity, the question still remains if the precision of a symbol that looks mathematical is just another kind of vagueness. The harshest critics of the mathemes see them as mystification because their use of mathematics is gratuitous: "The analysts manipulate mathematical symbols but they can't get anything from them because, in contrast to the use of such symbols in physics or even in economics, they are not using them to reach mathematical conclusions."

While the value of the mathemes for psychoanalytic theory construction remains the subject of heated debate, the
approach itself has done a lot to legitimate the presence of
non-analysts in the analytic institution. Jacques-Alain Miller,
who as a non-analyst was deeply and controversially involved
in the intellectual and political life of the Freudian School, has
put the relationship between the matheme and the psychoanalytic institution this way:

> The psychoanalytic matheme means that others besides analysts
> are in a position to contribute to the community which supports
> psychoanalytic experience. It is because the theory of mathemes
> underlies the Freudian School of Paris that from its beginnings,
> non-analysts—those "who are not engaged in the analytic act" (as
> I am often reproached by those who are too quick to see psycho-
> analysis as a secure career) and those who are not analyzed—have
> always had their place at the Freudian School. And as long as the
> Freudian School remains faithful to its orientation they shall con-
> tinue to have their place.[27]

Miller is a philosopher interested in academic research on
a new psychoanalytic science. But what gives a powerful emotional charge to the presence of the non-analyst in the analytic institution is the fear that non-analysts will not simply
philosophize but will authorize themselves to analyze. This of
course is the same fear that underlies putting psychoanalysis
in the university in the first place. Will students take learning
about psychoanalysis as tantamount to learning to *do* psychoanalysis? At Censier, this fear led to an explicit policy of psychoanalytic "prudence" in which psychoanalysis was doled
out in measured and neutralized dosages. And for five years,
right through the summer of 1976, the Lacanians at Vincennes
made official, emphatic statements that the task of the Department of Psychoanalysis "cannot be to deliver the right to

exercise as a psychoanalyst: one of the foundations of analytic theory is that only a personal psychoanalysis can authorize a psychoanalyst."[28] But in October 1976 the plot thickened considerably. The *Champ freudien* group at Vincennes announced a new two-year program of study called "The Psychoanalytic Clinic." Its title seemed to invite what had long been considered an abuse: it suggested that *clinical* psychoanalysis could be taught in a university.

Reaction to the announcement of the new program in the psychoanalytic world was convulsive and mostly outraged. For most of the objectors, giving a diploma in "The Psychoanalytic Clinic" was a contradiction of the principle that only a personal analytic experience could authorize psychoanalytic practice. Some Lacanians found the program in contradiction with twenty-five years of Lacanian criticism of a "curriculum" for psychoanalytic study and certainly in contradiction with the initial spirit of the Vincennes department, which had been resistant to giving a course credit, not to mention a university diploma that had psychoanalysis written on it. Many people who knew the situation at Vincennes believed that the new diploma would only serve to feed already rampant student fantasies about learning to be a psychoanalyst in a university.

Three members of the Fourth Group, Piera Castoriadis-Aulagnier, Jean-Paul Valabrega, and Nathalie Zaltzman, all Lacan's students who had broken with him in 1969 over the pass, denounced the new program as a threat to psychoanalysis and tried to marshal support in the psychoanalytic community to act against Lacan.[29] Their denunciation of the program was unconditional: first, the Vincennes group could only be playing malicious word games if they thought that a diploma in "The Psychoanalytic Clinic" would be taken as anything but a sign that its bearer was a psychoanalytic clinician and, since the French language allows for no distinction between clinician and practitioner, that he or she was a psychoanalytic practitioner as well. Second, the program constituted "a disavowal of Freud and psychoanalysis" because by nowhere mentioning the necessity for a personal analysis it implied that "two years of indoctrination with Lacanian theory would replace it most advantageously—in effect, what an economy of time and money."[30]

Their article in *Topiques*, the official journal of the Fourth Group, interpreted the Vincennes program as an extension of Lacan's policy of relegating practicing analysts to a second-class status, well below that of the "pure" analysts who busy themselves with "pure" theory and "pure" training analyses. Lacan's denigration of the "average psychoanalytic clinician" in his "Proposition of October 9, 1967" had led to the 1969 split in the Freudian School and to the formation of the Fourth Group. Now the members of the Fourth Group felt that Lacan had further reduced the status of "impure," "mere practitioners" by assimilating them into the group of Vincennes's "non-analyst psychoanalytic clinicians." The three authors wondered if Vincennes was just a first phase. Would a second phase follow in which analytic training at the Freudian School would disappear altogether, to be replaced by the "recitation of Lacanian dogma"? The fear was not only that non-analysts would take over the analytic world but that the analytic world would be divided into two groups of practitioners, one group that could afford to be trained in the "old style" in the psychoanalytic institution, and a second group that could only afford the registration fee at Vincennes. They would get the "short course." In this second group would be the mass of teachers, social workers, psychologists, speech and physical therapists who would go on to work in state-supported institutions. The "impure" practitioner trained at Vincennes and the "pure" theoretician trained by a personal analysis would treat different groups of patients.

> Neurotics and psychotics who have a certain economic standing will be counseled—and of this you can be sure—to go into treatment with the "pure" analysts. The have-nots will become the patients of the "non-analyst psychoanalytic practitioners" who work in public psychiatric institutions.[31]

In this sense, the Vincennes program was reminiscent of other programs led by psychoanalysts in the Paris area, where an analytic underclass is being trained to treat the social lower class. At Vincennes, however, said the Fourth Group analysts, insult is added to injury because there is actually a "diploma of clinical psychoanalysis." Although other programs have not gone so far, this distinction between theoretical study and study that looks forward to clinical practice had, in the three authors' opinions, "become a matter of pure form" at several universities. The three authors hope that this final line crossed by Lacan in the escalation of diplomas will prod "several Parisian departments directed by psychoanalysts" into critical reflection on what they are doing.[32]

A neutral observer reading the *Topiques* article might find some of its arguments overstated. A program is organized for non-analysts, school psychologists, for example, involved in a variety of aspects of clinical work. Through this course, the school psychologist would come to have an understanding of some aspects of psychoanalytic thinking. Can this be a bad thing? The representatives of the Fourth Group say it is because this school psychologist might then take to practicing psychoanalysis. But is it the responsibility of the holders of scientific knowledge to police the misapplication of this knowledge by people who have attended a certain course or read a certain book? The usual answer to this question has been no, but the authors object that in this case the title of the diploma being offered actively encourages the misapplication of knowledge. But the program's defenders, chiefly Jacques-Alain Miller, could argue that the program was designed for people who had *already* been engaged in some form of clinical activity.

Back in 1969, the *Topiques* authors left the Freudian School largely because Lacan was relegating the psychoanalytic practitioner to second-class status. Now at Vincennes, they saw some mental health professionals being elevated to the admittedly ambiguous status of non-analyst psychoanalytic practitioners. Since the authors already saw Lacan as holding the practitioner in contempt, his willingness to allow the line between the analyst and the non-analyst psychoanalytic practitioner (such as the school psychologist who now counsels his or her students with a psychoanalytic ear) to be blurred was seen as ominous. They saw Lacan as being in the process of liquidating their profession and seemed to feel that Lacan's actions at Vincennes were aimed at getting back at his old enemies.

Of course, the charge on these issues is overdetermined by a quarter of a century of psychoanalytic politics. What is new is that the struggles were now being played out in the university. This is not accidental. The old disputes within the psychoanalytic institution were about defining knowledge, transmitting knowledge, and legitimating certain "knowledge holders" as licensed to act on their knowledge. This is what universities are all about.

When Freud created a separate institution for the development of psychoanalytic knowledge, he created a tension between the university and the psychoanalytic institution.

The tension remains latent if psychoanalysis concentrates on the ways in which it is different from other disciplines and can afford to remain within its own institution. But it comes to the surface when psychoanalysis starts to take itself seriously as a science that cannot grow in isolation from other sciences. It is not surprising that when it did surface, as it has in France, the effect would be so explosive.

IV Psychoanalysis in Popular Culture

8 Psychoanalysis as Popular Culture: The Perils of Popularity

In the years after 1968, French psychoanalytic politics was played out in the world of the psychoanalytic societies and extended into worlds peopled by political activists, psychiatric patients, medical professionals, university students, and a bourgeois intelligentsia that has traditionally made a career out of keeping up with what is new. But the social diffusion of psychoanalysis extended even further, deep into French popular culture. Books, magazines, newspapers, radio, television, and casual conversation communicated how to use "psychoanalytic" ideas to many millions of French people who may never have been and may never be inside a psychoanalyst's office.

This chapter deals with psychoanalysis as it is woven through French popular culture. The picture that emerges can be characterized by three propositions. First, there is a very real diffusion and penetration of psychoanalytic ideas into French society. Second, these ideas, even when we find them on television or in women's magazines, reflect the political valence and highly charged internal politics of French psychoanalysis. Third, although some aspects of the French Freud are well represented in popular manifestations, other aspects are not, in particular, the idea that psychoanalysis is a subversive way of thinking about the individual. In the popular culture, psychoanalysis often is represented as a source of answers instead of as a practice that leads the individual to layer after layer of increasingly difficult questions. I have noted the very marked differences between the French and the American readings of Freud. This chapter shows how many of them are expressed in popular culture, although this also is a place where many of the differences break down.

Freud once wrote to Abraham: "I did not like the idea that psychoanalysis should suddenly become fashionable because of purely practical considerations."[1] Yet, in both France and America, Freud for the masses has passed through the prism of pragmatism. The psychoanalytically "useful" is what has made its way into the Sunday supplements. This is not surprising. Most people, busy with maintaining the necessities of life, can rally to revolutionary doctrines during revolutionary moments, but most of the time, they are trying to ease the burdens of a difficult daily life. In America, the ideology of organized psychoanalysis was in harmony with this popular pragmatism. In France, it comes into conflict with the beliefs of much of the psychoanalytic movement which sees psychoanalysis as incompatible with "making things a little better" or with "plastering over" social conflict with psychoanalytic language.

The widespread diffusion of psychoanalytic ideas into French popular culture was a relatively late phenomenon. Indeed, a study of the social image of psychoanalysis done by French social psychologist Serge Moscovici in the mid-1950s suggested that psychoanalysis was not widely diffused in French popular culture at all.[2] Twenty years later, I went back over some of the terrain that Moscovici had covered and talked with over two hundred Parisians of all ages and walks of life about what they knew and felt about psychoanalysis. My work did not fully replicate the earlier study, which had contacted over a thousand informants, but by using the data from the 1950s as a baseline, I was able to establish some major trends in how the new French psychoanalytic culture has been growing.[3] In the mid-1970s, it was common for people of all ages and classes to describe their interest in psychoanalysis as new, "really only a few years old," and to know more about psychoanalysis than had their counterparts of twenty years before. In the 1950s, even very well-informed people had fairly stereotyped ideas about what happens in an analysis ("You tell your dreams"). Today, people seem far more likely to reflect some knowledge of what is in fact the psychoanalytic "basic rule": the patient is to say everything that comes to mind.

> You can get un-blocked in analysis. Say what you can't say to family and friends.

> It is hard to be in analysis . . . to force yourself to say everything. In school and family you learn to say things "just right" or else to shut up.

It is not surprising that people seem to have more information about the psychoanalytic process. We know that there are more analysts (from dozens to thousands in the past twenty years), and because of the "short sessions" policy of many of them, the number of patients has increased more than proportionally. The percentage of middle-class respondents who claimed that psychoanalysis "was a frequent subject for conversation" was six times greater in 1974 than it had been in the 1950s, going from 5 to 31 percent. In the 1950s, when most people knew little about psychoanalysis, it was most commonly described as a religion or a philosophy. By the mid-1970s, its image had changed. When it was described with religious images, the comment was usually critical: "People go to the psychoanalyst the way they went to confession. But that is not what psychoanalysis should be." Or: "Lacan's School works like a religious order. It is closed, esoteric. It mystifies things." Although students and intellectuals still spoke of the philosophical importance of psychoanalysis, it was most often described as offering help for dealing with problems of daily life: "good for getting along with children," "good for marital troubles," "good for relaxing because people are too nervous these days," "makes people more secure . . . makes people less guilty."

Although people in all age groups showed a greater interest in psychoanalysis than their counterparts of the 1950s, high school and college students were the most knowledgeable and enthusiastic about the new French psychoanalytic culture. Since 1968, French students study Freud in high school and can choose to write about him in the philosophy section of their baccalaureate examination. Their teachers may well have been students of Althusser, and the French "high school Freud" tends to be fairly heady stuff. A seventeen-year-old French high school student gave a dizzying overview of what the past year in his philosophy course had been like: the curriculum had included "psychoanalysis and the notion of the epistemological break," "the formal character of the symptom," and "the dialectic of Master and Slave in Hegel and Lacan."

Things have changed and people are aware of it. One hundred and three of the over two hundred Parisians I interviewed in 1974 formed a representative sample of the Paris population distributed by age, sex, and class. The majority of them felt that psychoanalysis had become more important in the general culture in recent years, and most supported this contention by saying that there was more about psychoanalysis in the media. Indeed, most people in this representative sample had had their interest in psychoanalysis piqued by radio, television, or popular magazines. Even people who said that their primary source of information about psychoanalysis was books or formal study claimed to use the popular press to "keep up." In the 1950s, there was no way that someone could have used commercial media to "keep up" with psychoanalysis. Commercial media publish and broadcast what "sells," and psychoanalysis did not start to "sell" until late in the 1960s.[4]

To begin with, even in the early 1960s, one could not have kept up with psychoanalysis by reading even the most intellectual of the daily newspapers. Paris's *Le Monde*, for example, carried only one or two articles a year that even touched on it. But the number of articles about psychoanalysis "took off" in 1965–66, and by 1973 *Le Monde* was running over sixty articles a year about psychoanalysis and nearly one hundred more on psychiatry. In the early 1960s, the articles about psychoanalysis were usually about its stormy relations with the Catholic Church, but from 1968 on, the news was about psychoanalysis and politics, psychoanalysis and antipsychiatry, and on the internal politics of the psychoanalytic movement. When the International Psychoanalytic Association held its congress in Paris in August 1973, it was the subject of several news and feature articles, including some that focused on the story of why the Lacanian group was not invited. By the mid-1970s, Lacan had been the subject of several double-page features, and Wilhelm Reich, R. D. Laing, Herbert Marcuse, Bruno Bettelheim, Gilles Deleuze, and Félix Guattari have all received similar treatment. From 1966 and the publication of the *Ecrits*, reviews of psychoanalytic books have flooded the literary section of *Le Monde*, reflecting a major trend in French publishing.

Through the mid-1960s, only three French publishers (Presses Universitaires de France, Gallimard, and Payot) shared the small, "highbrow" trade of books related to psychoanalysis. The demand for books by and about Freud was small, not very different from what it had been in the 1920s when these three companies had first contracted for their publication rights. There was not even enough demand to justify a standard edition of Freud in French. Old and very poor translations of Freud were republished; new books about psychoanalysis were written for a specialized professional audience. Few copies were printed, and those rarely made any money.

Then in the mid-1960s, things began to change. Lacan's *Ecrits* sold out its first printing in advance sales alone. Work on a long-planned standard edition of Freud suddenly received high priority. New publishing houses that specialized in psychoanalytic works sprung up like mushrooms, and major publishing houses developed special psychoanalytic book series. By the early 1970s, French publishers were running no fewer than fifty of these series. American publishers, who had almost stopped trying to sell French publishers the translation rights to their psychoanalytic titles, suddenly found that these were the very books in demand. Psychoanalysis had become big business in French publishing.

In our conversations in 1973 and 1974, French editors described the market for a good psychoanalytic title as "infinitely elastic": "I usually try to search out where the market for a book is, but with a book by a well-known analyst, it is as though the market comes to find me . . . and keeps springing up in new places. . . . In this area of publishing, the demand definitely preceded the supply."

They made it very clear that keeping up with the demand often meant trying to squeeze books that were only very marginally about psychoanalysis into the magic circle that seems to protect publishing ventures in this area: "Sometimes I just put the word 'psychoanalysis' or 'Freud' into the titles of new books in my series . . . that way it will sell . . . and all by itself . . . and we can always add something about Freud to the text."

Publishers know that their lives began to change after 1968, but it is the people who run bookstores who see the changes in consumer taste from day to day.

The owner of a bookstore that specializes in psychology ran a modest business in the 1960s, catering to psychiatrists and educational psychologists:

> It used to be that I dealt with a few publishers, a few titles, a few journals, made a predictable amount of money and could pretty much run my business alone. Now I need a staff. I carry thousands of titles, there seems to be a new journal, a new pirated edition, a new antipsychiatric newspaper every week. The customers all seem to be studying psychology or psychoanalysis, or at least they seem to be part of a network from Vincennes or Censier that keeps them up on what is new.

The "magic circle" around psychoanalysis is found in other media. Jacques Lacan had his own prime-time two-part television special, and a call-in radio show that its hostess, Menie Grégoire, describes as "collective psychoanalysis" was one of the most popular programs in the history of French broadcasting. Since 1970, France has its own highly successful version of *Psychology Today*, and its reader surveys show that the most popular part of the magazine is the psychoanalysis section. For decades, the French edition of *The Reader's Digest* had stayed away from articles about psychology and psychoanalysis, but in the 1970s, even it had jumped on the psychoanalytic bandwagon.

In the 1950s, Moscovici found that people who learned about psychoanalysis from the popular media were likely to have negative feelings about it. At that time, the media generally portrayed psychoanalysis as an American export, which, like supermarkets, superhighways, and food chains, was being "artificially" injected into French life. People picked up an image of the United States as the "perpetrator" of psychoanalysis on the French. Psychoanalysis was "American propaganda spreading to Europe." In the 1970s, the people I interviewed who used the popular media to learn about psychoanalysis were very positive about it. The media presented psychoanalysis as interesting, useful, and timely. Women's magazines cited Freud as one might a contemporary, and glossy magazines carried features on psychoanalysis under the heading of *nouveautés* or *nouveautés de Paris*, "what's new in Paris."

One-half of the representative sample of Parisians whom I interviewed in 1974 had definitely gotten the message that psychoanalysis was somehow "new" and a recent French discovery. In response to a question that asked what they knew about psychoanalysis, many people were careful to distinguish the psychoanalysis they were talking to me about from that which they had so long and so negatively associated with the Americans: "In America, everybody has to have their own psychoanalyst. In France people are more balanced"; "In America, psychoanalysis is psychiatry and that equals social repression. Here psychoanalysis is not conservative."[5]

Everyone had different reasons for disassociating French and American psychoanalysis. Middle-class people did not like permissive child-rearing, which they associated with American psychoanalysis and the evils of Dr. Spock; working-class people distinguished the French from the "crazy Americans," who always "had to run to their psychoanalyst whenever they had a problem"; and the intelligentsia referred to Lacan's critique of "denatured" American psychoanalysis. The net result was dramatic. Over half of the people I interviewed in 1974 found a way to distinguish American psychoanalysis from the "new" French kind.

Much of what I have noted as novel in the French Freud is carried over into the representation of psychoanalysis in French popular culture. There seems to be a general awareness that psychoanalysis has taken on a new political valence. In the 1950s people were skeptical about the compatibility of psychoanalysis and an active political life (with people on the political Left registering the most skepticism); twenty years later most people saw psychoanalysis and politics as compatible, and people on the Left felt this most strongly. This finding is reflected in another trend: in the 1950s psychoanalysis was most popular and considered most efficacious among people who declared themselves to be on the Center and Right (with people on the Left expressing skepticism); twenty years later things were just the other way around. Not surprisingly, the most dramatic changes of attitude were among Communist Party members, whose party has gone through the most abrupt "about-face" in its attitude toward psychoanalysis. For example, a twenty-five-year-old Party member, a teacher, explained that "psychoanalysis need not be the arm of reaction. . . . It can work in the community to bring the advantages that the bourgeois have always had, right to the workers."

The association of psychoanalysis with political people and political ideas has left some interesting traces. In the 1950s, most people thought that intellectuals, artists, and the rich were the more likely groups to be in analysis. In the mid-1970s, the "typical" analysands were portrayed as students, the rich, and "people on the Left." In the 1950s, when people were asked to describe a psychoanalyst, they often used images that referred to physical qualities of personal magnetism ("a bearded man with glasses," "a demonic presence," "a man with piercing eyes"). By 1974, descriptions of analysts were as likely to make reference to their politics ("a wild-eyed radical in a center for emotionally disturbed children").

Psychoanalysis by and for radicals is a new phenomenon in France. In several interviews, a question about psychoanalysis and its relation to politics provoked a reverie about a new tolerance for things psychological among radicals. One sociologist spoke as follows:

> When I was in radical political circles in the fifties and early sixties, if a member of our political group had an emotional flare-up, he was out. Psychiatry was taboo. If someone was a known homosexual, he was out. That was disapproved of. Now, political *militants* even write about psychoanalysis, let it be known that they are homosexuals. The world has changed.

In chapter 3 we saw how psychoanalytic discourse has given a new flavor to radical politics. A manager of a large Latin Quarter bookstore was well placed to watch the development of the politicized psychoanalytic culture.

> People started coming in and asking for Marcuse. We didn't get the translation of *One Dimensional Man* until after the events, but then it sold like hotcakes. Then, Payot brought out Reich and since we were stocking nearly a hundred books about the May events, we put the Marcuse and the Reich in with the books on May. But people were still asking for Marcuse and Reich and then Laing, Lacan, and company long after we could no longer sell the May 1968 stuff.

The trend that started in May 1968 with some Reich and Marcuse continues:

> Customers come to me because they know I stock the political-psychoanalytic reviews by militant nurses, militant mental patients,

> militant social workers, militant feminists, militant god-knows-whats. They come in to buy a magazine, and then they buy more and more. Political psychoanalysis is good for business.

Merchants made it clear that political psychoanalysis was "good for business," and editors said that in their view a sure path to publishing success in the mid-1970s was finding "the golden ones," that is, the books that are both psychoanalytic and political: "*Anti-Oedipus*, that's a golden one: 'Freudo-Lacano-*gauchiste*.' The phrase may make you smile, but don't. You may laugh, but these are the books that sell."

Many of the people I interviewed who said that they had "recently" become more interested in psychology or psycho-analysis used May 1968 as a "marker" for when things had changed for them. This would not have been surprising even if the psychoanalytic explosion had had nothing to do with the events. In France, "normal" life stopped during the 1968 crisis (there were no cars, no work, no school). It was a time-out-of-time, and French people naturally use it as a point of reference. But we have seen that, in the development of the psychoanalytic culture, May 1968 was more than an arbitrary fixed point. It made connections among people and among ideas that set the stage for what was to come. How did people involved in May talk about psychoanalysis? May participants tended to see psychoanalysis as relevant to politics and were far more likely than other people to have positive things to say about Jacques Lacan and to associate him with "currents on the Left." In the 1950s, most people in Moscovici's study associated psychoanalysis with Christian religion, existential-ism, and surrealism. As we have seen, the events provided a moment of encounter for many of the currents—social, politi-cal, and intellectual—that define the specificity of what has emerged as the new "French Freud." As might have been expected, it was the May participants who were most likely to connect psychoanalysis with its "new" relations, specifically, Marxism and structuralism.

Thus, the social representation of psychoanalysis in France is exceptional in its association to politics and even to a particular political event. Another peculiarly French characteristic is the degree to which popular images of psychoanalysis reflect the politics of the psychoanalytic movement. Unlike analysts in other cultures, French analysts have brought their struggles to the public: anti-Lacanian propaganda, for example, is not confined to psychoanalytic circles. This could not have occurred were it not for the fact that the French public was interested in the psychoanalytic movement. There is a fascination with Lacan that has little to do with whether one feels positively or negatively about him. Among the public, as in the world of analysts, Lacan does not inspire neutrality. He has been described as: "a dangerous fraud," "a clown, a buffoon," "the eternal father . . . he creates a circus," "the most profound thinker since Freud . . . he has saved psychoanalysis."

I have written here of ways in which Lacan's theoretical approach is resonant with French intellectual traditions and with what I have described as an emergent modern mythology, but his popularity with the public seems based on other things. People who knew virtually nothing about what Lacan thinks saw him as the first strong French contender in a ring formerly monopolized by Americans and Germans. Books sell well if they are by Lacan, about Lacan, for Lacan, or against Lacan. There is even a novel, *Le Pitre* by François Weyergans, that recounts the story of a psychoanalysis with Lacan.[6] The narrator of the book, Eric, is the patient of *Le Grand Vizir*, unmistakably Lacan, down to his style of dress and his address. The novel includes Eric's reactions to the publications of Lacan's *Ecrits*, which are referred to in the novel as two volumes called the *Textes*. In the novel, Eric feels compelled to read and reread them: "As for his *Textes*, there are few books that I have held and caressed as much as those . . . which I acquired at the very first hour of the very first day that they were being sold."[7]

As Eric rushed to procure the writings of *Le Grand Vizir* and combed them for echoes of his own analysis, so did people in analysis with Lacan rush to procure Weyergans's novel, combing it for reference to Lacan's practice which might have been a part of their own experience with him. Psychoanalysis is an intensely private experience, but all of an analyst's patients share a certain intimacy, even in their isolation from one another. There is a thirst to share some sign of it, to acknowledge in some way that all their heads lie on the same pillow and look up, day after day, at the same portrait on the wall. The intimacy is only rarely expressed. But when the analyst is as controversial a figure as Lacan, it is much more likely to come to the surface. So, for example, after the publication of *Le Pitre*, some of Lacan's patients became preoccupied with determining whether or not Weyergans had really been in analysis with Lacan. If so, they teased one another, which details of the highly unorthodox analysis had really happened? Patients in analysis with Lacan would tell stories of Weyergans having approached them with such questions as "What are the color of the cushions on Lacan's armchair?" In the novel, the cushions appear as green (they *are* green), but the young woman in treatment with Lacan who claimed to have been the source for this bit of detail used it to attack Weyergans for his unfavorable portrayal of Lacan: "If you were really in analysis with Lacan, you wouldn't have to ask the color of anything in that room." *Le Pitre* has scarcely hurt Lacan's popularity, which in any case is not founded on a reputation for sobriety, chastity, and a fifty-minute hour.

Lacan's two-part television special during the spring of 1974 made this last point dramatically. Lacan appeared in a smoking jacket and began the proceedings by announcing that most of his audience were surely idiots and that he was surely in error in trying to make them understand.[8] It was an uningratiating remark, but it set the tone for two evenings of superb, outrageous theater. Many found that in two hours of insults, incomprehensibilities, and flashes of genius Lacan established himself as the undisputed master of the media, or as one analyst, who has always been hostile to Lacan but who said he was "overwhelmed by a virtuoso performance," described him: "The psychoanalyst for the Age of McLuhan." Like a neurotic's symptom, Lacan's *Télévision* was a program that people loved to hate.

The fascination with Lacan extended to his struggles and thus to psychoanalytic politics. The French are used to a schismatic, highly ideological national politics, and they approach French psychoanalytic quarrels much as they would the history of Fourth Republic coalitions. And the public, like the analytic world, tends to be partisan.

In a situation where the number of people who have been analyzed has only recently shot up from a few hundred to many hundreds of thousands, "the analyzed" constitute a new social group. In most settings, this group remains an invisible community, but in France, where psychoanalysis has become a part of political culture, there seems to be some interest in "organizing the analyzed." And so, for example, former analysands have advertised in the personals section of *Le Monde* and *Le Nouvel Observateur* in order to form clubs on the assumption that the analyzed share a common view of the world. The instinct to ideologize the analytic experience seems typically French and is certainly intensified by the fact that French analysands have had their analytic experience in a divided analytic community. They know more about its internal politics than analysands in most other settings. There seem to be very few French patients who choose an analyst without knowing whether he or she is Lacanian. In France, the image of psychoanalysis as a medical specialty has broken down. If the psychoanalyst is not part of a professional group with claims to a uniform, neutral form of knowledge, then the analyst's values become increasingly salient. Among the students and liberal professionals, people frequently said that it was important to know an analyst's politics in order to choose an analyst wisely. Many also said they would want to know the analyst's "psychological politics": What school was the analyst in? Was he or she a Lacanian?

Analysands form camps "for or against Lacan," in which the quarrels of the analysts are reflected in the allegiances of the patients. When there were plans afoot to start clubs for the veterans of the analytic experience, part of the idea was to publish information about the practices of various analysts— what were their politics, what did they charge, who were the most "silent," who held short sessions, who did not? And thus, among other things: were they Lacanians, and if so, what were the pros and cons of getting involved with them? Stories of quarrels, jealousies, and eccentricities inevitably make for lively conversation. Thus, conversations about psychoanalytic politics are frequent, perhaps even more frequent than conversations about psychoanalysis itself. The result is that anecdotes from the private world of psychoanalytic practice spread quickly into the public domain.

In *Les Analysés Parlent,* Dominique Frischer describes interviews with thirty analytic patients about their experiences with
psychoanalysis.[9] The analysands in Frischer's book give the flavor of how the factions of French psychoanalytic politics come
to be represented in the population of analysands and then
in the popular culture. The Paris Psychoanalytic Society (usually referred to as "The Institute") is portrayed as the place to
go if you really need help; Lacan's Freudian School is typically
described as offering the most "interesting" analysis and the
most serious training experience. In my conversations with
students and liberal professionals, Lacanians were described as
brilliant, bohemian, and intellectual. It often was made clear
that being accepted as a patient by a well-known Lacanian can
raise one's social and intellectual standing because it is taken
to mean that you have the intellectual qualities that will allow
the technique to work and that you are sufficiently interesting to interest an "interesting" analyst.[10] Needless to say, being
in analysis with Lacan can constitute an identity in itself. For
example, when university professors brag about their ten-year
"relationships" with Lacan, they are not talking about a "cure";
they are talking about an apprenticeship in a philosophical
discipline, a new way of seeing. In other words, the Freudian
School is represented as a place where new horizons are opened
to those "in the know." Patients in analysis at the Institute
spoke of wanting to do another analysis with a Lacanian when
they "were able." The idea has gotten around that to be in
analysis at the Freudian School requires being equal to the task:

> When I began my analysis there was absolutely no chance of my
> going into treatment with a Lacanian. I was terrorized by the
> very idea . . . afraid that I wasn't at a sufficiently high intellectual
> level . . . that I wouldn't be interesting. . . . I said to myself: "I am
> not an interesting case, suffering and illness are not interesting."[11]

Being in analysis with a Lacanian seemed to carry virtually none of the stigma of being involved with psychiatry; it was seen as something that people do even if they do not "need help," and in fact, the popular images of an analysis with a Lacanian indicate that the experience might be good "for the strong" but could easily crush the meek. There was folklore about patients being driven crazy or driven to suicide by the rigors of a Lacanian analysis. Patients claimed that Lacanians keep them waiting forty-five minutes for a five-minute "hour" and charge them the same rate as a "classical" analyst would for a forty-five-minute session (i.e., in 1976 at about eighty to one hundred fifty francs or twenty to thirty dollars). Lacan's original idea in proposing sessions of variable length was to keep patients from turning the "analytic hour" into too much of a routine, but from the patient's point of view, there is nothing surprising about a ten-minute session if you have one every day. In this situation, shortening the session to seven minutes hardly constitutes a shock. And of course, patients wanted to know why the Lacanian analyst never wants to "shake up" the routine by keeping them for more rather than less time.

Working a ten- to twelve-hour day divided into five-, ten-, and fifteen-minute sessions means that the Lacanian analyst can see a lot of patients. For many patients, this "crowd" had become a preoccupation. Patients count the new faces in the waiting room at different times of the day, and some claim to resort to even more subtle means to figure out how many patients their analyst is seeing and how much money he or she is making. One analyst who used new Kleenex tissues for each patient to protect the head cushions on his couch had one patient who claimed to count the number of discarded Kleenex generated by the end of the analyst's day.[12]

The method was hardly scientific, but the head counts and Kleenex counts do go on, and the rumors about "the dozens" and "the hundreds" of patients who pass through a Lacanian office spread. A wider public becomes involved in taking positions on the same issues that have plagued the analytic community.

A patient's description of what is happening in his or her analysis is a highly subjective account. Any sketch of what patients are saying does not establish the facts about analytic practice but illustrates the kinds of raw materials that go into public images of the analytic community. The Lacanians are portrayed as incomprehensible, an image that Lacan's television special probably did a lot to strengthen. Word seems to be out that one needs to be an intellectual to "keep up." In America, where the word "egghead" was once turned into a political slur, a reputation for incomprehensibility would be damning. In France, there is irritation, but people also seem to find it *piquant*. The French have lived with a series of postwar intellectual movements that seem to many to have made a virtue out of opacity, and it seems that in France banality is the greater vice. What many French patients bring to their analysts is conditioned both by the drama of their private worlds and by very powerful preconceptions, including ideas about whether they expect their analysts to be conservative or radical, comprehensible or incomprehensible, concerned with making them "well" or with something else entirely. Some people felt that they couldn't talk to an analyst about "getting better," but had to use an acceptable language with which to express their desire for symptom relief. One very cynical analytic patient, a philosophy professor in a *lycée*, made a list for me of some acceptable terms. It was short: "You're allowed to talk about 'feeling your anguish differently,' about 'going beyond the symptom,' and that's about all." The comment suggests a socialization into treatment analogous to that of American patients who in recent years have learned to talk of "getting in touch with feelings," "being centered," and "getting it."

In France, the "well-socialized" patient lives in a highly ideological psychoanalytic culture and comes to his analyst weighted down by some very heavy baggage of "dos" and "don'ts" that reflect the public's understanding of the differences among psychoanalysts. The following chapter turns from the patient's *divan* to the *fauteuil* behind and looks at what psychoanalysts have to say about the effects of such sophistication on psychoanalysis itself.

While some features of the French Freud, notably its preoccupation with politics and the "for or against Lacan" question, found their way into popular representations of psychoanalysis, others did not. For example, an important aspect of the Lacanian influence within the French psychoanalytic world was to insist on a series of radical propositions, among these the ideas that there is an unconscious, that people are not the autonomous thinkers and actors they often believe themselves to be, that the ego is not a coherent entity, and finally, that our every action has a meaning, one that often is so threatening that we work hard not to let it surface. These propositions break down the everyday, commonsense categories that people use to describe and navigate through their world. These are *not* the propositions that are popularized. Quite the contrary.

The media present psychoanalysts alternately as elegant experts on daily life, as therapists and counselors for "you and me," and as contemporary philosophers. Psychoanalysts are seen as operating either in a world of abstract, philosophical discourse or in a world of normal, everyday problems, being called in as experts on such subjects as how women can adjust to being in the workforce, how to grow old gracefully, how to decide what contraceptives to use.

And when the subject of the popularization was Lacan himself, who stated many of the radical psychoanalytic propositions in their sharpest form, he was often appreciated in terms of his value as fashion or as theater. The major publishing trend around Lacan could not have been sustained if it rested solely on the buying habits of people with strong enthusiasms for his ideas. Other clienteles came into the picture. The owner of a small bookshop in a fashionable Parisian residential neighborhood works in an atmosphere that is far removed from Latin Quarter pressures, but she too has set up a little "psychoanalysis department" in her shop:

> I picked up the *Ecrits*, and I couldn't make any sense of it—and I have sold it to hundreds of people whom I can't imagine doing any better than I did. I think I sell the *Ecrits* the way I sell expensive art books to people who are indifferent to art but who like having the books on their coffee tables. I have a lot of fairly well-to-do customers; they can afford to buy things just for show.

The image of "coffee-table Lacan" epitomizes a tension between the subversive message of much of French psychoanalytic thinking and its real social impact.

So, for example, advice columns in women's magazines are liberally sprinkled with psychoanalytic conceptualizations of the problem at hand, but the advice itself is about the same as when the columns dished out clichés from the accumulated wisdom of the *bon bourgeois*.

The same is true of the advice that people got when they called in to Menie Grégoire's popular radio show with a problem. The tone was often self-consciously psychoanalytic, but the advice was prescriptive.[13] Psychoanalysts bristled when Menie Grégoire likened her enterprise to theirs, but she was quite insistent in announcing her view of what psychoanalysis and her radio show had in common: "One voice speaks little . . . straining to hear the silences, the hesitations, the lies and tears which may lurk beneath the surface."[14]

Although not everyone I interviewed could define psychoanalysis, everyone had an opinion on Menie Grégoire:

> I hate when people make fun of her. She has the courage to speak . . . the masses have faith in her.

> I prefer Madame Soleil. . . . Soleil does an honest astrology which I prefer to pseudo-psychoanalysis.

> Her advice helps me in my relations with my family. My friends and I talk about the show. I think it makes us more open.

There is no doubt that Grégoire's listeners were being educated into a new way of talking about their problems. When her program first went on the air, most of the letters to her did little more than sketch the outlines of a catastrophe in the lives of their authors. Often, the only hint about a possible psychological source for the problem would be in how the letter was signed, for example as "Orphan" or as "Child of an Alcoholic Father." When Grégoire discussed such letters on the radio, she would begin with the signature and what might be behind it. After only a year and a half on the air, the letters were different. They talked about feelings, family life, and sex; information about an author's background would no longer be confined to how people signed their names. For about a quarter of the Parisians I interviewed, the messages that Menie Grégoire tried to get across on her program are understood as the "lessons" of psychoanalysis: all people have problems, most have some sexual problems, feeling guilty is bad, talking about problems and anger is good, seeking help is not shameful, and psychoanalytic expertise can be a big help.

The editor in chief of the French version of *Psychology Today* felt that the magazine owed its success to the fact that its readers do not associate psychoanalysis with psychopathology, but with useful ideas that can be good for everybody. Indeed, in my own interviews, people used words like "drugs," "asylum," and "crazy" in talking about psychiatry, but psychoanalysis was a different matter. It was spoken of as a strategy which could help people, perhaps to be "happier" or "better parents." Among students, liberal professionals, and upper-middle-class people, there were even frequent claims of using psychoanalytic ideas in daily life, especially in dealing with family problems. The association of psychoanalysis with child raising was particularly strong, perhaps reflecting the French media's steady message that psychoanalysts are authorities on children. It is one of the few images of psychoanalytic "helpfulness" that is shared among all classes.[15]

But popular images of psychoanalytic "helpfulness" are far away from the images of a kind of psychoanalysis that shatters assumptions and helps the individual grasp the contradictions of his or her situation. Although many have picked up the idea that psychoanalysis puts in question their conscious interpretation of experience, they also see it as pragmatic and nonthreatening. Two middle-class Parisian housewives I interviewed typified the paradox. When asked to "define psychoanalysis," each was able to give a concrete, specific definition. For the first, analysis is "a way of exploring what lies beneath our conscious selves." For the second, "The analyst listens to dreams and reveries and sees the hidden meanings that slip through."

Yet, in the course of the forty-five-minute interviews which followed, each talked about psychoanalysis in ways that dissolved its specificity. For the first woman:

> Psychoanalysis is used in schools when students are having trou-
> bles going from one grade to the next higher on. . . . Politicians
> use psychoanalysis—when there is a decision they must make or
> when they have suffered a defeat. . . . Drug addiction. . . . The
> French need psychoanalysis more now to calm them down. They
> are becoming more pressured and nervous. Not the way they used
> to be.

And for the second:

> Psychoanalysis is good for couples in trouble. It is for marriage
> counselors. . . . Excellent for stammering.

The world of people in France whose vision of psychoanalysis is that of a social practice that breaks down traditional
assumptions is large. But this group is embedded in a larger
society primarily interested in a psychoanalysis which can
help them build things up. The tension is ironic: the loss of
traditional anchors forms the basis for widespread interest in
the psychoanalytic culture, but then the demand is for psychoanalysis to provide new anchors. In France, this tension
appears more sharply than elsewhere, to the point of suggesting to some practitioners that the conditions for the social
success of psychoanalysis undermine the possibility for its
meaningful practice.

9 "Saving French Freud"

Freud was the first to point out that ideas shape symptoms: he noted, for example, that in the hysterical paralysis of an arm, the paralysis corresponded to the "idea" of an arm, rather than to the "anatomical" arm. In this case, a socially shared idea about a body part affected the symptom, but socially shared ideas about the mind can have similar powers. Generations of eighteenth-century women suffered from "the vapors," but as systems of explanation changed, so did the form of their swoons, and their daughters and granddaughters suffered instead from neurasthenia and hysteria.

In Freud's day, psychoanalysis was a radically new way of looking at the world, but now, three-quarters of a century later, it is so deeply embedded in our culture that it is psychoanalytic ideas themselves that influence our symptoms. So, although the subject here has often been the sociology of superficial psychoanalytic knowledge, its impact is not superficial. As the language of psychoanalytic interpretation becomes commonplace, the therapist begins to incarnate what is seen as a shared way of looking at the world. In this situation, pinning down exactly what is happening in an individual analysis poses some new problems: when is the analyst serving as a mirror for the patient and when is the patient reflecting the psychoanalytic beliefs of the culture?[1]

In our usual model, "natural" science does not change in its predictive ability as a function of the number of people who know about it. When a lot of people have information or misinformation about molecules or rat behavior, chemical reactions and the way in which rats run through a maze do not change. But when people are both the subject and object of a scientific inquiry, the situation is more complex. And when a therapeutic strategy is involved, things are even more dependent on their cultural context.[2] Specifically, the diffusion of the psychoanalytic culture, how much people know, what they know, and what they feel about psychoanalysis does impact on psychoanalytic therapy itself.

To illustrate, let us take an example offered by a French psychoanalyst, although perhaps the point is made more dramatically than in most routine practice. The analyst, François Roustang, described how, after two or three completely silent sessions, a hospitalized aphasic woman with paralyzed legs said: "It is my memory," after which she remembered her married name, her mother's name, and finally, with great difficulty, her father's name. Several days later, the symptom-free patient walked out of the hospital. Roustang concluded that his patient had been cured by being conscious of psychoanalytic theory several steps ahead of the cultural situation of her symptom. In other words, twentieth-century theory had triumphed over nineteenth-century neurosis:

> The spectacular cure . . . can only be explained as a phenomenon of cultural lag. An hysteric who conformed to Charcot's model abandoned her symptoms thanks to Freudian theory (of memory traces), and then Lacanian theory (of the *nom-du-père*, the father's name). . . .[3]

Here, a woman was cured through her modern understanding of her culturally regressive symptomatology. But what happens with twentieth-century symptomatology? Roustang suggests that to be effective, psychoanalysis has to run ahead of its cultural diffusion. Despite the fact that the conjecture is a bit dizzying, it is not unpopular in French psychoanalytic circles. The recent and widespread popularization of psychoanalysis has left many French analysts preoccupied with its impact on their work. Many admit that their most prized patients are the psychoanalytically "naive." The naive may be prized, but they are a dying breed. Most French patients and their analysts are struggling together with the challenges of the "sophisticated symptom."

The notion of the sophisticated symptom provides a powerful image for how the psychoanalytic culture might impact on the psychoanalytic symptom and cure. A series of related problems raise similar questions about the practice of psychoanalysis in a psychoanalytic culture. First, French analysts, like analysts throughout the world, must deal with their patients' use of "book learning" as a form of resistance. In France, however, the issue is more salient, both because of the intellectual emphasis of the prevailing psychoanalytic doctrine and because so many patients look to their analysis as a training experience and are trying to "keep up with the literature" as they go along. It is possible that French analysts face the world's most sophisticated patient population.

Some analysts are untroubled by patient sophistication:

A patient comes in with the expectation that we are going to be talking about his relationship to his "father's name." Sure enough, he brings it up within five sessions. So what? If it's important, we may well be talking about it in five years. If it is coming up only because the patient has just walked out of Lacan's seminar,

the issue will quickly fade away to be replaced by what is really
important.

Others find it a more troublesome obstacle and fear that the
theoretically sophisticated patient is making psychoanalysis
more lengthy and complex: "It is harder to separate out the
insights that come from the patient's guts from those that
come from his reading." And some stress that even a little
knowledge can be a dangerous thing. One analyst told the
story of a patient who had been making very little progress
in over a year of analysis although things seemed to have
started very well. Finally, the patient confided to him: "At first,
I was very provoked by your silences. They reminded me of
my father who hardly ever speaks to me. But then, I found
out that it is just the method. . . . So I don't take it as personally now."

In France, the intensity of psychoanalytic politics can give
intellectual resistance to analysis a new twist. Patients come
to analysts with a lot of information about their theoretical
and political preferences, their conduct with other patients,
and where they stand on issues of psychoanalytic politics. The
information explosion leads to the predictable results: Freudian School analysts told stories of how their patients suddenly
discover that "Lacan is a fraud and his theories are paranoid
junk," and analysts outside of the Freudian School had stories of analyses punctuated by their patients becoming "rabid
Lacanians" and insisting that "they were learning more about
themselves in fifteen minutes of Lacan's seminar than in four
years of analysis with me":

> I have a patient who comes in every day with a copy of the *Ecrits*
> under his arm. But of course, I am not a Lacanian. He is trying to
> tell me something, and of course, in the analysis, it will be said, it
> must be said and analyzed.

Analysts on both sides of the Lacanian divide had similar attitudes about patients using intellectual sophistication or knowledge of psychoanalytic politics as a weapon to fend off analysis. Although some were more concerned than others, they all agreed that, ultimately, everything is grist for the analytic mill. But in general, they did seem more agitated by something over which they felt less control: the image of psychoanalysis in the culture.

For example, patients make it clear that being in analysis can raise one's social standing. This is clearly in some tension with a vision of psychoanalysis as a process that calls the fundamental categories of our experience into radical doubt. Patients and analysts also share normalization through psychoanalytic careerism. Patient rosters in all the analytic societies are filled by psychologists, teachers, family counselors, and speech therapists who need psychoanalytic experience as well as academic diplomas in order to find work. Some analysts insist that the issue of career obligation, like everything else, is simply grist for the analytic mill; others are more concerned: "Would Freud have talked about psychoanalysis as the plague if he knew it was going to become a rubber stamp for certifying marriage counselors and dance therapists?"

With university legitimation and flattering coverage in the media, psychoanalysis in France is popularly portrayed as a literary, educational, even a political discipline. Shown on television working with normal children or philosophizing in the isolation of his study, the analyst comes to be seen as a nonthreatening figure, close to the world of everyday concerns, an expert on everyday problems. Although the neutralization of psychoanalysis may make it easier for people to approach an analyst, many analysts make it clear that their first job in the clinical situation is to undo the cultural image of the psychoanalyst as an expert, a fix-it man for specific problems. French analysts, like their colleagues in other cultures, talk about the necessity of refusing a "first request" (*la première demande*) for specific help that masks a more global desire for analysis. But in France, this classic sequence has a new complication: the relative psychoanalytic hegemony in the French therapeutic world (psychoanalytic ideology has infiltrated an astounding range of specialties from gynecology to massage therapy and acupuncture) is so great that things may often be the other way around. Some bourgeois patients may live in worlds where talking about "being in analysis" is the most acceptable way of asking for help. So a desire for information or social support may actually find a masked expression in a desire for "analysis."

Analysts have blamed the public's "misunderstanding" of what they really are about on misrepresentation by journalists and their psychoanalyst colleagues who set themselves up as experts. But the frequent reports by analysts that people ask for psychoanalysis when what they really want is a kind of support more appropriately given by a family member or clergyman, make it clear that the misunderstanding goes beyond the "misrepresentations" of the media to raise a more fundamental contradiction. The growth of psychoanalytic culture seems to depend on significant numbers of middle-class people feeling dislocated and disoriented in a society that they once felt was "theirs." When support from the community becomes too abstract to rely on, the individualistic analytic relationship turns into a valued resource. But the private problems which the patient brings to the analyst are rooted in the social conditions which made the psychoanalytic culture possible in the first place, and so it is not surprising that the patient seeks a solution from the analyst in terms of what he or she has lost:

rules, roots, and shared meaning. The patient's fantasy that the analyst has "answers" is fed by real needs as much as by media misrepresentations. French analysts claim that for the past ten years patients have come in not with a "symptom," but with a request for advice on how to live.

> I used to get patients who were suffering from a tic, a hearing disorder, a phobia. Now I get people who seem to be suffering from a way of life. They were brought up Catholic, but the Church has worked its way into a position of irrelevance in their lives. They were brought up to believe in their studies; now diplomas come cheap and mean nothing, especially when it comes to getting a job. They were brought up to live in communities; now they don't even know their neighbors. They want me to be a priest, a neighborhood, an authority on how they should live. . . .
>
> My patients cannot stand the fact that there are no longer clear-cut rules about what behavior is appropriate to the well brought up bourgeois child. Should your seventeen-year-old daughter take the pill, should you give her money to set up housekeeping with her boyfriend? And if she does, should this be kept a secret from family and friends?

Social dislocations condition an environment in which individual psychoanalytic therapy flourishes, but then people come into that therapy hoping that it will give them answers that society no longer provides. The conflict is apparent; perhaps it is inevitable.

> Each analyst has always had to struggle against his patients' desires that he or she take over their lives. But now that analysts live in a society that treats them like experts on living, they have to struggle against becoming gurus. . . . To do so would mean the end of analysis, but everything in the society pushes toward it. It is no longer a problem for individual analysts, it is *the* problem for contemporary psychoanalysis.

These tensions between psychoanalysis and the psychoanalytic culture are certainly not unique to the French scene, but perhaps French psychoanalysts are more aware of them because they have been faced with them so suddenly and in such an intense and explosive form. In the 1950s, when Serge Moscovici was interviewing members of the public at large for his study of the social image of psychoanalysis in France, he also tried to interview some analysts. Few would cooperate. They seemed to feel that it would compromise them in their role as analysts. One analyst who knew about Moscovici's work in the 1950s said that he would "never have gotten involved" because "the idea of a sociologist studying psychoanalysis as a social phenomenon seemed objectionable."

> But now, here I am, twenty years later, talking with a foreign sociologist who is studying psychoanalysis as a social phenomenon. . . . But you see, after the whirlwind of the past five to ten years, I no longer have any doubts that psychoanalysis is a social phenomenon.

Twenty years after Moscovici's work, French analysts responded enthusiastically to my project. Few declined to be interviewed, and once the project had gotten underway, many requested to be interviewed and reinterviewed. Twenty years ago, French analysts pictured themselves as marginal and believed that their effectiveness depended on their "neutrality," that is to say, on not taking public stands. Now things are different. Analysts came out of the events of May–June to discover that, far from being marginal they were very much at the center of things. Their sense of their roles has changed dramatically.

This new position affects the profession; there is a possible contradiction between the subversive aspirations of psychoanalysis and the new acceptability and prestige of the psychoanalytic career in France. It used to be easier to feel that one was doing something subversive because family, friends, and professional associates disapproved.

I started in 1949. My friends and family considered me mad . . .
feared I would get sick by contamination. . . .

When I began my analysis in 1960, my family was angry, saw it as
destined to hurt family relationships . . . saw it as courting disas-
ter . . . and it had to be hidden from my colleagues in medicine. . . .

The change in the social acceptance of the analytic career has
meant that it has a new normalized recruitment. If you were
French and chose to be an analyst in the 1930s, 1940s, 1950s,
or even the early 1960s, you were choosing a "path less taken,"
and like the men and women who joined Freud's circle, you
had to have a good reason for doing so—a neurosis whose
treatment drew you into psychoanalytic circles, a passion for
psychoanalytic theory. The road was rough: one's status was
marginal. Now, medical students talk about their decisions to
pursue analytic careers with the same language, if perhaps not
with the same feelings, that they use to talk about the pros
and cons of careers in ophthalmology: the market is good,
the referral network is reliable, the prestige is high, the hours
are predictable. We cannot know the power of their analytic
experience. But the question still remains if the assurance of
being launched in what the French call a *belle carrière* is easily
reconcilable with the psychoanalytic enterprise.

Psychoanalytic careerism is by no means confined to the
medical community. The rise of Lacanianism and the decline
of the French university have made psychoanalysis an attractive career choice for philosophers as well as for physicians.
The same students who once studied philosophy at the Ecole
Normale Supérieure know that an *agrégation* or a doctorate
may not get them a job, but an analytic career can provide
intellectual community and steady work. Many young analysts came to see Lacan's inner circle at the Freudian School
as the 1970s' equivalent of the university *mandarinat*, a closed

circle for the Parisian best and brightest. "After all," said one dropout from the *agrégation*, who was now cultivating the good graces of powerful Lacanians, "they're the only visible intellectuals around—the existentialists' cafés have given way to the psychoanalysts' couches."

Such analysts might be more interested in the mathemes than in the routine of daily practice. When patients reported incomprehensible sessions during which their analysts seem to be "talking to someone else or giving a speech," it may reflect that their analysts were rehearsing for the *really* important encounter with a Freudian School luminary or an editor. The problem of the philosopher-manqué may have appeared more sharply at the Freudian School, where a highly politicized, theoretical, and even mathematically formalized psychoanalytic doctrine had near hegemony, but militant intellectualism runs through the entire French psychoanalytic community. The Freud who has "caught on" in almost all French analytic circles is more structuralist and poeticized than he ever has been before. During the international conferences at which psychoanalysts meet, American and British analysts describe even the more "medical" French analysts as "intellectual terrorists." Those who are dazzled by their theoretical leaps are not always sure where the leaps are leading; some suspect they are leading nowhere at all, but they are dazzled all the same.

At the Freudian School, where Lacan was everyone's *Maître*, young analysts reported feeling particularly strong pressure to differentiate themselves from their patients, and this could lead to trying to impress patients by intellectual intimidation, and to some other problems as well. These analysts made a radical distinction between themselves and *le reste*, the mass of psychologists, nurses, social workers, and teachers who crowded Lacan's seminar. One young analyst, a patient of

Lacan and a teacher at Vincennes, had nothing but disdain for the "average" Lacanian consumer: "These people know nothing of Lacan. Perhaps they go to the Seminar, perhaps they own a copy of the *Ecrits* to impress their friends. For them, knowing a little makes them feel that they are part of something, but they don't really belong at all." This young analyst's condescension may well be toward his own patients. Most of the people who "don't understand" and who "don't belong" tend to have little money, the wrong diplomas, and few connections. They go to the Lacanians who are just starting their practices—newly authorized *analystes practiciens*. These young analysts may charge them prices they can afford, but are the very ones who are most likely to see their patients as a psychoanalytic "subproletariat."

French analysts have often criticized American psychoanalysts for "giving in" to the social pressure to provide "answers." But French analysts face the same problem, and it seems that their model of American "normalization" as "giving in" was too simple. What is most subversive about psychoanalysis, its insistence on the ever-presence of another level of explanation, may be more denatured by the integration of psychoanalysis into everyday life and everyday language than by analysts' participation in everyday institutions.

French analysts struggle to get their bearings in a situation in which many feel psychoanalysis is deeply threatened. Some try to "strike back" by a strategy of "militant retreat," others by political militancy. The first group argues that there was a virtue as well as a necessity in the way things used to be in France when psychoanalysis was invisible to the public and was scorned by all establishments, including, as one analyst put it, the "anti-establishment establishment." This group of "nostalgics" includes a broad spectrum of analysts, politically

radical and conservative, and psychoanalytically Lacanian
and non-Lacanian. They have little in common except a belief
that psychoanalysis is "definitionally" subversive, but only
when it is marginal. For them, psychoanalytic purity can only
be recaptured if psychoanalysts "stay home" in private practice, off television and out of schools, hospitals, and universities. Their attempt to save a "revolutionary" psychoanalysis by
beating a retreat into traditional practice may be rather futile:
the popular diffusion of psychoanalysis follows analysts right
into the privacy of their consulting rooms, brought in by their
patients. Beyond the limitations of this nostalgic strategy lies
the irony of arguing that psychoanalysis can be "revolutionary" only when conducted in its most classical, which is also
to say in its most upper-class, setting.[4]

While some analysts are turning from the public back to
the private, others are taking the opposite tack, and look to
radical politics as a way to counter psychoanalytic normalization. We have already met these analysts many times: they
are the veterans of May, the university activists, the antipsychiatric radicals. Their actions have given the "French Freud"
much of its special flavor, but their strategy also suffers from
contradictions.

Some of these contradictions may be local to France, where
radical politics often degenerates into a radical chic. Other
tensions seem more universal. First, since the subversiveness
of psychoanalysis lies in its assertion of a radical discontinuity between a hidden reality with which it is in touch and the
world of the everyday, analysts may undermine their impact
by making it possible for the psychoanalytic relationship to
become a continuation of political interests that they share
with patients. One analyst put it this way: "Sharing a patient's
political world by standing next to him at a demonstration can

stop an analysis dead. Complicity is bad for analysis whether the complicity is for a good cause or a bad one, on the Right or the Left." Second, the marriage of psychoanalysis and radical politics may not work because, even when it has a strong political flavor, psychoanalysis may depoliticize people. The May events left a political legacy to French psychoanalysis, but the ensuing psychoanalytic culture also took many people who had been working for social change and refocused their energies on the possibilities for personal change, a pattern not unique in the history of failed social movements.

Analysts who are committed to integrating psychoanalysis and political activism in their own lives are pained to watch some of their own patients drop out of politics as they become involved with their psyches. One analyst, a Communist, was anguished by this aspect of his practice: "The most painful is when patients talk about former political colleagues with the condescension of the enlightened."

French analysts I interviewed expressed yet another "hope" in their description of efforts to combat or at least to run ahead of psychoanalytic normalization. This was Jacques Lacan.

Freud's technique was designed to create a relationship whose rules (and most specifically, whose golden rule "to say everything that comes to mind") defied social conventions and facilitated an openness about sexual matters that was forbidden elsewhere. In Freud's day, psychoanalysis was "beyond the law," but times have changed. The erotic is banalized, "everyone knows" how analysts behave, and "playing analyst" with one's friends and family has become a way for people to express caring and intimacy. Some French analysts were preoccupied with the question of what psychoanalysis must become and what psychoanalysts must do to remain "beyond the law" as Freud intended:

I feel that if I made the kinds of interpretations with my patients that Freud reports that he made with his, I would be doing something that my patients would find banal, perhaps funny. I would be laughed at for saying the obvious. It would seem pitiful, obvious, gross.

The power of analysis is the power of the unspoken, the imagined, the unexpected. My analysands are programmed to expect that they will imagine strange things about me, fall in love with me, hate me, dream about me—programmed, in short, to expect the unexpected. The power of the analysis is in the refusal to gratify the first level of demand [*la premiere demande*], but if my patients come to me with the desire to be in analysis with someone who "behaves" like an analyst, unless I invent and invent . . . and perhaps invent things that have never been associated with the analytic . . . I can end up by essentially gratifying this desire and the analysis can stop.

Many analysts saw Lacan's refusal to act in expected ways, or even to act in those unexpected ways that have come to be expected of him, as positive responses to psychoanalysis having become routine and predictable. In France today (where an illustrated book called *Freud Explained to Children* has become a popular birthday gift), it is hard to create the feeling that psychoanalysis is unfamiliar or illegitimate. In many ways, Lacan succeeded in doing both.

Lacan made a career out of standing against the professionalization and normalization of psychoanalysis, but the Lacanian response to normalization, like the withdrawal from institutions and the advance into politics, had its limitations. If he succeeded in disrupting the psychoanalytic "professional" routine, he may also have succeeded in creating a movement with religious overtones of which he was the guru. If he succeeded in bringing psychoanalysis back to what is most radical in the Freudian field of the unconscious, he may also have created a theory so abstract that its practice is in constant danger of degenerating into intellectual games. Analysts complain that their colleagues tend to be unnecessarily abstruse with their patients and with each other. Critics charge that they do this to reassure themselves that they are in a league with Lacan's intellectual virtuosity. But even on this question of psychoanalytic opacity, some analysts see a possible virtue in the "over-intellectualization" that most people think of as the French psychoanalytic vice. They feel that the use of Lacanian opacity serves the social function of restoring a distance between public and analyst, a distance that is necessary for the transference and that has been badly eroded by popularization.

Americans criticize Lacan's style as the "opposite of American clarity and frankness," but for the French, this is exactly the point. There is nothing clear or frank about the unconscious. In any case, the French are convinced that the threat to psychoanalysis is oversimplification rather than its opposite. They were comforted by Lacan's attacks on those who have taken the difficult and made it simple: "If Lacan brings us to new difficulties, isn't it precisely in order to liberate us from so much that is facile."[5] Many analysts believe that what is most radical in the psychoanalytic vision is the search for the "unacceptable" *within* and that Lacan repeatedly brought them back to it by confronting them with the unacceptable in himself. In large part, this was the power of Lacan's seminar, where Lacan put himself in the position of the analysand, publicly expressing, analyzing, and theorizing his own symptoms much as Freud did in his early work.

It was not easy for analysts who had broken away from Lacan to appear at his seminar: even with a thousand listeners, Lacan was known to note publicly such a "significant presence." But analysts who had bitter ruptures with Lacan and who claimed that it would be "political suicide" to be seen at his seminar almost wistfully expressed the desire to attend once again, as if to recapture a closeness to a kind of touchstone. Analysts spoke of the seminar as a place to make contact with something precious that they could not find in other places and that they feared they were losing in the routine practice of analytic work:

> What Lacan is doing is taking his own hysterical capacities and using them to present the discourse of the unconscious in public, and although he brings it to a theoretical and poetic level, he captures the very tonality of what happens between analyst and patient. He can do this because he has no choice; he must . . . it is really happening there for him. . . . That he has taken his audience as his analysts, there is the mark of his symptom, his megalomania . . . but that is not important. . . . What is important is that he brings to our attention something very powerful that we tend to smooth over, even to erase because it frightens us: that our power as analysts comes from our confrontations with our own neuroses.

There were many who felt that Lacan's contribution to keeping French psychoanalysis in touch with the power of the unacceptable came not only from his ability to theorize his symptom in his seminar and in his writing, but more basically, from who he was. Analysts whom Lacan considered as enemies and traitors felt that Lacan offered them the hope of relief from the dilemma of psychoanalytic familiarity and acceptability, not in spite of his unorthodox practice and often outrageous public persona, but in part, as a result of them.

> The temper tantrums, the aristocratic expectations that the caviar will be perfectly chilled, the toasts perfectly buttered, the champagne perfectly dry, the habit of summoning friends to see him, asking them a question and then dismissing them "until tomorrow" as though they were analytic patients in for their five-minute

sessions rather than colleagues, all of these are part of Lacan's power.

One afternoon during Lacan's visit to Boston in December 1975, he and a small party (a mathematician, several visiting analysts, friends of Lacan) went to lunch at the Ritz. Lacan was wearing a silk shirt with a high clerical collar and a long fur which he placed on the back of his chair. The maître d' of this very formal dining room informed Lacan that the rules required that he check his coat and wear a tie. Lacan stormed out, past Boston matrons and bankers looking grave over their business lunches, hurling obscenities to the waiter, to the maître d', and to the world. When I told this story of Lacan's noisy brush with Yankee propriety to two of Lacan's colleagues, each had an immediate response for or against Lacan. For one:

> Of course! That is his greatness. The man who is comfortable with the outrageous. The obscenity that is on all of our lips but that we never dare say. All is permissible. He is analysis. The unthinkable. The forbidden-to-touch.

For the other:

> Everything he does—how he eats, his stares, his dress, his histrionics—all of this provokes the most massive violent transference to him. The abusive father. The castrating mother. He is out of control, dangerous. It must stop.

Freud did not bring the plague to America. Much of what he considered to be the most revolutionary aspects of his thought was downplayed by American psychiatrists who wanted the acceptance of psychoanalysis to go smoothly. Freud shattered the notion of the self as a conscious, coherent actor, but American ego psychology went far toward pasting its parts back together again. Freud's pessimism about the limits of personal change without social restructuring and his sense that "cure" was a notion that could do psychoanalysis as much harm as good got lost in the appropriation of psychoanalysis by American medicine.

In America, the tone of nonthreatening good citizenship continues. When, for example, in the 1970s American psychoanalytic institutes had trouble recruiting new candidates and finding patients for candidates to treat in supervised analytic work, institutes turned unabashedly to public relations. They held press conferences in which they stressed the usefulness of their service to the community and held "open house" cocktail parties where everyone could see that analysts were not mysterious but just "plain folks." In short, American psychoanalysis has tried to fit in by stressing its proximity rather than its distance from the world of the everyday.

Many French psychoanalysts feel that what the Americans did with Freud was psychoanalytic suicide. Others, less hostile, take it as a warning about the price of popularity. Psychoanalysis may be accepted if it presents itself as acceptable, but the essence of psychoanalysis is its contact with an almost definitionally unacceptable truth: people are not their own centers. The question for the majority of French analysts is whether things can be different for them. Their effort to make them different through a policy of nostalgic retreat seems like an exercise in futility, but politics and Lacanism *are* making a difference and their synergism has created an environment that is unique in the history of psychoanalysis.

We know that Freud took a certain comfort when he saw resistance to psychoanalysis because he believed that when people really understood his message they had reason to feel hesitant and afraid. So, on the grounds that resistance was a sign of a significant measure of understanding, Freud predicted that psychoanalysis would have won its final and decisive battle when it had "won over" the culture that had been most hostile to it. We may already have seen this happen: the French resistance to psychoanalysis was exceptional, and the acceptance equally so. But what Freud may not have seen is that psychoanalysis faced more significant battles that were not over conquest, but over its internal contradictions, battles not with the outside but with the inside.

There is an irony in Freud's blind spot. He who taught us that the individual's greatest battle is within himself somehow imagined that psychoanalysis would triumph if it dealt with external enemies. In France, the struggle with internal contradiction has lasted long after the external enemies have been defeated or, as in the case of existentialists and Marxists, have been turned into friends. In this book, we have met some of these contradictions, which range from the contradiction between psychoanalysis and the psychoanalytic institution to the contradiction between psychoanalysis and its social success. In France, these contradictions are being lived, not just theorized. France is the stage for a battle that has the greatest significance for the future of psychoanalysis. But it is not the battle for acceptance that Freud imagined. It is the battle of psychoanalysis against itself.

V Lacan in Contemporary Culture

10 Lacan in America: Poetry and Science

When Freud came to America in 1909, he courted American medicine. In November 1975, at the age of seventy-four, Jacques Lacan made a second visit to the United States, knowing that Freud had lived to regret his too easy successes with American physicians and believing that American medicine had failed psychoanalysis for over half a century. His agenda had to be more complex.

Lacan's American itinerary brought him to New Haven, New York, and Cambridge, where he was to meet with the American analysts he had denigrated as technicians and who had rejected him as a renegade, and with mathematicians, linguists, and logicians whose work had become part of the theoretical scaffolding for his own contributions. The American visit was highly charged; analysts could accept or not accept him as a colleague, and mathematicians and linguists could recognize or not recognize a kinship with his efforts at constructing a psychoanalytic science.

Lacan stood in front of an expanse of green chalkboard in a conference room at the Massachusetts Institute of Technology School of Engineering. Behind him, painstakingly sketched in colored chalk, was a series of knots (see figure 10.1). These, he

Figure 10.1
Adapted from *Scilicet* (Paris: Seuil, 1976), p. 56.

explained, were Borromean knots made of interlocking circles. When one is cut, the whole chain of circles becomes undone. Wherever Lacan went in America, he spoke of these knots. Before each talk, he spent hours drawing the knots in four colors, designating the imaginary, the real, the symbolic, and a fourth circle which he called the "symptom" (*symptôme*). When Lacan was speaking to audiences of psychoanalysts, the drawings of complex knots and the language of topology were themselves a barrier to communication.

But now, at MIT, formal representation and mathematical rigor presented no problem. The problem was in what Lacan

was saying. After carefully describing manipulations to prove
that a series of representations on the board were all the same
knot, Lacan went on to give the knot a name.

> I call the knot with three circles the figure of psychic reality, and
> S, is the symptom. The symptom is the special mark of the human
> dimension. Perhaps God has symptoms, but his understanding is
> most probably paranoid. . . . We encounter the Trinity all the time.
> Notably in the sexual domain. There, it is not held fixed by an
> individual alone but also by another. . . . The pretended mystery of
> the divine Trinity reflects what is in each of us; what is illustrated
> best is paranoid knowledge. . . .

For most of the mathematicians, linguists, and philosophers
in his audience, the question of whether this man was doing
poetry or science did not even present itself. He simply seemed
incomprehensible. How can one begin to make a bit more
sense out of Lacan's attempt to pull together topology, trini-
ties, and symptoms?

There are several ways in which mathematicians might
enter a theoretical discourse about human nature. Mathematics can be used metaphorically; or it can be used very literally
in the construction of precise and delimited mathematical
models. Lacan's use of topology fits neither of these familiar
categories. It is too sustained on a technical level to be dismissed as "pure metaphor"; it is not delimited enough to be a
model. What is it? Understanding its several differences from
more typical uses of mathematical models in psychology is a
way to begin to answer the question.

Often the purpose of a mathematical model in psychology is to calculate the consequences of a given manipulation on a given situation. The formula is the instrument that
lets you "crank the handle." There is nothing of this predictive intent in what Lacan is doing with the knots. Often the

psychologist's use of a mathematical model is more concep-
tual than predictive; certain problems are elucidated by being
presented entirely within the framework of a mathematizable
microworld. These mathematizable phenomena are factored
out of the rest of reality which is left for another time and
another theory. They deliberately have been made function-
ally invisible to the scientist. Lacan wants to capture some
aspect of the mind through mathematization, what he calls a
"mathematizable minimum," but he is not willing to filter out
the rest even temporarily. Thus he might begin a paragraph
with a description of how to manipulate knots and end it with
a question about God. For the mathematical psychologist, the
justification for a theory is its product, that is, the true statements it will generate. For Lacan, the process of theorizing
itself takes on a privileged role. He speaks of how manipulating
and perforating spheres in the "praxis of knots" is "the thing
to which the spirit is most rebel." The circles that make up the
knots are sections of spheres, "man's first representations of
his own body and his first conceptions of science." The knots
"so contradict our global sense of our bodies as enveloped and
enveloping that to try oneself in the praxis of knots is to shat-
ter inhibition," perhaps because it threatens our images of our
bodies and our images of our science by reminding us of a
connection between them.

It is clear that for Lacan the role of mathematical theory
is psychoanalytic. Doing the theory—working on the knots,
practicing the manipulations—enters as an integral element,
indeed, the critical element in the emergence of insight about
the self, in the same sense that psychoanalytic insight grows
out of the lived relationship with an analyst.

The mathematical modeler often sees his or her enterprise
as scientific and precise, as opposed to literary or poetic. Lacan

refuses this dichotomy. He cuts across a line between poetry and science that has become axiomatic in the philosophy if not in the practice of Western science.

Occasionally physicists or mathematicians describe what they do in poetic terms. Their discourse may be seen as interesting, but it is judged peripheral to the fundamentals of their "science." Even if its relation to philosophical issues is granted, it is considered to be irrelevant to scientific practice. For the physicist, the question of the line between poetry and science can be a matter for Sunday morning rumination because on Monday morning he or she can relegate it to the philosophers of science and get back to the "real business" of being a physicist. Physicists can factor out poetry from scientific function because for them there is a clear distinction between their creative, partly intuitive mental processes, which lead them to discover the fundamental particles, and the fundamental particles themselves. For the psychoanalyst, the distinction is less clear: process and product may be one.

Lacan's MIT audience, used to a polished university discourse, found the Lacanian presentation confusing; some of them even interpreted it as an insulting lack of preparation. The discussion period made matters worse. Lacan answered a question about the relationship between interior and exterior by stating that, as an analyst, he was not at all certain that people even have an interior:

> The only thing that seems to me to testify to it is that which we produce as excrement. The characteristic of a human being is that—and this is very much in contrast with other animals—he doesn't know what to do with his shit. He is encumbered by his shit. Why is he so encumbered while these things are so discreet in nature? Of course it is true that we are always coming across cat shit, but a cat counts as a civilized animal. But if you take elephants, it is

striking how little space their leavings take up in nature, whereas
when you think of it, elephant turds could be enormous. The discretion of the elephant is a curious thing. Civilization means shit,
cloaca maxima.

The seminar came to an end soon after this digression on
the excrement of elephants and others. By the time his audience shuffled out of the seminar and on to dinner at the Ritz,
grumblings about Lacanian incomprehensibility had given
way to protests about his deliriousness or senility. A rational
discourse, the kind of discourse that would be accepted in the
university, can be about topology, or it can be about elephant
shit as an example of Dadaist poetry. But Lacan was not speaking *about* mathematics or poetry or psychoanalysis. He was
trying to *do* them.

When Lacan was asked why he came to the United States,
he said, "I have come to speak." In other words, he would not
speak *of* psychoanalysis; his speech itself would *be* a psychoanalytic discourse. He distinguishes this psychoanalytic discourse, which he himself characterized at MIT as "a discourse
close to delirium," from a university discourse, where language is taken over by its object. In a certain sense, in the psychoanalytic discourse all objects are taken over by language.
For Lacan, "language is the condition of the unconscious";
the message about the unconscious in the psychoanalytic discourse is deeply embedded in its medium, in its language and
style. The American audience was expecting an expert who
would spell out for them his new theory of the mind; instead,
they got a man who simply spoke and who made it clear that,
despite their expectations, "I don't have a conception of the
world; I have a style."

When Americans heard Lacan speak of Borromean knots,
Greek science, paranoia, the concept of number, of symptoms,

of phonemes, of spheres, and elephant shit, they were baffled. They tried to find a code to decipher the communication. They may have missed the point. Lacan wants his audience to enter into the circle of his language without trying to understand it from the "outside." Lacan takes his structuralism seriously. If you assume that people are inhabited by language, then the suggestion that you relate to a psychoanalytic discourse, in particular *his*, by letting it inhabit you, makes sense. And as in any psychoanalytic experience, there should be no expectation that things will happen quickly. Lacan makes it clear that understanding him requires time and a process of "working through": "It is empirical fact . . . that after ten years time, what I have written becomes clear to everyone."[1] Americans think of themselves as a pragmatic people; and they also like to think of themselves as responsive to intellectual humility. They found cold comfort in Lacan's assurance that with ten years' work they would be sure to understand or in his idea that what he had to say was embedded in his style.

Americans often fear that when style is stressed, it is stressed at the expense of substance. Lacan the stylist was mistrusted, seen as frivolous and uninterested in "getting a message across." Lacan was trying to get a message across, but he was trying to do it across an ocean of differences in cultural and intellectual traditions.

Americans are quick to equate the gestural with the superficial; but in France, a nation of stylists, style and substance are not so sharply dichotomized. Style of dress, speech, and physical bearing are seen as expressions of the inner man; gesture is studied and significant. Even small differences in the formulas for closing a letter carry subtle nuances. In France, stylized gesture becomes art: mime. Charlie Chaplin and Buster Keaton are beloved.

French structuralism has intellectually legitimated the French national preoccupation with style by erasing the line between what is said and how it is said and by arguing that style is the key to substance. While American behavioral scientists are encouraged to "get their results out" in easily abstractable articles, the model that is set by the dean of French structuralism, Claude Lévi-Strauss, is to write one's books in elaborate homologies with their subjects. So, for example, Lévi-Strauss structured *The Raw and the Cooked* in the form of a musical concerto.[2] Scholars justified this extrapolation from music on intellectual grounds, but it also can be seen as consonant with a long French tradition of intellectual play, even intellectual teasing.

In the early years of the twentieth century, a group of young French mathematicians invented Nicholas Bourbaki, and by signing their collaborative articles in his name, they made "him" the founder of one of the most important movements in twentieth-century mathematics. Lévi-Strauss put the picture of a wild pansy on the cover of his masterwork on primitive thought, *La Pensée sauvage*, punning "wild pansy" (*pensée*) with "wild thought" (*pensée*).[3] When Americans are faced with Lévi-Strauss's "Overtures" and pansies, with the Bourbaki School, or with the infinite regress of Lacanian literary conceits, they want to know if this is "play" or if this is "serious." They seem to have the idea that if it is not the one it must be the other. But for Lacan himself, wit, word games, jokes, mythology making, the materials of the poet, were all part of a kind of play that is inseparable from what is most serious about the psychoanalytic enterprise. If analysts do not subvert the line between work and play, they are doing neither science nor poetry, and if analysts do not subvert the line between science and poetry, they are not psychoanalysts at all.

In France, Lacan was celebrated and notorious; he was hated, loved, and feared. He was at the center of a web of complex personal relationships and at the center of a psychoanalytic school with complex internal politics. For many French psychoanalysts, Lacan was either their analyst, their analyst's analyst, or their analyst's enemy. Lacan became a prisoner of the psychoanalytic mythology, history, and politics that he created around himself. In France it is often difficult for people to discuss Lacan's psychoanalytic ideas apart from the psychoanalytic and extra-psychoanalytic political contexts in which they have found expression. Lacan's ideas about involving mathematicians and linguists in psychoanalytic research are "heard" through the filter of what he did at Vincennes. Lacan's ideas about psychoanalysis and topology are "heard" through the filter of the division among Lacanians between those who are for the matheme and those who are against it. Lacan's interest in the process by which someone authorizes him or herself to assume the position of an analyst is "heard" as part of the debate on the pass that tore apart the Freudian School.

In America, the fundamental question addressed in the pass, once removed from the institutional context in which an answer to it might mean "promotion" to Lacan's inner circle, was heard as simple, direct, and important. And Lacan asked it whenever he was before a group of analysts small enough to allow for an open conversation. He asked each analyst to speak of "how one day . . . and it did happen 'one day' because being an analyst is not a natural state . . . you believed yourself authorized to put yourself in the position of an analyst." As with the academicians, Lacan did not speak about psychoanalysis but asked for collaboration in an enterprise of a psychoanalytic order. And it was a collaboration because, wherever he asked the question, he was willing to answer it for himself as well. Lacan spoke of how as a young psychiatrist he studied and wrote about paranoia and found himself increasingly preoccupied with it. He found himself turning to psychoanalysis, which "Freud had called a kind of 'reasoned paranoia.'" Lacan made it clear that for him the decision to become an analyst had had nothing to do with rational planning: he described it as a "slipping," a "slide," "something I had to do."

In a dialogue with an analyst who claimed that she had chosen her profession out of her sense of being the sort of strong person whom others could turn to for help, Lacan admitted that he had come to analysis "in just the opposite way," drawn to the way Freud had emphasized not man's strength but his vulnerability. Lacan spoke of the analyst as someone deeply in touch with the sense of being at risk and deeply in touch with the knowledge "that it is possible for each of us to go mad." And in response to an analyst who claimed to have become one because a given psychoanalytic society was receptive to candidates at just the right time, Lacan spoke of how he had found himself angry, even enraged at the psychoanalytic institution, perhaps because he feared that it could rob him of his powers: "I was struck by the relative incapacity of Freud's disciples . . . at a certain moment, they didn't seem able to say anything anymore."

Implicit in Lacan's question about becoming an analyst, and in his own answers to it, was his belief that the only meaningful way to talk about the authorization to become an analyst is in terms of an authorization from within. At a meeting of analysts in Boston, he made the point explicit. He said that he was interested in "an authentic response" to his question, and this had to go beyond the question of an institution,

> beyond the question of what happened in the Boston Psychoana-
> lytic Society. The fact of an analytic society means a recruitment.
> But what is important is what happened within each of you . . . this
> is a question of differences that goes beyond recruitment where
> you are told: come here, join us . . . you will make as good a soldier
> as another.

At other moments in his career, Lacan had been critical and
shrill in his attitude toward American psychoanalysis, attacking its medical professionalization in the name of a subversive
psychoanalytic poetry and attacking its biologism and psychologism in the name of a subversive psychoanalytic science.
Now he neither criticized nor proselytized. He simply asked
people to share his idea of a "psychoanalytic reformation."
Luther cried out against the institutionalization of faith in a
church bureaucracy that traded on good works and rewarded
people for following rules and a clear chain of command.
From the point of view of psychoanalytic Protestantism, the
psychoanalytic institution sells its indulgences for the price
of a medical degree, a psychiatric residency, a training analysis, and promises of obedience to dogma. Lacan, like Luther,
was trying to draw attention to the moment when each must
stand alone and make a personal commitment, not to an institution, but to a belief or vocation.

To commit oneself and declare oneself is a process of making oneself. The word "poetry" derives from the Greek *poi-
ein*, "to make." Lacan's psychoanalytic Protestantism stresses
the person as he makes himself; it is a kind of poetry of the
person. For Lacan, the poet and the psychoanalyst are closely
related through their relationship to language. People "make"
and produce language; yet they are also made by language,
inhabited by it. The poet and the analyst both carry this universal relation to language to a higher power: the poet makes

a poem; yet these verses also "make" the poet . . . the analyst too is specially inhabited by the word and "is more made than others." Lacan's question about the authorization of an analyst is designed to grasp how individuals come to accept the special relation to language that, for analysts as for poets, puts them at some risk. Lacan believes that they both are trying to grab hold of something that Freud called the psychoanalytic "impossible" and that he calls the real. In America, Lacan characterized the real by its elusiveness: "When we bang our heads against a stone wall, we are struggling with the real." The search for the real can lead to a kind of delirium—or in any case to a delirious discourse. This is how Lacan sees both psychoanalysis and poetry. When Lacan described the "icy road" that had brought him to his life as an analyst, he was clearly describing himself as someone whose own attempts to understand had put him in some peril. He spoke of being "haunted" and "troubled" by his own formulations and by his attempts to be rigorous about the real, which "only the mad" fully believe in. At Yale, he put it this way: "Psychosis is an attempt at rigor. In this sense, I would say that I am psychotic. I am psychotic for the simple reason that I have always tried to be rigorous."

Lacan clearly had a sense of walking on a precarious line that divides science from poetry, rigor from delirium; he was involved in a constant process of balancing. Indeed, it sometimes looked as though his strategy was to bounce from the scientific to the poetic, using "doses" of each as a corrective to the other in order to protect psychoanalysis from overpoetization as well as from scientific reductionism. This strategy created a tension between Lacan and most audiences, and such tensions surfaced many times during his American trip.

At a seminar at Yale, Lacan was surrounded by literary scholars, psychoanalysts, and philosophers. Most members of this audience were believers in the value of a hermeneutic approach to all sciences of the mind. When the idea was expressed that perhaps psychoanalysis and linguistics were science enough since, by whatever means, both "brought us closer to an unknown reality," Lacan cut the comment short: the answer was no. That was not science. More was needed. Genuine science had to follow in the line of Galileo and Newton. In other words, science was only science when it was expressed in equations. And although

> we use language to teach science, scientific formulas must be expressed in little letters. To explain $\frac{1}{2} mv^2$, the relationship between mass and acceleration, by using language is only a long detour. . . . Science is that which holds together in its relation to the real due to the usage of little letters.

But when, in a conversation with Noam Chomsky at MIT, a highly formalized view of science was expressed, Lacan sensed that a different antidote was needed and swung to the other pole. Lacan was telling Chomsky why he was preoccupied with *lalangue*, his way of denoting a specific language with its own particular "equivocations," its special pattern of internal resonance and multiple meanings. On the blackboard of Chomsky's office, Lacan wrote:

> *Deux*
> *D'eux*

These are the French words for "two" and "of them," and in French, their pronunciation is identical. In a corner of the board, Lacan wrote another French word, *Dieu*, "God," a word which is pronounced only slightly differently from the other two.

Lacan asked Chomsky the same question that he had asked of Roman Jakobson the day before: Are such puns, the stuff from which psychoanalytic interpretation is made, intrinsic to language or merely accidental features of particular ones? Chomsky responded to Lacan much as Lacan had responded to the hermeneuticists at Yale the week before. He confronted Lacan with a view of linguistic science in the spirit of the Newtonian equations that Lacan had been praising, a formalized statement of laws that are universal across all languages. Lacan had asked if linguistics could help the analysts with the problem of punning and equivocation, and Chomsky responded that these were not even problems for a scientific linguistics. Scientific linguistics had to study similarities in language, not the differences among them. The language function, according to Chomsky, "was like an organ of the body, an ear, for example." When we look closely at different people's ears, we are going to see differences, but if we focus on the differences we will be distracted from the real job of trying to understand what all ears have in common, how they work. Lacan, visibly moved, declared that, next to Chomsky's approach, "I am a poet."

Lacan's behavior in these two incidents was not all modulated. He asserted the need for equational science among those who he felt use poetic justifications to avoid the hard and rigorous work ahead and asserted the need for poetry among others who may be allowing scientific rigor to narrow their field of vision. The lack of modulation extended into the assumptions that Lacan seemed to be expressing about the nature of science itself. In the discussion at Yale, for example, when he spoke of the "science of little letters," he seemed to consider as science only those activities of inquiry that closely fit a natural science model. At Yale, Lacan did say that for the moment he was only formalizing "a mathematizable minimum," but he left his vision of the future unclear. Many people who listen to Lacan feel that his work encourages a disquieting vision of an ultimate de-poetization of psychoanalysis through formalism. The question was raised as to whether Lacan's conception of poetics in psychoanalysis is that it constitutes an interim measure, what you have to fall back on while you still do not have a complete and coherent scientific theory. Is science the vision of the future and poetry the paltry means of the past that has now become the means of the meantime?

In France, these problems of interpretation have become issues for heated debate. In particular, people who followed Lacan through a career in which he fought against mechanistic theory and rigid institutions, and in which he has continually drawn people back to the existential statement within the psychoanalytic vocation, have a hard time accepting that his vision is that, in the end, all will be matheme. It certainly is true that Lacan's words often seem to support this literal reading of his views on psychoanalytic science, but this interpretation is not wholly plausible and certainly does not tell the whole story. If one focuses on Lacan's behavior and his own level of discourse, one may be led to a different attitude in which the image of the matheme is taken seriously, but taken seriously as a poetic device. In this second view, the mathematization of psychoanalysis will never really be complete, but its presence as an aspiration will be used to keep psychoanalysis working in a positive relation to science. This means that the psychoanalytic bias will be toward discovery and innovation rather than reliance on dogma or falling back on technique with no sense of experiment. Whereas the first interpretation devalues poetry by seeing it as expediency, the second devalues science by seeing it as fiction.

These two interpretations of what the Lacanian vision implies for the future of psychoanalysis accept the division between poetry and science. But it seems that Lacan *lived* a different vision. He was a poet whose ambition was to rediscover psychoanalysis as a science. In trying to place him on one side or another of the line that divides science from poetry, the line itself comes into question. He struggled to articulate a new way of thinking about the interrelationship among psychoanalysis, mathematics, science, and poetry. Why was Lacan working with knots? The question came up many times during his American visit, and most usually, it was asked with considerable skepticism. During his stay at Yale, Lacan answered in terms of his need for models of how things tie together in complex ways. Lacan explained that in order to understand the interconnections of the psyche (the symbolic, the imaginary, the real, and the symptom), he was trying "to invent another geometry," a geometry "of the chain." He envisages a mathematics that is not detached from our sense of our bodies, but deeply rooted in it. At MIT, Lacan described how he became preoccupied with "little loops of string" in an attempt to think about body and psyche at the same time.

Lacan explained how people have always been preoccupied with spheres and circles as abstractions of their own forms. In the hands of mathematicians, topology took off to become apparently detached from the body, but the detachment is only superficial, and perhaps defensive. Lacan explained that a full experience of the knots in which we let ourselves become deeply involved with the twists and turns and intricacies of the little circles of string leads to a *choc de retour*, something like a return of the repressed. This is because we can make our own circle back from an abstract notion of topology to what Lacan believes were its primitive roots as a way of experiencing the body. But the circle in which Lacan has led us has not returned us to our point of departure. Our vision of mathematics and its relation to the unconscious has changed.

For Lacan, mathematics is not disembodied knowledge. It is constantly in touch with its roots in the unconscious. This contact has two consequences: first, that mathematical creativity draws on the unconscious, and second, that mathematics repays its debt by giving us a window back to the unconscious. Lacan has often said that "the unconscious is structured like a language." Perhaps in some important ways, it is structured like mathematics as well; so that doing mathematics, like dreaming, can, if properly understood, give us access to what is normally hidden from us. When we describe poetic, intuitive theories of psychology, we tend to speak of them as "warm," "human," "humanistic." The adjectives imply that we find them appropriate to the description of a whole, physically and socially rooted human being. But theories that use mathematical formulation are seen as "cold," "impersonal." Definitionally, something that is cold leaves out the warmth of the body. But Lacan's ideas powerfully suggest that when we think about the future of psychoanalytic theory, or indeed about future theories of the mind, whose content we can as of now only dream of, we need not feel that we are faced with a choice between poetic warmth and the cold, dry fruits of the Pythagorean tree.

11 Thinking Things Through in Lacanian Space

No wonder the ancient cultures of conceit
in his technique of unsettlement foresaw
        the fall of princes, the collapse of
    their lucrative patterns of frustration:

if he succeeded, why, the Generalised Life
would become impossible, the monolith
        of State be broken and prevented
    the co-operation of avengers.

—W. H. Auden, "In Memory of Sigmund Freud"

Although Freud certainly saw psychoanalysis as revolutionary in its implications, he might not have recognized himself in Auden's description as an agent of the fall of princes
and the destruction of the monolith of the state. The politics of the theorist bear no necessary relation to the political
impact of the thought. For example, the first American ego
psychologists were sympathetic to the Left and believed that
they were radicalizing psychoanalysis by theorizing it in a way
that allowed the individual more freedom for action. Yet their
model of the autonomous individual drew people away from
politics toward a search for personal solutions. Similarly, the

human potential theorists of the 1960s were self-styled radicals who believed that their attempts to "green America" were consonant with their earlier attempts to change it through the civil rights and antiwar movements. Yet their theories seemed to offer the promise that one could escape from society into self-actualization. The politics of the theorist are not necessarily the politics of the theory.

Thus the Lacanians and Althusserians who exhort a return to a politically "subversive" Freud are neither returning to Freud's political positions nor to what Freud wrote about politics. Freud's own attempts to apply his theory to social analysis are given no privileged status; for the French, far from spelling out the radical consequences of his more fundamental ideas which challenge standard ways of knowing and standard methodologies of testing our knowledge, they reduce history and sociology to processes suggested by the more mechanistic elements of the metapsychology. What is subversive is to be found in the core of his theory: in the model of the unconscious, in its laws and the effects of symbols. This is Freud's science of the unconscious. And as we have seen, for Althusser and Lacan "only the science is subversive."

It is most subversive in its methodology of interpretation and analysis of contradiction. In this it is central to the concerns of Marxists who share with Freudians the belief that there is contradiction inherent in every advance and that every advance proceeds from an analysis of contradiction. But as we have seen, Freud's French Revolution has not recruited its troops primarily among those whose first concern is the development of psychoanalytic science. It has offered images that have proved highly evocative to many people who have not necessarily used these images with great rigor. The images have been "good to think with." For example, we have seen

Lacan's portrait of the social linguistic construction of the subject in the symbolic dimension become a common idiom in French political discourse, where in the decade since 1968 much of social thought has situated itself in "Lacanian space." That is to say, it has accepted some of the fundamentals of Lacan's theory: in particular, the notions that people are constituted by language, that our discourse embodies the society beyond, and that there is no autonomous ego.

Of course, people have situated themselves somewhat differently even within this space; for some, representative of a new, naturalistic political thought, Lacan was the theorist of a return to the imaginary. For others, among them Maoists deeply concerned with the nature of superstructure, he was the theorist of a transformation of the symbolic. But for all, he has offered a new way of thinking about the social and linguistic construction of the self. The influence of Lacan's ideas on how people put together their thoughts about politics and language is illustrated by an example of French popular philosophy and by the French appreciation of Alexander Solzhenitsyn.

The events of May 1968 and the Russian invasion of Czechoslovakia which followed later that summer left a bitter legacy. In this atmosphere, Solzhenitsyn's novels about the prison camps in Russia had a waiting audience. His work, which portrayed the encounter between the individual and the Gulag (the system of Soviet prisons and places of exile), was read as resonant with Lacan's description of our encounter with the symbolic. The prevalence of a psychoanalytic culture that stressed that there is a politics in our language prepared Solzhenitsyn's audience to read his descriptions of the coherent discourse of the Soviet camps as a significant political statement, as significant as his exposés of Soviet brutality.

It is an old idea that stone walls do not always make the most effective prisons, that people can be more deeply enmeshed by their own "mind-forged manacles." This image from Blake can be read to suggest that autonomous humans have tragically let themselves become the agent of their own enslavement. But in Solzhenitsyn's Gulag, an internally coherent discourse possesses, even reconstitutes, people, both guards and prisoners. The Gulag inhabits the people as much as the people inhabit the Gulag. Heavily influenced by a Lacanian perspective which might analogize the Gulag's discourse to that of the symbolic, recent French writers have in effect asked: "Does the discourse of the Gulag owe its power to what it shares with the discourse of the Soviet Marxist state or, indeed, of all bureaucratic states?"

"The Soviet camps are Marxist, as Marxist as Auschwitz was Nazist," was the message that Bernard-Henri Lévy took from Solzhenitsyn's writing.[1] For Lévy, one of a group of young philosophers known as the "new philosophers," the lesson of Solzhenitsyn was that Marxism was not in crisis, compromised by "deviations," but that the "deviations"—prison camps and the rest—were consistent with the whole Marxist enterprise. May was not a failed revolution; what it failed to achieve could never be achieved: the Marxist myth of an end to history. There would be no end to history, no withering of the state, no classless harmony among men: "The world is not going well and without a doubt things are not going to get better."[2]

These philosophers, who wrote of "life as a lost cause and history a played out idea," had a fabulous publishing success in Paris in 1977–78.[3] Ten years after the May rebels had declared "everything is possible," a powerful, popular philosophy of pessimism gained ground. These "new philosophers" saw all ideologies which envisage an end point to history (whether the classless society or the society of desiring-machines) as dangerous: theories that promise an end to power relations convince people that they can judge present means by that future end and so rationalize labor camps and mass slaughter. But according to Lévy, these theories are wrong. Deeply rooted in the unconscious is the inevitability of power. It is the fundamental social fact, "the fatality that bends history to its rule."[4] The only ethical way to live, says Lévy, is to take the goal of limiting power as a basis for one's actions without believing that power can ever really be eliminated.[5]

When in the early 1950s Albert Camus wanted to express a similar message, he searched for an image deeply embedded in his culture, an image which would convey the paradox of action without hope of a final solution. He turned to Greek mythology and to the myth of Sisyphus who labors to push a giant boulder up a mountain only to have it roll back down the slope. The gods may laugh, but Sisyphus labors eternally, because if he should cease for even a moment he would then be crushed. When, a quarter of a century later, Lévy searched for a metaphor, he chose differently and told his story through the symbology of the Lacanian trinity: the imaginary, the symbolic, and the real.

A decade of naturalistic social theory and a decade of Marxist thought had expressed themselves using a Lacanian idiom. Now Lévy, who attacked both naturalism and Marxism for their myths of the dissolution of power, turned to this idiom himself: Lévy was drawn to Lacan as the theorist of the "impossible." His ethical project, a project of contradiction, is easily analogized to the psychoanalytic one. We conceptualize the reconstitution of the associative chains as though we could reach the ultimate signifier although we know we cannot. For Lévy, a Freudian politics that understands constraint, contradiction, and the inevitability of power is our only hope, and it is Lacan who suggests its form with his theory of knots, his topographical image for the indissociability of the imaginary, symbolic, and real. Power is tied to desire and to the impossibility of final resolutions just as the symbolic is tied to the imaginary and the real. There is no escape to the imaginary except through psychosis, and for Lévy this is not a workable political solution. There is no utopia, no "beach under the cobblestones."

The May events, that most optimistic of social festivals during which people acted without stopping to reflect or theorize, gave way to a profound pessimism in theory that expressed itself in the metaphor of the psychoanalytic culture and looked toward a Freudian politics of the impossible. While May had left some with new hope for a politics of language and desire, for Lévy the event had been decisive in exactly the opposite sense. It led him to imagine an encyclopedia definition of socialism from the year 2000 as:

> Socialism. [masculine noun] born, Paris, 1843. died, Paris, 1968.[6]

I began this reflection on the French psychoanalytic culture with the 1968 events, and I end with them. In terms of traditional economic and political analysis, the events were *impensable*, "unthinkable"; they *should* not have happened. And when they were over, there was no one way to think them through and make coherent what to many people seemed like a dream only a few days after things had returned to normal. Even while they were on the barricades, student leaders signed publishing contracts and—along with sociologists, journalists, economists, political scientists, literary critics, philosophers, and psychoanalysts—made writing books about May–June 1968 into a new French cottage industry. In the two years after the events, over a thousand books appeared in France which "made sense" of them. The May–June events became a giant projective test. As with a Rorschach, the shape was inchoate and ambiguous, and everybody saw what they wanted or "needed" to see. Sociologists who had spent their careers analyzing bureaucratic dysfunctions saw the events as a crisis of French bureaucratic society, existential Marxists saw the beginning of a new society of self-management, while the Communist Party saw a petit bourgeois farce.

But the events were more than a projective screen. They were a powerful personal experience. French people who had lived all their lives in a society whose Napoleonic bureaucracy had once been a point of national pride and whose bureaucratic procedures for life's simplest matters had long since become an object of national satire, found themselves in a two-month period when structures dissolved, where there were no rules. People who had grown up with rigid notions of privacy and a sense that the informal was almost always inappropriate had found themselves on the street in a festival atmosphere where everybody spoke to everybody.

The power of the May events was heightened by the fact that they were only the most recent expression of what has always been a major theme in French political history: the tension between the individual and the constraints of a highly structured society. This tension has led to wild pendulum swings from government by bureaucracy or authoritarian leaders to the negation of constraint in assertions of antistructure like the Paris Commune and May 1968. While the flood of books about May–June may have stopped by the early 1970s, the preoccupation with the issues raised by the events was far from over. As has been suggested throughout this book, involvement with the new psychoanalytic culture was a way of continuing contact with the personal and political issues which May 1968 brought to the surface.

Among many other things, May–June 1968 left people thinking about the question of how desire, sexuality, and self-expression could be part of a revolutionary movement, and "thinking through the events" required a theory which could integrate politics and the person. This theory was psychoanalysis.

I have suggested a similar relationship between the Occupation and Resistance, which left people preoccupied with questions of choice, freedom, and constraint, and the existentialist movement, which took these questions as its theoretical scaffolding. When I speak of "thinking the Resistance" by "thinking existentialism" or "thinking May–June" by "thinking psychoanalysis," I am not merely describing a use of theory to explain social events. People can also use a theory to "think through" powerful cultural images, to help them to arrange these images into new and clearer patterns. In the case of May–June and psychoanalysis, people used contact with the theory to keep in touch with the stuff of which the events were made. For a person to use theory in this way does not require a full understanding of its subtleties. This theoretical "tinkering" can serve as the object of a sociology of "superficial knowledge" which does not trivialize the meaning of that knowledge in the life of the person, or of the society.

The argument that the French psychoanalytic "take off" was fueled by its ability to serve as a carrier for issues raised by May is strengthened by recognizing how other popular trends in recent French intellectual life serve the same function. Lacan, Solzhenitsyn, and the "new philosophers" have all been read as theorists of the tension between the individual and society.

We have seen how Lacan described the construction of the subject by society and language; for many French intellectuals, Solzhenitsyn made it impossible to ever again see the Soviet concentration camps as "errors" and again forcefully raised the question of the politics of discourse. Involvement with Solzhenitsyn's literature or with Lacan's reflection on the transaction among the imaginary, symbolic, and real was a way for May themes to go underground and find expression in realms that were of, but not in politics. But with the new philosophers, the May criticism of systems, structures, and ideologies broke to the surface in a frankly political discourse whose basic message was that all ideologies are bad, including, and perhaps most of all, the radical "Protestant" ideologies that encourage their believers to "do what they wish." The injunction to freedom is a paradox.[7] The *Maître* is still present. In this book we have seen this paradox at work in psychoanalytic politics. We have seen it in Lacan's relation to disciples at the Freudian School, where the policy of self-authorization is in conflict with the presence of a *Maître* whose authority authorizes the self-authorization. This conflict may be paradigmatic for political contradiction beyond the psychoanalytic world.

Lacan is a psychoanalyst; the new philosophers are political writers: Solzhenitsyn is a novelist. There is no intention here to equate what they have to say, their intents, or the quality of their work. There is, however, the suggestion that they have captured the public imagination in France for similar reasons.

Understanding this resonance between the French Freud, other intellectual movements, and the larger society is part of the ethnography of the French psychoanalytic culture. But looking at the story of contemporary French psychoanalysis has consistently raised questions that go far beyond that framework. Lacan's description of the transaction between the imaginary and symbolic has been a powerful heuristic for social theorists who have wanted to think through the relationship of individual and society, the role of language in politics, and the role of ideology. More popularized versions of psychoanalytic ideas have helped the French think through their contemporary social experience where rules and certainties are in the process of eroding. And finally, thinking about the history of psychoanalysis has offered a way to "think through" issues that go beyond it: the relationship between politics and the person, the tension between a subversive science and its social acceptance, the contradiction between a scientific stance of radical self-doubt and the presence of a *Maître*.

Freud believed his theory was subversive because it told "unacceptable truths." Among its unacceptable truths, Freud emphasized the sexual foundation of psychoanalytic theory. Writing in the world of early twentieth-century "civilized" morality, he feared that this would be the first thing that others would water down. Since Freud's day there has been continuing debate on the question of whether or not psychoanalysis is revolutionary. Many argue that psychoanalysis was revolutionary but only in the sexually repressive society from which it sprung. Now, they argue, with more permissive sexual codes and with its integration into mass culture, psychoanalysis is part of the status quo.

Contemporary French psychoanalytic thought suggests a more fundamental way in which psychoanalysis is unacceptable. It insists on the presence of social forces within the individual, on the interpenetration of individual and society. This perspective seeks to analyze the truth of the subject and the society in relationship to each other, and in doing so it underscores another psychoanalytic "unacceptable truth": the individual is not his or her own center; each of us is inhabited by society through use of language. The domination by language is inevitable. Only the psychotic escapes. For the individual this eliminates the possibility of personal transcendence. For a political movement, it eliminates the possibility of mechanistic materialism, the dream that it might be possible to make a new social order without making new people.

In the past, most ideas about radical change have been dichotomized. Some have looked more to changing social institutions, and others have believed that revolutions could be made by the liberation of the mind and the purification of the heart. A psychoanalytic politics refuses this dichotomy. It sets a new agenda for political thought, demanding that it continually confront the essential complexity inherent in strategies of change: If society inhabits each individual, who among us can take up arms against society? In the years after the First World War, the theorists of the Frankfurt School argued that such questions were central to Marxist science and Marxist politics.

As we look at the development of the French Freud, we see two different, equally important ways in which it breaks new ground in dealing with this problem. The first is in the realm of theoretical analysis. Lacan's theorization of the symbolic order has offered a powerful framework for thinking about the transaction between the individual and society. The second is of a sociological order. In the past, concern with the problem of subjectivity in revolution remained within the confines of academic seminars and activist study groups. In the 1960s in America, carried in part by the popularity of Marcuse's ideas, it broke out into a wider student movement. In France, carried by Lacanian thought, it has been able to spread further and sustain itself longer. It is not enough for a revolutionary theory to satisfy the theorists. It must also have the power to move out, to become a culture. In France this has happened. In its details, the French psychoanalytic culture betrays some contradiction and immaturity, but its integration of theoretical depth and social resonance gives new plausibility to the idea that a psychoanalytic politics may yet reveal itself as one of our century's most revolutionary forces.

12 Dynasty 1991

The first edition of *Psychoanalytic Politics* concluded in 1976, a time when the pace of events in the world it described was accelerating. In particular, the tensions within Lacan's Freudian School were becoming harder to contain, and a struggle for power and succession was occurring, at the center of which was Lacan's son-in-law, Jacques-Alain Miller. Here I bring the story of the Freudian School and its descendants up to date. It is a drama of internal contradictions and bitter vendettas that did not end with Lacan's death in 1981 but continues to this day [1991]. I begin with the history of Lacan's relationship with Jacques-Alain Miller and return to the story of Miller's rise to power in the Department of Psychoanalysis at Vincennes. In retrospect, Lacan's increasing dependence on Miller and Miller's stronghold within the French university system foreshadowed what was to follow: the dissolution of the Freudian School, a milestone that marked, before the event, the mourning of the death of the *Maître*.[1]

In the early 1960s, the Marxist philosopher Louis Althusser turned toward Lacanian thought and brought his students at the Ecole Normale Supérieure with him, among them the brilliant Jacques-Alain Miller. In 1963, Miller, then nineteen, had just completed his *license* in philosophy under Althusser's direction; he had not yet read a line of Lacan. Miller recalls that in the fall of 1963, Althusser called him into his office to urge him to begin a serious study of the analyst's work. Following Althusser's advice, Miller says he went directly to the bookstore of the Presses Universitaire de France and bought all the back issues of *La Psychanalyse*, the publication of the French Psychoanalytic Society to which Lacan had belonged since the schism of 1953. With his new purchases in hand, Miller then left Paris for the country with a friend who was studying for the *agrégation* in philosophy. "I remember quite well beginning my reading of the *Rome Discourse* on the second floor and then coming downstairs at lunchtime to tell my friend, who had spent the morning reading Spinoza, that I had just read something unprecedented."[2]

Jacques-Alain Miller entered Lacan's world at a fateful moment. Even as Miller was reading his first Lacan texts, the International Psychoanalytic Association was demanding that Lacan's name and that of his colleague Françoise Dolto be removed from the approved list of training analysts at the French Psychoanalytic Society. A month later, in November 1963, the decision of the International was ratified by the Society itself. Lacan declared himself "excommunicated" and charged that the International was more like a church than a scientific organization. In protest, he shut down his weekly seminar at Saint Anne's hospital. When he resumed teaching in January 1964, it was on Althusser's turf at the Ecole Normale Supérieure. The move was symbolic. Excluded from internationally recognized psychoanalysis, Lacan was now determined to seek recognition in other worlds. Miller was intellectually well suited to help him. Unlike Althusser, Miller was not interested in integrating Lacan's ideas with those of Freud but in stressing their differences. Miller saw Lacan's work as a theoretical whole that needed to be systematized and formalized in order to put it in a better position for dialogue with other formal theories of discourse. What these theories had in common was what Althusser had already commended in Lacan's reading of Freud: they specifically excluded the psychological subject.

In June 1964, Lacan founded the Freudian School. Unlike traditional psychoanalytic societies, it welcomed non-analysts as members. It was there that Miller and a small group of Althusser students formed a study group on "the theory of discourse." In January 1966, this group, known as the Cercle d'Epistémologie de l'Ecole Normale Supérieure, began to publish its own journal, *Cahiers pour l'analyse*. Its first issue included a paper by Miller that linked Lacanian ideas to the mathematics of Gottlob Frege. The paper analyzed the operations of thought from the point of view of formal and symbolic logic. Surveying this period of intellectual history, psychoanalytic historian Élisabeth Roudinesco remarks that "the Millerian interpretation of the theory of the signifier led to a rearticulation of Lacanianism which was to have two immediate consequences, one theoretical and the other political."[3] Theoretically, Lacanianism became a model for a new kind of Freudian science, purified of all reference to psychology and historical contingency. From 1966 to 1969, *Cahiers pour l'analyse* built up an extra-analytic, theoretical Lacanianism, oriented toward logic, formalism, and science. The journal became a vanguard for the Lacanian colonization of the larger intellectual culture. In its issues, Lacan appeared next to such writers as Georges Canguilhem, Louis Althusser, Jacques Derrida, and Georges Dumézil.

Politically, the reference to an objective science meant that adversaries could be identified and labeled "deviationist" in relation to a pure and absolute doctrinal norm. While Lacan produced concepts that were deliberately ambiguous and open to multiple interpretations, Miller sought to rationalize them in the direction of greater logical coherence and uniformity. This "corrected," more "coherent" version of Lacan facilitated attacks on now more easily identifiable theoretical enemies. Before he met Miller, Lacan had called his theory scientific, hoping that this might afford him some protection from being "revised" as Freud had been, but Lacan had never accused wayward disciples of deviationism. In his very first presentation at Lacan's seminar, however, Miller applied the language of deviation to attack theoretical impurities in Lacan's followers (in that particular case, the analyst Piera Aulagnier). Aulagnier refused Lacan's invitation to respond to Miller's attack, claiming that the charge of deviationism had no meaning in a clinical context. This very first interchange established a pattern that was to mark the history of the Freudian School: Miller pitted a "pure" and "scientific" philosophy against "impure" clinical work. With Miller, the reference to science in Lacan's work lost its neutrality; the claim of objectivity became a tool of Lacanian psychoanalytic politics.

In an interview with Roudinesco, Miller recalls that during this early period he saw his relation to Lacan in terms of Hugo's *La Légende des siècles*, where he identified with the character of Aymerillot. The story is revealing.

> Charlemagne was sad upon returning from Roncevaux. He had lost Roland and wanted to conquer Narbonne. He addressed his barons, his old comrades in arms, but none was willing to take up the challenge. All were mortified and stared at the ground. Suddenly, Aymerillot stepped out of the ranks. He was wan and frail. "I have come to ask you for what no man wants, the honor of being, oh my King!, if God does not forsake me, the man of whom it will

be said: It was he who took Narbonne. . . . I will enter Narbonne and I will be its conqueror. Later, I will punish scoffers, should any remain." More radiant than an archangel, Charlemagne said to Aymerillot, "You will be a count paladin." The following day the youth took the city.[4]

In 1969, after its tenth issue, Miller interrupted the publication of *Cahiers pour l'analyse* to turn his full attention to politics. He was now a committed Maoist, a member of La Gauche Prolétarienne. At this turn of events, there were already those at the Freudian School who were pleased that Miller would be occupied elsewhere than on their home turf. But they were naive to rejoice so soon. Miller *was* to take Narbonne, although to his foes he resembled less a chivalric knight than an implacable Jacobin, more Saint Just than Aymerillot. In 1966, he married the king's beloved daughter, Judith Lacan. In 1969 he began his step-by-step takeover of the Department of Psychoanalysis at Vincennes, a campaign waged to full victory by 1976. And in 1972, while still a member of La Gauche Prolétarienne, he was passed what in retrospect was Lacan's most potent symbol of succession: Lacan decided that it was Miller who should edit and control the texts of his seminars. It was Miller who would inherit the rights to the word.

Lacan began his weekly seminar in 1953; by the early 1970s, there were transcripts, notes, unauthorized and pirated versions, as well as a series of incomplete attempts to edit them. In June 1972, Lacan challenged Miller to do better. Miller agreed and left for Italy, where he worked with a stenographer's transcript of the seminar of 1963–64, the first seminar he had attended, the first seminar after Lacan's excommunication. A month later, Miller returned to Paris with a first draft. Lacan was pleased but thought this version of his seminar was so much Miller's work that he offered him coauthorship.

Miller refused. In his view, the intellectual and commercial value of the seminars was tied to Lacan's being sole author. But when Miller raised the possibility of other transcriptions by other editors, Lacan objected. It was at this point that his son-in-law accepted Lacan's second challenge; Miller agreed to do them all himself.

Lacan made Miller legal owner of the transcriptions of his seminars and in doing so bequeathed him a life's work. Miller's was no simple editorial job. He was not "editing" but, as he put it, "establishing" the texts of the seminars. He added language where there were gaps and removed contradictions and ambivalences. As Miller did this work, Lacan's dependence on him grew; some would say their relationship became the dominant force during the last fifteen years of Lacan's life. On the one hand, Miller was a scribe, writing out what the *Maître* had said, or perhaps meant to say. On the other, Miller clearly revised and changed Lacan's work as he "established" it. To some degree, Miller renounced his own voice to pledge himself to his version of Lacan's. The resulting symbiosis had fateful consequences for the history of Lacanianism. If by the 1980s, Miller seemed to feel justified in speaking for Lacan, by that point he was acting not only out of habit but out of a profound sense of Lacan's wanting and needing him in this role.

In 1974, Miller entered a new relationship with the Lacanian enterprise. He went into analysis with Charles Melman, a prominent Freudian School analyst. Now on his way to becoming an analyst, Miller could present himself as the legitimate heir not only to Lacan's science but to his analytic kingdom as a whole, and then could "punish scoffers, should any remain."

Miller was helped in his rise at the Freudian School by his position in the Lacanian-controlled Department of Psychoanalysis at the Experimental University Center at Vincennes, created in July 1968 in the aftermath of the May events. At that time, Michel Foucault was put in charge of the Department of Philosophy and invited Lacan to form a Department of Psychoanalysis. Lacan refused but asked Serge Leclaire to head the project in his stead. Both Leclaire and Foucault asked Jacques-Alain Miller (then teaching at Besançon) to join them at Vincennes. Miller chose the Department of Psychoanalysis.[5] Teaching began in January 1969; by the spring, Miller had joined La Gauche Prolétarienne. Since this Maoist organization had the destruction of the university as one of its theoretical goals, Leclaire became uncomfortable. He wrote to Miller and asked him to move to the Department of Philosophy. Miller refused. The relationship between the two men became strained, but Leclaire soon had more urgent crises to attend to. As we have seen in chapter 7, Leclaire was attacked by analytic colleagues and by student radicals for his participation at Vincennes, all of this in an atmosphere that threatened to devour itself over the very premises of its existence.

Leclaire, a brilliant theoretician, had long suffered from the fact that at the Freudian School there could be only one voice. He saw Vincennes as an opportunity to breathe less suffocating air while remaining faithful to Lacan. But when a pirated student edition of Leclaire's Vincennes seminar appeared in September 1969, Lacan became angry. It appears that he could not tolerate this second voice, this second seminar. Although Leclaire made it clear that he was displeased by the unofficial publication, Lacan seized the opportunity to punish him. At Lacan's prodding, the Board of Directors of the Freudian School accused Leclaire of authorizing the publication of his seminar without the School's approval. Lacan also undermined Leclaire in a December 1969 visit to

Vincennes during which he attacked the Department of Psychoanalysis for its policy of giving course credits. Although Leclaire made it clear that the Department was not training psychoanalytic clinicians, he believed that its courses should confer academic credit; Lacan at this point disagreed. After a second visit by Lacan to Vincennes in early summer 1970, Leclaire resigned.

Now, Jean Clavreul was nominally in charge of the Department of Psychoanalysis, but for the next four years it took its orders straight from Lacan's office. During this period, Miller's influence grew as his relationship with Lacan became much closer. It was Miller who supported Lacan's work on the mathemes, an effort to systematize psychoanalytic theory mathematically. It was Miller who took charge of establishing the texts of the seminars. And, of course, it was Miller who was now a member of the family.

In 1974, Miller sensed his strength and decided to take aggressive action. He convinced Lacan to reorganize the Department around the elaboration of the mathemes. As we have seen, the result was a new power structure at Vincennes. The Department was now run by a triumvirate that included Clavreul but left real power to Miller and Charles Melman, both of whose authority came from the fact that they acted as Lacan's agents. When in November 1974 the president of Vincennes asked Lacan if he would now be willing to head the teaching program, Lacan agreed to be scientific advisor on the condition that Miller be in full administrative charge. This decision met with protests from Department faculty, but Miller won the assignment. Vincennes was now his, close to a personal fiefdom within the university.

In the two years that followed, Miller transformed the Department of Psychoanalysis. Once reluctant to give any regular courses lest it be perceived as training clinicians, the Department now granted diplomas and doctorates, and began a continuing education program for psychologists, nurses, and social workers.[6] Only a few years before, Lacan had scorned Leclaire for allowing course credits. Now he supported Miller's October 1976 announcement that the "clinical section of the Freudian Field" would divide its educational program between Vincennes and the Freudian School itself. For many Freudian School analysts this was the last straw. Miller was now a clear enemy who was stealing not only Lacan but their clinical principles and analytic society from them.

By 1979, the Freudian School was increasingly dominated by Miller; Lacan had become withdrawn and silent. The school was a powder keg waiting to explode. It had grown to 609 members, and from Miller's point of view, "Lacan no longer held an ideological majority."[7] An incident in which Lacan acted imperiously (but no more so than he had done many times before) finally set it alight. Perhaps Lacan did not realize that by distancing himself from his "subjects" and by imposing Miller on them, he had broken his side of the political contract that kept the School together. There could be an absolute monarch but it had to be Lacan, not his designate. Perhaps Lacan wanted the keg to explode.

In February, Denis Vasse, vice president of the Freudian School, had participated in a meeting of Confrontations, a group that brought together psychoanalysts from all schools for colloquia, presentations and debates on special topics. As the formal and mathematical Millerian line became more dominant at the Freudian School, its analysts had increasingly turned to Confrontations, which served them as a kind of counterweight. Lacan himself had never taken a public position against Confrontations, although he clearly was upset by its growing role as a meeting place for his disaffected students. But now Lacan dismissed Vasse from his post as vice president. The response at the Freudian School was immediate outrage.

At a meeting of the Freudian School's Administrative Council, Françoise Dolto pointed out that over the years many of the School's senior members had participated in Confrontations. Charles Melman responded that as vice president, Vasse should have shown greater discretion. Dolto insisted that titles had nothing to do with this matter and that in an analytic society, no one should have to ask "Papa" for authorization to act as an adult. At her remark, Lacan left the room in silent rage.

Françoise Dolto had been with Lacan since the first schism of 1953. With Lacan, she had been accused of unorthodox practices and "excommunicated" from the International Psychoanalytic Association in 1963. For fifteen years she and Lacan had been firm allies at the Freudian School, but beginning in 1978, Dolto began to speak openly about the School's problems. In the course of the controversy about Denis Vasse, she became a symbol of resistance for many Freudian School analysts who felt distanced from Lacan, confused by his silence, and angered by Miller's growing power.

In the middle of the controversy over Vasse, a special general assembly of the Freudian School was called for September 30, 1979. The first agenda item was to vote an amendment to the School's statutes. Lacan and Miller proposed to enlarge the School's Administrative Council from seventeen to twenty-five members; many feared that their purpose was to bring in more supporters of the Millerian line. The vote on this amendment was urgent because the Council was due for a turnover in its membership. Indeed, the second item on the general assembly's agenda was to vote on Lacan's new membership slate for the Council, a slate that included Françoise Dolto but excluded Denis Vasse.

The general assembly was marked by high emotion and parliamentary confusion, so much so that Lacan's new membership slate (of twenty-five members) was voted on before the expansion of the Council's membership had been approved. Moreover, neither of the two proposals had won by the requisite two-thirds majority. There had been clear parliamentary irregularities; they became symbols of Lacan's arbitrary use of power. Outraged, some members of the School openly called Lacan a tyrant. Until this point, such feelings had only been expressed in private. In the weeks that followed, the divisions within the School became a matter of public record and discussion in the mass media.

The September 30 meeting and its aftermath made it clear that the Freudian School was divided into three factions with different ideas about what the School was and what it should become. A first group, loyal to Miller, supported Lacan's work on the mathemes, the mathematical symbolizations of psychoanalytic research. Although this group included some analysts, its strong base was among philosophers. This group was favored by Lacan and increasingly it spoke in his name.

Picking up the metaphor drawn from Miller's dreams of Charlemagne, Roudinesco called the second group the "great barons." These were the old guard of the Lacanian clinical tradition, many of whom had been Lacan's loyal followers since the schism of 1953. This group, whose members included Jean Clavreul, Françoise Dolto, Serge Leclaire, and Octave and Maud Mannoni, carried the authority of distinguished individual careers and long-tested relationships with Lacan. Miller had taken the barons as his natural enemies for many years.

When the crisis hit, most of them would support Miller out of loyalty to Lacan and in the hope that Miller might be satisfied with his control of Vincennes and the establishment of Lacan's seminars and leave the training of psychoanalytic clinicians to them. In fact, Miller wanted it all. As Lacan became increasingly ill and Miller increasingly ambitious, most of the barons would turn against the young man and accuse him of seizing Lacan's power by falsely speaking in his name, indeed, by forging Lacan's signature.

A third faction was composed of young analysts, openly hostile both to the mathemes and to Miller. Many of them had been analyzed by the generation of the barons, but unlike their analytic parents, their loyalty was not to Lacan but to the Freudian School as an institution. They felt that it was being put in jeopardy and that the future of the Lacanian movement was in their hands. Angered by what they saw as Lacan's arbitrary use of personal power, this group, whose members included Michèle Montrelay and Claude Rabant, began to explore the unprecedented idea of countering Lacan's actions with an appeal to legal authorities. After fifteen years of accepting absolute monarchy, this third group "discovered" that the Freudian School could be held accountable to the rules of its incorporation under France's "1901 law for public associations." But at the Freudian School, the position of the *Maître* had always stood in place of the law. The challenge to this unspoken assumption went like a shock wave through the School; it would not survive.

In the days after the general assembly, Miller warned those who sought outside legal jurisdiction: "The Freudian School is Lacan's School, period. . . . Those close to Lacan are now being encouraged to become turncoats: 'Think of the future!' whispers a viper into the ears of the faithful. One must realize that for some time now, when they have said 'the future,' analysts have meant nothing other than Lacan's death."[8] On December 10, Charles Melman issued a bulletin attacking the "feminist, obscurantist, and religious elements of the School" (Here his targets were Montrelay, Leclaire, Xavier Audouard, and Dolto) and interpreting the divisions that had emerged at the September 30 general assembly as a split between those who follow Lacan and those "with a fundamental opposition to his teaching." Melman concluded by telling the dissidents that if they didn't like the direction the Freudian School was taking, they should simply leave.[9] On December 13, Miller disparagingly called the dissidents "anarlysts" (anarchist/analysts) and made it clear that Lacan despised them.

According to Miller, Lacan had raised the possibility of dissolving the Freudian School on the Sunday following the September 30 general assembly but was not ready to act at that time. By the end of December, however, he was ready. According to Solange Faladé, a School vice president, the decision to disband was made at a Christmas meeting at Miller's home. Lacan was ill, those close to him knew that he had been diagnosed with cancer of the colon, and there was a pressure to act quickly "in order to create something while there was still time." According to Faladé, "Lacan could no longer write. It was decided that Miller would compose the letter and Lacan would correct it. He eliminated passages that were not to his liking. I did not return to Guitrancourt, but during the first weekend of the new year, Miller telephoned me to say the letter was typed up and ready to be sent out."[10] Miller's version of the composition of the letter is somewhat different. He claims that on January 6 at the Lacan country home at Guitrancourt, Lacan gave him the text of the letter of dissolution that he wished to have circulated the following day.

On Tuesday, January 8, at the usual meeting time for his seminar, Lacan read the letter of dissolution, dated Guitrancourt, January 5. It specified that the legal dissolution of the Freudian School would take place after the vote of a general assembly, a vote presumed to be only a legal formality. Lacan called on those who wished to avoid the "deviations"—note the Millerian word!—and "compromises nourished by the Freudian School" to make their wishes known to him within ten days. The letter closed with a statement that would be much quoted in the press: "Je n'ai pas besoin de beaucoup de monde et il y a du monde dont je n'ai pas besoin." ("I don't need many people and there are many people whom I don't need.") By the following Friday, Lacan had the stenographic transcripts of his seminars withdrawn from the Freudian School library.

When he founded the Freudian School in June 1964, Lacan had said: "I hereby found—as alone as I have always been in my relation to the psychoanalytic cause—the Ecole Francaise de Psychanalyse."[11] (The name of the School would change three months later to the Ecole Freudienne de Paris.) In his mind, since he had founded the Freudian School alone, he could now dissolve it alone. Others felt differently. The School was a public institution. It was not his to dissolve. The battle lines were drawn between two groups: those who saw psychoanalytic organizations as being about personal power and theoretical brilliance and those who thought these organizations must also obey the law. The first group held that from the moment Lacan signed the letter of dissolution, the School had ceased to exist. They were the party of symbolic dissolution. The second group rallied around a demand for legal dissolution. This did not mean that they wanted the School to be legally dissolved; on the contrary, they insisted on legal dissolution as a way to assert that the School was not Lacan's personal possession. His letter did not in itself mean that the Freudian School was no more; it belonged to them as well as to him.

A parallel with Vienna would of course be inexact, but imagine that in the early 1930s Freud had informed his disciples that with the support of his daughter Anna he was shutting down the Vienna Psychoanalytic Society to begin a new group and that such members as Jones, Sachs, Rank, Erikson, Deutsch, and Abraham insisted that since they had participated in the development of the organization, Freud really could not act without their approval. Freud treated psychoanalytic organizations as though he owned them. Lacan was stunned when there was any question of the Freudian School not belonging to him.

Beyond the issue of Lacan's rights, the letter of dissolution raised a question about his competence. Who was the true author of the letter? Lacan or Miller? Lacan's commitment to the contents of the letter was never disputed. Lacan presented the letter as his, supported and defended it as his, and behaved in accord with the intentions it announced. But the question of the origins of the letter (that is, whether it was Lacan himself who put ink to paper) took on great symbolic importance. In the crisis of dissolution, the osmotic—some said fusional—relationship between Miller and Lacan which Lacanians implicitly tolerated when they accepted Miller's words as Lacan's seminar, became intolerable. People became preoccupied with the degree to which Lacan was *alone* responsible for the dissolution of the School and the degree to which he had simply become Miller's puppet.

Week after week, month after month, the French press covered the drama of the Freudian School dissolution and the French public showed a seemingly insatiable appetite for following its twists of plot, much as Americans read almost anything about the Kennedys and the British follow their royal family. At the Freudian School, the dramatis personae were in costume for a spectacle that crossed *King Lear* with *Dynasty*. There was the dying *Maître*, who pronounced the words "Delenda est" (from Cato the Elder's *Delenda Carthago*— Carthage must be destroyed) and announced the destruction of his kingdom; the scheming son-in-law, positioned to inherit the property, the woman, and the power; the obedient daughter, dominated by father and husband; and the jealous students, divided in their frustration at not having familial access to their beloved *Maître* and reduced to fighting over the spoils of the kingdom. Finally, there were the *Maître*'s aging comrades, who had never had their place in the sun. Remarkably, for a troupe of psychoanalysts, the actors in this drama played willingly on the most public of stages. During the May events, psychoanalysts had anguished over speaking and writing in public. Now, they behaved as though it was perfectly natural for them to heap invective and venom on each other in the pages of *Le Monde* and *Libération* and on the airwaves of the radio station Europe no. 1. In the January 10 issue of *Libération*, Miller attacked Dolto as "pitiful" and Félix Guattari as "hypocritical" and gave voice to a private "jubilation" that "at last we shall know who are the pupils of Lacan and who are the pupils of little nobodies." Not to be outdone, in the same issue, Melman concluded an attack on the dissidents by saying, "I vomit them."

The barons who supported Miller and the dissolution seemed to be doing so in the hope that if the new Lacanian organization included them, some of France's best-known clinicians, Miller could be isolated in the university. However,

when Jean Clavreul publicly criticized Miller in an open letter published in *Le Monde* on January 10, it became clear that
Miller could not be easily isolated. Only four days later, *Le
Monde* published a reply to Clavreul signed by Lacan in which
he disavowed his old friend and supported Miller. Once again
the rumors flew that Miller had written the letter and Lacan
had simply signed it.

Meanwhile, on the other side, the partisans of legal dissolution had called for the emergency intervention of the
French legal system. On January 17, the unthinkable occurred:
a summons was served to Lacan for fifteen years of administrative irregularities at the Freudian School. This complaint
was signed by twenty-eight members of the School, including Michèle Montrelay, Claude Rabant, Michel de Certeau,
Xavier Audouard, and François Roustang. The summons was
not really about specific complaints; since the founding of
the School Lacan had been an absolute monarch who ruled
with the free consent of his subjects. Rather, the purpose of
the summons was strategic: to force those who believed that
the Freudian School had already been symbolically dissolved
to play the legal game. Miller's enemies hoped that this would
improve their chances of retaining the Freudian school after
Lacan and Miller left it.

The court hearing took place on January 21. Lacan did not
appear but was represented by his lawyer, Roland Dumas,
accompanied by Jacques-Alain Miller. Five days later the court
made its ruling public and both sides claimed victory. Montrelay had wanted the judge to appoint a court administrator
who would have been empowered to strip the School of its
rights. Instead, the judge simply appointed a court representative, Maître Zécri, whose only instructions were to investigate
procedural irregularities in the School's functioning. Zécri's

first act was to set a date for a new general assembly: March 16. The School still had to vote on the statutory amendment (to increase the size of the Administrative Council) that had not been legally approved the previous September.

Meanwhile Lacan's call to his true followers had produced a remarkable result. In the week that followed his public presentation of the letter of dissolution, Lacan received over a thousand letters from people wanting to continue with him or, in his terms, *père-sévère* (persevere with a severe, punishing, and severing father). Only about three hundred of these letters were from members of the Freudian School; the rest were from teachers, psychiatric interns, psychologists, social workers, and physiotherapists, all of whom had in one way or another affiliated themselves with the Lacanian adventure. They formed the mass from which Lacanian patients were drawn. They were the audience, the clientele, the proletariat of Freud's French revolution. The popular success of the Lacanian movement had rested on this waiting, fascinated public whose members had occupied the couches of the ever-swelling ranks of Freudian School analysts. They were the underclass of the French psychoanalytic movement, and they had responded to Lacan's call for love and allegiance. To almost everyone's great surprise, they all received an invitation to a new dance: "To the thousand whose letters attest their desire to go with him, Jacques Lacan replies that as of today, February 21, 1980, he founds the Freudian Cause."

The Freudian School had been designed as a democratic organization; Lacan's extraordinary powers followed from a consensus of its membership. The statutes of the Freudian Cause described a very different kind of organization. Essentially, until further notice, the association was controlled and directed by Lacan, assisted by his personal secretary, Gloria

Gonzalez. These casual and arbitrary arrangements provoked a great deal of anger. On March 10, Lacan responded to the anger by inviting the loyal to support him against his critics: "Otherwise the name which you owe to me, the Freudian School, will fall into the hands of known frauds." Eric Laurent of the Miller camp supported Lacan's letter with a petition of loyalty and collected three hundred signatures. But it was widely believed that some analysts pushed their patients into signing it "to defend Lacan's cause."

Three days after reading the letter of dissolution, Lacan announced a meeting of all members of the Freudian School who were in favor of the dissolution. It was held on the evening of March 15 at the Hotel St. Jacques. On sale there was the first issue of *Delenda*, the "newsletter of the dissolution." Three hundred and eight people presented their invitations to the security guard at the door. That evening, the security arrangements were strict, embarrassingly so. Althusser showed up without an invitation, saying that he had been asked to come by "Libido and the Holy Spirit." At first he was turned away; finally he was recognized and admitted. After Lacan's speech to his disciples ("The School is coming to the end of its course. You are still here with me. I left because it was dead and didn't realize it"), Althusser took the floor. He spoke of Lacan as a pitiable clown and of his speech as monotonous and long-winded and then turned his attack on the analysts, whom he accused of forgetting their patients as they dithered in their conflicts, each "like a woman attempting to sift out lentils while war was breaking out."[12] Seventeen years after he had delivered Miller to Lacan, Althusser was returning Lacan's evening to the surrealists.

The general assembly of March 16 called by Maître Zécri did not succeed in achieving a two-thirds vote to adopt the statutory amendment that would raise the membership of the Freudian School's Administrative Council to twenty-five. The vote on this amendment did, however, become a context in which to measure the strength of the proponents of both symbolic and legal dissolution. Those who now supported the Lacan–Miller line had two hundred and seventy-one votes, those opposed one hundred and eighty-eight, with fourteen abstentions. Another general assembly was called for April 27. The opposition to dissolution now included Dolto and Leclaire. Dolto announced that she was going to vote against dissolution and be part of an opposition slate for the Administrative Council, as were Jenny Aubry, Michèle Montrelay, Claude Rabant, and Irène Roublef.

At the general assembly of April 27, Dolto made good on her promise to stand up and fight and denounced the candidates on Lacan's slate as "commandos." Nevertheless, those in favor of dissolution knew they had won even before the vote. With two competing slates, they only needed a simple majority to elect the list presented by Lacan. And they had it. Jacques-Alain Miller was placed in charge of a Department of Dissolution. Eric Laurent circulated a letter that proposed an amicable divorce to the opposing parties. But by May 1980, there was nothing amicable in the relationship between the competing groups. The minority had started its own journal, *Entre-temps*, an answer to *Delenda*, and the sentiments expressed on its pages were increasingly bitter. Jean-Pierre Lehman wrote of Lacan's desire as analogous to that of the destructive mother; Jenny Aubry borrowed Lacan's own language and complained of the minority's excommunication. Lucien Mélèse described the partisans of the Freudian Cause as "mutants who change skins, all together on command." Meanwhile the four analysts who were effectively in charge of directing the Freudian

Cause (Jacques-Alain Miller, Eric Laurent, Michel Silvestre, and Colette Soler) began a program called "Dissolution Mondays" whose objective seemed to be the demonstration of the theoretical errors of the minority.

At the same time as he was leading these exercises in recrimination, Miller was also planning the international expansion of Lacanianism. Since the early 1970s, Lacanianism had spread not only through Europe but to Latin America, competing with—and to some degree displacing—Kleinian allegiances in that part of the world. Since 1974, Latin American "Freudian Schools" had sprung up in Argentina, Brazil, Peru, Mexico, Uruguay, and Venezuela. By 1979, the Foundation of the Freudian Field, with Lacan's daughter Judith Miller as President, was organizing international exchanges and supervising international developments. The idea was to rival the British- and American-dominated International Psychoanalytic Association in those places that might be sensitive to Anglo-American imperialism. In November 1979, Miller was in Venezuela, where he made plans for Lacan to attend an international Lacanian congress to be held in Caracas the following fall. At his seminar on June 10, 1980, Lacan announced his intention to go to Caracas; it was there that he would officially launch the Freudian Cause. On that same day, the "Assembly of Dissolution of the Freudian School" was set for July 5.

At that Assembly of Dissolution, Montrelay called for those opposed to dissolution to remain in opposition "to the end," picking up this phrase from Lacan's most recent letter on "bringing things to an end." Montrelay asked: "What desire to destroy must gnaw at the person who expresses himself thus? We are not questioning his right to found elsewhere, or to disavow whomever he wants. That's his right and we respect it. But why can't Jacques Lacan bear that what he removes himself from should continue to live?"[13] Once again, the majority didn't get a two-thirds vote and only abstentions kept the School legally alive. But since the School was legally alive, Dolto and thirty other analysts made one final "formal demand" to Lacan to reestablish its functioning. Their letter received no reply until September 8, when Solange Faladé made it public and ridiculed its contents: "Do you really believe that the association can function and remain itself thanks to a few abstentions?"[14] On September 18, Montrelay and Rabant came forward with a new compromise: the majority should resign from the School, the School's name should change, and its assets should be divided. Just as Faladé had mocked Dolto's proposal, the majority now scorned this latest effort, comparing it to "the story of the fine knife whose blade was changed after its handle was replaced. Is the psychoanalyst a hermit crab who needs to protect himself with an empty shell?"[15]

Although the Freudian Cause was presenting a united front to the outside world, within its inner circle relationships were becoming strained and fidelity to Miller was becoming more complicated. Members of its inner circle were in the best position to know how little Lacan was really in charge of things, in the best position to know the degree to which Miller had appropriated his voice. Faladé later recounted that from May onward "Lacan was no longer interested in what was going on, and everything had to be discussed with Miller."[16] But for members of the inner circle, a commitment to dissolution meant that until it was achieved, Miller could not be dissociated from Lacan. Admitting that Lacan was no longer involved could play into the hands of the minority by calling into question the authenticity of the original letter of dissolution. Thus until September 27, the date of the general assembly where the fate of the Freudian School would be decided, the Administrative Council was unanimous in its support of Miller. In contrast, even the semblance of unity among those who opposed the dissolution was falling apart. Finally, their quarrels intensified to the point that Rabant changed sides. On the evening before the general assembly, he informed Lacan that he would now vote for dissolution. Rabant's action was critical; his allies changed sides with him. On September 27, 1980, the dissolution was voted: three hundred and forty-three votes to seventy-seven, with thirty-three abstentions.

Lacan had invited most of the members of the Freudian School to a reception at the Maison de l'Amérique Latine on the evening after the general assembly. It was there that Jacques-Alain Miller told Lacan that they had won. In *La Seconde mort de Jacques Lacan*, Claude Dorgeuille provides a revealing portrait of Lacan's demeanor on that evening of triumph. Dorgeuille describes Lacan as indifferent, vaguely smiling, giving no sign of satisfaction at the good news. "Lacan shook hands in an automatic way when hands were offered to him, often not recognizing his own colleagues. On the second floor of the building, the Administrative Council had a brief meeting to draft the press release announcing that the Freudian School was dissolved. Lacan left without having said a word."[17]

As soon as the battle for the dissolution of the Freudian School was won, the coalition behind Miller began to crumble. Lacan was mortally ill, withdrawn, and incoherent in this final year of his life. Yet the accusations against Miller were implicitly or explicitly addressed to Lacan, even as Miller's accusers expressed doubt and disbelief that Lacan was capable of writing, or even of responsibly signing, any communication he might send them in return. And in the same spirit, Miller's defense consisted of a series of letters signed by Lacan.

There was soon to be yet another dissolution, this time of the Freudian Cause. Although its story proceeds as if it turned on a succession of revelations about Jacques-Alain Miller, in fact, it reveals little new about him. What it does reveal is how those closest to Lacan faced and could not face the end of his life.

On October 22, 1980, modifications to the statutes of the Freudian Cause were filed with the Paris Prefecture of Police over Lacan's signature. The amendments note that their origin was an "assembly" held on October 19, but no record of the meeting exists. It is possible that the assembly included only Lacan and Miller or only Lacan and his secretary, Gloria Gonzalez. Or perhaps, went the rumors, only Miller attended. The meeting was important because it was widely felt that the new statutes which emerged from it had dealt a final blow to any semblance of democracy within the Freudian Cause.

By now, hundreds of pages have been written agonizing over the question of whether Lacan wrote or even approved these new statutes. There had, of course, been controversy over the authorship of the original letter of dissolution, but in that case even if Lacan did not write the letter himself, he clearly intended and supported its contents. But now, Lacan seemed too weak and confused for his actions to indicate clear intentions. Yet his signature and his "letters" were still being used to give direction to the "thousand" of the Freudian Cause. If earlier, Miller had perhaps taken the intentions of a weakened Lacan, turned them into prose, and submitted the words for Lacan's signature, knowing that his father-in-law stood behind them, now, if Miller was involved, the meaning of his actions would have to be different. The architects of the dissolution accused Miller of using a senile Lacan as a rubber stamp for political intrigues that he could not possibly understand. Having supported Miller in Lacan's name, it was now difficult for senior analysts at the Freudian Cause to denounce him in Lacan's name. Yet it would seem that for many of them, this solution was preferable to facing the painful truth that Lacan had done everything he could to ensure that his legacy (his money, his property, his daughter, his texts, and his School) would go to Miller. It was easier to construct a version of the story in which a feeble, trapped, even imprisoned Lacan was powerless against the energetic, obsessed, tyrannical Miller. Miller presented an enemy that you could love to hate. Perhaps being enraged at Miller was a way of refusing to mourn Lacan, of refusing to accept that Lacan wished to leave his legacy not to an experienced clinician or to a lifelong follower but to a professional philosopher and a member of the family.

In December 1980, tensions at the Freudian Cause came to the surface in a crisis nominally about real estate. Miller had asked Charles Melman to help him secure permission for the Cause to rent the Freudian School's former headquarters. When this had been achieved, Miller submitted a lease to Melman that the latter found unacceptable because, among other things, it stipulated that it could be rescinded by the tenant alone. Furthermore, Miller announced plans for a renovation of the headquarters so that it could be used as a library and editorial office. The renovation would have effectively closed the space to analytic teaching.[18] In this symbolic harbinger of the "après-Lacan," the philosopher was taking yet another revenge on the clinicians. Melman, a clinician who had loyally supported Miller throughout the crisis of the dissolution, was enraged and was about to do something that broke all the rules. Melman was about to denounce his patient.

On December 7, Melman sent a letter attacking Miller, although it did not mention him by name, to three hundred former members of the now-defunct Freudian School.[19] The letter aired grievances about the lease, about Miller's ambitions and dishonesty, and about the questionable legality of the October 22 amendments to the statutes of the Freudian Cause. Melman claimed that although both he and Solange Faladé were on the Board of Directors of the Cause, neither of them had seen its new statutes before they were officially registered with the legal authorities. ("My wife had to go search them out at the Prefecture of Police!") Most important, Melman said what no member of the inner circle had yet dared to say: he questioned the authenticity of the many letters supposedly sent by Lacan over the past year. Melman spoke of "apocryphal texts" with the inference that Miller had been running the show all along, manipulating Lacan's supposed "wishes" and his signature:

> The current situation demands that one of the "old guard" takes the liberty to say where we are. The Freudian Cause, although in its cradle, has a malformation which runs the risk of killing it or turning it into a monstrosity. Why? Because everything is decided and inscribed in Lacan's name although it is clear that he himself has nothing to do with these actions except for adding his signature, now become automatic. That is the painful fact.

Melman admitted that this painful fact had been hidden because Lacan's students hoped that he would start a new organization "to which they could belong with honor."

> However, one must now face the fact that the Freudian Cause is being made without Lacan, even if we are fortunate enough to have him still among us.
>
> His deficiency due to age and fatigue leaves a free field to those who dispose of his signature if not his voice, and thus get him to

endorse, and even pronounce, apocryphal texts that are put in the
service of a cause that has very little to do with Freud.

In a futile effort to show respect for the principles of clinical
confidentiality, Melman insisted that his letter did not draw
on information confided to him in the privacy of the analytic
encounter. Psychoanalytic politics always mixes institutional
and analytic affairs—the internal conflicts of a psychoanalytic
society are fought out among people who are or were each other's patients, analysts, supervisors, lovers, ex-lovers, spouses,
and ex-spouses. But even in the Lacanian milieu, which by the
early 1980s had more or less seen everything, Melman's letter
went beyond acceptable bounds.

Melman's letter was, in fact, a toned-down revision of an
even more violent first draft. Melman had shown that first
version to Faladé, asking her to sign it with him. She refused
and also counseled him to rewrite it. Two weeks later Faladé
sent out her own letter.[20] Addressed to "those who have asked
to belong to the Freudian Cause," it was calmer than Melman's
letter but essentially supported his story.

According to Faladé, the October modifications of the statutes of the Cause had never been approved by the Board of
Directors. All discussion of the amendments had been cut
short with the words "Doctor Lacan has signed the statutes."
Similarly cut short was all discussion of the statutes for what
was supposed to be the training program for the organization, the School of the Freudian Cause. Faladé was supposed
to be one of the analysts in charge of the School, but she was
left uninformed about its basic structure. To add insult to
injury, her teaching program on "Texts and Experiences" had
been canceled. Melman told her that he "had been told that
it was of no interest." Indeed during November, Miller had
told analysts who wished to form study groups on Freudian

or Lacanian texts that from now on this function would be reserved for the Department of Psychoanalysis at Vincennes. The clinicians were being squeezed out of teaching.

Faladé had one final difference with Miller, which concerned money and honor. Faladé claimed that at the first meeting of the Board of Directors of the Cause, the group decided to pay off the debts of the former Freudian School, a sum of about fourteen thousand francs. But two weeks after this decision was made, on the day before she was to prepare the checks to pay overdue salaries to Freudian School staff, Miller telephoned her and objected, claiming that he had not realized how large the debt was, that he had gotten confused between "old" and "new" francs. According to Faladé, Miller complained that "fourteen thousand francs were the equivalent of fourteen million old francs." Since it had been twenty years since the old franc had been exchanged for the new, Faladé's comment on Miller's confusion seems apt: "In 1980, I could not believe my ears!" It seemed to her that Miller was willing to use any excuse to block payment. He proposed that the Cause buy the assets of the Freudian School, specifically its library, to help meet the School's debt, but offered what Faladé felt was a ridiculously low price. Faladé's letter ends with a touching reiteration of her loyalty to Lacan. It is only by *refusing* "to accept all demands which are *presented* as though they come from Jacques Lacan, that I can remain faithful as I have always tried to be, to his teaching and example."

Five days later, Jean Clavreul supported Melman and Faladé with his own letter, addressed to Lacan but sent to the membership of the Freudian Cause and the now-defunct Freudian School.[21] It touched on many by now familiar points, using a directly political metaphor to make its case. As Clavreul saw it, the new political structure at the Cause was designed to mask the fact that Lacan was no longer in charge. The texts that were said to come from him were highly suspect. The plans for the governance of the Cause would have it run by a Soviet-styled "democratic centralism" that would destroy all grassroots initiatives. Clavreul believed that in this new bureaucratic regime, clinical psychoanalysis would be discredited and demanded that a general assembly of the Freudian Cause be held to discuss the current crisis. In the meantime, Clavreul invited members of the Cause and former members of the Freudian School to join him in a new Psychoanalytic Study Group to "constitute a place sheltered from the conformist terrorism" of the Cause. Faladé, too, moved in the direction of creating a new group, but it never got off the ground.

Miller's response to the deluge of criticism was indirect: he released a transcript of an "anonymous" and undated interview which was recorded and then transcribed by two of his supporters, Maryse Clastres and Gérard Pommier. In the interview Miller pointed to flaws in his adversaries' arguments: Melman and Faladé could not have been unaware of the modifications to the statutes of the Cause since they admit that these were discussed at a meeting of the Board of Directors. As far as the lease was concerned, Miller reminded everyone that he was only a tenant. If the landlord (Melman) hadn't liked his tenant's proposal, it had been up to the landlord to suggest another. Finally, Miller declared that it was inconceivable that faced with a silent Lacan, Melman and Faladé had let themselves be cut off by "young Turks."[22]

Delenda had been created to do the "work of the dissolution," but Miller turned it into his weapon in new struggles within the Cause long after the dissolution had been achieved. His opponents felt that meetings were politically orchestrated so that there was not much room to ask embarrassing questions: a silent and confused Lacan was brought to these gatherings, some thought in order to stifle dissent. But by January 1981, Miller's students were asking for explanations and the visibly ill Lacan stopped attending meetings, perhaps because his presence was deemed more harmful than helpful. By some admittedly partisan accounts, the meetings of *Delenda* brought democratic process in psychoanalytic politics to a new low. When at a meeting on January 22 the jurist Pierre Legendre interrupted the tightly controlled program to criticize the statutes proposed for the School of the Freudian Cause, Claude Dorgeuille recounts that the lights in the auditorium kept going out. At the time, people assumed it was a power failure, but it turned out that it was Gérard Miller (Jacques-Alain Miller's brother) playing with the switch.[23] In the February 2 issue of *Delenda*, devoted to criticizing Miller's critics, Gérard Miller accused Melman of wanting Lacan to die.

Although most analysts could not condone Melman's letter because it publicly discussed one of his patients, many believed its contents to be true. January 1981 brought a flood of resignations from the Cause, so many in fact that its Board of Directors decided to abandon the organization and start a new one: the *School* of the Freudian Cause. Created on January 19, the School's statutes were attributed (as usual) to Lacan. Tragedy had already repeated itself as farce. This third act was pure politics. Miller was not going to take the chance of having barons again. At the School of the Freudian Cause, no titles were to be permanent. (Even the much-coveted status of School Analyst would be held for only three years.) Nor would Miller tolerate grassroots democracy or coalition politics. In this organization, all votes would be by a public show of hands. Dissenters would be seen before they could be heard.

The cover letter that was sent out with the organization's statutes made its politics clear: "We know that many of you have wanted an opportunity to look at the statutes before they were formally adopted in an assembly. But there were no criteria that could establish the competence of such an assembly, and so this was impractical." In other words, the authors of the statutes for the new organization did not doubt their competence to write them, but the "thousand" who followed Lacan were considered too motley a crew to have a say. Yet in the spirit of a Napoleonic plebiscite, that same "thousand" were asked to legitimate statutes they had never seen or discussed. Six days later, a group of twenty-two former School Analysts who had been loyal to Miller through the dissolution resigned from the Cause. This group included Jean Allouch, René Bailly, Louis Beirnaert, Jean Clavreul, Claude Dorgueille, Claude Dumézil, Solange Faladé, Maud Mannoni, Octave Mannoni, Charles Melman, Thérèse Parisot, Guy Sapriel, and Christian Simatos. For them, the Cause or its "replacement," the School of the Freudian Cause, had "broken its contract" with the "thousand" and no longer existed except as an example of "the intimate link between psychoanalysis and politics, a relationship in which political intrigue will prevail when the specificity of psychoanalytic discourse is ignored."[24] Within six months, most of the twenty-two would be the head of their own schools in the post-dissolution Lacanian diaspora.

The day after the group resignation, another letter signed by Lacan appeared in the mail: an appeal for love and for the School of the Freudian Cause. On the subject of the School were the following words: "It is the School of my students, those who still love me. I open its doors to them. I say to the thousand: 'This is worth the risk. It is the only solution possible—and decent.'"[25] In this letter Lacan announced that for the past month he had withdrawn from all activity except for his analytic practice. Now, turning his attention to the crisis, he called for a "Forum (of the School), where everything will be open for debate." He named an eight-member committee of advisors to prepare the program for this Forum (Claude Conté, the president of the School of the Cause, Lucien Israël, Robert Lefort, Patrick Lemoine, Pierre Martin, Jacques-Alain Miller, Moustapha Safouan, and Colette Soler) and asked them to write if they were willing to accept this charge.

This latest Lacan letter provoked the strongest outcry ever. Jean Clavreul pointed out that although Lacan said that he had withdrawn from all activity for the past month, important decisions had been made during that time that had been advertised as "with Lacan's agreement." "Who lies?" asked Clavreul. "Lacan or Conté?"[26] For Octave and Maud Mannoni:

> An analyst cannot believe that Lacan—at least the Lacan that we know—would have been able to write a sentence where he calls on "those who still love me." He knows Freud's "Group Psychology" too well to speak thus. . . . Lacan would not have had the naiveté to make allusions to love.
>
> You can bet with no risk that this sentence was originated by a non-analyst; otherwise it is not believable.[27]

Lacan's state of confusion coupled with this new and disturbing letter increased the suspicion that Miller was writing Lacan's texts. Yet there was an obvious contradiction when analysts used the contents of this most recent letter ("I have not done any of the actions attributed to me this past month") to call into question the letters that had come before. One could not both disbelieve the authenticity of Lacan's letters and use their contents to criticize the person presumed to have composed them. But if the letters were not being written by Lacan, analysts asked, why were they being presented as his, why were they written in near parodies of his style? Why was Miller insulting their intelligence and demeaning Lacan? What was this masquerade?

The analyst Claude Poncin found his answer to these questions in *Oedipus at Colonnus*:

> My daughter, what have the oracles revealed?
> That the people, for their well being, will search you out, dead or alive.
> But what can one get from an old man like me?
> It is said that their power depends on you.
> They want to keep you near the country and you will no longer be able to come and go as you wish.[28]

Not surprisingly, given that Lacan had called on loyalists, the advisors he chose did agree to work on the Forum. One of them, however, Moustapha Safouan, insisted that their letter of acceptance specify that "no one will present himself or herself as Lacan's representative."[29] In many ways, Safouan's gesture was too little and too late. Critics pointed out not only that the advisors *were* Lacan's representatives but that their letter of acceptance had a troublesome political tone. The advisors' letter expressed the hope that their work would lead to "articulated results" that could "be communicated to all" in order to "be discussed and voted by all." For Pierre de Cabarrus, this put matters back to the kind of plebiscite politics that had marred the presentation of the statutes of the Freudian Cause in the first place: "Thus you will know everything, you will vote on everything . . . one falls into *l'utopie totalisante*."[30]

The "thousand," Cabarrus underscored, had been invited to join the Cause without any process of selection. Some were analysts, some were simply fans. Others were practicing psychoanalysts but had subminimal training even by Lacanian standards. Thus the composition of the Cause did not put a general assembly of all its members in a good position to formulate, discuss, and ratify the statutes of a psychoanalytic society or institute. And no one (except presumably the Board of Directors) knew whether new members had been recruited since the declaration by the "thousand" at the time of the dissolution. And if there had been recruitment, who had joined? Lacan and Miller had set up an organization in which there was little room for its full membership to play any role other than that of an electoral mass.

Although the advisors had publicly accepted Lacan's charge, they were far from unanimous in their enthusiasm for the project. Lucien Israël expressed his doubts to Lacan: "I cannot and do not want to work with just anyone. The flight [from the Freudian Cause] that we are seeing now attests to the fact that it wasn't only Freud who was afflicted with a 'bande.'"[31] Safouan and Israël felt that the Forum could only take place if it declared its independence from the School of the Freudian Cause. Lacan's letter of January 26 called for a "Forum (of the School)." The parentheses gave some hope that Lacan was willing to call the School into question in order to have an open debate on the future. Although Miller objected, Safouan insisted that the February 7 letter announcing the plans for the Forum go out on plain paper without the School heading. Safouan was enraged that after having worked so hard for this concession on the letter, it went out in *envelopes* that bore the return address of "the School of the Freudian Cause."

On February 9, Octave and Maud Mannoni asked the advisors for their resignations or for the dissolution of the School of the Freudian Cause, insisting that these were the only two ways to give some credibility to the advisors' claim that what they wanted was to "take the debate from point zero." The next day, Safouan and Israël wrote to Lacan, pointing out that the existence of the School of the Freudian Cause was standing in the way of an open Forum. They asked Lacan to clarify that the call for the Forum constituted the dissolution of the School of the Freudian Cause. For them to serve in good faith, there had to be at least the possibility that the outcome of the Forum's debate would be the creation of a new psychoanalytic institution.

Two members of the Board of Directors of the School of the Freudian Cause, Jean-Pierre Bauer and Michel Ritter, resigned their positions to facilitate an open Forum, but on February 17, the remaining members of the Board stated that maintaining the School was not incompatible with the Forum. Now, Claude Conté resigned as Director, declaring his support for Bauer and Ritter. Conté felt that the Board of Directors of the School should not be in place while the very existence of the School was in question, and the Forum was meaningless if the School was not in question. Conté made it clear that if his position was not accepted at the next meeting of the advisors, he would resign as an advisor as well.

That meeting of the advisors on February 23 was violent. Each had just received a new urgent letter from Lacan, who asked for their counsel within the week in the form of a letter of not more than a page in length. The letter concluded: "I said Forum of the School. Thus there must be a School."[32] Safouan, who doubted that this letter came from Lacan, nevertheless responded by writing Lacan and asking him to dissolve the School or to let him resign from his functions. That same day, Lucien Israël resigned from the group of advisors; Conté resigned two days later.

On March 11, members of the School of the Freudian Cause received the final letter signed by Lacan before his death, a letter announcing the March 28 and 29 convocation of the

Forum. On March 25, a letter of information from the School
of the Freudian Cause concerning participation in the Forum
made it clear that "those who have already decided not to
participate in the constitution of the School of the Freudian
Cause or who even consider its dissolution as an objective cannot legitimately participate in the debate concerning it."[33] In
other words, the Forum specifically excluded the very people
whose objections made it happen in the first place. As might
be expected, the Forum was something of a nonevent. Interventions from the floor were held to five minutes. No debate
was allowed. Lacan was not present. No vote was taken. Spiritually now, as well as legally, the dissolution of the Freudian
School was complete.

After the Forum, and with the resignation of almost all of its
experienced analysts, the energies of the School of the Freudian Cause went into the publication of a new psychoanalytic
review, *L'Ane*, with an emphasis on literature and culture. In
May, Lacan attended the party that celebrated the publication
of its first issue, which included a collection of documents that
presented the story of the dissolution from the perspective of
its partisans; his health was so deteriorated that he did not
recognize anyone there. The explanation given was that he
had a cataract.

At the end of the summer of 1981, at Guitrancourt, alone
with his secretary Gloria, Lacan began to hemorrhage and
was rushed to the hospital at Neuilly for emergency abdomi-
nal surgery. A few days later he fell into a coma. Lacan died
on Wednesday, September 9. His last words were unyielding:
"Je suis obstiné. . . . Je disparais" (I am stubborn. . . . I am
disappearing.)[34]

Lacan's body was brought to Miller's home, where he had
lived during the last months of his life. A few members of the

School of the Freudian Cause were authorized to pay their
last respects. On Friday, Jacques Lacan's brother, a member of
the Benedictine order, came to Paris to celebrate a mass in his
memory. The next day Lacan, an atheist, had a secular burial at
Guitrancourt. About thirty people accompanied the hearse to
the small village. There were friends of the family and a small
delegation from the School of the Freudian Cause. The "compa-
gnons de Lacan," the "barons," the analysts who had been his
closest collaborators for more than a quarter of a century, were
all absent. In the end, the Lacanian journey was a family affair.

When Lacan rose to preeminence in the 1960s, French
intellectual life was divided into politicized factions, mobi-
lized by true believers. And his work itself became a system
that competed on these ideological grounds. "Lacanianism
served as an ideological alternative to Catholicism and gauchisme," wrote Eric Conan in *L'Express*. "It was a blessed time
when Jesuits seized by doubt and stalled Althusserians could
join the new Lacanian institution."[35] Writing the history of
this period, Élisabeth Roudinesco went further, believing that
without the "Lacanian adventure" a certain number of young
French intellectuals of the 1968 generation would have been
"drifting toward terrorism."[36] Lacan died as the decade of the
1970s ended; the one that followed had a very different political tenor. In the 1960s and 1970s, the Left had been in the
opposition; in the 1980s with the Socialist victory, the Left was
in power but no longer recognizably the Left. In the structuralist 1960s, French intellectual culture was predominantly Marxist; in the postmodernist 1980s, this was no longer the case.
In the 1960s, when intellectuals spoke of conservative forces,
they were likely to be referring to the Communist Party; in
the 1980s, the Communist Party all but disappeared as a force
to contend with, and conservatives were now on a reborn

nationalist Right. In the 1960s, social theory nurtured the idea of the decentered subject. In the 1980s, there was a rebirth of liberalism and humanism; theories that spoke of an intentional actor were newly relegitimated in political thought.[37]

The "Lacano- *gauchiste*" moment had made a commitment to a program that integrated politics with psychology, right action with personal reflection. The tone of that moment survives in French feminist writing, which still takes Lacanianism as a discourse of liberation, and in the School of the Freudian Cause, which has consecrated itself to keeping the flame alive.[38] At the School of the Freudian Cause, criticism of Lacan is met with staunch defense and a closing of the ranks. If the organization seems authoritarian in its management and doctrinaire in its theoretical commitments, this is at least in part because it functions as would a group of embattled missionaries fighting for the truth.

In April 1981, in the aftermath of the Forum, the School of the Freudian Cause was in disarray. It had lost its most experienced analysts and was left only with analysts of Miller's generation and a group of much younger members, many of whom had not yet begun analytic training. Within five years, however, the School had a new lease on life. The generation of younger analysts was willing to accept Miller as an "elder" and was now creating its own analytic children. By 1988, when the School celebrated its seventh birthday, it had 236 members and 63 associates, with 25 offices outside Paris, and an affiliated branch in Belgium.[39] To the outside world, it appeared as the center of a successful empire, protected and defended by a publishing house (Navarin), a literary and cultural magazine (*L'Ane*), and a university stronghold, now at Saint-Denis. In addition the School was the center of an international organization.

In the years before his death, Lacan (through Miller) had put in place an instrument of potential revenge against those who had banished and humiliated him. La Fondation du Champ Freudien, the Foundation of the Freudian Field, originally created in 1979 to organize international conferences, gradually took on a political aspiration and an international vocation: to organize the non-French Lacanian world under the umbrella of the Paris organization. By 1990, there were over sixty affiliated groups in twenty countries. In most cases what the affiliated groups want and get is no more than Miller's blessing, a symbol that they are part of the true Lacanian family.[40] Unlike its rival, the International Psychoanalytic Association, the Foundation does not impose rules for analytic technique or training. In practice, however, its affiliated groups are under pressure to maintain a certain ideological purity. Perceived disloyalty to Miller is not well tolerated.

Indeed, what most distinguishes the School of the Freudian Cause from other psychoanalytic organizations is its pronounced tone of political militancy. For example, on its seventh birthday the School published a four-point overview of its history, summarized below, which specified political enemies and political purpose.

Point one: Psychoanalysis, born in Central Europe, takes the United States as its center of gravity with the rise of Nazism. There, it becomes dominated by a deviationist tendency: ego psychology. Jacques Lacan is the strongest and most persistent force who struggles against this trend under the banner of a return to Freud.

Point two: Ten years later, the final consummation of the political rupture: Lacan ratifies the irremediable drift of the IPA and decides to found his own School "to restore truth" to psychoanalysis. The Freudian School grows within France and internationally, the success of Lacan's Seminar associates him with Freud's renown.

Point three: In 1980, Lacan criticizes the functioning of his school and decides to dissolve it in order to reconstitute it on new lines. The dissolution was achieved by a large majority vote, but the dynamic of the events inhibits the wished-for reconstitution in the Freudian Cause. Instead there is a dispersion, then, during the 1980s, a reappearance of groups with a common reference point. Nevertheless, the first of these groups to be created and the most important of them (because of the number of the members of the dissolved school who joined and because it is the only one presided over by Lacan until his death) is the School of the Freudian Cause.

Point four: The School of the Freudian Cause is both the continuation and the counter experience of the original Freudian School through its permutative structures, decentralized teaching, promotion of clinical psychoanalysis, ongoing criticism of the psychoanalytic movement, and international program. Seven years after its creation, these structures are confirmed in their stability. The School recognizes its clear success, but is not complacent in this recognition.[41]

This history is both revisionist and highly politicized. It presents deviationism to fight, a slogan to fight it under, and a charismatic leader who has passed the torch to a new generation of militants. History is rewritten so that key actors make decisions rather than do the best they can under the pressure of events. (For example, in this official School history, Lacan "ratified" the irremediable deviations of the International

Psychoanalytic Association rather than being excluded from it against his will.) The School is said to embody a permanent revolution that is given a Lacanian pedigree and a label with a not surprising mathematical resonance: "l'instance de la per-mutation."[42] At the School of the Freudian Cause, "permuta-tion" means that study groups, administrative bodies, even the status of School Analyst, are periodically dissolved. Finally, the School is placed in the vanguard of a historical struggle. According to its analysis, social crisis has created an acceler-ating demand for psychoanalysis that Lacan had termed an epidemic. It is being met by a false and bureaucratic psycho-analysis, the kind of psychoanalysis that Lacan spent his life opposing. It is the School's mission to confront and challenge this false psychoanalysis by preaching the word of Lacan.

The rhetoric of action in these 1988 texts is dialectical and touched by a certain Maoism: extend true psychoanalysis and challenge the symptom-psychoanalysis; spread the word of Freud and Lacan in the university and participate in the decon-struction of the university.[43] The texts have a self-confident tone as they present the School as a unified and politically focused association. But behind the public presentation, there was another reality. By April 1989, little more than a year later, it had become commonplace for its membership to qualify the School as in crisis. By the following fall, Miller himself described the School as threatened "as to its very existence."[44]

Throughout the 1980s, that is, during its period of rebuild-ing, the School of the Freudian Cause had been involved in a series of controversies, most of them centered on its relation to Lacan and its right to claim legitimacy through him. In one sense, there was ample room to invoke the sturdy French aph-orism "The more things change, the more they are the same." However, unlike the politics of previous analytic generations but like the final days of the Freudian School, several of these controversies brought the School of the Freudian Cause into contact with the legal system. In 1980, most analysts found it unthinkable that Michèle Montrelay and Claude Rabant would actually call Lacan into court. The legacy of the dissolution was to change all that.

Jacques Lacan had given Miller exclusive rights to his literary estate, including the responsibility of "establishing" the texts of his seminars for publication at Le Seuil. In 1985, however, a group of analysts joined together in an association devoted to the transcription of Lacan's seminar (Association Pour la Recherche et l'Etablissement de Séminaires), known by the acronym APRES ("after"). APRES published a version of Lacan's seminar of 1960–61, based on stenographic transcripts, in the journal *Stécriture*. Miller tried to stop APRES, but the organization insisted that Miller's "establishment" of the seminars was an admitted act of literary interpretation. The seminars were a spoken act, and not allowing the original words to circulate was inadmissible censorship. Thus did the "question of the passage of Jacques Lacan's spoken work through writing" come before the French courts.

When the high court of Paris declared that it was not competent to make a simple ruling, Jacques-Alain Miller sued for a trial and asked for an end to the publication of *Stécriture*, the destruction of all printed copies of unauthorized versions of the seminar, and monetary compensation for damages. In December 1985, Miller won his case. Many found his victory a troubling chapter in the politics of ideas. The court had upheld Miller's right to declare illegal the circulation of any traces of Lacan's words except those that he chose to let out.

Two years later, Miller was back in court. This time he was being sued by Gérard Pommier, an analyst at the School of the

Freudian Cause and one of his staunchest supporters during the period of the dissolution. The media tended to portray the suit as part of a struggle for the control of a "post-Lacanian psychoanalytic International with high stakes both in terms of power and money."[45] Understandably, Pommier saw it otherwise. From his point of view he was fighting to clarify the relationship between psychoanalysis and the law.

In September 1985, Pommier, who directed a small publishing house, wrote several confidential letters to Spanish colleagues in which he criticized Miller and the School of the Freudian Cause and discussed plans for a new psychoanalytic review. One of the Spaniards with whom Pommier corresponded was in analytic treatment with Jacques-Alain Miller and gave him one of Pommier's letters. Pommier accused Miller of using information obtained from this letter to interfere with his professional plans. Pommier claimed that Miller had violated the rules of professional confidentiality by using a letter furnished by a patient against him, a colleague. The principle of confidentiality is, of course, traditionally thought of as protection for the patient. Pommier's case raised the question of whether protection can also be claimed by third parties who consider themselves damaged by analytic indiscretion. At the time of Miller's alleged indiscretion, Pommier asked the School of the Freudian Cause to take action against him. But the School, loyal to Miller, turned the case around, declaring that it was Pommier who was guilty of professional misconduct.[46] It was then that Pommier took Miller to court. And so Pommier's case also raised the question of whether psychoanalysts are capable of settling their own quarrels given the close interweaving of familial, educational, transferential, political, financial, and sexual relationships in their circles. Pommier was himself deeply entangled in this web. At the time of the lawsuit, Catherine Millot, Lacan's final mistress and also an analyst at the School of the Freudian Cause, had been Pommier's companion for many years. Feelings about their relationship and Pommier's challenge to Miller ran high.

The court dismissed Pommier's lawsuit for lack of evidence, but Pommier did not let matters drop. He saw Miller's breach of confidentiality as only one manifestation of larger problems endemic to psychoanalysis: analytic practice tempts analysts to think of themselves as above the law and analytic legitimacy tends to become a family affair. In an April 1989 article in the review *Passages*, Pommier charged that although Miller did not have analytic training that corresponded to the "standard norms," he nevertheless had been "seeing patients since Lacan's death," supported by the weight of his "family heritage."[47] That same month, Pommier distributed this article and other writings about his lawsuit to colleagues at the School of the Freudian Cause. The documents were sent out with a cover letter that outlined his position both on Miller and the larger question of the transmission of psychoanalysis.

Since J. Lacan's death, the Lacanian movement has been faced with a serious problem. Although the movement continues to grow, the criteria to practice psychoanalysis remain vague. The problem is not in theoretical divergences, but rather in the question of ethics. This question must be successfully resolved before psychoanalysis can realize its full potential.

However, since the death of Freud, we have seen the repetition of a ludicrous mode of transfer of legitimacy. The I.P.A. claimed a legitimacy by its association with Anna Freud, although neither her practice nor her theories justified it. As long as family ties serve as the means of recognition, to speak of ethics in psychoanalysis is senseless.

Today, Judith Miller, who has never even undergone analysis, heads a foundation whose objectives are the same as those of the

I.P.A.: to control theory and to install bureaucracy. It is true that in France the methods and objectives of J.-A. Miller have been rejected by the vast majority of psychoanalysts, obliging him to look abroad for the recognition he didn't receive in Paris. Further-more, he allows himself to practice psychoanalysis even though he never received the training normally required by all schools of psychoanalysis. (It is known that his analyst refused to continue his training. At the time, J.-A. Miller was writing the last "Lacan" texts which were then signed by J. Lacan.)

It is once again a serious problem of ethics which is posed and because of repeated manipulations of patients for political ends, I have decided to bring the question before the courts.

Pommier concluded: "The rights to an inheritance, which J.-A. Miller possesses, cannot possibly imply that he has the right to exercise the profession of psychoanalyst. Equally, the publication of the works of Lacan does not imply the right to lead the Lacanian movement, whose development doesn't require a guardian."[48]

Pommier was looking for a way to challenge Miller; not surprisingly the two were soon on opposing sides in another legal proceeding. In the fall of 1989, Pommier published *La Névrose infantile de la psychanalyse*, which elaborated his ideas about the "familial" transmission of legitimation in the psy-choanalytic movement, noting the cases of Anna Freud and the Lacan family. Pommier's essential points were that Anna Freud's power in the psychoanalytic movement was based on a familial relationship that has no place in legitimating a role as an analyst. The same is true for Lacan's daughter and son-in-law. Judith Miller has no analytic training, yet is at the head of the Freudian Field. Jacques-Alain Miller practices analysis although his training is incomplete and his analysis broken off by Charles Melman for the reasons outlined in Melman's famous letter, primarily that "Jacques-Alain Miller wrote Lacan's last seminars."[49] Pommier's controversial book was published right before the fall scientific meetings of the School of the Freudian Cause on October 14 and 15, 1989. Books published by School authors are often sold at these meetings, and Pommier wanted his book to be among them. It was not to happen that way.

For several years, Gérard Miller had been in charge of all book sales at the scientific meetings. On September 22, Pommier wrote him asking that *La Névrose infantile de la psychanalyse* be put on sale. On October 2, Miller replied that School procedure required that the Board of Directors be informed of his request. Pommier complied although he insisted that this had never before been the School's procedure. On October 11, Danièle Silvestre, the School's director, received Pommier's formal request, which she presented to the Board of Directors at its general meeting the next evening. At this meeting, the Board decided that since none of its members had either read or seen Pommier's book, it was in no position to authorize its sale. On October 13, Silvestre called Pommier and informed him of this decision.

The next day, Pommier showed up at the scientific meetings with the statutes of the School of the Freudian Cause and several cartons of his book and insisted on his right to place his book on sale.[50] Pommier claimed that he showed the relevant statutes to three members of the Board, Danièle Silvestre, Pierre Bruno, and Marie-Hélène Brosse, who agreed that there had been a mistake and authorized him to place his books on the sale table. But some time in the course of the morning, Gérard Miller removed the books. When another analyst put them back on sale, Miller removed them for a second time. At this, Pommier blew up and in his anger knocked over the exhibit table on which books for sale were displayed.

That evening, Pommier distributed a press release, claiming censorship.

On Sunday afternoon, the Board of Directors learned of Pommier's press release and asked him to withdraw it. Pommier told Jacques-Alain Miller that he would withdraw his complaint if his book was now placed on sale at the meeting. Miller refused and called a special meeting for that same evening so that the School could review the entire incident. From Pommier's point of view, the meeting was an exercise in "collective hysteria," at which twenty members of the School took turns denouncing him. Pommier feels that "a responsible leadership would have closed such a meeting as quickly as possible. But this meeting was encouraged to continue, as quite calmly, one analyst stood up to make judgments about my mental state, another about my masochism, a third about my 'jouissance.'"[51] Pommier was accused of lying to the press and of committing an act of public vandalism that had humiliated the School in front of 1,200 conference participants. The Board of Directors insisted that it had exercised no censorship; when it turned down Pommier's book, it was simply exercising its right to read works before authorizing their sale.

Ten days later, the School's Council asked Pommier to attend a Council meeting on November 13 in order to explain his actions. In response, Pommier wrote to Serge Cottet, president of the School, and asked a series of procedural questions about the forthcoming meeting. Among other things, he asked if the purpose of the meeting was simply to collect information, if the Council would be making an immediate decision, and if he could bring a lawyer. Pommier was told that no decision would be taken during the meeting nor directly following it and that the Council did not want his lawyer to attend.[52] But the very next day after the meeting, the Council asked Pommier to leave the School of the Freudian Cause. The School's statutes required that this Council recommendation be ratified by another administrative body, the Assembly. Therefore, Pommier was asked to appear before the Assembly on December 2. When Pommier protested what he saw as procedural irregularities, the Council excused its behavior by saying, first, that they had not wanted Pommier to bring a lawyer because they had hoped that their meeting with him could be a cordial interchange, a cordiality that his demeanor had made impossible, and second, that they had changed their mind about deferring a decision on his case because after his appearance they had been close to unanimity about subsequent action. Their only disagreement had been about which manner of implementing the action would be psychoanalytically correct.[53] Since several members of the Council lived far from Paris, immediate action seemed appropriate.

The weeks between the Council's decision to remove Pommier from the School and the December 2 Assembly that would be asked to ratify that decision brought a flurry of registered letters from both sides that made it clear that legal cases were being prepared. Pommier reiterated his points about the procedural irregularity of the meeting on November 13 and further complained that he had not been paid for those books that had been sold during their brief appearance on the sale tables. For its part, the Council reiterated its position that although Pommier had excused his behavior as a "capricious act," they had to disagree; if it had been so benign, Pommier would have apologized. Instead, he had written a press release. The Council saw Pommier's actions as serious and motivated. In its view, he *wanted* a furor and hoped the scandal would boost sales of his book.

Pommier's protests about procedural irregularities at the School were made in the context of a global critique of Millerian psychoanalytic politics and of the relationship of psychoanalysis to the law.[54] Pommier saw the Council as a "kangaroo court"; he likened the School's objections to his press release to the International Psychoanalytic Association's now-defunct rule that had barred analysts from all recourse to the media, and he represented the current fracas as a smoke screen for a larger scandal concerning the legitimacy of the School and the authorship of Lacan's final seminars. The controversy about these seminars had last flared up in 1982, when the School had published its first directory of members. In addition to listing School members, the directory had included a collection of Lacan texts: the 1962 "Act of Foundation of the Freudian School," the "Proposition of October 1967" (on the pass), the January 1980 letter of dissolution, and a group of circulars signed by Lacan concerning events from February 1980 to March 1981. When the directory was published, Laurence Bataille, Lacan's stepdaughter and an analyst at the School, resigned, protesting the inclusion of the post-1980 texts as official documents on the same level as Lacan's earlier writing. "The utilization of texts signed by Lacan starting in 1980," she wrote, "may have been useful at one time." But continuing to use them could not be justified. "Would those who receive their training at the School have been incapable of sustaining themselves without that comfort?"[55]

Pommier claimed that at the time of her resignation Laurence Bataille told him that she knew that Lacan's final texts were fraudulent and that Miller was their author. Pommier had supported Miller when Bataille made her accusation. Now, however, he insisted that the true authorship of the texts be made clear because the false documents were still being used to maintain the fiction that Lacan had founded the School of the Freudian Cause, a fiction that Miller had used to transfer the allegiance of analysts from Lacan to himself. "Jacques-Alain Miller should stop trying to profit from these ambiguities. He should clarify this past or start his own [psychoanalytic] group. Doing so, he would have the right—and for the first time—to my respect and he would moderate the scorn that most French psychoanalysts, both Lacanians and non-Lacanians, feel for him."[56]

Miller's response to Pommier's challenges was to announce that the very existence of the School was now in question.[57] In preparation for the December 2 Assembly, he reminded his colleagues that although at the Freudian School abstentions could block action, this was no longer true at the Freudian Cause. Now, decisions were made by a majority of those who voted by open ballot either for or against a proposal. Nevertheless, wrote Miller, although abstentions could not block action, they could destroy the School's viability. He warned his colleagues that he himself was going to be measuring this viability by the proportion of those who voted for removing Pommier in relation to the number of abstentions. "It is important to know this before abstaining."[58]

Miller got the vote he wanted. The Assembly had fifty-six members; fifty-one voted to exclude Pommier. (There were four abstentions, and Catherine Millot refused to participate in the vote, even to abstain.)[59] Pommier's next move was to sue the School, citing procedural irregularities. Miller's next move was to declare an official crisis and like Lacan, to ask for love. On December 11, Miller wrote an open letter to all members of the School which sounded like the announcement of a cultural revolution: the School must be born again and its challenged foundations made once again transparent. For Miller, the School was in crisis, gripped by the pathologies that had destroyed the Freudian School, and everything needed to be rebuilt from zero. The crisis of 1990, announced Miller, would be good for the School. "Born in crisis, it would know how to nourish and replenish itself through crisis." "The crisis of 1990," said Miller, "I want it cold, clean, and without acrimony. This is why I am making it into a quasi-matheme."[60] In his declaration of crisis, Miller characterized the logic of the School's enemies as dialectical. First, according to Miller, they contrast Lacan with the School: he is the good, the School is the bad. Then, Lacan himself is split into two: the good Lacan and the bad, the "final Lacan." With this split, it is possible to be against both Lacan and the School. Finally, one might even be against the bad Lacan and for the School *if the latter could be purged of the bad Lacan, now represented by the "famous son-in-law."* Miller stood fast on the legitimating authority of the final Lacan. He wrote: "The 'final Lacan' is inseparable from the destiny of a School that was created to be his cortège. Some who objected have already left. If there are those at the School who now think they made an error in their youth and that what they have heard from this one or that one has made them lose their innocence, now they should leave in their turn."[61]

With this letter, Miller announced a dissolution without a dissolution. "It is not necessary to have a formal dissolution to feel the necessity to renew the pact which unites us."[62] Reminiscent of how Lacan had handled the dissolution of the Freudian School, Miller asked his colleagues to write him letters of support. His letter to them bore the title "Acier l'Ouvert." The letters to him would be published in collections entitled "A Ciel Ouvert." Unsheathed steel and skies open for the deluge—the wordplays announced a period of crisis and cleansing.

On April 2, the leadership that had declared the start of the crisis announced that it was almost over. Miller had received letters of strong support and commitment; now it was time to get back to work. There would be a plenary session of the School membership on October 8, 1990, that would "mark the end of the crisis and the beginning of a new era for the School."[63]

Three weeks later, the Council of the School of the Freudian Cause informed its membership that Pommier had won his lawsuit. The court noted that Pommier should have been advised to bring a lawyer to the November 13 Council meeting, a ruling the Council interpreted as signifying that Pommier had won his suit on the most narrow technical grounds. Its response was to start a new set of procedures to exclude Pommier, this time conforming to the requirements set by the courts. To that end, Pommier was convoked to another special meeting of the Assembly on June 23. The Board of Directors had already made it clear that "even if we had known of Pommier's latest book in plenty of time, we still would not have authorized its sale" because it was defamatory toward Lacan's memory and Pommier's colleagues at the School.[64] At the Assembly, Pommier was once again charged with "vandalism and public scandal," and four new charges were added as well, each concerning Pommier's generally critical stance toward the School, for example, his case against Miller for violation of professional confidentiality and "participating or helping groups which were deliberately founded against the School of the Cause and her friends."[65] With this last charge, the School's language seemed to return full circle to the 1979 censure of Denis Vasse for participating in Confrontations. But the 1990 School of the Freudian Cause was a very different kind of organization from the 1979 Freudian School. Its dissidents were already gone. Its members were prepared to take the role of militants, increasingly stigmatized by the rest of the French analytic and even Lacanian landscape. Indeed, in the 1990s, French psychoanalysis seems to have a new myth in the making: that there are good Lacanians, defined as Lacanians who abandoned Miller, who can get along with almost everybody, and that the only significant cleavage is between the School of the Freudian Cause and the others.

Consider the way the School of the Freudian Cause was represented at the February 1990 conference "The Question of the Dissolution: Ten Years After," which was sponsored by the Freudian Circle, one of the Lacanian groups born of the dissolution. There, Claude Conté, former president of the Freudian Cause, captured the mood when he described the School of the Freudian Cause as a "residual symptom of the dissolution" whose isolation permitted other groups to work in a new and more productive way.[66] Jean-Pierre Winter likened the meetings of the School of the Freudian Cause to "those of the Eastern bloc before their recent revolutions." Michel Fennetaux said that the constructive pluralism and the heterogeneity of the French psychoanalytic world faced two enemies: the International Psychoanalytic Association and the School of the Freudian Cause. Pommier agreed, adding that, for psychoanalysts, the International Psychoanalytic Association is like the Church and the School of the Freudian Cause is like the Army.[67]

When reporting on this meeting to the School of the Freudian Cause, Anne Dunand noted that its participants used the strategy of "splitting Lacan" that Miller had described in "Acier l'Ouvert," his declaration of the 1990 crisis. "The speakers were able to identify with each other," wrote Dunand, "because what they share is loss, the loss of Lacan, the true and the real. Each speaker wanted to hold on to a little piece of real Lacan, who must exist somewhere: not in the writings (falsified), not in the act of dissolution (qualified by them as a non-act), not in his teaching . . . not in the Pass . . . not in the work. . . ."[68] The bad Lacan could be projected onto other people or onto institutions, the School of the Freudian Cause being an obvious target and Miller an even easier one.

Miller interprets other analysts' resentment of him as an expression of their shame for leaving Lacan. "I am their 'living tort' (*leur tort vivant*), their insupportable object. It is unbearable for them. But I cannot cure them."[69] And he believes that at bottom they cannot tolerate that Lacan chose him over them.

> This conflict goes back to 1964 when I first met Lacan, before I had met his daughter. The two of us got along from the very first, and this itself has always displeased certain of his other students. It was me, still a student at the time, that he invited for weekends at his country house! It was me to whom he gave the mission of transcribing [the seminars]. He had always refused to have the seminar published, that is, until I established the text of the "Fundamental Concepts" in a way that won his approval because he recognized himself in it. He put his hand on my shoulder; we made a pact. He gave me this task, he didn't give it to the others. And he chose me from the crowd to make me promise that I would take on all of the seminars. . . . It is this that they cannot tolerate: they dream to get from me that which they lost of the Freudian field because of their conflict with Lacan. I symbolize the living signifier of their castration![70]

Whether or not one agrees with Miller's general interpretation of events, on one point he is clearly right. French Lacanians without Lacan (and to some extent, non-Lacanians as well) are preoccupied with him. They are preoccupied with him as a member of Lacan's family, the inheritor of his literary estate, the favored disciple, and finally, as the one who dared to put himself in Lacan's place in the establishment of the Seminars. Miller has described his method of establishing the Seminars in terms of effacing himself in order to assume Lacan's position. Miller attempts to find "a position where when I write 'I' it is the 'I' of Lacan."[71] During the trial against *Stécriture*, Miller's lawyer put it another way: Miller "is the continuation of the author, he who prolongs him beyond death."[72] During Lacan's life, analysts found the notion of Miller as Lacan's extension and alter ego hard to take; with Lacan gone, it became intolerable. Analysts now allow themselves to express a hostility toward his relationship with Miller that they did not permit themselves when Lacan was alive. During Lacan's life, Miller's establishment of the Seminars was applauded. Now analysts feel free to attack it as a travesty. It seems part of a pattern that attempts to protect Lacan's memory from the reality of Lacan's choices in his final decade. And since Lacan cannot be mourned before he is accepted, it seems part of a profound inability to mourn Lacan.

The widespread preoccupation with Miller is striking in all recent discussions among French analysts about how to respond to proposals for government licensing of psychoanalysts or indeed to proposals that suggest that analysts should regulate themselves. Since the early 1980s, psychoanalysts have feared that the government might decide to require state certification to practice psychoanalysis, a "statut de la psychanalyse." At that time, the Lacanians were waging their battles in the media, and analysts feared that if the authorities believed half the charges they were leveling against each other, it might well be inferred that large numbers of analysts were unfit to practice. Most French analysts did not want government intervention, but many found it hard to resist the opportunity to use its discussion as a forum in which to denounce Lacanians, or if they were Lacanians, to denounce Millerians. And indeed, some analysts find the Lacanians so offensive that they genuinely welcome government intervention as a way to get rid of them. For example, André Green of the Paris Psychoanalytic Society believes that the government should not only control the number and duration of analytic sessions but should standardize the clinical indications for analysis as well. This is harsh medicine for a profession that has traditionally insisted on complete autonomy, but Green believes that such stringent rules are necessary because Lacan and his followers have put analysis in mortal danger and have left the general public totally unprotected from clinical abuses by poorly trained practitioners."[73]

Although not many analysts would go as far as Green, there has been growing sentiment that there is a need for analysts to put their own house in order. In December 1989, Serge Leclaire and Jacques Sédat, along with colleagues Philippe Girard, Lucien Israël, and Daniele Lévy, proposed that analysts create a formal mechanism for self-regulation. They called it an "instance ordinale de la psychanalyse," an "Order of Psychoanalysts" that would determine which practitioners had a right to call themselves analysts."[74] They argued that the current situation in analytic practice was out of control.

In the 1980s, the number of French analysts increased, but since the dissolution of the Freudian School, a growing number of them choose not to identify with any formal group. Indeed, by 1989, half the analysts practicing in France were working outside any institutional framework. Lacan intended his statements about the self-authorization of psychoanalysts

to underscore his belief that psychoanalysis is more like a calling than a traditional profession, more like the priesthood
than the law. The only person, insisted Lacan, who can know
if an analysand is ready to assume the position of an analyst
is that analysand. No list of completed courses and grades can
validate an analyst's right to practice. Self-authorization was
a cornerstone of what I have termed Lacan's "psychoanalytic
Protestantism." In France, where all analytic schools have
been profoundly influenced by Lacan, it made the notion
of licensing psychoanalysts profoundly countercultural. But
when the notion of self-authorization became a popular slogan, it had unintended effects. In the 1970s, the label "analyst" became prestigious, chic, and financially rewarding. The
doctrine of self-authorization gave a wide range of French
therapeutic practitioners (marriage counselors, group therapists, social workers) who had had some experience with a
personal analysis the justification they were looking for to
declare themselves analysts. By the time Leclaire made his proposals in 1989, there was no longer any way to know who was
doing what.

Other European countries (Sweden, Holland, West Germany) had prevented such disorder by integrating psychoanalytic practice within their state medical systems. Leclaire found
this an unacceptable course of action. For him, the medicaliza-
tion of psychoanalysis transformed it into an instrument of
social adaptation whereas its true vocation was subversive. True
analysis, argued Leclaire and his colleagues, stands in opposition to "conservative guardians of the discourse of order and
propriety" because it demands that "everything be spoken."[75]
Leclaire feared that with the planned economic integration of
the European Community in 1992, the regulations adopted by
other countries might be imported to France unless she had

her own respected formulae in place. So, paradoxically, the most widely debated proposal for giving psychoanalysis an official legal status came from an analyst who claimed to be motivated by the desire to *avoid* its normalization. Analysts, not outsiders, said Leclaire, must be the ones to identify true analytic practitioners.

But, of course, the problem of how to select "true" from "false" in this domain is not so simple. Leclaire's proposal revived the controversies of the early 1960s when the International Psychoanalytic Association excommunicated Lacan and Dolto for not meeting its standards but was willing to welcome their students on condition that they renounce their mentors. The paradox was apparent: if the teachers were flawed, what made the students acceptable? To the generation of French analysts who had grown up in an atmosphere charged with this history, it was clear that psychoanalytic standards often boil down to psychoanalytic politics. Was this any less true in 1989 when analysts were motivated by a desire to exclude Miller than it had been in the 1960s when they wanted to exclude Lacan?

Jean-Paul Valabrega, a veteran of the schism of 1963, reminded Leclaire that analysts have no formulae for deciding who should be in and who should be out. Whom exactly would Leclaire exclude? "Everyone knows," said Valabrega, writing in *Le Monde*, "that the immense majority of abuses, aberrations, and scandalous practices are taking place among Lacanians. [Here, the understood reference is to Miller and his colleagues at the School of the Freudian Cause.] Yet Leclaire and his collaborators have always supported this tendency, and have tacitly or explicitly stood behind its dubious practices. They have never clearly disavowed or abandoned them."[76] Thus Valabrega fears that Leclaire's proposal would lead to legislation that would not punish the worst offenders. And even if Miller and company could be excluded from this "order," Valabrega believes that the lesson of history would indicate that, once again, Lacanians would play the role of martyrs and gain sympathy and new adherents in the process. "When analysts try to legislate their identities," said Valabrega, "they are deputies, delegates, presidents, general secretaries, perhaps dictators, but they are not psychoanalysts."[77]

Jean Clavreul, another veteran of decades of psychoanalytic politics, wrote passionately on this point:

> The psychoanalyst is something altogether different from the pale silhouette of a civil servant who emerges in the framework of the Order, something altogether different from what the medical order expects, a hack who cures neuroses, and finally, something altogether different from a member of a corporate group inscribed in the social order that the authorities wish for.[78]

And Clavreul added a practical note to the debate. Whatever its intent, he warned, an Order of Psychoanalysts would end up discriminating against nonmedical practitioners, because even if a physician-analyst were excluded from it, he or she could still legally practice; even the long-established Order of Physicians (L'Ordre des Médecins) cannot prevent physicians from using whatever recognized therapeutic techniques they deem appropriate. How could an Order of Psychoanalysts do better? Finally, Clavreul reminded Leclaire that his call for standards went against Lacan's long insistence that psychoanalysis must never reduce itself to a standard technique.

There is a final source of resistance to Leclaire's proposals. Not everyone is disturbed by the cacophony of psychoanalytic politics in the "après-Lacan" era. Maud Mannoni believes that conflict is inherent in psychoanalysis and that Leclaire's proposals express dangerous fantasies of unity, power, and control that are dangerous to the analytic enterprise. In this respect, she sees them as paradoxically allied with Miller's politics. For her, the post-dissolution years were a long period of mourning that has come to an end. Ten years after Lacan's death, she sees a new space for creative work and a long overdue spirit of communication between analytic groups. "The only problem today is with relations with the group of the Cause and its terribly dogmatic functioning," says Mannoni.[79] Her caveat is crucial. It comes close to being the "received wisdom" about the French analytic landscape of the 1990s. It allows analysts to split off a good from a bad Lacan, the Lacan of the Freudian School from the Lacan of the dissolution, "their" Lacan from the Lacan who was seduced by Miller.

The dissolution, the Forum, the Melman scandal, the Bataille resignation, the Pommier case—all of these are chapters in recent French psychoanalytic history in which patients denounce their analysts, analysts denounce their patients, and colleagues of long standing turn against each other. What are we to infer from their bitter quarrels?

Does the fact that these men and women are psychoanalysts call psychoanalysis itself into question? Isn't it the job of psychoanalysts to help people understand and thus master such emotions? Are these out-of-control institutional warriors able to do that kind of work? What do their political struggles say about their qualities as analysts? And what do their public scandals say about their analytic theories?

In physics, theories are not shaken by the neuroses of their creators. But in our scientific culture, opinions about psychoanalytic theory are colored by an image of the well-analyzed analyst, a person whose judgment is legitimated by having achieved a degree of calm and distance about his or her own life. Just as each new analysand develops a fantasy about the

successful analysis of his or her analyst, the analytic movement perpetuates myths about the successful analyses of its
founder and major theorists. A myth of the well-analyzed analyst is used to legitimate analytic theory.

When analysts talk about their anxiety about the release
of Freud's private papers, they fear scandal—an affair or an
indiscretion—and, more important, they fear the banal. Will
Freud be further revealed as a man who struggled like the rest
of us with his demons and his pettiness, a man whose self-
analysis got him so far and no further and, most damagingly, a
man whose unresolved conflicts are transparently spelled out
in his theories?

In every part of the world where psychoanalysis has flourished, the myth of the well-analyzed analyst brings together
the psychoanalytic movement and the psychoanalytic culture. The myth is in the culture because it speaks to common
sense. After all, asks the reasonable man and woman, how
could Lacan have been a good clinician if he was so obviously
hysterical? And the myth has the complicity of the professionals who want to use it to legitimate their theories and right to
practice. The importance of the myth helps to explain why
the identity of Anna Freud's analyst was kept in the shadows
for so long. Would a well-analyzed Freud have undertaken the
analysis of his daughter? And could a daughter analyzed by
her father be well analyzed? Was she in a good position to
train a new analytic generation? What is the status of theoretical ideas born of such illegitimate unions?

Freud was protected by well-guarded secrets when he was
alive and by a loving biographer and closed archives when he
died. In contrast, Lacan's life was an open book. His private
affairs were public knowledge; his indiscretions, jealousies,
rages, and pettiness were covered as front-page news. The man

whom many hailed as the greatest psychoanalytic theorist since Freud was from the beginning hard to place in the category of the "well analyzed." His own analyst testified against him. In a 1953 letter to Marie Bonaparte, Rudolf Loewenstein wrote that Lacan never completed his analysis. Although he promised Loewenstein he would continue, Lacan dropped out of analysis as soon as he had been elected to membership in the Paris Psychoanalytic Society. Loewenstein wrote:

> What you tell me about Lacan is distressing. He has always represented a source of conflict for me; on one hand there is his intellectual worth which I value highly, though I disagree violently with him. Nevertheless the misfortune is that much as we agreed that he would continue his analysis after his election [to membership in the Society], he did not do so. One does not cheat on such an important point with impunity (this between us). I certainly hope that his hastily analyzed (that is to say incompletely analyzed) trainees will not be admitted.[80]

And Lacan's analysands testified against him. For example, Didier Anzieu of the French Psychoanalytic Association, who left Lacan during the schism of 1963, recounted his experience of what it was like to be on Lacan's divan:

> During the sessions, Lacan was intermittently attentive. Sometimes, instead of sitting in his analyst's chair, he paced back and forth in the room in order to stretch his legs, to take a book; he sat at his work table and read, leafing pages covered with Chinese letters, which, apparently, he was learning. . . . Sometimes, his maid knocked on the door, to bring tea, sandwiches, the mail, or to alert him that he was wanted on the telephone. Lacan gave instructions for the answers or even went to answer himself. "Don't let this prevent you from continuing your session during my absence," he told me once as he disappeared from the office.[81]

In France, such examples of Lacan's self-indulgence and aggression have been talking points for challenges to his theory for nearly half a century. The debate began in analytic circles but ended up reaching far beyond. Certainly, in the popular press, the thousands of pages written on Lacan's bad behavior and on the ongoing squabbles among his closest descendants usually imply that psychoanalysis is delegitimated by psychoanalysts who are portrayed as unpleasant, unethical, and unanalyzed. Within the French psychoanalytic world, however, the need to come to terms with Lacan has provoked serious investigation of the tension between theorist and theory, as well as between theory and its institutionalization.

Wladimir Granoff and François Roustang are two French analysts who have directly addressed such questions. Their work weaves together the history of the schisms within the French movement with the history of dissidence in Freud's circle to focus on the psychological and sociological issues raised by the transmission of psychoanalysis.[82] Their insights on the cycle of dependence on a beloved *Maître*, conflict with a dominating *Maître*, and preoccupation with a lost *Maître* are as applicable to the psychoanalytic politics of the "aprés-Lacan" as they were to the stormy years before Lacan's death. More recently, Roustang has focused specifically on the problems of the transference to Lacan within the Freudian School; specifically asking, "Why did we follow him for so long?"[83] And Didier Anzieu has attempted a direct confrontation with the myth of the well-analyzed analyst. In *L'Auto-analyse de Freud et la découverte de la psychanalyse*, Anzieu examined the limitations of Freud's theory in terms of the limitations of Freud's personality. Anzieu analyzes Freud as a man who could only see the world through the prism of depressive anxiety and who was dominated by the desire to protect an idealized image of the maternal. Because Freud was "hysterophobic," the maternal dimension of psychoanalysis had to be added by others, most notably by Melanie Klein. But, of course, there were things that Freud could see that Klein was not able to. "Just as Freudian psychoanalysis is the fruit of the formation of the depressive position, Kleinian psychoanalysis is the fruit of the formulation of the schizoparanoid position.[84]

Anzieu's thesis is that in the case of psychoanalysis, a science of self-reflection, theories embody the personalities of their theorists; elements of character etch themselves in the theory, leaving traces both of strengths and limitations. Anzieu speculates that if psychoanalysis had been invented by a hysteric, such as Fliess, it would have been too taken with the physical experience of fantasy, and if by an obsessional, such as either Breuer or Charcot, it would have been made too systematic. A prepsychotic, like Tausk or Reich, would have swung between making psychoanalysis too subjective and too abstract. The limitations of each theorist and each theory means that psychoanalysis is best seen as an art form where theorist and patient, theory and symptom, need to be delicately matched. The construction of theory is a social process; theorists with different personality structures must collaborate on the edifice.

If one accepts the myth of the well-analyzed analyst, materials that cast doubt on the psychological state of the theorist cast in doubt the validity of the theory. Lacan's theory of the analyst rejecting the place of the "subject presumed to know" would be called into question, since he insisted on taking that place himself.[85] The status of Melanie Klein's work on reparation to a mother would be called into question, since she never made peace with her own.[86] But this point of view is too simple. Anzieu's work is a contribution to the development of an epistemology that would capture how deep truths about the issues that psychoanalysis touches are very often best understood and communicated by individuals who have experienced them in a raw form.

In 1987, a play adapted from Phyllis Grosskurth's biography of Melanie Klein opened on the London stage.[87] *Mrs. Klein* shows psychoanalysis as a calling that can excite damaging passions. Melanie Klein, like Sigmund Freud, analyzed her children. The play explores the tragic dimensions of this undertaking; to feed the theory, the most creative minds in the early history of psychoanalysis had a form of intercourse with their children that the theory itself would dismiss as impossible, and as destructive in its impossibility. In the play the analyst Klein is at war with herself and her offspring. Indeed, she does not seem to know who her true offspring are. Are they her biological children, her analytic candidates, or are they in the theory? Her biological child, Melitta Schmideberg, and an analytic daughter, her disciple Paula Heimann, are locked in battle for her allegiance. And, incredibly and cruelly, as the last act of the play unfolds, the daughter by blood does not win. We are far from a Hollywood popularization of psychoanalysis in which a rich and beautiful analytic patient (in American films, Ginger Rogers was the actress most likely to play this role) tells all to an omniscient, silent, and bearded analyst. We are in the rag-and-bone shop of the psychoanalytic life. It is a world that Jacques Lacan and Jacques-Alain Miller, joined to each other through marriage, ambition, and a fusional intellectual relationship, would surely understand.

Many British analysts, especially Kleinians, did not like the play *Mrs. Klein*, finding it disrespectful of their beloved mentor and friend. That British analysts are troubled by the story of Melanie Klein and her children reflects their fear that telling it undermines the legitimacy of the Kleinian enterprise. It was, after all, the same fear that caused the story of Anna

Freud's analysis by her father to remain, until recently, cloaked in taboo. But to my mind, *Mrs. Klein* responds to one of the most important challenges faced by psychoanalysis.

The passions of *Mrs. Klein* and the excesses of the Lacanian saga illuminate but do not necessarily undermine the power of their contributions. Only when psychoanalysis faces all aspects of its history can it fully address the question of the relationship between psychoanalytic theory and the psychological vulnerability of its theorists. For me, confronting this question stands between where we are today and a mature psychoanalytic culture.

Notes

The notes for chapters from earlier editions are unrevised.

Preface [1991]

1. Those readers who would like to learn about the history of the French psychoanalytic movement in greater detail will be richly rewarded by Élisabeth Roudinesco's two-volume work, *L'Histoire de la psychanalyse en France: La Bataille de cent ans* (Paris: Seuil, 1986). Volume 1 covers the years from 1885–1939 and volume 2 from 1925–1985. Volume 2 has been translated into English by Jeffrey Mehlman as *Lacan and Company: A History of Psychoanalysis in France, 1925–1985* (London: Free Association Books, 1990).

2. Sigmund Freud, "The Psychopathology of Everyday Life," in *The Complete Psychological Works of Sigmund Freud*, Standard Edition, vol. 6, trans. James Strachey et al. (London: Hogarth Press, 1953–66), p. 59.

3. For an example of an information-processing perspective on the Freudian, see Donald Norman, "Post-Freudian Slips," *Psychology Today* (April 1980), pp. 41–44 ff.; Donald Norman, *Slips of the Mind and an Outline of a Theory of Action* (San Diego: Center for Human Information Processing, University of California, November 1979); Donald Norman, "Categorization of Action Slips," *Psychological Review* 88 (January 1981): 1–15.

4. The notion of programs as agents is well represented in computer science. Among the most explicit of the "social" metaphors is found

in Marvin Minsky, *The Society of Mind* (New York: Simon and Schuster, 1986).

5. Claude Lévi-Strauss, *The Savage Mind* (Chicago: University of Chicago Press, 1966).

6. Peter Berger, "Towards a Sociological Understanding of Psychoanalysis," *Social Research* 32 (Spring 1965): 38.

7. Edith Kurzweil, *The Freudians: A Comparative Perspective* (New Haven: Yale University Press, 1989), p. 1.

8. See, for example, Stanley Fish, *Is There a Text in This Class? The Authority of Interpretive Communities* (Cambridge, MA: Harvard University Press, 1980).

9. Susan Rubin Suleiman, *Subversive Intent: Gender, Politics, and the Avant Garde* (Cambridge, MA: Harvard University Press, 1990), p. 193.

10. Eric Conan, "Les Psychanalystes, sont-ils dangereux?," *L'Express*, no. 1976 (May 19–25, 1989), p. 72. Danièle Lévy estimates the number of French analysts as between 4,500 and 5,000. Cited in Caroline Brizard, "Les huit questions que vous posez sur votre analyste," *Le Nouvel Observateur*, no. 1313 (January 4–10, 1990), p. 12. In France, it is hard to pin down the number of analysts in practice because the Lacanian doctrine of "self-authorization" means that an unknown number of analysands begin analytic practice as soon as they are able to recruit patients. And since Lacan's dissolution of the Freudian School in 1981 and the resulting dispersion of Lacanian analysts into looser groupings, many analysts are not "registered" with any analytic society but practice independently.

11. Conan, "Les Psychanalystes sont-ils dangereux?," p. 73.

12. Ibid.

13. Ibid., p. 72.

14. Marie Cardinale, *The Words to Say It* (Cambridge, MA: VanVactor and Goodheart, 1983); anonymous, *Séductions sur le divan ou le malentendu amoreux* (Paris: La Découverte, 1989); Joëlle Augerolles, *Mon analyste et moi* (Paris: Editions Lieu Commun, 1989).

15. Jacques Lacan, *The Seminar of Jacques Lacan, Book I*, trans. John Forrester (Cambridge, Eng.: Cambridge University Press, 1988), p. 16.

16. Ibid.

17. Sherry Turkle, *The Second Self: Computers and the Human Spirit* (New York: Simon and Schuster, 1984); Sherry Turkle, "Romantic Reactions: Paradoxical Responses to the Computer Presence," in *Boundaries of Humanity: Humans, Animals, Machines*, ed. Morton Sousna and James Sheehan (Berkeley: University of California Press, 1991).

18. Jacques Lacan, *The Seminar of Jacques Lacan, Book II*, trans. John Forrester (Cambridge, Eng.: Cambridge University Press, 1988), p. 11.

Introduction

1. Sigmund Freud, "On the History of the Psychoanalytic Movement (1914)," in *Collected Papers* (London: Hogarth Press, 1949), p. 314.

2. Ibid., p. 316.

3. Ibid., pp. 316–317.

4. See Paul Roazen, "Freud and America," *Social Research* 29, no. 1 (Winter 1972): 720–732.

5. The American neo-Freudians (Erich Fromm, Karen Homey, Clara Thompson, Harry Stack Sullivan) shifted the emphasis of dynamic psychology from the unconscious to the conscious, from id to ego, and most generally from depth psychology to cultural psychology; in doing so, they gave psychoanalysis a more optimistic tone. In a sense, they did their job too well, and the next generation of American theoreticians usually referred to as the "post-Freudians" (Abraham Maslow, Gordon Allport, Carl Rogers) were not responding to Freud but contented themselves with revising his revisionists. On this point, see Russell Jacoby, *Social Amnesia: A Critique of Contemporary Psychology from Adler to Laing* (Boston: Beacon Press, 1975). Jacoby's book deals with the "forgetting of psychoanalysis" and the emergence of a primarily American "conformist psychology." A less critical treatment of what America did with Freud's ideas is Hendrik Ruitenbeck, *Freud and America* (New York: Macmillan, 1966).

6. See David Riesman, *The Lonely Crowd* (New Haven: Yale University Press, 1950).

Chapter 1

1. See Anne Parsons, "La Pénétration de la psychanalyse en France et aux Etats-Unis: Une étude de psychologie sociale comparative" (Thèse du doctorat. Faculté des Lettres, Paris, 1954).

2. See Paul Roazen, "Freud and America," *Social Research* 29, no. 1 (Winter 1972): 720–732. This provocative essay is a discussion of two books that are important in tracing the early development of "the American Freud." The first is Nathan Hale, *Freud and the Americans*, vol. 1 (New York: Oxford University Press, 1971). The second is Nathan Hale, ed., *James Jackson Putnam and Psychoanalysis: Letters between Putnam and Freud* (Cambridge: Harvard University Press, 1971). Another excellent work on this theme is John C. Burnham, *Psychoanalysis and American Medicine: 1894–1918*, monograph no. 20, *Psychological Issues* 5 (1967).

3. Hale, *Freud and the Americans*, especially chapter 17, "'Civilized' Morality and the Classical Neuroses, 1880–1920: The Social Basis of Psychoanalysis," pp. 462–480.

4. Ibid., p. 21.

5. Ibid., p. 46.

6. Ibid., p. 477.

7. Stanley Hall to Sigmund Freud, October 7, 1909, Clark University Papers.

8. See Peter Berger, "Towards a Sociological Understanding of Psychoanalysis," *Social Research* 32 (Spring 1965): 26–41.

9. Philip Rieff, *The Triumph of the Therapeutic: The Uses of Faith after Freud* (New York: Harper and Row, 1968). In this work, Rieff argues that the development of modern industrial societies has been accompanied by their "deconversion" from the belief systems and symbols of traditional "positive communities" to those of "negative communities"

that share only the symbols of science and where each individual must create his own personal world of meaning. In positive communities, the culture itself can serve as its own therapeutic order because members of the culture can interpret their experiences through the categories it furnishes. After deconversion, this is no longer possible.

10. Hale, *Freud and the Americans*, p. 36.

11. The description of the Republican synthesis and the image of France as a "stalemate society" in this chapter follow the argument of Stanley Hoffmann, "Paradoxes of the French Political Community," in *In Search of France*, Stanley Hoffmann et al. (Cambridge, MA: Harvard University Press, 1963), pp. 1–117.

12. See Laurence Wylie, "Social Change at the Grass Roots,' in ibid., pp. 159–234.

13. Michael Crozier, *The Bureaucratic Phenomenon* (Chicago: University of Chicago Press, 1964).

14. Hale, *Freud and the Americans*, p. 49.

15. See Michel Foucault, *Madness and Civilization: A History of Insanity in the Age of Reason*, trans. Richard Howard (New York: Pantheon Books, 1965).

16. The classic literary statement of fear of "uprootedness" was, of course, that of Maurice Barres in *Les Déracinés* (Paris: Plon, 1947). Psychiatrist Pierre Janet explored related themes in his *De l'angoisse à l'extase* (Paris: Alcan, 1926–28), where he argues that French people run grave psychological risks when they abandon traditional patterns of rural life.

17. For a history of French psychiatry, see Henri Baruk, *La Psychiatrie française de Pinel à nos jours* (Paris: Presses Universitaires de France, 1967); Henri Ellenberger, *The Discovery of the Unconscious* (New York: Basic Books, 1970); Yves Pelicier, *Histoire de la psychiatrie française* (Paris: Presses Universitaires de France, 1971).

18. On Janet, see Ellenberger's excellent chapter "Pierre Janet and Psychological Analysis," in *The Discovery of the Unconscious*, pp. 331–417.

19. See Parsons, "Pénétration de la psychanalyse en France et aux Etats-Unis."

20. Henri Claude, preface to R. Laforgue and R. Allendy, *La Psychanalyse et les névroses* (Paris: Payot, 1924).

21. Claude's ambivalence toward psychoanalysis is illustrated by the fact that at times he justified Laforgue's presence in his service by saying that Laforgue was doing statistical studies for him. These studies do in fact offer some interesting information about the early French psychoanalytic world: the longest analytic "cure" done in Claude's service took several weeks.

22. In 1965, psychiatrist Yves Bertherat published a survey of 10 percent of French psychiatrists that asked whether the psychiatrist being questioned provided some form of "psychotherapy" to his patients. Only 50 percent said that they did, but their descriptions of what this meant made it clear that most of their therapy was didactic ("setting a good moral example," teaching patients how to "organize" life) rather than an occasion for the patient to explore feelings, relationships, irrational fears, and desires. See Yves Bertherat, "Enquête sur l'exercise de la psychiatrie en France," *L'information psychiatrique* (March 1965): 219–251.

23. See Roger Bastide, *Sociologie des maladies mentales* (Paris: Flammarion, 1965).

24. See Serge Moscovici, *La Psychanalyse son image et son public* (Paris: Presses Universitaires de France, 1961) for a profile of French attitudes toward psychoanalysis in the mid-1950s.

25. For example, Henri Baruk, a member of the "moral school" of French critics of Freud, charges that psychoanalysis "destroys individual morality," encourages weakening of the social personality, all leading to a "neurotic culture." See Baruk, *La Psychiatrie française de Pinel à nos jours*, p. 29. A more recent attack on Freud on the issue of his lack of scientificity is Pierre Debray-Ritzen, *La Scholastique freudienne* (Paris: Fayard, 1972).

26. Carol Pierson Ryser, "The Influence of Value Systems in the Practice of Psychiatry: The French Case" (PhD diss., Harvard University,

1967). On the basis of an analysis of historical, literary, and social scientific writing, Ryser chose a set of dominant French cultural values (rationalism, realism, individualism, creativity, loyalty to an in-group, sense of the "dual nature of reality"). She then went on to analyze French psychiatric writing from 1954–66 to check for the presence of these values.

27. See Jean-Paul Sartre, *Being and Nothingness*, trans. Hazel Barnes (New York: Philosophical Library, 1956), especially part 1, chap. 2, and part 4, chap. 2. These chapters are reprinted as a separate volume. *Existential Psychoanalysis* (Chicago: Henry Reznery, 1962).

28. John Demos, "Oedipus in America," unpublished manuscript.

29. Psychologists help to "track" students into academic or vocational programs. This weeding out turns out to be along class lines. Students can be retracked at several points, but in practice, the "second chances" for a classical bourgeois education are taken advantage of only by the children of the bourgeoisie.

30. See Bernard Penot, "Un psychiatre à l'école," *Psychiatrie Aujourd'hui*, no. 11 (November 1972).

31. See *Le Monde*, Dossiers et Documents, no. 17, série A, "L'Eglise de France" (January 1975).

32. Protestant pastors express their new identification with *le psy* in much the same terms as the Catholic clergy. For example: "I don't want to speak from the pulpit or preside or consecrate from above. I want to speak to people where they are and share their lives with them, myself engaged as they are, in a professional activity." See *Le Monde*, Dossiers et Documents, "L'Eglise de France."

33. Berger, "Towards a Sociological Understanding of Psychoanalysis."

Chapter 2

1. When we speak of a French psychoanalytic culture we do not mean to imply that French psychoanalysis is a monolith. Not all French psychoanalysts are Lacanian. Indeed, some are interested in things

that are antithetical to the Lacanian vision. Some are interested in integrating psychoanalysis and ego psychology. There is even nascent interest in psychoanalysis and behaviorism. In its theoretical referent, however, most French psychoanalysis bears the unmistakable stamp of Lacanianism. In this book, the emphasis is on Lacan as the best representative of a clearly "French" reinterpretation of Freud. For an overview of the movement as a whole, see Ilse and Robert Barande, *Histoire de la Psychanalyse en France* (Paris: Privat, 1974).

2. For a discussion of the May events as an expression of existential Marxist political thought, see David Poster, *Existential Marxism in Postwar France* (Princeton: Princeton University Press, 1977), pp. 361–398.

3. For a discussion of the social "fit" of therapeutic systems, see Peter Berger and Thomas Luckmann, *The Social Construction of Reality* (New York: Doubleday and Company, 1966), pp. 112 ff.; Jerome Frank, *Persuasion and Healing* (New York: Schocken, 1973); Claude Lévi-Strauss, "The Sorcerer and His Magic" and "The Effectiveness of Symbols," in *Structural Anthropology*, trans. Claire Jacobson and Brooke Grundfest Schoepf (New York: Basic Books, 1963).

4. Stuart Hughes, *The Obstructed Path: French Social Thought in the Years of Desperation, 1930–1966* (New York: Harper and Row, 1966), p. 290.

5. Jacques Lacan, "The Function and Field of Speech and Language in Psychoanalysis," *Ecrits: A Selection*, trans. Alan Sheridan (New York: W. W. Norton, 1977), p. 62.

6. Ibid.

7. Ibid., p. 64. Of course when Lacan made this critique of behaviorism, he was certainly not alone in his insistence that problems of human meaning could not be reduced to behaviorist mechanisms. Such authors as Merleau-Ponty, Sartre, and Piaget were advancing similar positions at about the same time.

8. The italicized word appears in English in the original text.

9. Lacan, "The Freudian Thing," *Ecrits: A Selection*, p. 135.

10. Ibid., p. 134.

11. Lacan, "The Direction of the Treatment and the Principles of Its Power," *Ecrits: A Selection*, pp. 230–231. The italicized word appears in English in the original text. Lacan footnotes his use of the English term "non-conflictual-sphere" in the following way: "Hartmann, Kris and Loewenstein, various joint contributions in *The Psychoanalytic Study of the Child*, since 1946."

12. For example, in the case of the Rat Man, Freud demonstrated how a person comes to associate the same word (or sound) with essential elements of his neurotic conflict. The man was plagued by fears of torture by rats (*Ratten*, in German), but these fears were associated with a series of other conflicts that all involved words resembling "rat": conflict over his late father's unpaid gambling debts (*Raten* in German means "installments"), over the loss of a sister, Rita, who had died in infancy, and over whether to marry (*heiraten*).

13. To clarify this point about metaphor formation and repression, we compare a non-psychoanalytic metaphor with the psychoanalytic paternal metaphor we have just described, making use (as does Lacan) of linguist Ferdinand de Saussure's notation for the relationship of a signifier to what it signifies. This is S/s where S is the signifier and s is the signified and the line between them (the "bar") stands for the relationship of signification. So, for example, the word combination "brave man" is a signifier (S) for the fact that someone is a brave man (s). When we introduce the word "lion" as a metaphor, the new signifier "lion" (S) stands in place of the statement "brave man" (the former signifier) and also signifies being a brave man (the original signified). "Lion" now signifies "brave man" (just as "father's name" now signifies "desire for mother"), but the original signifier has been pushed down to a deeper level. This sequence from "He is a brave man" to "He is a lion" can be expressed as:

$$\frac{S'(\text{"lion"})}{S(\text{"brave man"})} \bullet \frac{S(\text{"brave man"})}{s(\text{the fact of being a brave man—the signified})} \to \frac{S'}{s} \text{ or,}$$

"lion signifies the fact of being a brave man"

When we apply this reasoning to the origin of the paternal metaphor during the Oedipal crisis, "pushing a signifier down to a deeper level" (below the bar of signification) means its repression into the unconscious. The father's name serves as a metaphor, a new signifier, which causes the old signifier (the mother's desire) and the old signified (the phallus) to descend more deeply into the unconscious.

We recall our formula for metaphor, but this time, again following Lacan's usage, we substitute $ for the original signifier, which is designed to be expulsed by the new signifier, and indicate that in the case of psychoanalytic metaphor, being below the bar of signification in the final term means being in the unconscious (U). So we have:

$$\frac{S'}{\$} \cdot \frac{\$}{s} \to S' \frac{U}{s} \text{ or}$$

$$\frac{\text{the "name of the father" } (S')}{\text{the mother's desire } (\$)} \cdot \frac{\text{the mother's desire } (\$)}{\text{the signified to the subject}}$$

$$\to \text{ the name of the father} \frac{U}{\text{the phallus}}$$

(This formula is adapted from Lacan, "On a Question Preliminary to Any Possible Treatment of Psychosis," *Ecrits: A Selection*, p. 200).

14. Lacan, "Function and Field of Speech and Language," *Ecrits: A Selection*, p. 56.

15. Lacan, "The Mirror Stage as Formative of the Function of the I," *Ecrits: A Selection*, p. 2.

16. For Lacan, this absolute Other, which he calls the Other with a capital *O* (in French, *l'Autre, grand A*), stands for the symbolic order and Freudian unconscious. We recall the reason why: the capacity for symbolic functioning was built around the repression through a process of metaphor formation of an absolute and irreducible desire to be the desire of an other. The Freudian unconscious was born of the repression of the desire for the absolute Other. In contrast, Lacan refers to the ego's identificational objects as "objects a" (in French, *l'object, petit a*). In this case, the lowercase letter is a reminder that these objects are substitute objects. These "objects a" do not constitute the subject. The subject comes into being through a relationship with the symbolic order, the order of language and society, which is also the order of the Freudian unconscious. The Other stands for all of these. Thus, for Lacan, the alienated self (the *ego* or *moi*) is constituted

by the subject addressing himself in imaginary relationships to "objects a" and the subject (S) is constituted by the symbolic order.

17. Jacques Lacan, cited in Maud Mannoni, "Psychoanalysis and the May Revolution," in *Reflections on the Revolution in France: 1968*, ed. Charles Posner (Hammondsworth, Eng.: Penguin, 1970), p. 219.

18. The phallus signifies a fundamental absence, a lack in the being of the subject, what Lacan calls the *manque-à-être*. The subject *cannot* be the other's desire and this frustration was the condition for entrance into the symbolic. This formulation of frustration is Hegelian and, indeed, we cannot fully appreciate Lacan's position without entering a world of dialectical discourse in which it is not considered either obscure or illogical to maintain that the real is impossible and the impossible is the real. Indeed, this is exactly what Lacan does maintain when he describes the real as the third order.

19. Jacques Lacan, "Seminar on 'The Purloined Letter,'" in *Yale French Studies*, "French Freud: Structural Studies in Psychoanalysis," 48 (1972): 39–72. See note on p. 38 by translator Jeffrey Mehlman.

20. Lacan, "The Direction of the Treatment," *Ecrits: A Selection*, p. 231. The italicized words appear in English in the original text.

21. Lacan, "Function and Field of Speech and Language," *Ecrits: A Selection*, p. 37.

22. Jacques Lacan, *Télévision* (Paris: Seuil, 1974), p. 33 ff.

23. The best known of these antipsychiatric experiments is at the Clinique de la Borde at Cour-Cheverny, home of "institutional psychoanalysis" as developed by Lacanian analyst Félix Guattari. See Félix Guattari, *Psychanalyse et transversalité* (Paris: Maspero, 1972); *Perspectives Psychiatriques*, no. 45 (1976), "Psychotherapie institutionelle à Cour-Cheverny"; Jean-Claude Polack and Danielle Sivadon-Sabourin, *La Borde ou le droit à la folie* (Paris: Calmann-Levy, 1976).

Chapter 3

1. Henri Lefebvre, *La Proclamation de la commune* (Paris: Gallimard, 1965), p. 389.

2. René Vienet, *Enragés et situationnistes dans le movement des occupations* (Paris: Gallimard, 1968), p. 136.

3. See Epistémon, *Ces Idées qui ont ébranlé la France* (Paris: Fayard, 1968).

4. Jacques Lacan, cited in Maud Mannoni, "Psychoanalysis and the May Revolution," in *Reflections on the Revolution in France: 1968*, ed. Charles Posner (Hammondsworth, Eng.: Penguin, 1970), p. 219.

5. See Edwin Schur, *The Awareness Trap: Self-Absorption Instead of Social Change* (New York: Quadrangle, 1976).

6. See Martin Jay, *The Dialectical Imagination* (Boston: Little, Brown, 1973); Russell Jacoby, *Social Amnesia* (Boston: Beacon Press, 1975).

7. Theodor Adorno, "Die revidierte Psychanalyse," cited in Jacoby, *Social Amnesia*, pp. 33–34.

8. Jacoby uses the concept of "second nature," accumulated and sedimented history, in his discussion of the Frankfurt theorists. *Social Amnesia*, p. 31.

9. See Jacques Lacan, "The Signification of the Phallus," *Ecrits: A Selection*, trans. Alan Sheridan (New York: W. W. Norton, 1977), pp. 281–291. For some interesting reflections on the reconciliation of French feminists with Lacan, see Juliet Mitchell, *Psychoanalysis and Feminism* (New York: Random House, 1974). The "Daddy-Mommy-Me" characterization of the patriarchal, Oedipal family is from Gilles Deleuze and Félix Guattari, *Anti-Oedipus: Capitalism and Schizophrenia*, trans. Robert Hurley, Mark Seem, and Peter R. Lane (New York: Viking, 1977).

10. Lacan, "The Function and Field of Speech and Language in Psychoanalysis," *Ecrits: A Selection*, p. 65.

11. Ibid., p. 68.

12. Mark Poster, *Existential Marxism in Postwar France* (Princeton: Princeton University Press, 1977), p. 340.

13. Michel Foucault, *Madness and Civilization: A History of Insanity in the Age of Reason*, trans. Richard Howard (New York: Pantheon Books, 1965); *Birth of the Clinic*, trans. A. M. Sheridan Smith (New York:

Pantheon Books, 1973). Foucault also sponsored the group project that led to *Moi, Pierre Rivière, ayant egorgé ma mère, ma soeur et mon frère, un cas de parracide au XIXe siècle* (Paris: Gallimard/Julliard, 1973).

14. See J. Simon, "A Conversation with Michel Foucault," *Partisan Review* 2 (1971), p. 201. Italics are mine.

15. The quotation is part of a longer manifesto by the radical political group Scription Rouge in an antipsychiatric magazine, *Gardes Fous*, no. 1 (February–March 1974).

16. Lacan, "Function and Field of Speech and Language," *Ecrits: A Selection*, p. 65.

17. Philippe Sollers, "A propos de la dialectique," in *Psychanalyse et politique*, ed. Armando Verdiglione (Paris: Seuil, 1974), p. 31.

18. Ibid., pp. 29, 30.

19. Ibid., p. 30.

20. Ibid., p. 34.

21. Ibid.

22. Julia Kristeva, "Sujet dans la langage et pratique politique," in Verdiglione, *Psychanalyse et politique*, p. 62.

23. Ibid., p. 68.

24. Ibid., pp. 68–69.

25. Louis Althusser, "Freud et Lacan," *La Nouvelle Critique*, nos. 161–162 (December–January 1964–65), p. 97.

26. Félix Guattari, "Micropolitique du désir," in Verdiglione, *Psychanalyse et politique*, p. 47.

27. Lacan, "The Direction of the Treatment and the Principles of Its Power," *Ecrits: A Selection*, p. 254.

28. Ibid.

29. Maud Mannoni cites this comment, made by Lacan during his seminar at the Ecole Normale Supérieure on June 19, 1968, in

"Psychoanalysis and the May Revolution," in Posner, *Reflections on the Revolution in France*, p. 215.

30. "A Reporter in Europe," *The New Yorker*, July 4, 1977, p. 72.

31. Herbert Tonka, "Fiction de la contestation alienée." The pamphlet, published in June 1968, shows no other information about its publication.

32. Georges Politzer, *Ecrits*, vol. 2, *Les fondements de la psychologie* (Paris: Editions sociales, 1969), especially pp. 12, 18.

33. Ibid., pp. 288, 293, 302.

34. "La psychanalyse: Ideologie réactionnaire (Autocritique)," *La Nouvelle Critique* 20, no. 7 (June 1949), pp. 52–73. Among the eight authors of the declaration was Dr. Serge Lebovici, who has since left behind both the Communist Party and his criticisms of psychoanalysis. In 1973, Lebovici, a member of the Paris Psychoanalytic Society and a determined opponent of Lacan during the first schism in the psychoanalytic movement, became the first French president of the International Psychoanalytic Association.

35. Althusser, "Freud et Lacan," p. 91.

36. Ibid., p. 89.

37. Ibid., p. 107.

38. Catherine Backes-Clément, Pierre Bruno, and Lucien Sève, *Pour une critique marxiste de la théorie psychoanalytique* (Paris: Editions sociales, 1974). Backes-Clément and Bruno are at the Freudian School. By the time of the first publication of this book, favorable articles about psychoanalysis were appearing regularly in Party publications aimed at a mass audience.

39. The phrase "Communist Party intellectuals" is misleading because it does not represent a homogeneous group of people. For example, both Louis Althusser and Roger Garaudy were "Communist Party intellectuals," and we already have noted that their positions on most matters were in direct opposition. There are serious disagreements on

theory within the Party and, of course, some of these are expressed in different perspectives on psychoanalysis. The main source of contention is whether Freud and Lacan, and Marx for that matter, are to be read as theorists who reject or who leave room for an existential voluntarist psychology, what is usually referred to as a "humanist" psychology. Lucien Sève, one of Althusser's intellectual rivals within the Communist Party, represents a more humanist position than Althusser does. The Party's "practical" side, the people in the Party who worry about concrete policies in the mental health field, are similarly divided on the role of psychoanalysis. See, for example, the positions of two Party psychiatrists: Lucien Bonnafé, *Une psychiatrie différente, dites-vous*, supplement to *La Nouvelle Critique*, no. 63 (April 1973); Bernard Muldworf, "Les Communistes et la psychanalyse," *La Nouvelle Critique*, no. 30 (January 1970), pp. 17–23.

40. Jacques Lacan, "Le Seminare sur 'La Lettre Volée'" and "Position de l'inconscient," both found in the French edition of the *Ecrits* (Paris: Seuil, 1966), pp. 45, 52, 833. These comments are not unique. Lacan's work is studded with such. For example, Lacan's disdain for the Americans is clearly expressed in his introductory remarks to the "Discourse of Rome": "Function and Field of Speech and Language in Psychoanalysis."

There he writes:

> In any case, it appears incontestable that the conception of psychoanalysis in the United States has inclined towards the adaptation of the individual to the social environment, towards the quest for behaviour patterns, and towards all the objectification implied in the notion of "human relations." And the indigenous term "human engineering" strongly implies a privileged position of exclusion in relation to the human object.
>
> Indeed, the eclipse in psychoanalysis of the most living terms of its experience—the unconscious and sexuality, which apparently will cease before long even to be mentioned—may be attributed to the distance from the human object without which such a position could not be held.

See *Ecrits: A Selection*, p. 38.

41. Lacan put forth this claim in "Position de l'inconscient," an essay which does not appear in the selections of the *Ecrits* which have been translated into English. See the French edition of *Ecrits*, p. 833.

Chapter 4

1. The French expression for psychoanalytic training is *formation psychanalytique*. In some ways the acuity of the conflict in France is lost in this English translation of what the French analysts have been fighting about. To "train" someone implies that you have a concrete skill to teach and that a "candidate" in a "training analysis" has something almost tangible to learn, whereas in France one of the major contentions in the debate on the *formation* of an analyst through the *analyse didactique*, or "training analysis," is that the latter does not even exist as a separate entity. A similar point has, of course, often been made about the English translations of other Freudian terms. Where the English have translated *es* as *id*, the French have used the earthier and less literary translation of *es* as the "it," the *ça*. The Latin words have an abstract quality and seem far less threatening than having to accept the presence of an it, in French *ça*, a stranger that dwells within us.

2. Jacques Lacan, "The Function and Field of Speech and Language in Psychoanalysis," *Ecrits: A Selection*, trans. Alan Sheridan (New York: W. W. Norton, 1977), p. 39.

Lacan first formulated his ideas about psychoanalysis as a scientific enterprise in opposition to a doctrine (which Lacan refers to as neo-Freudian and which he strongly identifies with the development of psychoanalysis in America) that sees Freud as a doctor who was "lucky enough" to make some discoveries of great therapeutic value (this unfortunate phrase belongs to Ernest Jones), but whose theoretical work was too rigid and focused on sexual concerns. Since the neo-Freudians believe that Freud's own attempts to formulate a general theory for what he had discovered were insufficient and led him into inconsistency and mysticism, the things about psychoanalysis that they feel are to be preserved at all costs are its outward forms: the interview, the training method, and the most mechanical features of interpretation.

Lacan's position, on the other hand, is that Freud was not "lucky" but knew exactly what he was doing when he delimited and described the unconscious as an object for scientific investigation and pointed toward how it could be studied.

3. See Erich Fromm, *Sigmund Freud's Mission* (New York: Grove Press, 1959), p. 86; Paul Roazen, *Freud: Political and Social Thought* (New York: Knopf, 1968), pp. 90–101.

4. Lacan, "Function and Field of Speech and Language," *Ecrits: A Selection*, p. 31.

5. Ibid., p. 39.

6. André Gide gave Madame Sokolnika literary immortality in his novel, *The Counterfeiters*, where she is thinly disguised as Madame Sophrosnika, the analyst of "Petit Boris."

7. According to a letter written by René Laforgue, French psychoanalytic pioneer, to Freud on January 30, 1926, the French psychoanalytic group was made up of Laforgue and nine colleagues: Madame Sokolnika, E. Pichon, R. Allendy, G. Parcheminey, A. Borel, A. Hesnard, R. Loewenstein, and two Swiss analysts, R. de Saussure and C. Odier. The eleventh member of the French group was to be Princess Marie Bonaparte of Greece, who was in Vienna with Freud at the time that this letter was written. The official founding of the Paris Psychoanalytic Society was in November 1926; by December 1926, the group co-opted its first full member, Madame O. Codet, and its first associate member, Mlle. Anne Berman, who became one of the principal translators of Freud's work into French.

8. For some interesting discussion of the early days of the French psychoanalytic world, see a special issue, "Freud," of *Europe* 52, no. 539 (March 1974). Our account of French psychoanalytic history in this and the following chapter focuses on psychoanalytic politics and on Lacan. For a more inclusive picture, see Ilse and Robert Barande, *L'Histoire de la psychanalyse en France* (Paris: Payot, 1974).

9. René Laforgue, cited by P. Denis, "Psychanalyse d'hier," *Psychiatrie Aujourd'hui* 6 (November–December 1971), p. 36.

10. Indeed, the lack of interest was so great that the original French analysts did little of the training of their own "second generation." Most of the prewar training was done by Laforgue, Loewenstein, and the Swiss analysts, Odier and de Saussure, and then by Spitz and Hartmann during their visits to Paris. In the "second generation"

of analysts who made the first schism, Jacques Lacan and Daniel Lagache were analyzed by Rudolf Loewenstein, Sacha Nacht by Heinz Hartmann, and Françoise Dolto by Réne Laforgue.

11. The reflections of Anaïs Nin on her analysis with Allendy testify to the fact that the picturesque style of Laforgue's practice, which often is described as "thaumaturgical" or "wonder-working," was not exceptional for its day. *Diary of Anaïs Nin, 1931–34* (New York: Swallow Press, 1966).

12. Lacan sees Clerambault as his "only master in psychiatry." Lacan acknowledges that Clerambault's work on mental automatism is to be criticized for its "mechanistic ideology of metaphor," but it also gets Lacan's homage: "In its grasp of the subjective text [it is] closer to that which can be obtained from a structural analysis than any other clinical effort in French psychiatry." See Lacan, "De nos antécédents," *Ecrits* (Paris: Seuil, 1966), p. 65. This paper does not appear in the English edition.

13. Lacan's thesis consisted of a critical survey of the then extant theories of paranoid psychosis followed by the detailed study of a female psychotic given to literary endeavor. The patient wrote love letters to celebrities, some of which Lacan analyzed in his text. The thesis has been republished as *De la psychose paranoiaque dans ses rapports avec la personalité suivi de premiers écrits sur la paranoia* (Paris: Seuil, 1975).

14. For example, Lacan's publications in 1934 went from the "classically psychiatric," "Un cas de perversion infantile par encéphalite épidémique précoce diagnostiqué sur un syndrome moteur fruste" (in *Annales Medico-psychologiques* 2 [1933]: 221–223) to "Motifs du crime paranoiaque: Le crime des soeurs Papin" (in *Le Minotaure* 3 and 4 [1933]: 25–28) by way of a poem, "Hiatus Irrationalis" (in *Le Phare de Neuilly* 3–4 [1933]: 27) of which we quote a few lines.

> Celui qui couve en moi, le même vous souleve,
> Formes, que coule en vous la sueur ou la sève
> C'est le feu qui me fait votre immortel amant.

15. The text of 1936 appears in Lacan's *Ecrits* (French edition) as "Au-delà du 'principe de réalité," pp. 73–92. An English translation of

the 1936 paper appeared in the *International Journal of Psychoanalysis* 18, part 1 (January 1937) under the title "The Looking-Glass Phase." Lacan gave his theory of the mirror phase fuller elaboration at the Sixteenth Congress of the International Psychoanalytic Association in Zurich in 1949, where he presented "Le Stade du miroir comme formateur de la fonction du Je telle qu'elle nous est revélée dans l'experience psychanalytique." This is the text translated by Alan Sheridan as "The Mirror Phase as Formative of the Function of the I as Revealed in the Psychoanalytic Experience," in *Ecrits: A Selection*, pp. 1–7.

16. Lacan, "The Mirror Stage," *Ecrits: A Selection*, p. 6.

17. Ibid.

18. The Paris members were R. Laforgue, M. Bonaparte, G. Parcheminey, Cenac, O. Codet, J. Lacan, D. Lagache, J. Leuba, S. Nacht, B. Reverchon-Jouve, and M. Schlumberger.

19. See "Réglement et doctrine de la Commission de 1'Enseignement" (by Jacques Lacan), in Jacques-Alain Miller, ed., *La Scission de 1953: La Communauté psychanalytique en France*, 1, supplement to *Ornicar?, bulletin périodique du Champ freudien*, no. 7 (1976), pp. 29–36. This book is a collection of documents relevant to the first schism in the French psychoanalytic movement. A second volume, also edited by Jacques-Alain Miller, contains documents relevant to the second schism. This is *L'Excommunication: Le Communauté psychanalytique en France*, 2, supplement to *Ornicar?, bulletin périodique du Champ freudien*, no. 8 (1977).

20. Miller, *Scission*, p. 56.

21. A great deal of anger toward Nacht had been generated around the reporting of a vote that was taken in late December 1952. Nacht reported that a decision on the rules for the new Institute had been reached unanimously. When a third of the Paris Society's membership wrote him to object that this could not be true because they had voted *against* the majority position, the word went around that his reply was cavalier, something like: "What do numbers matter since in any case the rules have been voted in?" See Miller, *Scission*, p. 81.

22. Documents from this period of controversy (letters, voting rosters, proposals) can be found in Miller, *Scission*, pp. 65–91.

23. The phrase is from a letter of complaint written by Jenny Roudinesco, a student at the Paris Society during the time of the schism. It was signed by fifty-one of the Society's seventy analytic candidates. Ibid., p. 73.

24. Ibid., p. 110.

25. In the days that followed, Hesnard, Berge, and Laforgue also joined the dissidents.

26. Miller, *Scission*, pp. 95–96.

27. Miller, *Scission*. The letter is printed on the back cover.

28. A sample of their efforts to gain support is a letter of sixty-four handwritten pages that Lacan wrote to his analyst, Rudolf Loewenstein, on Bastille Day 1953, in which Lacan tried to defend himself against what he was experiencing as "treason," "betrayal," and "an attempt to turn my students away from me." In the letter, Lacan describes how Marie Bonaparte traded her political support for special treatment. He defends his experimentation with short sessions in the training analysis as theoretically motivated research. He claims that, despite the seriousness of his research, he had respected his colleague's wishes and had abandoned the short sessions since January 1953. At the end of the letter, Lacan asks Loewenstein to intercede on behalf of the new French Psychoanalytic Society with his close friend, Heinz Hartmann, then president of the International Psychoanalytic Association. For the text of Lacan's letter to Loewenstein, see ibid., pp. 120–135.

29. This committee was composed of Drs. Eissler, Greenacre, Lamp-de Groot, Winnicott, and Mrs. H. Hoffer.

30. The minutes of the discussion can be found in the *International Journal of Psychoanalysis* 35, part 2 (1954): 272–278.

31. Ibid., p. 277. The irony here is considerable. Anna Freud had been analyzed by her father.

32. Lacan, "Function and Field of Speech and Language," *Ecrits: A Selection*, pp. 31–32. This paper is the work translated and commented on in Anthony Wilden's *The Language of the Self* (Baltimore: Johns Hopkins University Press, 1968).

33. Ibid., p. 33.

34. See Serge Moscovici, *La psychanalyse, son image et son public* (Paris: Presses Universitaires de France, 1961), for a picture of how the French public saw psychoanalysts in the 1950s.

35. The other members of this committee were Dr. Paula Heimann, Mme. Ilse Hellmann, and Dr. P. J. van der Loeuw.

36. According to the rules of the International Psychoanalytic Association, the French Psychoanalytic Society could not become a study group unless three of its members were regular members of the IPA. But of course, all of its members had been excluded from the International in 1953. To get around this requirement, the International reinstated Daniel Lagache and Juliet Favez-Boutonier and awarded membership to Serge Leclaire, who had seen a student of Lacan.

37. The French Psychoanalytic Society tried to make distinctions between the International's demands on "issues of principle" which they were willing to accept and on "issues of persons" which they could not See, for example, a letter of September 28, 1961, from the president of the French Psychoanalytic Society, Juliette Favez-Boutonier, to Dr. Maxwell Gitelson, the president of the International Psychoanalytic Association. In Miller, *L'Excommunication*, p. 25.

38. Notes taken by François Perrier, secretary of the French Psychoanalytic Society, on the presentation of the Turquet Report to the French analysts are in ibid., pp. 41–45.

39. The conflict had finally crystallized around Lacan; the demand for the exclusion of Françoise Dolto became a non-issue. For the minutes of the International Psychoanalytic Association's Twenty-Third Congress at Stockholm at which the case of the French Society was discussed, see *The International Journal of Psychoanalysis* 45, parts 2–3 (April–July 1964): 468, 481.

40. Maud Mannoni, in Miller, *L'Excommunication*, p. 65.

41. Wladimir Granoff claims to have instigated the motion to the Education Committee. The motion to strike Lacan's name was also signed by Juliette Favez-Boutonier, Daniel Lagache, and Georges Favez. The motion is reprinted in Miller, *L'Excommunication*, p. 87.

42. Ibid., pp. 110–111.

43. See *The International Journal of Psychoanalysis* 47, part 1 (1966): 88–90.

44. Miller, *L'Excommunication*, p. 130.

45. Miller, *L'Excommunication*. The excerpt from Lacan's seminar appears on the back cover.

Chapter 5

1. Jacques Lacan, *Les quatre concepts fondamental de la psychanalyse* (Paris: Seuil, 973), pp. 210–211.

2. Karl Abraham, *A Psycho-Analytic Diologue: The Letters of Sigmund Freud and Karl Abraham, 1907–1926*, ed. Hilda C. Abraham and Ernst L. Freud, trans. Bernard Marsh and Hilda C. Abraham (New York: Basic Books, 1965), p. 351.

3. Sigmund Freud, "Group Psychology and the Analysis of the Ego," *The Complete Psychological Works of Sigmund Freud*, Standard Edition, vol. 18, trans. James Strachey et al. (London: Hogarth Press, 1953–66), pp. 67–143.

4. In Wladimir Granoff, *Filiations: L'Avenir du complexe d'Oedipe* (Paris: Editions de Minuit, 1975), references to the schisms in France are woven together with the history of dissidence in Freud's circle and with a theoretical discussion of the problem of paternity in psychoanalysis. François Roustang, *Un Destin si funeste* (Paris: Editions de Minuit, 1976) concentrates specifically on the problem of the *Maître* in the psychoanalytic society.

5. Roustang, *Un Destin si funeste*, p. 28.

6. The text of Lacan's announcement that founded the Freudian School appears in Jacques-Alain Miller, ed., *L'Excommunication: La Communauté psychanalytique en France*, 2, supplement to *Ornicar?, bulletin périodique du Champ freudien*, no. 8 (1977), pp. 149–153.

7. Lacan's phrase is "tout psychanalyste ne s'autorise que de lui-méme."

8. Lacan's proposal for the pass and for the introduction of a new category of "School Analysts" at the Freudian School appears in his "Proposition du 9 octobre 1967 sur le psychanalyste de l'Ecole." A version of the text appears in *Scilicet: tu peux savoir ce qu'en pense l'Ecole Freudienne du Paris*, no. 1 (1968).

9. This particular passage from Lacan's plans for the pass made clinicians and anti-elitists bristle. It became the focus of controversy. It was cited in Piera Castoriadis-Aulagnier, "Sociétiés de psychoanalyse et psychanalyse de société," *Topiques*, no. 1 (October 1969), p. 40.

10. Ibid., p. 42.

11. In the July 1964 text that founded the Freudian School, the first section of the School's activity is listed as "section of pure psycho-analysis, that is, of the practice and doctrine of genuine psychoanalysis which is no other (and this will be established in its place) than the training analysis." The text is reprinted in Miller, *L'Excommunication*, pp. 149–153.

12. In telling the story of the schisms, we have abandoned each psychoanalytic group after its break with Lacan, but not unlike the dynamics of political parties in France, the conflict and schism in the French psychoanalytic movement live on in the ideology and institutions of each group.

The Fourth Group worked out its training policies largely in reaction to its members' bad experiences at the Freudian School. First, the Fourth Group requires somewhat greater rigor in training. In practice, analysts in training at the Freudian School do supervised analytic work, but as we have seen, this work is not formally listed as a requirement before the School will list a member as a practicing analyst. In the Fourth Group, there is a requirement of supervised analytic work before a candidate is recognized as an analyst.

Second, the Fourth Group, embittered by its experience with Lacan's "School Analysts," has allowed virtually no possibility for hierarchy among its analysts. An analyst becomes a full member of the Fourth Group by presenting a statement of his theoretical or clinical interests to a group of colleagues. In this process, very similar in tone to a Quaker meeting, the Fourth Group is staying very close to Lacan's psychoanalytic Protestantism.

Third, the Fourth Group insists on a greater respect for clinical psychoanalysis than the group's members found with Lacan.

The Fourth Group keeps itself egalitarian and flexible so that it can serve as a meeting ground for analysts of all the societies. As at the Freudian School, one need not be an analyst or even a member of the group to participate in its activities. Although only a few dozen analysts use the Fourth Group as a primary professional affiliation, many hundreds of analysts participate in it. In particular, the group seems to have found colleagues and support in the Paris Psychoanalytic Society.

The weight of psychoanalytic history has identified the Paris Psychoanalytic Society with its Institute of Psychoanalysis, and so the Society is almost universally referred to as "The Institute." The Institute, with a total membership of about three hundred, is organized in a traditional hierarchy of training analysts, associate and affiliate members, and candidates. One legacy of Nacht's long and unsuccessful attempt to have the state recognize an Institute medical diploma in clinical psychoanalysis is the strong implantation of the Institute in the medical milieu. Although 40 percent of the members of the Institute are nonmedical analysts, they do not occupy positions of power in the organization in proportion to their numbers. They complain of being treated like second-class citizens and feel that they require the protection of a strong "medical" member of the group in order to carve out successful careers. About 40 percent of the Association's members are lay analysts as compared with about 60 percent nonmedical membership in the Fourth Group and at the Freudian School.

In the years immediately following its break with Lacan in 1953, the Institute developed the reputation of being an anti-Lacanian monolith, but this is no longer the case. Several of its most influential members, among them André Green and Conrad Stein, are profoundly influenced by Lacan's ideas and participate in numerous research and publishing efforts with Lacanians. Far from presenting a "united front," the Institute struggles with its own internal psychoanalytic politics. Of all the French psychoanalytic societies, it was the one most severely challenged from within during the events of May–June 1968, when its bureaucratic and hierarchical structures came under sharp fire.

It is, of course, the members of the Institute who have had the most regular contact with the Anglo-American psychoanalytic community through their participation in the International Psychoanalytic Association. In fact, in 1973 a new president and secretary of the International took office, and for the first time they both were French, Serge Lebovici and Daniel Widlöcher. Both were veterans of psychoanalytic schisms: Lebovici broke with Lacan in 1953, Widlöcher in 1963.

The French Psychoanalytic Association, the product of the 1963 schism, has roughly had the same internal structure as the Paris Society, but it is far smaller, with less than a hundred members, which gives it a less formal tone. The Association has an image of being academic and intellectual. It sponsors a journal of considerable breadth, *La Nouvelle Revue de Psychanalyse*, and many American readers may have gotten their first taste of Lacanianism via the work of two of his former students, now at the Association, Jean Laplanche and J.-B. Pontalis, who wrote the *Vocabulary of Psychoanalysis* (Baltimore: Johns Hopkins University Press, 1968).

13. See Roustang, *Un Destin si funeste*, especially chapters 1, 2, and 4.

14. See ibid., especially chaps. 1, 2, 3, and 5.

15. Miller, *L'Excommunication*, p. 97.

16. Didier Anzieu, "Contre Lacan," *La Quinzaine Littéraire*, January 20, 1967, p. 15.

17. Granoff, *Filiations*, p. 241.

18. Ibid.

19. Forculsion is the term which Lacan uses to translate Freud's *Verwerfung.*

20. See Paul Roazen, *Brother Animal: The Story of Freud and Tausk* (New York: Knopf, 1969); Kurt R. Eissler, *Talent and Genius: The Fictitious Case of Tausk contra Freud* (New York: Quadrangle Books, 1971).

Chapter 6

1. The saliency of psychiatric struggles for the Left is quite concrete. Psychiatry in France as in the United States becomes part of systems of oppression and discrimination in schools, factories, and prisons. And, of course, there is the fact that 80 percent of French mental patients are from the working class.

2. Sigmund Freud, in Joseph Breuer and Sigmund Freud, "Studies in Hysteria," in *The Complete Psychological Works of Sigmund Freud,* Standard Edition, vol. 2, trans. James Strachey et al. (London: Hogarth Press, 1953–66), p. 305.

3. Nathan Hale, ed., *James Jackson Putnam and Psychoanalysis* (Cambridge, MA: Harvard University Press, 1970), pp. 90–91.

4. The psychoanalyst community mental health reformers can trace their heritage back to the origins of "antipsychiatry" in France. The marginality of psychoanalysis to psychiatry until the mid-1950s meant that the critique of asylum psychiatry, which began to emerge after World War II, did not develop against psychoanalysis. In fact, it developed in close alliance with a brand of psychoanalysis that was willing to see itself in the service of psychiatry. Tens of thousands of French mental patients had been allowed to starve to death during World War II; after the war, public horror at the atrocity gave momentum to a nascent movement for the reform of the psychiatric hospital system which had been growing up around the practice of psychiatrist François Tosquelles at Saint-Alban Hospital. The principles behind the Tosquelles movement included improving material conditions within the hospital, diminishing the then total separation between the hospital and the outside world, and employing a therapeutic team whose members would engage patients in a variety of relationships

and activities. The original group of reformers with Tosquelles (among them L. Bonnafé, G. Daumezon, and L. LeGuillant) worked in an eclectic spirit of medical empiricism. Their goal was to rationalize and humanize an absurd and inhuman system, and they were open to whatever they thought might help: drug therapy, group techniques, occupational therapy, and certain psychoanalytic techniques.

Today's community mental health reformers include those who regard psychoanalysis as the technique that will make it possible for the psychiatric system to provide an adequate solution to the problem of psychosis. For them, the major obstacle to psychiatric therapy is the hospital model of practice, and they propose a marriage of psychiatric and flexible psychoanalytic ideas which will bring a modernized, supple psychiatry out into the community. According to this model, psychoanalysis exists to help psychiatry do its task better. The medical and psychiatric system and its hierarchies are accepted, not challenged. In the thirteenth *arrondissement*'s community health center, which was the first "pilot" project for what is now a national community program, psychoanalytic power tends to reinforce medical authority: the entire institution operates by a kind of consensus about psychoanalysis, but for the nonphysicians, access to psychoanalysis is through an identification with the psychiatrist-analyst-leader. In terms of the relation between psychoanalytic politics and the politics of psychoanalysis, it is not insignificant that the analysts who founded the pilot in the thirteenth *arrondissement* were all of the Paris Psychoanalytic Society and all militantly anti-Lacanian. See P.-C. Recamier, Serge Lebovici, Phillipe Paumelle, and René Diatkine, *Le psychanalyste sans divan* (Paris: Payot, 1970).

5. "Et l'être de l'homme, non seulement ne peut être compris sans la folie, mais il ne serait pas l'être de l'homme s'il ne portait en lui la folie comme limite de sa liberté." Jacaues Lacan, *Ecrits* (Paris: Seuil, 1966), p. 176.

6. Gilles Deleuze and Félix Guattari, *L'Anti-Oedipe: Capitalisme et schizophrénie* (Paris: Editions de Minuit, 1972). Translated by Robert Hurley, Mark Seem, and Helen R. Lane as *Anti-Oedipus: Capitalism and Schizophrenia* (New York: Viking, 1977). All citations are from the English edition.

7. The fact that when Lacan "uses" linguistics he transforms terms and meanings is a source of contention in the French psychoanalytic world because, although the intention of using other disciplines is to open up psychoanalysis to them and vice versa, this idiosyncratic *Lacanian* usage can close down communication with other disciplines. If a linguist cannot criticize Lacan on the basis of how he uses terms from linguistics, there is a serious problem.

8. Ludwig Wittgenstein, *The Tractatus* (New York: Humanities Press, 1963). This idea of using philosophy not to convey explicit "knowledge" but as a "therapeutic" vehicle has been developed by the British school of philosophers influenced by Wittgenstein and is explicitly formulated as such by Brian Farrell in his paper, "An Appraisal of Therapeutic Positivism," *Mind* 55, nos. 217, 218 (January, April 1946): 25–48 and 133–150.

9. Deleuze and Guattari, *Anti-Oedipus*, pp. 1–2.

10. Ibid., p. 54.

11. Ibid., p. 55. Italics are mine.

12. Ibid., p. 54.

13. Ibid., p. 116.

14. Ibid., p. 118.

15. Ibid., p. 116.

16. Ibid., especially pp. 34, 222 ff., 296 ff.

17. Ibid., p. 54.

18. Deleuze and Guattari take a cure among the African Ndembu reported by anthropologist Victor Turner as an example. See ibid., p. 167.

19. Ibid., p. 360.

20. Ibid.

21. Robert Castel, *Le Psychanalysme* (Paris: Maspero, 1972), p. 21. *Anti-Oedipus* appeared just as Castel's book was going to press, and

Castel makes the point that *Anti-Oedipus* represents the kind of criticism of psychoanalysis that he has been looking for.

22. See Michel Foucault, *Madness and Civilization: A History of Insanity in the Age of Reason*, trans. Richard Howard (New York: Pantheon Books, 1965).

23. Castel, *Le Psychanalysme*, p. 22.

24. The GIA (Groupe Information Asiles) tries to organize former patients in neighborhood groups to form a "counter-sector." Their goal is to inform patients so that they can better deal with the psychiatric establishment.

25. "Sept theses pour une lutte," *Gardes Fous*, no. 1 (February–March 1974).

26. Ibid.

27. Indeed, radical groups, such as Scription Rouge, whose interests are certainly not restricted to the politics of psychology, publish in *Gardes Fous*, and the line between the political analysis of capitalism and the political analyses of psychiatry dissolves.

Chapter 7

1. Sigmund Freud, "On the Teaching of Psychoanalysis in Universities," in *The Complete Psychological Works of Sigmund Freud*, Standard Edition, vol. 17, trans. James Strachey et al. (London: Hogarth Press, 1953–66), pp. 169–175.

2. Louis Althusser, "Freud et Lacan," *La Nouvelle Critique*, no. 161–162 (December 1964–January 1965), p. 93.

3. See Jacques Hassoun, "Quand le psychanalyste se fait freudologue," *Etudes Freudiennes*, no. 5–6 (January 1972), p. 9. Psychoanalysts had been professors in the French university system before 1968 (Juliette Favez-Boutonier and Daniel Lagache, for example), but they were there as experts in psychology or psychiatry, not to profess psychoanalysis.

4. The unevenness of French medical education has slowed down Common Market plans for reciprocity in the recognition of health

professionals among member countries. Before 1968, even the post of *externe* (i.e., the possibility of having some clinical experience during medical school) was competitive and open to only a limited number of students.

5. Political and psychoanalytic themes are developed together in the "Livre blanc de la réforme en médecine" and the "Livre blanc des sciences humaines," two mimeographed works of synthesis produced by reformers at the medical school during the summer of 1968.

6. "Livre blanc de la réforme en médecine."

7. "Information CHU [Centre-Hospitals-Universitaire] Saint-Antoine, Commission 8 (Sciences Humaines)," report of June 5, 1968.

8. There were three French psychoanalytic societies by 1968: the Paris Psychoanalytic Society, the French Psychoanalytic Association (both recognized by the International), and Lacan's Freudian School. Interviews with medical students of 1968 indicate that they were perceived as two camps: Lacanian and non-Lacanian.

9. Patrick Weiller, "Tentative de mise en question de la psychanalyse à propos du mouvement étudiant de mai 1968 à la Faculté de Médecine de Paris" (thèse, Faculté de Médecine de Montpelier, 1969), pp. 131–132.

10. There was one teacher for fifty students in the medical school as a whole, the worst student-faculty ratio in Europe, but only one teacher for each one hundred students of psychiatry.

11. Plans for the Psychiatric College are found in the mimeographed "Project d'un institut pluridisciplinaire de psychiatrie" (September 26, 1968).

12. The reforms achieved were in general those that had been outlined in the 1965 *Livre blanc de la psychiatrie française*, a publication of *L'Evolution Psychiatrique*, 3 vols. (Toulouse: Edouard Privat, 1965, 1966, 1967).

13. Since 1968, French higher education has been divided into Unités d'Etudes et de Recherches (UERs), which function somewhat

analogously to departments in American universities. For example, each UER gives courses for credits (known as *Unités de Valeur*, or UVs). The Department of Clinical Human Sciences at Censier is technically not a "department," but a UER; the Department of Psychoanalysis at Vincennes is another UER.

14. The Institute has preserved some of the outward forms of the Critical University. For example, the Critical University had spoken of integrating theory and practice, and the Institute of Psychology does not permit a student to enroll unless he also is doing paid work as a psychologist.

15. It is increasingly difficult for the French university system to justify eight years of post-baccalaureate training for a psychology diploma that has little real value unless it is "validated" by a psycho-analysis. The two major movements to reform the situation shared a hidden agenda to squeeze out the Freudian School. The first was spearheaded by Didier Anzieu, former student of Lacan's, member of the French Psychoanalytic Association, professor of psychology at Nanterre. The Anzieu plan tried to upgrade the psychology diploma by only certifying those psychologists trained by an analytic society that is recognized by the International Psychoanalytic Association (which is to say, a non-Lacanian society). The second, the Boulin Decree, was a government plan to give psychologists less training and lower their status to that of medical paraprofessionals. Physicians lobbied for the Boulin plan, which would have forced people who wanted to be psychotherapists into medicine and forced many Laca-nian psychologist-analysts out of practice.

16. Jean Laplanche, "Psychanalyse à l'université," *Psychanalyse à l'Université* I (December 1975): 5–10.

17. Laplanche, "Psychanalyse à l'université," pp. 8–10.

18. Of course, this feeling was not limited to the Vincennes campus. The question of whether or not to participate in student-faculty com-mittees (*commissions paritaires*) kept students all over France busy fighting with each other rather than with the government for several years after the May events.

19. Hassoun, "Quand le psychanalyste se fait freudologue," p. 9.

20. Jacques Lacan, "Impromptu de Vincennes," *Magazine Littéraire*, no. 121 (February 1977): 21–25.

21. For a description of the new direction for the department, see *Ornicar?, bulletin périodique du Champ freudien*, no. 1 (January 1975): 12–15.

22. Luce Irigaray, *Spéculum, de l'autre femme* (Paris: Editions de Minuit, 1974).

23. Jacques Lacan, "Yale University, Kanzer Seminar," *Scilicet: Tu peux savior ce qu'en pense l'Ecole Freudienne de Paris*, nos. 6–7 (1976), p. 26.

24. Jacques-Alain Miller, "Théorie de la langue (Rudiment)," *Ornicar?, bulletin périodique de Champ freudien*, no. 1 (January 1975).

25. Ibid.

26. François Roustang, *Un Destin si funeste* (Paris: Editions de Minuit, 1976), p. 96.

27. Miller, "Théorie de la langue," p. 34.

28. "Départment de Psychanalyse: Annonces et Informations," *Ornicar?, bulletin périodique de Champ freudien*, no. 7 (June–July 1976), p. 119.

29. Piera Castoriadis-Aulagnier, Jean-Paul Valabrega, and Nathalie Zaltzman, "Une néoformation du lacanisme," *Topiques*, no. 18 (January 1977), pp. 3–9.

30. Ibid., p. 6.

31. Ibid., p. 8.

32. Ibid.

Chapter 8

1. Sigmund Freud, *A Psycho-Analytic Dialogue: The Letters of Sigmund Freud and Karl Abraham, 1907–1926*, ed. Hilda C. Abraham and Ernst

L. Freud, trans. Bernard Marsh and Hilda C. Abraham (New York: Basic Books, 1965), pp. 279–280.

2. See Serge Moscovici, *La Psychanalyse, son image et son public* (Paris: Presses Universitaires de France, 1961). All references to popular attitudes of the 1950s in the chapter are from Moscovici's study.

3. Moscovici assembled a wide range of materials in his profile of psychoanalysis and society in the 1950s, including a content analysis of the press, and of Communist Party and Catholic opinion. In this chapter, we focus on some of the more notable changes in French attitudes since the 1950s which emerge from comparing Moscovici's work with interviews I did twenty years later. Of course, there are similarities as well, particularly in how the French voice objections to psychoanalysis and in their characterization of "American psychoanalysis." Moscovici worked with data collected from a representative sample of the Parisian population and a sample of subpopulations (liberal professionals, upper- and lower-middle classes, workers, and students). My 1974 study took up many of the questions raised in Moscovici's work, examining, for example, each subject's level of knowledge, attitudes, and experience in regard to psychoanalysis and other forms of psychotherapy. It also raised new issues which seemed relevant to the evolving social role of psychoanalysis in France, for example, attitudes about abortion, sex education, the 1968 events.

My study was in the form of an interview protocol which took about two hours to complete. Over two hundred subjects were interviewed. One hundred and eighty-two of them were used in tabulating the statistical results. I did seventy-eight of the interviews myself; the remaining one hundred and four were done by two assistants. The instructions to the interviewers were to take down everything that the subject said verbatim, as one would do if giving a Rorschach. Thus, I had one hundred and eighty-two full transcripts to work from. Proceeding in the same manner as Moscovici, subjects were quota sampled to constitute subpopulation samples. One hundred and three of the subjects form a "representative" sample of the Parisian population, distributed by age, sex, and class. This 1974 sample enables us to make comparisons with the responses of Moscovici's similarly constituted, representative sample. For a full description of my study, including the protocol, statistical analysis, and detailed information on the responses of the different subpopulations, see Sherry Turkle, "Psychoanalysis and Society: The Emergence of French Freud" (PhD diss., Harvard University, 1976). In this chapter, which focuses on the one hundred and three members of the representative sample of 1974, no finding is presented if it was not significant to the .01 level using the chi-square test of association.

4. My comments on the publications world are based on a count and content analysis of articles published in *Le Monde* from 1960–74 that touched on psychology, psychiatry, and psychoanalysis; on an analysis of books published in these fields during the same period; on a survey of French television and radio programming; and on interviews with editors, publishers, and booksellers. For more detail, see Turkle, "Psychoanalysis and Society."

5. Feelings about what psychoanalysis is like in America seemed virtually unchanged from the 1950s when Moscovici collected the following reflections:

> Americans go to a psychoanalyst the way they go to a grocer.
>
> The French wouldn't take it—they don't need it. In America, they are naive and childlike—they take to anything.
>
> In America, there are many crazy people—perhaps so is the population as a whole. They have the medicine and the politics they deserve.

What *had* changed was feelings about what psychoanalysis is like in France.

6. François Weyergans, *Le Pitre* (Paris: Gallimard, 1973).

7. Ibid., p. 118.

8. See Jacques Lacan, *Télévision* (Paris: Seuil, 1974).

9. Dominique Frischer, *Les Analysés parlent* (Paris: Editions Stock, 1977).

10. Ten of the thirty patients whom Frischer interviewed made it very clear that for them being in analysis had raised their social standing. This sentiment was expressed many times by the people I

interviewed. It partially explains why the public has a tendency to use the word "analyst" to cover a much larger group of counseling professionals. Association with an "analyst" brings prestige. A wide range of mental health professionals also try to "promote" their status to the analytic by using the term loosely. Patients as well as practitioners want to share in *le pouvoir analytique*, "psychoanalytic power," an expression that exists today as a common French idiom whereas to the American reader the expression may have little meaning.

11. Frischer, *Les Analysés parlent*, p. 114.

12. Ibid., p. 144.

13. Grégoire claims that her analyst, René Laforgue, encouraged her to turn her talents toward the diffusion of psychoanalysis to the general public. Women's magazines and the Grégoire radio show are only two examples of how the language that French people find appropriate for giving advice about their problems has slipped from the moral to the psychological. Mme. Soleil, France's best-known and best-loved astrologer, is yet another. Soleil, who also has her own radio show, has taken to using a quasi-therapeutic language to talk about reading the stars: "People come to see me to engage in a dialogue, to discover themselves . . . to confide in someone anonymous with whom they can speak freely and without consequence."

14. Menie Grégoire, *Les Cris de la vie* (Paris: Tchou, 1971), p. 13.

15. The only contact with psychoanalysts that any of the working-class people I spoke with had had was in public institutions, usually for children. Contact with psychoanalysis in institutions seems to breed contempt for it. While the liberal professional imagines his child in a private consulting room, a poorer person imagines a crowded waiting room in a state institution. While the liberal professional feels confident that "one can choose one's own analyst," workers and lower-middle-class people know that for them there is usually no choice. One passes through a series of offices and a battery of tests, and a therapist is "assigned." For poor people, contact with *les psy* puts them in relationships in which they have little control, and the sense of personal humiliation associated with public health facilities interferes with any sense of psychoanalysis as liberating.

Chapter 9

1. See Serge Moscovici, *La Psychanalyse, son image et son public*, 2nd ed. (Paris: Presses Universitaires de France, 1976), pp. 19–30.

2. The efficacy of priests and shamans and specialists in internal medicine is related to their society's belief in the legitimacy and power of their methods. Psychoanalysts are no different. For an overview of the question of the "social leverage" of the healer, see Jerome Frank, *Persuasion and Healing* (New York: Schocken, 1963).

3. François Roustang, *Un Destin si funeste* (Paris: Editions du Minuit, 1976), p. 91.

4. For the best critical discussion of this strategy of nostalgia and retreat, see Robert Castel, *Le Psychanalysme* (Paris: Maspero, 1973).

5. Maud Mannoni, "Le Malentendu," *L'Arc*, no. 58 (1974), p. 74.

Chapter 10

1. Jacques Lacan, *Télévision* (Paris: Editions du Seuil, 1974), p. 71.

2. Claude Lévi-Strauss, *The Raw and the Cooked* (New York: Harper and Row, 1969).

3. Claude Lévi-Strauss, *La Pensée sauvage* (Paris: Plon, 1062).

Chapter 11

1. Bernard-Henri Lévy, *La Barbarie à visage humaine* (Paris: Grasset, 1977), pp. 181–182.

2. Ibid., p. 16.

3. Other authors in the "new philosopher" group include André Glucksmann, *Les Maîtres penseurs* (Paris: Grasset, 1977); Guy Lardreau and Christian Jambet, *L'Ange* (Paris: Grasset, 1977).

4. Lévy, *La Barbarie à visage humaine.*

5. Ibid., p. 224.

6. Ibid., p. 11.

7. See Glucksmann, *Les Maîtres penseurs*, especially chap. 1, "Panurge hors les murs."

Chapter 12

1. For a personal and insightful account of Lacan's last years and the beginning of this mourning process, see Stuart Schneiderman, *Jacques Lacan: The Death of an Intellectual Hero* (Cambridge, MA: Harvard University Press, 1983). The history of the dissolution of the Freudian School has been admirably chronicled in Élisabeth Roudinesco's *Lacan and Company: A History of Psychoanalysis in France 1925–1985* (London: Free Association Books, 1990). Roudinesco's invaluable second volume of her history of psychoanalysis in France is of the greatest interest to all students of the period. Roudinesco, a member of Lacan's Freudian School from 1969 until its dissolution in 1980, is a second-generation Lacanian, the daughter of Jenny Aubry, a psychiatrist who was in analytic training at the Paris Psychoanalytic Society at the time of the schism of 1953. Carefully researched, using archival and interview material never previously reported on, *Lacan and Company* recounts the Lacanian saga from a unique, insider's point of view. In telling the story of the dissolution, Roudinesco and I were often working from the same primary sources, in particular the circulars and letters that constitute the correspondence among the Lacanians, but I owe a special debt to her work. Embroidered with finely drawn portraits and personal reminiscences, her account provides a rich context for written source materials. For a fuller discussion by me of Roudinesco's work, see my review in *The London Review of Books* 12, no. 23 (December 1990), pp. 3–9.

In the translation of my own archive of circulated correspondence among Lacanians during the period of dissolution and in the years following, I wish to acknowledge the able assistance of Dr. Martin Roberts of the Department of French of Harvard University. I, of course, am responsible for any errors in the final result of these labors. Much of the correspondence protesting the dissolution and its aftermath has been anthologized in Claude Dorgeuille, *La Seconde mort de Jacques Lacan* (Paris: Actualité Freudienne, 1981). Other documents relevant to the story of the dissolution as seen by its protagonists appeared in *L'Ane* (April–May 1981) and were reprinted in *Almanach de la dissolution* (Paris: Navarin, 1986). Whenever possible, I provide a published source for documents I cite.

2. Roudinesco, *Lacan and Company*, p. 379.

3. Ibid., p. 402.

4. Ibid., pp. 403–404.

5. Besides Leclaire and Miller, the Department of Psychoanalysis at its inception in January 1969 included François Baudry, Jean Clavreul, Claude Conté, Claude Dumézil, Luce Irigaray, Michèle Montrelay, Claude Rabant, François Roustang, and René Tostain.

6. In 1991, the Department of Psychoanalysis, with its continuing education program and diploma in "la clinique psychanalytique" remains a Millerian enterprise, although it has moved from Vincennes to the university center at Saint Denis.

7. Interview with Jacques-Alain Miller, June 20, 1989.

8. *Almanach de la dissolution*, p. 10.

9. Ibid., pp. 10–11.

10. Cited in Roudinesco, *Lacan and Company*, p. 652. Miller's account of the decision to dissolve the Freudian School appears on pp. 651–652.

11. Jacques Lacan, "Founding Act," in Jacques Lacan, *Television*, ed. Joan Copjec, trans. Denis Hollier et al. (New York: W. W. Norton, 1990), p. 97.

12. Roudinesco, *Lacan and Company*, p. 659.

13. Ibid., p. 662.

14. *Almanach de la dissolution*, p. 18.

15. Ibid., p. 19.

16. Roudinesco, *Lacan and Company*, p. 662.

17. Dorgeuille, *La Seconde mort*, p. 26

18. The premises of the Freudian School, 69 rue Claude Bernard, had been purchased by a group of one hundred and twenty members of the School, who formed a realty corporation that then rented the premises back to the School. Its principal shareholders were Lacan and Melman, each with fifty shares, Dolto and René Bailly, with twenty-five, Clavreul with twelve, and Jenny Aubry, Pierre Martin, Mousapha Safouan, Christian Simatos, Jean Oury, and Irène Roublef, each with ten. René Bailly was the manager of the property. After the dissolution, Miller, apparently on Melman's advice, requested that the Freudian Cause rent the property. The form of the request was the by now predictable one: a signed letter from Lacan. To back up his suggestion, Melman had himself appointed co-manager of the realty corporation where he would serve jointly with Bailly. What Melman overlooked, although in retrospect the lapse seems almost inconceivable, is that once the dissolution of the Freudian School had taken place, those among the realty corporation shareholders who had opposed its dissolution, would scarcely want to rent it to the successor organization to which they had been so bitterly opposed. The simplest thing would have been to sell the premises and return the money to the shareholders. But instead, Melman had his way and the request for rental was approved at a November 14 meeting of the shareholders.

At this point, Miller, acting in his capacity as "Lacan's secretary," proposed the renovation of the former Freudian School headquarters, which would have closed it to analytic teaching, and proposed the lease that Melman found unacceptable. Melman and Bailly were, of course, under no obligation to sign this proposed lease. It would have been understandable if they had simply proposed an alternative. Instead, Melman used the unacceptable lease as an occasion to launch an attack on Miller.

19. The text of Melman's letter and appended documents appears in Dorgeuille, *La Seconde mort*, pp. 28–48. Three weeks after Melman sent his letter, there was a general assembly of the shareholders of the realty corporation that owned the property at 69 rue Claude Bernard. Now Melman threw his support to those who wished to sell the premises. His change of position was decisive; the decision was made

to put the former Freudian School headquarters up for sale, rather than rent to the Cause.

20. The text of Faladé's letter appears in Dorgeuille, *La Seconde mort*, pp. 49–51.

21. The text of Clavreul's letter appears in ibid., pp. 51–52.

22. Roudinesco, *Lacan and Company*, pp. 667–668.

23. Dorgeuille, *La Seconde mort*, p. 89.

24. The text of this letter of resignation appears in ibid., pp. 87–88. It specifies that the Cause had broken its contract in the following ways:

> By putting into place an organization, authoritarian in its principles and manipulative in its process which is incompatible with the ethics of psychoanalysis. By turning the Freudian field into a marketplace where people bargain for posts and jobs in exchange for submission. By making a lust for power come before any respect for Lacan's teaching. By using the authority of that teaching to justify schemes and intrigues, all foreign to his approach. By trying to impose unacceptable statutes—unacceptable because of the scorn they show vis-à-vis the members, a scorn that is evident even to the nonspecialist.
>
> These facts are grave and sufficient to discredit their authors. They disqualify the name of the Freudian Cause to those for whom psychoanalysis matters. They discourage those who have just begun to be raised in Lacan's teaching. Because we are students of Lacan and wish to follow his teaching, we must denounce this state of affairs and say that for us, the Freudian Cause and its replacement, the School, no longer exist.

25. *Almanach de la dissolution*, p. 24.

26. Dorgeuille, *La Seconde mort*, p. 96.

27. Ibid., pp. 97–98.

28. Ibid., p. 99.

29. Ibid., p. 90.

30. Ibid., p. 105.

31. Ibid., p. 124. The correspondence of Safouan, Israël, Conté, the Mannonis, Bauer, and Ritter on the subject of the Forum appear in ibid., pp. 123–130.

32. Ibid., p. 128.

33. Ibid., p. 136.

34. Roudinesco, *Lacan and Company*, p. 679.

35. Eric Conan, "Les psychanalystes, sont-ils dangereux?," *L'Express* (May 19–25, 1989), p. 81.

36. Roudinesco, p. 398.

37. Luc Ferry and Alain Renaut, *French Philosophy of the Sixties: An Essay on Antihumanism*, trans. Mary Schnackenberg Cattani (Amherst: University of Massachusetts Press, 1990).

38. For a critical discussion of the link between Lacanism and feminism, see David Macey, *Lacan in Contexts* (London: Verso, 1988).

39. Ecole de la Cause Freudienne, *La Lettre Mensuelle*, no. 69 (May 1988), p. 2.

40. The Foundation is headed by Lacan's daughter, Judith Miller, which enhances the sense that the organization is familial. In addition to the international activity of the Foundation, there have been some recent efforts by members of the International Psychoanalytic Association to take Lacanianism away from the family, indeed to "reappropriate" Lacanianism for itself, now that Lacan is dead. For example, a group of New York analysts began an "International Freudian Foundation for New Perspectives in Psychoanalytic Research," whose goal was to assemble all Freudian tendencies together, including Lacanians. Alain de Mijolla, a member of the Paris Psychoanalytic Society became its French coordinator; its first clinical symposium was held in Paris in June 1986. Members of many French analytic societies participated: Joyce MacDougall, André Green, and Michel de M'Uzan for the Paris Psychoanalytic Society, J.-B. Pontalis for the French Psychoanalytic Association, François Roustang for the College of Psychoanalysts and Maud Mannoni for the Center for Psychoanalytic Training and Research.

41. Ecole de la Cause Freudienne, *La Lettre Mensuelle*, no. 69 (May 1988), p. 2.

42. It was described by Lacan in his Seminar of March 18, 1980: "Collez-vous ensemble le temps qu'il faut pour faire quelque chose et dissolvez-vous après pour faire autre chose." "Stick together as long as it takes to do something and then break up to do something else." Ibid., p. 3.

43. Ibid., p. 29.

44. Jacques-Alain Miller, "Position de Jacques-Alain Miller à l'Assemblée du 2 décembre," Ecole de la Cause Freudienne, *Annexe Aux Pré-Rapports II*, letter of November 29, 1989, p. 25.

45. Michel Kajman, "Le divan à l'encan," *Le Monde*, April 1, 1989, p. 10.

46. In the confidentiality lawsuit, the School of the Cause stood with Miller as a united family. On his side, Pommier found support among analysts who could be counted on to stand against Miller. Françoise Dolto, Maud Mannoni, Jean Clavreul, and Claude Dumézil supported Pommier's case.

47. Gérard Pommier, "Psychanalyse: Au nom de la loi?," *Passages*, no. 16 (April 1989), p. 45.

48. I have this letter in my personal archive. I know of no published source.

49. Gérard Pommier, *La Névrose infantile de la psychanalyse* (Paris: Point Hors Ligne, 1989), p. 60.

50. The statute under the heading "La 'Librairie' des Journees" reads as follows: "During the Scientific Meetings, the sale of publications of the School of the Freudian Cause, the Freudian Field, and publications edited (*éditée*) by members of the School of the Freudian Cause is given to Gérard Miller, member of the School of the Freudian Cause, who will take in charge the organization of the bookstalls."

There is no mention of the Board of Directors. Its position that book sales require its authorization was based on a preceding paragraph, under the heading of "The School Bookstore, rue Huysmans," which specifies that "Publications of the School will be for sale at the reception: those of the Freudian Field and those of members, with the agreement of the Board of Directors based on a report of the library's secretary."

51. Gérard Pommier, letter of November 22, 1989, in Ecole de la Cause Freudienne, *Annexe Aux Pré-Rapports II*, p. 4.

52. Gérard Pommier, letter of November 14, 1989, in Ecole de la Cause Freudienne, *Annexe Aux Pré-Rapports I*, p. 16.

53. Directoire de l'Ecole de la Cause Freudienne, letter of November 20, 1989, in ibid., p. 23.

54. "In his report to our last Congress, two years ago," wrote Pommier, "the President of the School had already stated that a psychoanalyst need not be accountable to the law. That is a point of view which situates psychoanalysis above the law and which I consider to be a perverse conception of psychoanalysis, a conception whereby the analyst claims to make the law." See Pommier, letter of November 22, 1989, *Annexe Aux Pré-Rapports II*, p. 5.

55. Roudinesco, *Lacan and Company*, p. 693. Roudinesco's final comment on the charges and countercharges: "The authenticity of the circulars signed by Lacan after January 5 has been contested more forcefully still than the letter of dissolution. Nothing proves that those circulars were written by Lacan, but nothing proves that they were not." Ibid., p. 754.

56. Pommier, letter of November 22, 1989, *Annexe Aux Pré-Rapports I*, p. 6.

57. Miller, "Position de Jacques-Alain Miller à l'Assemblée du 2 décembre," *Annexe Aux Pré-Rapports II*, p. 25.

58. Ibid., p. 29.

59. At the Assembly, Pommier challenged Miller on Lacan's role in the foundation of the School. Miller responded that when at the end of 1980 several members of the Council became hostile to the Freudian Cause, there was a crisis. Those who remained needed to choose between continuing with the Cause or starting a new organization. "We asked Lacan and he told us to do what we wished,"

said Miller. "On my proposal, the Board of Directors decided on the creation of the School of the Freudian Cause and Lacan ratified the proposal." Miller added that Lacan added in his own hand to the first copies of its statutes (that is, on eleven or twelve copies of the document) the words "This is the school of those who still love me." "Only then," said Miller, "were the statutes sent to the prefecture." See "Un Compte-rendu de l'Assemblée du 2 décembre, rédigé par Guy Trobas sur ses notes," in Ecole de la Cause Freudienne, *Annexe Aux Pré-Rapports III*, p. 31.

60. Jacques-Alain Miller, "Acier l'Ouvert," in Ecole de la Cause Freudienne, *Lettre Mensuelle*, no. 85, January 1990, p. I.

61. Ibid., p. 5.

62. Ibid., p. 4.

63. Conseil de l'Ecole de la Cause Freudienne, "Communiqué du Conseil: Une Issue Pour la Crise," April 2, 1990, p. 9.

64. Directoire de l'Ecole de la Cause Freudienne, "Lettre du Directoire aux membres et membres associés," in Ecole de la Cause Freudienne, *Annexe Aux Pré-Rapports II*, p. 18.

65. Danièle Silvestre, "Rapport de la Directrice devant l'Assemblée du 23 juin 1990," in Ecole de la Cause Freudienne, "Information sur l'Assemblé du 23 juin," pp. 4–5. The School did remove Pommier from the ranks of its members at its June 23 Assembly. At that meeting Pommier remarked on the (increasingly) political nature of the charges: "You would only have political reasons to decide in favor of removing me from the ranks of members . . . and your problem is to have to choose between a decision which respects a fair taking account of the facts and political considerations." And he made a final effort to get to what he believed to be the heart of the matter, that the School of the Freudian Cause considered itself above the law. In his view, the statutes of January 1981 signed by Lacan were illegally modified in September 1981. This was, for Pommier, the moment when Miller should have begun a new organization. In his view, Miller refused to do so in order to keep Lacan's signature (and thus the fiction of him as the founder of the School) at any

price. Pommier made it clear that he would not go back to court, but called attention to what he called his "farewell present." "Any interested member of this association can tomorrow call its statutes into question . . . indeed, any association which considers itself morally implicated will be able to rightly protest if there is the continued public pretense that this School was founded by Lacan, which is not the case." (Gérard Pommier, "Déclaration aux délégués l'Assemblée générale du 23 juin 1990.)

66. Conté went so far as to say, "Lacan's seminars are not published, because I don't consider what is published at Seuil worthy of their name. I can give you information on where to read stenographers' versions of the originals." Cited in Anne Dunand, "La Pensée Naufrage: Compte-rendu," in Ecole de la Cause Freudienne, *A Ciel Ouvert*, March 1990, pp. 1–2.

67. The interventions of Winter, Fennetaux, and Pommier are cited in ibid., pp. 3, 6, and 7.

68. Ibid., pp. 8–9.

69. Eric Conan, "Entre deux mots de Lacan, comment choisir le pire," *Libération*, July 16, 1985, p. 29.

70. Ibid.

71. Jacques-Alain Miller, *Entretien sur Le Séminaire* (avec François Ansermet) (Paris: Navarin, 1985), p. 23.

72. Eric Conan, "La Parole Lacan sous license Miller," *Libération*, December 15, 1985, p. 37.

73. Eric Favereau, "La Question de l'ordre gêne les fils de Freud," *Libération*, January 17, 1990, p. 28.

74. The hope was that designated analysts would then be treated equally by the tax and social security systems. At present, French social security only reimburses patients who are treated by medically trained psychoanalysts. Non-physician analysts used to belong to the same tax category as fortune tellers and prostitutes; since 1983 analysts who are not physicians have to pay a T.V.A. or "value-added

tax," which is applied to the fees they earn in return for the service they provide their clients.

75. Serge Leclaire, Jacques Sédat, Philippe Girard, Lucien Israël, and Daniele Lévy, "'Utilité publique' et 'nécessité vitale,'" *Le Monde*, December 15, 1989, p. 13.

76. Jean-Paul Valabrega, "Réponse à Serge Leclaire," *Le Monde*, January 12, 1990, p. 2.

77. Ibid.

78. Jean Clavreul, "Mais si! Les psychanalystes aiment l'ordre," *Libération*, January 26, 1990, p. 4.

79. Maud Mannoni, interview with Eric Favereau, *Libération*, January 22, 1990, p. 28. The silence about Leclaire's proposals seems to have come from the government. When pressed, all that the health ministry would say is, "We will do nothing to interfere except if the analysts come to agreement among themselves."

80. Rudolf Loewenstein, letter of February 22, 1953. Cited in Marion Michel Oliner, *Cultivating Freud's Garden in France* (Northvale, NJ: Jason Aronson, 1988), p. 44.

81. Anzieu gives more details about the short sessions and ambience of the Lacan waiting room:

> At the beginning of my analysis, he gave me sessions of normal length, forty to forty-five minutes, and he saw me at the prearranged times. After two years of work with him, the analytic framework developed a snag. The length of the sessions was reduced to thirty then to twenty minutes. The waiting room became filled with persons anxious to know if they would be received—Lacan opened the door, designated the chosen one, who would retrace his steps ten or fifteen minutes later in order to leave. I read. Lacan tapped me on the shoulder: it was my turn to pass in front of everyone or to find myself sent away to come back another day. . . . The master, heaving a deep sigh, confided in me, as in a friend, that he was overloaded, that he had to make an unforeseen appointment, face a difficult case, giving me to understand that I was not one, that I could therefore come back, and that he was sure that I understood him. This reinforced my narcissism, which did not need this, and made it difficult for me to express my astonishment, my criticism, my disagreement, that is, a negative transference without which a psychoanalysis is not complete.

See Didier Anzieu, *Un Peau pour les pensées* (Paris: Clancier-Guenaud, 1986), p. 34. Cited and translated by Oliner, *Cultivating Freud's Garden in France*, pp. 123–124.

82. Wladimir Granoff, *Filiations: L'Avenir du complexe d'Oedipe* (Paris: Editions du Minuit, 1975); François Roustang, *Dire Mastery: Discipleship from Freud to Lacan*, trans. N. Lukacher (Baltimore: Johns Hopkins University Press, 1985).

83. François Roustang, *The Lacanian Delusion*, trans. Greg Sims (New York: Oxford University Press, 1990), chapter 1.

84. Didier Anzieu, *L'Auto-analyse de Freud et la découverte de la psychanalyse* (Paris: Presses Universitaires de France, 1975), p. 742.

85. François Roustang makes this point:

> In adopting the position of master and producing pupils who were supposed to remain such indefinitely, Lacan was no longer merely *supposed* to know, he *knew*, and even saw himself as the only one who knew. Indeed, did he not repeatedly tell us that, on any given question, we could not go beyond the stage he had reached himself, and that to make further progress, we would just have to wait until he was ready to take another step?

See Roustang, *The Lacanian Delusion*, p. 9.

86. Phyllis Grosskurth, Melanie Klein's biographer, had access to Melanie Klein's own unpublished autobiography. In that work, Klein did not seem able to separate fact from fiction. She presents her mother and brother as near saints; in reality they were jealous and intrusive. Her sickly brother did everything to make Klein feel guilty for her vitality and for the fact that she would outlive him. Her mother actively worked to promote her depressions and to undermine her marriage. See *Melanie Klein: Her World and Her Work* (New York: Alfred A. Knopf, 1986).

87. Nicholas Wright, *Mrs. Klein* (London: Nick Hern, 1988).

Index